Rev. ~~~~

P9-CKB-838

Mechanicsburg Presb.Ch.Lib.

THE FAMILY BOOK OF
Best Loved Poems

THE FAMILY BOOK OF

Best Loved Poems

Edited by

DAVID L. GEORGE

HANOVER HOUSE
Garden City, New York

1952

HANOVER HOUSE

Copyright 1952, by Doubleday & Company, Inc.

PRINTED IN THE UNITED STATES OF AMERICA

Acknowledgments

The editor wishes to express his thanks to the following publishers, authors, or authorized representatives, for their kind permission to reprint poems copyrighted or controlled by them:

ALICE E. ALLEN: For "My Mother's Garden."

APPLETON-CENTURY-CROFTS, INC.: For "The Elf and the Dormouse," from *Artful Antiks* by Oliver Herford.

ERNEST BENN LTD.: For "The Spell of the Yukon" and "The Shooting of Dan McGrew," from *The Complete Poems of Robert W. Service*.

JOHN BENNETT: For "In a Rose Garden."

BRANDT & BRANDT: For "God's World," from *Renascence and Other Poems* published by Harper & Brothers, copyright, 1913, 1941 by Edna St. Vincent Millay; for "Ashes of Life," from *Renascence and Other Poems* published by Harper & Brothers, copyright, 1915, 1943 by Edna St. Vincent Millay.

JONATHAN CAPE LIMITED and MRS. W. H. DAVIES: For "Leisure," from *The Collected Poems of W. H. Davies*. Also JONATHAN CAPE LIMITED: For "Tree at My Window," from *The Complete Poems of Robert Frost*.

THE CLARENDON PRESS, Oxford: For "I Will Not Let Thee Go," from the *Shorter Poems of Robert Bridges*.

BADGER CLARK and FRANCIS CASE: For "Pioneers," from *Sky Lines and Wood Smoke* by Badger Clark.

W. B. CONKEY COMPANY: For "I Love You" and "Optimism," by Ella Wheeler Wilcox.

DAVID CORY: For "Miss You."

CURTIS BROWN, LTD.: For "Up from the Wheelbarrow," from *I'm a Stranger Here Myself*, by Ogden Nash.

WALTER DE LA MARE and FABER & FABER: For "Miss T" by Walter de la Mare.

DODD, MEAD & COMPANY: For "Kashmiri Love Song" from *India's Love Lyrics* by Laurence Hope, copyright, 1902 by Dodd, Mead & Company, Inc., copyright renewed 1929; for "The Spell of the Yukon" and "The Shooting of Dan McGrew," from *The Complete Poems of Robert W. Service*, copyright 1916 by Dodd, Mead & Company, Inc.; for "The Rosary," from *The Rosary and Other Poems* by Robert Cameron Rogers.

DOUBLEDAY & COMPANY, INC.: For "The Ballad of East and West," from *Departmental Ditties and Ballads and Barrack-Room Ballads* by Rudyard Kipling; and for "If," from *Rewards and Fairies* by Rudyard Kipling, copyright 1910 by Rudyard Kipling; both reprinted by permission of Mrs. George Bambridge and Doubleday & Company, Inc.; for "Trees" from *Trees and Other Poems* by Joyce Kilmer, copyright 1914 by Doubleday & Company, Inc.

CONSTANCE GARLAND DOYLE and ISABEL GARLAND LORD: For "The Gold Seekers" by Hamlin Garland.

GERALD DUCKWORTH & CO. LTD.: For "Trees" from *Trees and Other Poems* by Joyce Kilmer.

MAX EASTMAN: For "Rainy Song."

BERTHA K. EHRMANN: For "A Prayer" by Max Ehrmann.

STRICKLAND W. GILLILAN: For "Finnigin to Flannigan."

LAURENCE GOMME: For "The Frog" by Hilaire Belloc.

HILDEGARDE HAWTHORNE: For "A Song."

WILLIAM HEINEMANN LTD.: For "Kashmiri Song," from *India's Love Lyrics* by Laurence Hope.

HENRY HOLT & COMPANY, INC.: For "Tree at My Window" from *Complete Poems of Robert Frost*, copyright 1930, 1949, by Henry Holt & Company, Inc.; for "Miss T" from *Collected Poems* by Walter de la Mare, copyright, 1920, by Henry Holt & Company, Inc. Copyright, 1948 by Walter de la Mare; for "At a Window" from *Chicago Poems*, by Carl Sandburg, copyright, 1916 by Henry Holt & Company, Inc., copyright, 1944, by Carl Sandburg; for "Loveliest of Trees" from *A Shropshire Lad* by A. E. Housman.

HOUGHTON MIFFLIN COMPANY: For "Out Where The West Begins" by Arthur Chapman; for "Jim Bludso" and "Little Breeches," from *Pike County Ballads* by John Hay; for "Waiting" by John Burroughs.

LITTLE, BROWN & COMPANY: For "Up from the Wheelbarrow" from *I'm a Stranger Here Myself*, by Ogden Nash; for "Constant" from *The Poems of Emily Dickinson*, edited by Martha Dickinson Bianchi and Alfred Leete Hampson.

LIVERIGHT PUBLISHING CORPORATION: For "My Grandmother's Love Letters" by Hart Crane, from *The Collected Poems of Hart Crane*. Copyright, Liveright, Inc., 1933.

LOTHROP, LEE & SHEPARD CO., INC.: For "The Coming American" and "The House by the Side of the Road," both by Sam Walter Foss.

THE MACMILLAN COMPANY: For "Spanish Waters" and "Sea Fever" both from *Collected Poems* by John Masefield, copyright 1918 and 1935; for "Spring Night" from *Collected Poems* by Sara Teasdale, copyright 1937; for "My Garden is a Pleasant Place" from *Garden Grace* by Louise Driscoll, copyright 1924; for "An Old Woman of the Roads" from *Wild Earth* by Padraic Colum, copyright, 1922.

ALBA R. MALONE: For "Opportunity" by Walter Malone.

VIRGIL MARKHAM: For "A Creed" by Edwin Markham.

ALIDA MONRO: For "Milk for the Cat" by Harold Monro.

DAVID MORTON: For "Who Walks with Beauty."

SILAS H. PERKINS: For "The Common Road."

THE REILLY & LEE COMPANY: For "Home" by Edgar A. Guest, copyright, 1928 by The Reilly & Lee Company; for "It Couldn't Be Done" by Edgar A. Guest, copyright 1934 by The Reilly & Lee Company.

JOHN JEROME ROONEY, JR.: For "The Men Behind the Guns" by John Jerome Rooney.

SYDNEY RUSSELL: For "Midsummer."

THE RYERSON PRESS, Toronto: For "The Spell of the Yukon" and "The Shooting of Dan McGrew" both by Robert W. Service. By permission of the author and The Ryerson Press, from *The Complete Poems of Robert W. Service,* published in Canada by The Ryerson Press.

CHARLES SCRIBNER'S SONS: For "These Are The Gifts I Ask," reprinted from *The Poems of Henry Van Dyke,* copyright, 1911 by Charles Scribner's Sons, 1939 by Tertius Van Dyke, used by permission of the publishers; for "Be Strong": Reprinted from *Thoughts For Everyday Living* by Maltbie D. Babcock, copyright 1901 by Charles Scribner's Sons, 1929 by Katharine T. Babcock, used by permission of the publishers.

THE SOCIETY OF AUTHORS, as the literary representative of the Trustees of the estate of the late A. E. Housman, and JONATHAN CAPE LIMITED, publishers of A. E. Housman's Collected Poems: For "Loveliest of Trees" by A. E. Housman. Also THE SOCIETY OF AUTHORS and DR. JOHN MASEFIELD, O. M.: For "Sea Fever" and "Spanish Waters," by John Masefield.

TURNER COMPANY: For "Let Me Grow Lovely" from *Dreamers On Horseback,* by Karle Wilson Baker.

BLANCHE SHOEMAKER WAGSTAFF: For "All Paths Lead to You."

MRS. NIXON WATERMAN: For "Far from the Madding Crowd," by Nixon Waterman.

A. P. WATT & SON, MRS. GEORGE BAMBRIDGE, THE MACMILLAN COMPANY OF CANADA, MACMILLAN & COMPANY LTD.: For "If" from *Rewards and Fairies* by Rudyard Kipling. Also A. P. WATT & SON, MRS. GEORGE BAMBRIDGE, THE MACMILLAN COMPANY OF CANADA, and METHUEN & COMPANY LTD.: For "The Ballad of East and West," from *Barrack-Room Ballads* by Rudyard Kipling.

VICTOR BLAINE WRIGHT: For "The Want of You," by Ivan L. Wright.

Introduction

Our chief purpose in assembling this new anthology of favorite poems has been to provide for all members of the family a satisfying collection of poems which have long endeared themselves to every American home. At the same time, we have introduced a certain number of other poems not so well known which seem to us to have the same popular appeal, including among them some outstanding choices from leading recent poets. In all cases the sentiment of the poem rather than the fame of the poet has been the deciding factor in determining its selection. The great poets, American and English, are well represented, along with others whose names are associated almost entirely with a single poem which has won a permanent place in the list of favorites. We have occasionally included a surprise poem by a writer better known in other fields than that of poetry, but whose chance excursion into verse has produced a poem of perennial appeal.

The poems are grouped in categories so varied as to suit almost every mood, and the reader can turn readily to the section which interests him most at any given time. Thus, the first category presents poems revealing the many aspects of love. Then, for contemplative moments there are sections devoted to faith and inspiration, nature, and reflection. Other groups give us great poems of adventure on land and sea, of legend and fantasy, of humor and satire. In a special group we bring together poems about America which vividly present great episodes in American history and convey profound devotion to our country. A separate section captures the flavor of frontier days. Much thought has been given to the placing of poems in relation to their neighbors within each section, so as to gain freshness from the continuity or contrast between poems which follow one another. Short poems, which convey their message or story rapidly, constitute the majority of the more than four hundred poems brought together here. Yet, we have made space so as to give in their entirety some outstanding long poems such as "The Rime of the Ancient Mariner" and "The Rubaiyat of Omar Khayyam." Thus, *The Family Book of Best Loved Poems* will be rewarding to readers who browse at random among its pages, as well as to those who read whole sections, and to those who are seeking a particular poem to fit a specific mood or occasion.

The editor wishes to mention here his appreciation and deep gratitude to Lawrence W. Lamm for his unerring guidance at every point from the conception to the completion of this volume.

It is the sincere hope of the editor that all the members of the family will turn frequently to the pages of this book for the inspiration and entertainment which it is sure to provide. For here are the poems that have pleased generations of readers, standing the test of time and change in popular taste, together with poems of our own day equally enduring in their feeling and expression. Here is a Family Book which, we feel sure, will have a welcome place on a handy table or a convenient bookshelf near a comfortable reading corner.

D. L. G.

Contents

Favorite Poems of
LOVE

Favorite Poems of
FAITH AND INSPIRATION

Favorite Poems about
AMERICA

Favorite Poems of
HOME AND FIRESIDE

Favorite Poems for
CHILDREN

Favorite Poems about
NATURE

Favorite Poems of
CONTEMPLATION

Contents

Favorite Poems of

ADVENTURE ON LAND AND SEA

Favorite Poems of
LEGEND AND FANTASY

Contents

Favorite Poems Of
LOVE

MY LOVE

NOT as all other women are
Is she that to my soul is dear;
Her glorious fancies come from far,
Beneath the silver evening-star,
And yet her heart is ever near.

Great feelings hath she of her own,
Which lesser souls may never know;
God giveth them to her alone,
And sweet they are as any tone
Wherewith the wind may choose to blow.

Yet in herself she dwelleth not,
Although no home were half so fair;
No simplest duty is forgot,
Life hath no dim and lowly spot
That doth not in her sunshine share.

She doeth little kindnesses,
Which most leave undone, or despise:
For naught that sets one heart at ease,
And giveth happiness or peace,
Is low-esteemèd in her eyes.

She hath no scorn of common things,
And, though she seem of other birth,
Round us her heart intwines and clings,
And patiently she folds her wings
To tread the humble paths of earth.

Blessing she is: God made her so,
And deeds of week-day holiness
Fall from her noiseless as the snow,
Nor hath she ever chanced to know
That aught were easier than to bless.

She is most fair, and thereunto
Her life doth rightly harmonize;
Feeling or thought that was not true
Ne'er made less beautiful the blue
Unclouded heaven of her eyes.

She is a woman: one in whom
The spring-time of her childish years
Hath never lost its fresh perfume,
Though knowing well that life hath room
For many blights and many tears.

I love her with a love as still
As a broad river's peaceful might,
Which, by high tower and lowly mill,
Seems following its own wayward will,
And yet doth ever flow aright.

And, on its full, deep breast serene,
Like quiet isles my duties lie;
It flows around them and between,
And makes them fresh and fair and green,
Sweet homes wherein to live and die.

JAMES RUSSELL LOWELL

A SONG

Sing me a sweet, low song of night
    Before the moon is risen,
A song that tells of the stars' delight
    Escaped from day's bright prison,
A song that croons with the cricket's voice,
    That sleeps with the shadowed trees,
A song that shall bid my heart rejoice
    At its tender mysteries!

And then when the song is ended, love,
 Bend down your head unto me,
Whisper the word that was born above
 Ere the moon had swayed the sea;
Ere the oldest star began to shine,
 Or the farthest sun to burn,—
The oldest of words, O heart of mine,
 Yet newest, and sweet to learn.

HILDEGARDE HAWTHORNE

LOVE

I LOVE you,
Not only for what you are,
But for what I am
When I am with you.

I love you,
Not only for what
You have made of yourself,
But for what
You are making of me.

I love you
For the part of me
That you bring out;
I love you
For putting your hand
Into my heaped-up heart
And passing over
All the foolish, weak things
That you can't help
Dimly seeing there,
And for drawing out
Into the light
All the beautiful belongings
That no one else had looked
Quite far enough to find.

I love you because you
Are helping me to make
Of the lumber of my life
Not a tavern
But a temple;
Out of the works

Of my every day
Not a reproach
But a song.

I love you
Because you have done
More than any creed
Could have done
To make me good,
And more than any fate
Could have done
To make me happy.

You have done it
Without a touch,
Without a word,
Without a sign.
You have done it
By being yourself.
Perhaps that is what
Being a friend means,
After all.

ROY CROFT

LIGHT

THE night has a thousand eyes,
    The day but one;
Yet the light of the bright world dies
    With the dying sun.

The mind has a thousand eyes,
    And the heart but one;
Yet the light of a whole life dies
    When its love is done.

FRANCIS W. BOURDILLON

TO CELIA

DRINK to me only with thine eyes,
    And I will pledge with mine;
Or leave a kiss but in the cup,
    And I'll not look for wine.
The thirst that from the soul doth rise
    Doth ask a drink divine;
But might I of Jove's nectar sup,
    I would not change for thine.

I sent thee late a rosy wreath,
Not so much honoring thee
As giving it a hope, that there
It could not withered be.
But thou thereon didst only breathe,
And sent'st it back to me;
Since when it grows, and smells, I swear,
Not of itself, but thee.

BEN JONSON

BEDOUIN SONG

FROM the desert I come to thee,
On a stallion shod with fire;
And the winds are left behind
In the speed of my desire.
Under thy window I stand,
And the midnight hears my cry:
I love thee, I love but thee,
With a love that shall not die
Till the sun grows cold,
And the stars are old,
And the leaves of the Judgment
Book unfold!

Look from thy window, and see
My passion and my pain;
I lie on the sands below,
And I faint in thy disdain.
Let the night-winds touch thy brow
With the heat of my burning sigh,
And melt thee to hear the vow
Of a love that shall not die
Till the sun grows cold,
And the stars are old,
And the leaves of the Judgment
Book unfold!

My steps are nightly driven,
By the fever in my breast,
To hear from thy lattice breathed
The word that shall give me rest.
Open the door of thy heart,
And open thy chamber door,
And my kisses shall teach thy lips
The love that shall fade no more

Till the sun grows cold,
And the stars are old,
And the leaves of the Judgment
Book unfold!

BAYARD TAYLOR

TO HELEN

HELEN, thy beauty is to me
    Like those Nicaean barks of yore,
That gently, o'er a perfumed sea,
    The weary, wayworn wanderer bore
    To his own native shore.

On desperate seas long wont to roam,
    Thy hyacinth hair, thy classic face,
Thy Naiad airs, have brought me home
    To the glory that was Greece
    And the grandeur that was Rome.

Lo! in yon brilliant window-niche
    How statue-like I see thee stand,
The agate lamp within thy hand!
    Ah, Psyche, from the regions which
    Are Holy Land!

EDGAR ALLAN POE

SHE WAS A PHANTOM OF DELIGHT

SHE was a Phantom of delight
When first she gleamed upon my sight;
A lovely Apparition, sent
To be a moment's ornament;
Her eyes as stars of Twilight fair;
Like Twilight's, too, her dusky hair;
But all things else about her drawn
From May-time and the cheerful Dawn;
A dancing Shape, an Image gay,
To haunt, to startle, and way-lay.

I saw her upon nearer view,
A Spirit, yet a Woman too!
Her household motions light and free,
And steps of virgin-liberty;
A countenance in which did meet
Sweet records, promises as sweet;

A Creature not too bright or good
For human nature's daily food;
For transient sorrows, simple wiles,
Praise, blame, love, kisses, tears, and smiles.

And now I see with eyes serene
The very pulse of the machine;
A Being breathing thoughtful breath,
A Traveller between life and death;
The reason firm, the temperate will,
Endurance, foresight, strength, and skill;
A perfect Woman, nobly planned,
To warn, to comfort, and command;
And yet a Spirit still, and bright
With something of angelic light.

WILLIAM WORDSWORTH

EROS

THE sense of the world is short,—
Long and various the report,—
    To love and be beloved;
Men and gods have not outlearned it;
And, how oft soe'er they've turned it,
    'Tis not to be improved.

RALPH WALDO EMERSON

AT A WINDOW

GIVE me hunger,
O you gods that sit and give
The world its orders.
Give me hunger, pain and want;
Shut me out with shame and failure
From your doors of gold and fame,
Give me your shabbiest, weariest hunger.

But leave me a little love,
A voice to speak to me in the day end,
A hand to touch me in the dark room
Breaking the long loneliness.
In the dusk of day-shapes
Blurring the sunset,
One little wandering, western star
Thrust out from the changing shores of shadow.

Let me go to the window,
Watch there the day-shapes of dusk,
And wait and know the coming
Of a little love.

CARL SANDBURG

SONNET

SHALL I compare thee to a summer's day?
Thou art more lovely and more temperate:
Rough winds do shake the darling buds of May,
And summer's lease hath all too short a date:
Sometime too hot the eye of heaven shines,
And often is his gold complexion dimm'd;
And every fair from fair sometime declines,
By chance, or nature's changing course untrimm'd;
But thy eternal summer shall not fade,
Nor lose possession of that fair thou ow'st,
Nor shall death brag thou wander'st in his shade,
When in eternal lines to time thou grow'st;
　　So long as men can breathe, or eyes can see,
　　So long lives this, and this gives life to thee.

WILLIAM SHAKESPEARE

WE HAVE LIVED AND LOVED TOGETHER

WE HAVE LIVED and loved together
　　Through many changing years;
We have shared each other's gladness
　　And wept each other's tears;
I have known ne'er a sorrow
　　That was long unsoothed by thee;
For thy smiles can make a summer
　　Where darkness else would be.

Like the leaves that fall around us
　　In autumn's fading hours,
Are the traitor's smiles, that darken
　　When the cloud of sorrow lowers;
And though many such we've known, love,
　　Too prone, alas, to range,
We both can speak of one love
　　Which time can never change.

We have lived and loved together
   Through many changing years;
We have shared each other's gladness
   And wept each other's tears.
And let us hope the future,
   As the past has been will be:
I will share with thee my sorrows,
   And thou thy joys with me.

CHARLES JEFFERYS

JENNY KISSED ME

JENNY kissed me when we met,
   Jumping from the chair she sat in.
Time, you thief! who love to get
   Sweets into your list, put that in.
Say I'm weary, say I'm sad;
   Say that health and wealth have missed me;
Say I'm growing old, but add—
            Jenny kissed me!

LEIGH HUNT

MISS YOU

Miss you, miss you, miss you;
Everything I do
Echoes with the laughter
And the voice of you.
You're on every corner,
Every turn and twist,
Every old familiar spot
Whispers how you're missed.

Miss you, miss you, miss you.
Everywhere I go
There are poignant memories
Dancing in a row,
Silhouette and shadow
Of your form and face
Substance and reality
Everywhere displace.

Oh, I miss you, miss you!
How I miss you, Girl!
There's a strange, sad silence
'Mid the busy whirl,

Just as tho' the ordinary,
Daily things I do
Wait with me, expectant,
For a word from you.

Miss you, miss you, miss you!
Nothing now seems true,
Only that 'twas Heaven
Just to be with you.

DAVID CORY

KASHMIRI SONG

PALE HANDS I loved beside the Shalimar,
    Where are you now? Who lies beneath your spell?
Whom do you lead on Rapture's Roadway, far,
    Before you agonize them in farewell?

Oh, pale dispensers of my Joys and Pains,
    Holding the doors of Heaven and Hell,
How the hot blood rushed wildly through the veins
    Beneath your touch, until you waved farewell.

Pale hands, pink-tipped, like lotus buds that float
    On those cool waters where we used to dwell,
I would have rather felt you round my throat
    Crushing out life than waving me farewell!

LAURENCE HOPE

SHE WALKS IN BEAUTY

SHE walks in beauty, like the night
    Of cloudless climes and starry skies,
And all that's best of dark and bright
    Meet in her aspect and her eyes,
Thus mellowed to that tender light
    Which heaven to gaudy day denies.

One shade the more, one ray the less,
    Had half impaired the nameless grace
Which waves in every raven tress
    Or softly lightens o'er her face,
Where thoughts serenely sweet express
    How pure, how dear their dwelling-place.

And on that cheek and o'er that brow
  So soft, so calm, yet eloquent,
The smiles that win, the tints that glow,
  But tell of days in goodness spent,—
A mind at peace with all below,
  A heart whose love is innocent.

GEORGE GORDON BYRON

MY LUVE'S LIKE A RED, RED ROSE

O MY LUVE's like a red, red rose,
  That's newly sprung in June:
O my Luve's like the melodie
  That's sweetly played in tune!

As fair art thou, my bonnie lass,
  So deep in luve am I;
And I will luve thee still, my dear,
  Till a' the seas gang dry.

Till a' the seas gang dry, my dear,
  And the rocks melt wi' the sun;
I will luve thee still, my dear,
  While the sands o' life shall run.

And fare thee weel, my only Luve,
  And fare thee weel a while!
And I will come again, my Luve,
  Though it were ten thousand mile.

ROBERT BURNS

SWEET PERIL

ALAS, how easily things go wrong!
A sigh too much, or a kiss too long,
And there follows a mist and a weeping rain,
And life is never the same again.

Alas, how hardly things go right!
'Tis hard to watch in a summer night,
For the sigh will come, and the kiss will stay,
And the summer night is a wintry day.

And yet how easily things go right,
If the sigh and a kiss of a summer's night
Come deep from the soul in the stronger ray
That is born in the light of the winter's day.

And things can never go badly wrong
If the heart be true and the love be strong,
For the mist, if it comes, and the weeping rain
Will be changed by the love into sunshine again.

GEORGE MACDONALD

HER FAIRNESS, WEDDED TO A STAR

HER fairness, wedded to a star,
Is whiter than all lilies are,
And flowers within her eyes more white
Than moonlight on an April night.

Her wonder like a wind doth sing,
Wedded to the heart of spring,
And April, dawning in her eyes,
Reflects the wonder of the skies.

Her beauty lights the April day
With radiance of her chastity,
And innocence doth slumber now
Upon her candid April brow.

EDWARD J. O'BRIEN

FIDELIS

You HAVE taken back the promise
    That you spoke so long ago;
Taken back the heart you gave me—
    I must even let it go.
Where Love once has breathed, Pride dieth;
    So I struggled, but in vain,
First to keep the links together,
    Then to piece the broken chain.

But it might not be—so freely
    All your friendship I restore,
And the heart that I had taken
    As my own forevermore.
No shade of reproach shall touch you,
    Dread no more a claim from me—
But I will not have you fancy
    That I count myself as free.

I am bound by the old promise;
    What can break that golden chain?

Not even the words that you have spoken,
  Or the sharpness of my pain:
Do you think, because you fail me
And draw back your hand today,
That from out the heart I gave you
  My strong love can fade away?

It will live. No eyes may see it;
  In my soul it will lie deep,
Hidden from all; but I shall feel it
  Often stirring in its sleep.
So remember that the friendship
  Which you now think poor and vain,
Will endure in hope and patience,
  Till you ask for it again.

Perhaps in some long twilight hour,
  Like those we have known of old,
When past shadows gather round you,
  And your present friends grow cold,
You may stretch your hands out towards me—
Ah! You will—I know not when—
I shall nurse my love and keep it
  Faithfully, for you, till then.

ADELAIDE ANNE PROCTER

THE FIRST DAY

I WISH I could remember the first day,
First hour, first moment of your meeting me,
If bright or dim the season, it might be
Summer or Winter for aught I can say;
So unrecorded did it slip away,
So blind was I to see and to foresee,
So dull to mark the budding of my tree
That would not blossom yet for many a May.
If only I could recollect it, such
A day of days! I let it come and go
As traceless as a thaw of bygone snow;
It seemed to mean so little, meant so much;
If only now I could recall that touch,
First touch of hand in hand—Did one but know!

CHRISTINA GEORGINA ROSSETTI

MY GRANDMOTHER'S LOVE LETTERS

THERE are no stars tonight
But those of memory.
Yet how much room for memory there is
In the loose girdle of soft rain.

There is even room enough
For the letters of my mother's mother,
Elizabeth,
That have been pressed so long
Into a corner of the roof
That they are brown and soft,
And liable to melt as snow.

Over the greatness of such space
Steps must be gentle.
It is all hung by an invisible white hair.
It trembles as birch limbs webbing the air.

And I ask myself:

"Are your fingers long enough to play
Old keys that are but echoes:
Is the silence strong enough
To carry back the music to its source
And back to you again
As though to her?"

Yet I would lead my grandmother by the hand
Through much of what she would not understand;
And so I stumble. And the rain continues on the roof
With such a sound of gently pitying laughter.

HART CRANE

RAINY SONG

DOWN the dripping pathway dancing through the rain,
Brown eyes of beauty, laugh to me again!

Eyes full of starlight, moist over fire,
Full of young wonder, touch my desire!

O like a brown bird, like a bird's flight,
Run through the rain drops lithely and light.

Body like a gypsy, like a wild queen,
Slim brown dress to slip through the green—

The little leaves hold you as soft as a child,
The little path loves you, the path that runs wild.

Who would not love you, seeing you move,
Warm-eyed and beautiful through the green grove?

Let the rain kiss you, trickle through your hair,
Laugh if my fingers mingle with it there,

Laugh if my cheek too is misty and drips—
Wetness is tender—laugh on my lips

The happy sweet laughter of love without pain,
Young love, the strong love, burning in the rain.

MAX EASTMAN

IN A ROSE GARDEN

A HUNDRED YEARS from now, dear heart,
    We shall not care at all,
It will not matter then a whit,
    The honey or the gall.
The summer days that we have known
Will all forgotten be and flown;
The garden will be overgrown
    Where now the roses fall.

A hundred years from now, dear heart,
    We shall not mind the pain;
The throbbing crimson tide of life
    Will not have left a stain.
The song we sing together, dear,
The dream we dream together here,
Will mean no more than means a tear
    Amid a summer rain.

A hundred years from now, dear heart,
    The grief will all be o'er;
The sea of care will surge in vain
    Upon a careless shore.
These glasses we turn down today
Here at the parting of the way—
We shall be wineless then as they,
    And shall not mind it more.

A hundred years from now, dear heart,
   We'll neither know nor care
What came of all life's bitterness,
   Or followed love's despair.
Then fill the glasses up again,
And kiss me through the rose-leaf rain;
We'll build one castle more in Spain,
   And dream one more dream there.

JOHN BENNETT

I LOVE YOU

I LOVE your lips when they're wet with wine
   And red with a wild desire;
I love your eyes when the lovelight lies
   Lit with a passionate fire.
I love your arms when the warm white flesh
   Touches mine in a fond embrace;
I love your hair when the strands enmesh
   Your kisses against my face.

Not for me the cold, calm kiss
   Of a virgin's bloodless love;
Not for me the saint's white bliss,
   Nor the heart of a spotless dove.
But give me the love that so freely gives
   And laughs at the whole world's blame,
With your body so young and warm in my arms,
   It sets my poor heart aflame.

So kiss me sweet with your warm wet mouth,
   Still fragrant with ruby wine,
And say with a fervor born of the South
   That your body and soul are mine.
Clasp me close in your warm young arms,
   While the pale stars shine above,
And we'll live our whole young lives away
   In the joys of a living love.

ELLA WHEELER WILCOX

THE ROSARY

THE hours I spent with thee, dear heart,
   Are as a string of pearls to me;
I count them over, every one apart,
   My rosary.

Each hour a pearl, each pearl a prayer,
   To still a heart in absence wrung;
I tell each bead unto the end and there
    A cross is hung.

Oh memories that bless—and burn!
   Oh barren gain—and bitter loss!
I kiss each bead, and strive at last to learn
    To kiss the cross,
      Sweetheart,
        To kiss the cross.
        ROBERT CAMERON ROGERS

CREED

I BELIEVE if I should die,
And you should kiss my eyelids when I lie
Cold, dead, and dumb to all the world contains,
The folded orbs would open at thy breath,
And, from its exile in the isles of death,
Life would come gladly back along my veins.

I believe if I were dead,
And you upon my lifeless heart should tread,
Not knowing what the poor clod chanced to be,
It would find sudden pulse beneath the touch
Of him it ever loved in life so much,
And throb again—warm, tender, true to thee.

I believe if on my grave,
Hidden in woody depths or by the wave,
Your eyes should drop some warm tears of regret,
From every salty seed of your dear grief
Some fair, sweet blossom would leap into leaf
To prove death could not make my love forget.

I believe if I should fade
Into those mystic realms where light is made,
And you should long once more my face to see,
I would come forth upon the hills of night
And gather stars, like fagots, till thy sight,
Led by their beacon blaze, fell full on me.

I believe my faith in thee,
Strong as my life, so nobly placed to be,
I would as soon expect to see the sun
Fall like a dead king from his height sublime,
His glory stricken from the throne of time,
As thee unworth the worship thou hast won.

I believe who hath not loved
Hath half the sweetness of his life unproved;
Like one who, with the grape within his grasp,
Drops it with all its crimson juice unpressed,
And all its luscious sweetness left unguessed,
Out from his careless and unheeding clasp.

I believe love, pure and true,
Is to the soul a sweet, immortal dew
That gems life's petals in its hours of dusk.
The waiting angels see and recognize
The rich crown jewel, Love, of Paradise,
When life falls from us like a withered husk.

                              MARY ASHLEY TOWNSEND

MIDSUMMER

You LOVED me for a little,
    Who could not love me long;
You gave me wings of gladness
    And lent my spirit song.

You loved me for an hour
    But only with your eyes;
Your lips I could not capture
    By storm or by surprise.

Your mouth that I remember
    With rush of sudden pain
As one remembers starlight
    Or roses after rain . . .

Out of a world of laughter
    Suddenly I am sad. . . .
Day and night it haunts me,
    The kiss I never had.

                    SYDNEY KING RUSSELL

SONNET

FIRST TIME he kissed me, he but only kiss'd
    The fingers of this hand wherewith I write;
    And ever since, it grew more clean and white,
Slow to world-greetings, quick with its "Oh, list,"
When the angels speak. A ring of amethyst
    I could not wear here, plainer to my sight,

Than that first kiss. The second pass'd in height
The first, and sought the forehead, and half miss'd,
Half falling on the hair. Oh, beyond meed!
That was the chrism of love, which love's own crown,
With sanctifying sweetness, did precede.
The third upon my lips was folded down
In perfect, purple state; since when, indeed,
I have been proud, and said, "My love, my own!"

ELIZABETH BARRETT BROWNING

BELIEVE ME, IF ALL THOSE ENDEARING YOUNG CHARMS

BELIEVE ME, if all those endearing young charms,
    Which I gaze on so fondly to-day,
Were to change by to-morrow, and fleet in my arms,
    Like fairy-gifts fading away,
Thou wouldst still be adored, as this moment thou art,
    Let thy loveliness fade as it will,
And around the dear ruin each wish of my heart
    Would entwine itself verdantly still.

It is not while beauty and youth are thine own,
    And thy cheeks unprofaned by a tear,
That the fervor and faith of a soul may be known,
    To which time will but make thee more dear!
No, the heart that has truly loved never forgets,
    But as truly loves on to the close,
As the sunflower turns to her god when he sets
    The same look which she turned when he rose!

THOMAS MOORE

TO DIANEME

GIVE ME one kiss,
And no more;
If so be, this
Makes you poor;
To enrich you,
I'll restore
For that one, two
Thousand score.

ROBERT HERRICK

YOU AND I

My HAND is lonely for your clasping, dear;
    My ear is tired waiting for your call.
I want your strength to help, your laugh to cheer;
    Heart, soul and senses need you, one and all.
I droop without your full, frank sympathy;
    We ought to be together—you and I;
We want each other so, to comprehend
    The dream, the hope, things planned, or seen, or wrought.
Companion, comforter and guide and friend,
    As much as love asks love, does thought ask thought.
Life is so short, so fast the lone hours fly,
    We ought to be together, you and I.

                                    HENRY ALFORD

ALL PATHS LEAD TO YOU

        ALL PATHS lead to you
            Where e'er I stray,
        You are the evening star
            At the end of day.

        All paths lead to you
            Hill-top or low,
        You are the white birch
            In the sun's glow.

        All paths lead to you
            Where e'er I roam.
        You are the lark-song
            Calling me home!

                    BLANCHE SHOEMAKER WAGSTAFF

THE ABIDING LOVE

It SINGETH low in every heart,
    We hear it each and all—
A song of those who answer not,
    However we may call;
They throng the silence of the breast,
    We see them as of yore—
The kind, the brave, the sweet,
    Who walk with us no more.

'Tis hard to take the burden up
　　When these have laid it down;
They brightened all the joy of life,
　　They softened every frown;
But, Oh, 'tis good to think of them
　　When we are troubled sore!
Thanks be to God that such have been,
　　Although they are no more.

More homelike seems the vast unknown
　　Since they have entered there;
To follow them were not so hard,
　　Wherever they may fare;
They cannot be where God is not,
　　On any sea or shore;
Whate'er betides, thy love abides,
　　Our God, forever more.

　　　　　　　JOHN WHITE CHADWICK

THE PASSIONATE SHEPHERD TO HIS LOVE

COME LIVE with me and be my love,
And we will all the pleasures prove
That valleys, groves, hills, and fields,
Woods, or steepy mountain yields.

And we will sit upon the rocks,
Seeing the shepherds feed their flocks,
By shallow rivers to whose falls
Melodious birds sing madrigals.

And I will make thee beds of roses
And a thousand fragrant posies,
A cap of flowers, and a kirtle
Embroidered all with leaves of myrtle;

A gown made of the finest wool
Which from our pretty lambs we pull;
Fair linëd slippers for the cold,
With buckles of the purest gold;

A belt of straw and ivy buds,
With coral clasps and amber studs:
And if these pleasures may thee move,
Come live with me, and be my love.

The shepherds' swains shall dance and sing
For thy delight each May morning:
If these delights thy mind may move,
Then live with me and be my love.

CHRISTOPHER MARLOWE

SONNET

How do I love thee? Let me count the ways.
I love thee to the depth and breadth and height
My soul can reach, when feeling out of sight
For the ends of Being and ideal Grace.
I love thee to the level of everyday's
Most quiet need, by sun and candle-light.
I love thee freely, as men strive for Right;
I love thee purely, as they turn from Praise.
I love thee with the passion put to use
In my old griefs, and with my childhood's faith.
I love thee with a love I seemed to lose
With my lost saints,—I love thee with the breath,
Smiles, tears, of all my life!—and, if God choose,
I shall but love thee better after death.

ELIZABETH BARRETT BROWNING

A WOMAN'S LAST WORD

LET's contend no more, Love,
  Strive nor weep:
All be as before, Love,
  —Only sleep!

What so wild as words are?
  I and thou
In debate, as birds are,
  Hawk on bough!

See the creature stalking
  While we speak!
Hush and hide the talking,
  Cheek on cheek!

What so false as truth is,
  False to thee?
Where the serpent's tooth is
  Shun the tree—

Where the apple reddens
    Never pry—
Lest we lose our Edens,
    Eve and I!

Be a god and hold me
    With a charm!
Be a man and fold me
    With thine arm!

Teach me, only teach, Love!
    As I ought
I will speak thy speech, Love,
    Think thy thought—

Meet, if thou require it,
    Both demands,
Laying flesh and spirit
    In thy hands.

That shall be to-morrow
    Not to-night:
I must bury sorrow
    Out of sight:

—Must a little weep, Love,
    (Foolish me!)
And so fall asleep, Love
    Loved by thee.

                    ROBERT BROWNING

ASHES OF LIFE

Love has gone and left me, and the days are all alike.
    Eat I must, and sleep I will—and would that night were here!
But ah, to lie awake and hear the slow hours strike!
    Would that it were day again, with twilight near!

Love has gone and left me, and I don't know what to do;
    This or that or what you will is all the same to me;
But all the things that I begin I leave before I'm through—
    There's little use in anything as far as I can see.

Love has gone and left me, and the neighbors knock and borrow,
    And life goes on forever like the gnawing of a mouse.
And to-morrow and to-morrow and to-morrow and to-morrow
    There's this little street and this little house.

                    EDNA ST. VINCENT MILLAY

WHO IS SYLVIA?

Who is Sylvia? what is she,
    That all our swains commend her?
Holy, fair, and wise is she;
    The heavens such grace did lend her
That she might admired be.

Is she kind, as she is fair?
    For beauty lives with kindness.
Love does to her eyes repair
    To help him of his blindness—
And, being help'd, inhabits there.

Then to Sylvia let us sing
    That Sylvia is excelling;
She excels each mortal thing
    Upon the dull earth dwelling;
To her let us garlands bring.

                    WILLIAM SHAKESPEARE

NON SUM QUALIS ERAM BONAE
SUB REGNO CYNARAE

Last night, ah, yesternight, betwixt her lips and mine
There fell thy shadow, Cynara! Thy breath was shed
Upon my soul between the kisses and the wine;
And I was desolate and sick of an old passion—
Yea, I was desolate and bowed my head.
I have been faithful to thee, Cynara!—In my fashion.

All night upon mine heart I felt her warm heart beat,
Night-long within mine arms in love and sleep she lay;
Surely the kisses of her bought red mouth were sweet;
But I was desolate and sick of an old passion—
When I woke and found the dawn was gray:
I have been faithful to thee, Cynara!—In my fashion.

I have forgot much, Cynara! Gone with the wind,
Flung roses, roses riotously with the throng,
Dancing, to put thy pale, lost lilies out of mind;
But I was desolate and sick of an old passion—
Yea, all the time, because the dance was long:
I have been faithful to thee, Cynara!—In my fashion.

I cried for madder music and for stronger wine,
But when the feast is finished and the lamps expire,
Then falls thy shadow, Cynara! The night is thine;
And I am desolate and sick of an old passion,
Yea, hungry for the lips of my desire:
I have been faithful to thee, Cynara!—In my fashion.

ERNEST DOWSON

SPRING NIGHT

The park is filled with night and fog,
    The veils are drawn about the world,
The drowsy lights along the paths
    Are dim and pearled.

Gold and gleaming the empty streets,
    Gold and gleaming the misty lake,
The mirrored lights like sunken swords,
    Glimmer and shake.

Oh, is it not enough to be
Here with this beauty over me?
My throat should ache with praise, and I
Should kneel in joy beneath the sky.
O beauty, are you not enough?
Why am I crying after love
With youth, a singing voice, and eyes
To take earth's wonder with surprise?
Why have I put off my pride,
Why am I unsatisfied,—
I, for whom the pensive night
Binds her cloudy hair with light,—
I, for whom all beauty burns
Like incense in a million urns?
O beauty, are you not enough?
Why am I crying after love?

SARA TEASDALE

SONG

Now SLEEPS the crimson petal, now the white;
Nor waves the cypress in the palace walk;
Nor winks the gold fin in the porphyry font:
The firefly wakens: waken thou with me.

Now droops the milkwhite peacock like a ghost,
And like a ghost she glimmers on to me.
    Now lies the earth all Danaë to the stars,
And all thy heart lies open unto me.
    Now slides the silent meteor on, and leaves
A shining furrow, as thy thoughts in me.

Now folds the lily all her sweetness up,
And slips into the bosom of the lake:
So fold thyself, my dearest, thou, and slip
Into my bosom and be lost in me.

ALFRED TENNYSON

MY TRUE-LOVE HATH MY HEART

My true-love hath my heart, and I have his,
    By just exchange one to the other given:
I hold his dear, and mine he cannot miss,
    There never was a better bargain driven:
My true-love hath my heart, and I have his.

His heart in me keeps him and me in one;
    My heart in him his thoughts and senses guides:
He loves my heart, for once it was his own;
    I cherish his because in me it bides:
My true-love hath my heart, and I have his.

SIR PHILIP SIDNEY

SERENADE

Stars of the summer night!
        Far in yon azure deeps,
Hide, hide your golden light!
        She sleeps!
My lady sleeps!
        Sleeps!

Moon of the summer night!
        Far down yon western steeps,
Sink, sink in silver light!
        She sleeps!
My lady sleeps!
        Sleeps!

Wind of the summer night!
        Where yonder woodbine creeps,

Fold, fold thy pinions light!
　　She sleeps!
My lady sleeps!
　　Sleeps!

Dreams of the summer night!
　　Tell her, her lover keeps
Watch! while in slumbers light
　　She sleeps!
My lady sleeps!
　　Sleeps!
　　　　　　HENRY WADSWORTH LONGFELLOW

THE WANT OF YOU

THE WANT of you is like no other thing;
It smites my soul with sudden sickening;
It binds my being with a wreath of rue—
　　This want of you.

It flashes on me with the waking sun;
It creeps upon me when the day is done;
It hammers at my heart the long night through—
　　This want of you.

It sighs within me with the misting skies;
Oh, all the day within my heart it cries,
Old as your absence, yet each moment new—
　　This want of you.

Mad with demand and aching with despair,
It leaps within my heart and you are—where?
God has forgotten, or he never knew—
　　This want of you.
　　　　　　　　IVAN LEONARD WRIGHT

I WILL NOT LET THEE GO

　　I WILL not let thee go.
Ends all our month-long love in this?
　　Can it be summed up so,
　　Quit in a single kiss?
I will not let thee go.

　　I will not let thee go.
If thy words' breath could scare thy deeds,

As the soft south can blow
And toss the feathered seeds,
Then might I let thee go.

I will not let thee go.
Had not the great sun seen, I might;
Or were he reckoned slow
To bring the false to light,
Then might I let thee go.

I will not let thee go.
The stars that crowd the summer skies
Have watched us so below
With all their million eyes,
I dare not let thee go.

I will not let thee go.
Have we not chid the changeful moon,
Now rising late, and now
Because she set too soon,
And shall I let thee go?

I will not let thee go.
Have not the young flowers been content,
Plucked ere their buds could blow,
To seal our sacrament?
I cannot let thee go.

I will not let thee go.
I hold thee by too many bands:
Thou sayest farewell, and lo!
I have thee by the hands,
And will not let thee go.

ROBERT BRIDGES

LOVE'S PHILOSOPHY

The fountains mingle with the river,
    And the rivers with the ocean;
The winds of heaven mix forever,
    With a sweet emotion;
Nothing in the world is single;
    All things by a law divine
In one another's being mingle:—
    Why not I with thine?

See! the mountains kiss high heaven,
    And the waves clasp one another;

No sister flower would be forgiven
    If it disdained its brother;
And the sunlight clasps the earth,
    And the moonbeams kiss the sea:—
What are all these kissings worth,
    If thou kiss not me?

PERCY BYSSHE SHELLEY

LINES TO AN INDIAN AIR

I ARISE from dreams of thee
    In the first sweet sleep of night,
When the winds are breathing low,
    And the stars are shining bright;
I arise from dreams of thee,
    And a spirit in my feet
Has led me—who knows how?—
    To thy chamber-window, sweet!

The wandering airs they faint
    On the dark, the silent stream—
The champak odors fail
    Like sweet thoughts in a dream;
The nightingale's complaint,
    It dies upon her heart,
As I must on thine,
    Beloved as thou art!

Oh lift me from the grass!
    I die, I faint, I fail!
Let thy love in kisses rain
    On my lips and eyelids pale.
My cheek is cold and white, alas!
    My heart beats loud and fast,
Oh! press it close to thine again,
    Where it will break at last.

PERCY BYSSHE SHELLEY

THE GOOD-MORROW

I WONDER, by my troth, what thou and I
Did, till we loved? were we not wean'd till then?
But suck'd on country pleasures, childishly?
Or snorted we in the Seven Sleepers' den?
'Twas so; but this, all pleasures fancies be;
If ever any beauty I did see,
Which I desired, and got, 'twas but a dream of thee.

And now good-morrow to our waking souls,
Which watch not one another out of fear;
For love all love of other sights controls,
And makes one little room an everywhere.
Let sea-discovers to new worlds have gone;
Let maps to other, worlds on worlds have shown;
Let us possess one world; each hath one, and is one.

My face in thine eye, thine in mine appears,
And true plain hearts do in the faces rest;
Where can we find two better hemispheres
Without sharp north, without declining west?
Whatever dies, was not mix'd equally;
If our two loves be one, or thou and I
Love so alike that none can slacken, none can die.

JOHN DONNE

THE ROSE AND THORN

SHE's loveliest of the festal throng
    In delicate form and Grecian face,—
A beautiful, incarnate song,
    A marvel of harmonious grace;
And yet I know the truth I speak:
    From those gay groups she stands apart,
A rose upon her tender cheek,
    A thorn within her heart.

Though bright her eyes' bewildering gleams,
    Fair tremulous lips and shining hair,
A something born of mournful dreams
    Breathes round her sad enchanted air;
No blithesome thoughts at hide and seek
    From out her dimples smiling start;
If still the rose be on her cheek,
    A thorn is in her heart.

Young lover, tossed 'twixt hope and fear,
    Your whispered vow and yearning eyes
Yon marble Clytie pillared near
    Could move as soon to soft replies:
Or, if she thrill at words you speak,
    Love's memory prompts the sudden start;
The rose has paled upon her cheek,
    The thorn has pierced her heart.

PAUL HAMILTON HAYNE

AT NIGHTFALL

I NEED so much the quiet of your love
　　After the day's loud strife;
I need your calm all other things above
　　After the stress of life.

I crave the haven that in your dear heart lies,
　　After all toil is done;
I need the starshine of your heavenly eyes,
　　After the day's great sun.

　　　　　　　　CHARLES HANSON TOWNE

SALLY IN OUR ALLEY

OF ALL the girls that are so smart
　　There's none like pretty Sally;
She is the darling of my heart,
　　And she lives in our alley.
There is no lady in the land
　　Is half so sweet as Sally;
She is the darling of my heart,
　　And she lives in our alley.

Her father he makes cabbage-nets,
　　And through the streets does cry 'em;
Her mother she sells laces long
　　To such as please to buy 'em;
But sure such folks could ne'er beget
　　So sweet a girl as Sally!
She is the darling of my heart,
　　And she lives in our alley.

When she is by, I leave my work,
　　I love her so sincerely;
My master comes like any Turk,
　　And bangs me most severely:
But let him bang his bellyful,
　　I'll bear it all for Sally;
She is the darling of my heart,
　　And she lives in our alley.

Of all the days that's in the week
　　I dearly love but one day—
And that's the day that comes betwixt

A Saturday and Monday;
For then I'm dressed all in my best
    To walk abroad with Sally;
She is the darling of my heart,
    And she lives in our alley.

My master carries me to church,
    And often am I blamèd
Because I leave him in the lurch
    As soon as text is namèd;
I leave the church in sermon-time
    And slink away to Sally;
She is the darling of my heart,
    And she lives in our alley.

When Christmas comes about again,
    O, then I shall have money;
I'll hoard it up, and box it all,
    I'll give it to my honey:
I would it were ten thousand pound,
    I'd give it all to Sally;
She is the darling of my heart,
    And she lives in our alley.

My master and the neighbors all
    Make game of me and Sally,
And, but for her, I'd better be
    A slave and row a galley;
But when my seven long years are out,
    O, then I'll marry Sally;
O, then we'll wed, and then we'll bed—
    But not in our alley!

                              HENRY CAREY

MY OWN CÁILIN DONN

THE blush is on the flower, and the bloom is on the tree,
And the bonnie, bonnie sweet birds are caroling their glee;
And the dews upon the grass are made diamonds by the sun,
All to deck a path of glory for my own Cáilin Donn!

    Oh fair she is! Oh rare she is! Oh dearer still to me,
    More welcome than the green leaf to winter-stricken tree!
    More welcome than the blossom to the weary, dusty bee,
    Is the coming of my true love—my own Cáilin Donn!

O sycamore! O sycamore! wave, wave your banners green!
Let all your pennons flutter, O beech! before my queen!

Ye fleet and honeyed breezes, to kiss her hand ye run;
But my heart has passed before ye to my own Cáilin Donn.

Ring out, ring out, O linden, your merry leafy bells!
Unveil your brilliant torches, O chestnut! to the dells;
Strew, strew the glade with splendor, for morn it cometh on!
Oh, the morn of all delight to me—my own Cáilin Donn!

She is coming, where we parted, where she wanders every day;
There's a gay surprise before her who thinks me far away;
Oh, like hearing bugles triumph when the fight of freedom's won,
Is the joy around your footsteps, my own Cáilin Donn!

GEORGE SIGERSON

KATHLEEN MAVOURNEEN

KATHLEEN MAVOURNEEN! the gray dawn is breaking,
    The horn of the hunter is heard on the hill;
The lark from her light wing the bright dew is shaking,—
    Kathleen Mavourneen! what, slumbering still?
Oh, hast thou forgotten how soon we must sever?
    Oh! hast thou forgotten this day we must part?
It may be for years, and it may be forever!
    Oh, why art thou silent, thou voice of my heart?
Oh! why art thou silent, Kathleen Mavourneen?

Kathleen Mavourneen, awake from thy slumbers!
    The blue mountains glow in the sun's golden light;
Ah, where is the spell that once hung on my numbers?
    Arise in thy beauty, thou star of my night!
Mavourneen, Mavourneen, my sad tears are falling,
    To think that from Erin and thee I must part!
It may be for years, and it may be forever!
    Then why art thou silent, thou voice of my heart?
Then why art thou silent, Kathleen Mavourneen?

LOUISA MACARTNEY CRAWFORD

KATE KEARNEY

Oh! DID you ne'er hear of Kate Kearney?
She lives on the banks of Killarney:
From the glance of her eye, shun danger and fly,
For fatal's the glance of Kate Kearney.

For that eye is so modestly beaming,
You ne'er think of mischief she's dreaming:

Yet, oh! I can tell, how fatal's the spell,
That lurks in the eye of Kate Kearney.

O should you e'er meet this Kate Kearney,
Who lives on the banks of Killarney,
Beware of her smile, for many a wile
Lies hid in the smile of Kate Kearney.

Though she looks so bewitchingly simple,
Yet there's mischief in every dimple,
And who dares inhale her sigh's spicy gale,
Must die by the breath of Kate Kearney.

LADY MORGAN

THE GIRL I LEFT BEHIND ME

THE dames of France are fond and free,
    And Flemish lips are willing,
And soft the maids of Italy,
    And Spanish eyes are thrilling;
Still, though I bask beneath their smile,
    Their charms fail to bind me,
And my heart falls back to Erin's Isle,
    To the girl I left behind me.

For she's as fair as Shannon's side,
    And purer than its water,
But she refused to be my bride
    Though many a year I sought her;
Yet, since to France I sailed away,
    Her letters oft remind me
That I promised never to gainsay
    The girl I left behind me.

She says, "My own dear love, come home,
    My friends are rich and many,
Or else abroad with you I'll roam,
    A soldier stout as any;
If you'll not come, nor let me go,
    I'll think you have resigned me,"—
My heart nigh broke when I answered "No,"
    To the girl I left behind me.

For never shall my true love brave
    A life of war and toiling,
And never as a skulking slave
    I'll tread my native soil on;

But, were it free or to be freed,
    The battle's close would find me
To Ireland bound, nor message need
    From the girl I left behind me.

ANONYMOUS

ANSWER TO A CHILD'S QUESTION

Do you ASK what the birds say? The sparrow, the dove,
The linnet and thrush say, "I love and I love!"
In the winter they're silent—the wind is so strong;
What it says, I don't know, but it sings a loud song.
But green leaves, and blossoms, and sunny warm weather,
And singing, and loving—all come back together.
But the lark is so brimful of gladness and love,
The green fields below him, the blue sky above,
That he sings, and he sings; and for ever sings he—
"I love my Love, and my Love loves me!"

SAMUEL TAYLOR COLERIDGE

MY HONEY, MY LOVE

Hit's a mighty fur ways up de Far'well Lane,
    My honey, my love!
You may ax Mister Crow, you may ax Mister Crane,
    My honey, my love!
Dey'll make you a bow, en dey'll tell you de same,
    My honey, my love!
Hit's a mighty fur ways fer ter go in de night,
    My honey, my love!
My honey, my love, my heart's delight—
    My honey, my love!

Mister Mink, he creeps twel he wake up de snipe,
    My honey, my love!
Mister Bull-Frog holler, Come alight my pipe!
    My honey, my love!
En de Pa'tridge ax, Ain't you peas ripe?
    My honey, my love!
Better not walk erlong dar much atter night,
    My honey, my love!
My honey, my love, my heart's delight—
    My honey, my love!

De Bully-Bat fly mighty close ter de groun',
    My honey, my love!

Mister Fox, he coax 'er, Do come down!
        My honey, my love!
Mister Coon, he rack all 'roun' en 'roun',
        My honey, my love!
In de darkes' night, oh, de nigger, he's a sight!
        My honey, my love!
My honey, my love, my heart's delight—
        My honey, my love!

Oh, flee, Miss Nancy, flee ter my knee,
        My honey, my love!
'Lev'n big, fat coons liv' in one tree,
        My honey, my love.
Oh, ladies all, won't you marry me?
        My honey, my love!
Tu'n lef', tu'n right, we'll dance all night,
        My honey, my love!
My honey, my love, my heart's delight—
        My honey, my love!

De big Owl holler en cry fer his mate,
        My honey, my love!
Oh, don't stay long! Oh, don't stay late!
        My honey, my love.
Hit ain't so mighty fur ter de Good-by Gate,
        My honey, my love!
Whar we all got ter go w'en we sing out de night,
        My honey, my love!
My honey, my love, my heart's delight—
        My honey, my love!

                            JOEL CHANDLER HARRIS

ROBIN ADAIR

WHAT's this dull town to me?
    Robin's not near,—
He whom I wished to see,
    Wished for to hear;
Where's all the joy and mirth
Made life a heaven on earth?
O, they're all fled with thee,
    Robin Adair!

What made the assembly shine?
    Robin Adair:
What made the ball so fine?
    Robin was there:

What, when the play was o'er,
What made my heart so sore?
O, it was parting with
   Robin Adair!

But now thou art far from me,
   Robin Adair;
But now I never see
   Robin Adair;
Yet him I loved so well
Still in my heart shall dwell;
O, I can ne'er forget
   Robin Adair!

Welcome on shore again,
   Robin Adair!
Welcome once more again,
   Robin Adair!
I feel thy trembling hand;
Tears in my eyelids stand,
To greet thy native land,
   Robin Adair!

Long I ne'er saw thee, love,
   Robin Adair;
Still I prayed for thee, love,
   Robin Adair;
When thou wert far at sea,
Many made love to me,
But still I thought on thee,
   Robin Adair!

Come to my heart again,
   Robin Adair;
Never to part again,
   Robin Adair;
And if thou still art true,
I will be constant too,
And will wed none but you,
   Robin Adair!

CAROLINE KEPPEL

ANNIE LAURIE

MAXWELLTON braes are bonnie,
Where early fa's the dew,
And it's there that Annie Laurie,

Gave me her promise true;
Gave me her promise true,
Which ne'er forgot will be;
And for bonnie Annie Laurie,
I'd lay me doun and dee.

Her brow is like the snowdrift,
Her neck is like the swan;
Her face it is the fairest
That e'er the sun shone on;
That e'er the sun shone on,
And dark blue is her e'e;
And for bonnie Annie Laurie,
I'd lay me doun and dee.

Like dew on the gowan lying,
Is the fa' o' her fairy feet;
And like winds in summer sighing,
Her voice is low and sweet;
Her voice is low and sweet,
She's a' the world to me;
And for bonnie Annie Laurie,
I'd lay me doun and dee.

WILLIAM DOUGLAS

I WANT YOU

I WANT you when the shades of eve are falling
  And purpling shadows drift across the land;
When sleepy birds to loving mates are calling—
  I want the soothing softness of your hand.

I want you when the stars shine up above me,
  And Heaven's flooded with the bright moonlight;
I want you with your arms and lips to love me
  Throughout the wonder watches of the night.

I want you when in dreams I still remember
  The ling'ring of your kiss—for old times' sake—
With all your gentle ways, so sweetly tender,
  I want you in the morning when I wake.

I want you when the day is at its noontime,
  Sun-steeped and quiet, or drenched with sheets of rain;
I want you when the roses bloom in June-time;
  I want you when the violets come again.

I want you when my soul is thrilled with passion;

I want you when I'm weary and depressed;
I want you when in lazy, slumbrous fashion
  My senses need the haven of your breast.

I want you when through field and wood I'm roaming;
  I want you when I'm standing on the shore;
I want you when the summer birds are homing—
  And when they've flown—I want you more and more.

I want you, dear, through every changing season;
  I want you with a tear or with a smile;
I want you more than any rhyme or reason—
  I want you, want you, want you—all the while.

ARTHUR L. GILLOM

FORGET THEE?

"FORGET thee?" If to dream by night and muse on thee by day,
If all the worship deep and wild a poet's heart can pay,
If prayers in absence breathed for thee to Heaven's protecting power,
If winged thoughts that flit to thee—a thousand in an hour—
If busy fancy blending thee with all my future lot—
If this thou call'st "forgetting," thou, indeed, shalt be forgot!

"Forget thee?" Bid the forest-birds forget their sweetest tune;
"Forget thee?" Bid the sea forget to swell beneath the moon;
Bid the thirsty flowers forget to drink the eve's refreshing dew;
Thyself forget thine own "dear land," and its "mountains wild and
    blue."
Forget each old familiar face, each long-remember'd spot—
When these things are forgot by thee, then thou shalt be forgot!

Keep, if thou wilt, thy maiden peace, still calm and fancy-free,
For God forbid thy gladsome heart should grow less glad for me;
Yet, while that heart is still unwon, oh! bid not mine to rove,
But let it nurse its humble faith and uncomplaining love;
If these, preserved for patient years, at last avail me not,
Forget me then; but ne'er believe that thou canst be forgot!

JOHN MOULTRIE

WE MET ON ROADS OF LAUGHTER

WE MET on roads of laughter,
  Both careless at the start,
But other roads came after
  And wound around my heart.

There are roads a wise man misses,
    And roads where fools will try
To say farewell with kisses,
    Touch love and say good-bye.

We met on roads of laughter;—
    Now wistful roads depart,
For I must hurry after
    To overtake my heart.

CHARLES DIVINE

CONSTANT

ALTER? When the hills do.
Falter? When the sun
Question if his glory
Be the perfect one.

Surfeit? When the daffodil
Doth of the dew:
Even as herself, O friend!
I will of you!

EMILY DICKINSON

O, SAW YE THE LASS

O, SAW ye the lass wi' the bonny blue een?
Her smile is the sweetest that ever was seen;
Her cheek like the rose is, but fresher, I ween;
She's the loveliest lassie that trips on the green.
The home of my love is below in the valley,
Where wild-flowers welcome the wandering bee;
But the sweetest of flowers in that spot that is seen
Is the maid that I love wi' the bonny blue een.

When night overshadows her cot in the glen,
She'll steal out to meet her loved Donald again;
And when the moon shines on the valley so green,
I'll welcome the lass wi' the bonny blue een.
As the dove that has wandered away from his nest
Returns to the mate his fond heart loves the best,
I'll fly from the world's false and vanishing scene,
To my dear one, the lass wi' the bonny blue een.

RICHARD RYAN

THE GOLDEN WEDDING

O LOVE, whose patient pilgrim feet
   Life's longest path have trod;
Whose ministry hath symbolled sweet
   The dearer love of God;
The sacred myrtle wreathes again
   Thine altar, as of old;
And what was green with summer then,
   Is mellowed now to gold.

Not now, as then, the future's face
   Is flushed with fancy's light;
But memory, with a milder grace,
   Shall rule the feast to-night.
Blest was the sun of joy that shone,
   Nor less the blinding shower;
The bud of fifty years agone
   Is love's perfected flower.

O memory, ope thy mystic door;
   O dream of youth, return;
And let the light that gleamed of yore
   Beside this altar burn.
The past is plain; 'twas love designed
   E'en sorrow's iron chain;
And mercy's shining thread has twined
   With the dark warp of pain.

So be it still. O Thou who hast
   That younger bridal blest,
Till the May-morn of love has passed
   To evening's golden west;
Come to this later Cana, Lord,
   And, at thy touch divine,
The water of that earlier board
   To-night shall turn to wine.

DAVID GRAY

I'LL REMEMBER YOU, LOVE, IN MY PRAYERS

WHEN the curtains of night are pinned back by the stars,
   And the beautiful moon leaps the skies,
And the dewdrops of heaven are kissing the rose,
   It is then that my memory flies

As if on the wings of some beautiful dove
   In haste with the message it bears
To bring you a kiss of affection and say:
   I'll remember you, love, in my prayers.

Chorus:

Go where you will, on land or on sea,
   I'll share all your sorrows and cares;
And at night, when I kneel by my bedside to pray
   I'll remember you, love, in my prayers.

I have loved you too fondly to ever forget
   The love you have spoken to me;
And the kiss of affection still warm on my lips
   When you told me how true you would be.
I know not if fortune be fickle or friend,
   Or if time on your memory wears;
I know that I love you wherever you roam,
   And remember you, love, in my prayers.

When angels in heaven are guarding the good,
   As God has ordained them to do,
In answer to prayers I have offered to Him,
   I know there is one watching you.
And may its bright spirit be with you through life
   To guide you up heaven's bright stairs,
And meet with the one who has loved you so true
   And remembered you, love, in her prayers.

ANONYMOUS

LOVE ME LITTLE, LOVE ME LONG

Love me little, love me long,
Is the burden of my song:
Love that is too hot and strong
   Burneth soon to waste.
I am with little well content,
And a little from thee sent
Is enough, with true intent,
   To be steadfast friend.
Love me little, love me long,
Is the burden of my song.

Say thou lov'st me while thou live,
I to thee my love will give,
Never dreaming to deceive
   While that life endures:
Nay, and after death in sooth,

I to thee will keep my truth,
As now when in my May of youth,
　　This my love assures.
Love me little, love me long,
Is the burden of my song.

Constant love is moderate ever,
And it will through life persever,
Give to me that with true endeavor.
　　I will it restore:
A suit of durance let it be,
For all weathers, that for me,
For the land or for the sea,
　　Lasting evermore.
Love me little, love me long,
Is the burden of my song.

ANONYMOUS

IF YOU BUT KNEW

IF YOU but knew
How all my days seemed filled with dreams of you,
How sometimes in the silent night
Your eyes thrill through me with their tender light,
How oft I hear your voice when others speak,
How you 'mid other forms I seek—
Oh, love more real than though such dreams were true
If you but knew.

Could you but guess
How you alone make all my happiness,
How I am more than willing for your sake
To stand alone, give all and nothing take,
Nor chafe to think you bound while I am free,
Quite free, till death, to love you silently,
Could you but guess.

Could you but learn
How when you doubt my truth I sadly yearn
To tell you all, to stand for one brief space
Unfettered, soul to soul, as face to face,
To crown you king, my king, till life shall end,
My lover and likewise my truest friend,
Would you love me, dearest, as fondly in return,
Could you but learn?

ANONYMOUS

MID-RAPTURE

Thou lovely and belovèd, thou my love;
Whose kiss seems still the first; whose summoning eyes,
Even now, as for our love-world's new sunrise,
Shed very dawn; whose voice, attuned above
All modulation of the deep-bowered dove,
Is like a hand laid softly on the soul;
Whose hand is like a sweet voice to control
Those worn tired brows it hath the keeping of:—
What word can answer to thy word,—what gaze
To thine, which now absorbs within its sphere
My worshipping face, till I am mirrored there
Light-circled in a heaven of deep-drawn rays?
   What clasp, what kiss mine inmost heart can prove,
    O lovely and belovèd, O my love?

DANTE GABRIEL ROSSETTI

ON A PICTURE BY POUSSIN REPRESENTING SHEPHERDS IN ARCADIA

Ah, happy youths, ah, happy maid,
   Snatch present pleasure while ye may;
Laugh, dance and sing in sunny glade,
   Your limbs are light, your hearts are gay;
Ye little think there comes a day
   ('Twill come to you, it came to me)
When love and life shall pass away:
   I, too, once dwelt in Arcady.

Or listless lie by yonder stream,
   And muse and watch the ripples play,
Or note their noiseless flow, and deem
   That life thus gently glides away—
That love is but a sunny ray
   To make our years go smiling by.
I knew that stream, I too could dream,
   I, too, once dwelt in Arcady.

Sing, shepherds, sing; sweet lady, listen;
   Sing to the music of the rill,
With happy tears her bright eyes glisten,
   For, as each pause the echoes fill,
They waft her name from hill to hill—

So listened my lost love to me,
The voice she loved has long been still;
    I, too, once dwelt in Arcady.
                    JOHN ADDINGTON SYMONDS

TO ALTHEA FROM PRISON

WHEN LOVE with unconfinèd wings
    Hovers within my gates,
And my divine Althea brings
    To whisper at my grates;
When I lie tangled in her hair
    And fettered with her eye,
The birds that wanton in the air
    Know no such liberty.

When flowing cups pass swiftly round
    With no allaying Thames,
Our careless heads with roses crowned,
    Our hearts with loyal flames;
When thirsty grief in wine we steep,
    When healths and draughts go free,
Fishes that tipple in the deep
    Know no such liberty.

When, linnet-like confinèd,
    With shriller throat shall sing
The mercy, sweetness, majesty
    And glories of my King;
When I shall voice aloud how good
    He is, how great should be,
The enlargèd winds, that curl the flood,
    Know no such liberty.

Stone walls do not a prison make,
    Nor iron bars a cage;
Minds innocent and quiet take
    That for an hermitage;
If I have freedom in my love,
    And in my soul am free,
Angels alone, that soar above,
    Enjoy such liberty.
                    RICHARD LOVELACE

SONNET

If I HAD never known your face at all,
Had only heard you speak, beyond thick screen
Of leaves, in an old garden, when the sheen
Of morning dwelt on dial and ivied wall,
I think your voice had been enough to call
Yourself before me, in living vision seen,
So pregnant with your Essence had it been,
So charged with You, in each soft rise and fall.
At least I know, that when upon the night
With chanted word your voice lets loose your soul,
I am pierced, I am pierced and cloven, with Delight
That hath all Pain within it, and the whole
World's tears, all ecstasy of inward sight,
And the blind cry of all the seas that roll.

WILLIAM WATSON

SONNET

MEN call you fair, and you do credit it,
For that yourself ye daily such do see:
But the true fair, that is the gentle wit
And virtuous mind, is much more praised of me:
For all the rest, however fair it be,
Shall turn to naught and lose that glorious hue;
But only that is permanent and free
From frail corruption that doth flesh ensue.
That is true beauty; that doth argue you
To be divine, and born of heavenly seed;
Derived from that fair Spirit from whom all true
And perfect beauty did at first proceed:
    He only fair, and what he fair hath made;
    All other fair, like flowers, untimely fade.

EDMUND SPENSER

RONDEL

KISSING her hair, I sat against her feet,
Wove and unwove it, wound and found it sweet;
Made fast therewith her hands, drew down her eyes,
Deep as deep flowers and dreamy like dim skies;

With her own tresses bound and found her fair,
    Kissing her hair.

Sleep were no sweeter than her face to me,
Sleep of cold sea-bloom under the cold sea;
What pain could get between my face and hers?
What new sweet thing would love not relish worse?
Unless, perhaps, white death had kissed me there,
    Kissing her hair.

ALGERNON CHARLES SWINBURNE

A CERTAIN YOUNG LADY

THERE's a certain young lady,
Who's just in her hey-day,
    And full of all mischief, I ween;
      So teasing! so pleasing!
      Capricious! delicious!
    And you know very well whom I mean.

With an eye dark as night,
Yet than noonday more bright,
    Was ever a black eye so keen?
      It can thrill with a glance,
      With a beam can entrance,
    And you know very well whom I mean.

With a stately step—such as
You'd expect in a duchess—
    And a brow might distinguish a queen,
      With a mighty proud air,
      That says "touch me who dare,"
    And you know very well whom I mean.

With a toss of the head
That strikes one quite dead,
    But a smile to revive one again;
      That toss so appalling!
      That smile so enthralling!
    And you know very well whom I mean.

Confound her! de'il take her!—
A cruel heart-breaker—
    But hold! see that smile so serene.
      God love her! God bless her!
      May nothing distress her!
    You know very well whom I mean.

Heaven help the adorer
Who happens to bore her,
    The lover who wakens her spleen;
        But too blest for a sinner
        Is he who shall win her,
    And you know very well whom I mean.
                        WASHINGTON IRVING

WHEN SHE COMES HOME

WHEN she comes home again! A thousand ways
I fashion, to myself, the tenderness
Of my glad welcome: I shall tremble—yes;
And touch her, as when first in the old days
I touched her girlish hand, nor dared upraise
Mine eyes, such was my faint heart's sweet distress
Then silence: and the perfume of her dress:
The room will sway a little, and a haze
Cloy eyesight—soul-sight, even—for a space;
And tears—yes; and the ache here in the throat,
To know that I so ill deserve the place
Her arms make for me; and the sobbing note
I stay with kisses, ere the tearful face
Again is hidden in the old embrace.
                        JAMES WHITCOMB RILEY

WILL YOU LOVE ME WHEN I'M OLD?

        I WOULD ASK of you, my darling,
            A question soft and low,
        That gives me many a heartache
            As the moments come and go.

    Your love I know is truthful,
        But the truest love grows cold;
    It is this that I would ask you:
        Will you love me when I'm old?

        Life's morn will soon be waning,
            And its evening bells be tolled,
        But my heart shall know no sadness,
            If you'll love me when I'm old.

Down the stream of life together
    We are sailing side by side,
Hoping some bright day to anchor
    Safe beyond the surging tide.
Today our sky is cloudless,
    But the night may clouds unfold;
But, though storms may gather round us,
    Will you love me when I'm old?

When my hair shall shade the snowdrift,
    And mine eyes shall dimmer grow,
I would lean upon some loved one,
    Through the valley as I go.
I would claim of you a promise,
    Worth to me a world of gold;
It is only this, my darling,
    That you'll love me when I'm old.

ANONYMOUS

YOU KISSED ME

You KISSED ME! My head drooped low on your breast
With a feeling of shelter and infinite rest,
While the holy emotions my tongue dared not speak,
Flashed up as in flame, from my heart to my cheek;
Your arms held me fast; oh! your arms were so bold—
Heart beat against heart in their passionate fold.
Your glances seemed drawing my soul through mine eyes,
As the sun draws the mist from the sea to the skies.
Your lips clung to mine till I prayed in my bliss
They might never unclasp from the rapturous kiss.

You kissed me! My heart, my breath and my will
In delirious joy for a moment stood still.
Life had for me then no temptations, no charms,
No visions of rapture outside of your arms;
And were I this instant an angel possessed
Of the peace and the joy that belong to the blest,
I would fling my white robes unrepiningly down,
I would tear from my forehead its beautiful crown,
To nestle once more in that haven of rest—
Your lips upon mine, my head on your breast.

You kissed me! My soul in a bliss so divine
Reeled and swooned like a drunkard when foolish with wine,
And I thought 'twere delicious to die there, if death

Would but come while my lips were yet moist with your breath;
While your arms clasped me round in that blissful embrace,
While your eyes melt in mine could e'en death e'er efface—
Oh, these are the questions I ask day and night:
Must my lips taste no more such exquisite delight?
Would you wish that your breast were my shelter as then?
And if you were here, would you kiss me again?

JOSEPHINE SLOCUM HUNT

Favorite Poems Of

FAITH AND INSPIRATION

THESE ARE THE GIFTS I ASK

THESE are the gifts I ask
Of Thee, Spirit serene:
Strength for the daily task,
Courage to face the road,
Good cheer to help me bear the traveler's load,
And, for the hours of rest that come between,
An inward joy of all things heard and seen.

These are the sins I fain
Would have Thee take away:
Malice and cold disdain,
Hot anger, sullen hate,
Scorn of the lowly, envy of the great,
And discontent that casts a shadow gray
On all the brightness of the common day.

HENRY VAN DYKE

A PRAYER FOR EVERY DAY

MAKE ME too brave to lie or be unkind.
Make me too understanding, too, to mind

The little hurts companions give, and friends,
The careless hurts that no one quite intends.
Make me too thoughtful to hurt others so.
Help me to know
The inmost hearts of those for whom I care,
Their secret wishes, all the loads they bear,
That I may add my courage to their own.
May I make lonely folks feel less alone,
And happy ones a little happier yet.
May I forget
What ought to be forgotten; and recall
Unfailing, all
That ought to be recalled, each kindly thing,
Forgetting what might sting.
To all upon my way,
Day after day,
Let me be joy, be hope! Let my life sing!

                              MARY CAROLYN DAVIES

BE STRONG!

BE STRONG!
We are not here to play, to dream, to drift;
We have hard work to do and loads to lift;
Shun not the struggle—face it; 'tis God's gift.

Be strong!
Say not, "The days are evil. Who's to blame?"
And fold the hands and acquiesce—oh, shame!
Stand up, speak out, and bravely, in God's name.

Be strong!
It matters not how deep intrenched the wrong,
How hard the battle goes, the day how long;
Faint not—fight on! Tomorrow comes the song.

                        MALTBIE DAVENPORT BABCOCK

A PRAYER

LET ME do my work each day;
And if the darkened hours of despair overcome me,
May I not forget the strength that comforted me
In the desolation of other times.
May I still remember the bright hours that found me
Walking over the silent hills of my childhood,

Or dreaming on the margin of the quiet river,
When a light glowed within me,
And I promised my early God to have courage
Amid the tempests of the changing years.
Spare me from bitterness
And from the sharp passions of unguarded moments.
May I not forget that poverty and riches are of the spirit.
Though the world know me not,
May my thoughts and actions be such
As shall keep me friendly with myself.
Lift my eyes from the earth,
And let me not forget the uses of the stars.
Forbid that I should judge others,
Lest I condemn myself.
Let me not follow the clamor of the world,
But walk calmly in my path.
Give me a few friends who will love me for what I am;
And keep ever burning before my vagrant steps
The kindly light of hope.
And though age and infirmity overtake me,
And I come not within sight of the castle of my dreams,
Teach me still to be thankful for life,
And for time's olden memories that are good and sweet;
And may the evening's twilight find me gentle still.

MAX EHRMANN

TO A WATERFOWL

WHITHER, midst falling dew,
While glow the heavens with the last steps of day,
Far, through their rosy depths, dost thou pursue
    Thy solitary way?

Vainly the fowler's eye
Might mark thy distant flight to do thee wrong,
As, darkly seen against the crimson sky,
    Thy figure floats along.

Seek'st thou the plashy brink
Of weedy lake, or marge of river wide,
Or where the rocking billows rise and sink
    On the chafed ocean-side?

There is a Power whose care
Teaches thy way along that pathless coast—
The desert and illimitable air—
    Lone wandering, but not lost.

Mechanicsburg Presb.Ch.Lib.

All day thy wings have fanned,
At that far height, the cold, thin atmosphere,
Yet stoop not, weary, to the welcome land,
   Though the dark night is near.

And soon that toil shall end;
Soon shalt thou find a summer home, and rest,
And scream among thy fellows; reeds shall bend,
   Soon, o'er thy sheltered nest.

Thou'rt gone, the abyss of heaven
Hath swallowed up thy form; yet, on my heart
Deeply has sunk the lesson thou hast given,
   And shall not soon depart.

He who, from zone to zone,
Guides through the boundless sky thy certain flight,
In the long way that I must tread alone,
   Will lead my steps aright.

               WILLIAM CULLEN BRYANT

A CREED

THERE is a destiny that makes us brothers;
   None goes his way alone:
All that we send into the lives of others
   Comes back into our own.

I care not what his temples or his creeds,
   One thing holds firm and fast—
That into his fateful heap of days and deeds
   The soul of man is cast.

               EDWIN MARKHAM

THE SPACIOUS FIRMAMENT ON HIGH

THE SPACIOUS firmament on high,
With all the blue ethereal sky,
And spangled heavens, a shining frame,
Their great Original proclaim.
The unwearied sun from day to day
Does his Creator's power display,
And publishes to every land
The work of an almighty Hand.

Mechanicsburg Presb.Ch.Lib.

Soon as the evening shades prevail,
The moon takes up the wondrous tale,
And nightly, to the listening earth,
Repeats the story of her birth;
Whilst all the stars that round her burn,
And all the planets in their turn,
Confirm the tidings as they roll,
And spread the truth from pole to pole.

What though in solemn silence all
Move round the dark terrestrial ball?
What though nor real voice nor sound
Amid their radiant orbs be found?
In reason's ear they all rejoice,
And utter forth a glorious voice,
Forever singing as they shine,
"The Hand that made us is divine!"

JOSEPH ADDISON

FAITH

BETTER trust all and be deceived,
And weep that trust and that deceiving,
Than doubt one heart that, if believed,
Had blessed one's life with true believing.

Oh, in this mocking world, too fast
The doubting fiend o'ertakes our youth;
Better be cheated to the last
Than lose the blessed hope of truth.

FRANCES ANNE KEMBLE

THE WHITE PEACE

IT LIES not on the sunlit hill
    Nor on the sunlit plain:
Nor ever on any running stream
    Nor on the unclouded main—

But sometimes, through the Soul of Man,
    Slow moving o'er his pain,
The moonlight of a perfect peace
    Floods heart and brain.

WILLIAM SHARP

MIZPAH

Go THOU thy way, and I go mine,
    Apart, yet not afar;
Only a thin veil hangs between
    The pathways where we are.
And "God keep watch 'tween thee and me";
    This is my prayer;
He looks thy way, He looketh mine,
    And keeps us near.

I know not where thy road may lie,
    Or which way mine will be;
If mine will lead thro' parching sands
    And thine beside the sea;
Yet God keeps watch 'tween thee and me,
    So never fear;
He holds thy hands, He claspeth mine,
    And keeps us near.

Should wealth and fame perchance be thine,
    And my lot lowly be,
Or you be sad and sorrowful,
    And glory be for me,
Yet God keep watch 'tween thee and me;
    Both be His care;
One arm round thee and one round me
    Will keep us near.

I sigh sometimes to see thy face,
    But since this may not be,
I'll leave thee to the care of Him
    Who cares for thee and me.
"I'll keep you both beneath my wings,"
    This comforts, dear;
One wing o'er thee and one o'er me,
    Will keep us near.

And though our paths be separate,
    And thy way is not mine,
Yet coming to the Mercy seat,
    My soul will meet with thine.
And "God keep watch 'tween thee and me,"
    I'll whisper there.
He blesseth thee, He blesseth me,
    And we are near.

JULIA A. BAKER

INVICTUS

Out of the night that covers me,
  Black as the Pit from pole to pole,
I thank whatever gods may be
  For my unconquerable soul.

In the fell clutch of circumstance
  I have not winced nor cried aloud.
Under the bludgeonings of chance
  My head is bloody, but unbowed.

Beyond this place of wrath and tears
  Looms but the Horror of the shade,
And yet the menace of the years
  Finds and shall find me unafraid.

It matters not how strait the gate,
  How charged with punishments the scroll,
I am the master of my fate:
  I am the captain of my soul.

WILLIAM ERNEST HENLEY

UP-HILL

Does the road wind up-hill all the way?
  Yes, to the very end.
Will the day's journey take the whole long day?
  From morn to night, my friend.

But is there for the night a resting-place?
  A roof for when the slow dark hours begin.
May not the darkness hide it from my face?
  You cannot miss that inn.

Shall I meet other wayfarers at night?
  Those who have gone before.
Then must I knock, or call when just in sight?
  They will not keep you standing at that door.

Shall I find comfort, travel-sore and weak?
  Of labour you shall find the sum.
Will there be beds for me and all who seek?
  Yea, beds for all who come.

CHRISTINA GEORGINA ROSSETTI

ABOU BEN ADHEM

Abou Ben Adhem (may his tribe increase!)
Awoke one night from a deep dream of peace,
And saw, within the moonlight in his room,
Making it rich, and like a lily in bloom,
An Angel writing in a book of gold:
Exceeding peace had made Ben Adhem bold,
And to the Presence in the room he said,
"What writest thou?" The Vision raised its head,
And with a look made of all sweet accord
Answered, "The names of those who love the Lord."
"And is mine one?" said Abou. "Nay, not so,"
Replied the Angel. Abou spoke more low,
But cheerily still; and said, "I pray thee, then,
Write me as one that loves his fellow men."

The Angel wrote, and vanished. The next night
It came again with a great wakening light,
And showed the names whom love of God had blessed,
And, lo! Ben Adhem's name led all the rest!

LEIGH HUNT

MY EVENING PRAYER

If i have wounded any soul to-day,
If I have caused one foot to go astray,
If I have walked in my own wilful way—
    Good Lord, forgive!

If I have uttered idle words or vain,
If I have turned aside from want or pain,
Lest I myself should suffer through the strain—
    Good Lord, forgive!

If I have craved for joys that are not mine,
If I have let my wayward heart repine,
Dwelling on things of earth, not things divine—
    Good Lord, forgive!

If I have been perverse, or hard, or cold,
If I have longed for shelter in Thy fold,
When Thou hast given me some part to hold—
    Good Lord, forgive.

Forgive the sins I have confessed to Thee,
Forgive the secret sins I do not see,
That which I know not, Father, teach Thou me—
　　Help me to live.

CHARLES H. GABRIEL

WHAT I LIVE FOR

I LIVE for those who love me,
　　Whose hearts are kind and true;
For the Heaven that smiles above me,
　　And awaits my spirit too;
For all human ties that bind me,
For the task by God assigned me,
For the bright hopes yet to find me,
　　And the good that I can do.

I live to learn their story
　　Who suffered for my sake;
To emulate their glory,
　　And follow in their wake;
Bards, patriots, martyrs, sages,
The heroic of all ages,
Whose deeds crowd History's pages,
　　And Time's great volume make.

I live to hold communion
　　With all that is divine,
To feel there is a union
　　'Twixt Nature's heart and mine;
To profit by affliction,
Reap truth from fields of fiction,
Grow wiser from conviction,
　　And fulfil God's grand design.

I live to hail that season
　　By gifted ones foretold,
When men shall live by reason,
　　And not alone by gold;
When man to man united,
And every wrong thing righted,
The whole world shall be lighted
　　As Eden was of old.

I live for those who love me,
　　For those who know me true,

For the Heaven that smiles above me,
    And awaits my spirit too;
For the cause that lacks assistance,
For the wrong that needs resistance,
For the future in the distance,
    And the good that I can do.

                    GEORGE LINNAEUS BANKS

AN ANCIENT PRAYER

GIVE ME a good digestion, Lord, and also something to digest;
Give me a healthy body, Lord, and sense to keep it at its best.
Give me a healthy mind, good Lord, to keep the good and pure in sight,
Which, seeing sin, is not appalled, but finds a way to set it right.

Give me a mind that is not bound, that does not whimper, whine or
    sigh.
Don't let me worry overmuch about the fussy thing called I.
Give me a sense of humor, Lord; give me the grace to see a joke,
To get some happiness from life and pass it on to other folk.

                    THOMAS H. B. WEBB

EVENING CONTEMPLATION

SOFTLY now the light of day
Fades upon my sight away;
Free from care, from labor free,
Lord, I would commune with Thee.

Thou, whose all-pervading eye
    Naught escapes, without, within!
Pardon each infirmity,
    Open fault, and secret sin.

Soon for me the light of day
Shall for ever pass away;
Then, from sin and sorrow free,
Take me, Lord, to dwell with Thee.

Thou who, sinless, yet hast known
    All of man's infirmity!
Then, from Thine eternal throne,
    Jesus, look with pitying eye.

                    GEORGE WASHINGTON DOANE

WHO WALKS WITH BEAUTY

WHO WALKS with Beauty has no need of fear;
The sun and moon and stars keep pace with him;
Invisible hands restore the ruined year,
And time itself grows beautifully dim.
One hill will keep the footprints of the moon
That came and went a hushed and secret hour;
One star at dusk will yield the lasting boon;
Remembered beauty's white immortal flower.

Who takes of Beauty wine and daily bread
Will know no lack when bitter years are lean;
The brimming cup is by, the feast is spread;
The sun and moon and stars his eyes have seen
Are for his hunger and the thirst he slakes:
The wine of Beauty and the bread he breaks.

DAVID MORTON

WAITING

SERENE I fold my arms and wait,
    Nor care for wind, or tide, or sea:
I rave no more 'gainst time or fate,
    For lo! my own shall come to me.

I stay my haste, I make delays,
    For what avails this eager pace?
I stand amid the eternal ways,
    And what is mine shall know my face.

Asleep, awake, by night or day,
    The friends I seek are seeking me;
No wind can drive my bark astray,
    Nor change the tide of destiny.

What matter if I stand alone?
    I wait with joy the coming years;
My heart shall reap where it has sown,
    And garner up its fruit of tears.

The waters know their own, and draw
    The brook that springs in yonder height;
So flows the good with equal law
    Unto the soul of pure delight.

The floweret nodding in the wind
   Is ready plighted to the bee;
And, maiden, why that look unkind?
   For lo! thy lover seeketh thee.

The stars come nightly to the sky;
   The tidal wave unto the sea;
Nor time, nor space, nor deep, nor high
   Can keep my own away from me.

JOHN BURROUGHS

HOLD FAST YOUR DREAMS

HOLD FAST your dreams!
Within your heart
Keep one still, secret spot
Where dreams may go,
And, sheltered so,
May thrive and grow
Where doubt and fear are not.
O keep a place apart,
Within your heart,
For little dreams to go!

Think still of lovely things that are not true.
Let wish and magic work at will in you.
Be sometimes blind to sorrow. Make believe!
Forget the calm that lies
In disillusioned eyes.
Though we all know that we must die,
Yet you and I
May walk like gods and be
Even now at home in immortality.

We see so many ugly things—
Deceits and wrongs and quarrelings;
We know, alas! we know
How quickly fade
The color in the west,
The bloom upon the flower,
The bloom upon the breast
And youth's blind hour.
Yet keep within your heart
A place apart
Where little dreams may go,
May thrive and grow.
Hold fast—hold fast your dreams!

LOUISE DRISCOLL

IT COULDN'T BE DONE

SOMEBODY SAID that it couldn't be done,
    But he with a chuckle replied
That "maybe it couldn't," but he would be one
    Who wouldn't say so till he'd tried.
So he buckled right in with the trace of a grin
    On his face. If he worried he hid it.
He started to sing as he tackled the thing
    That couldn't be done, and he did it.

Somebody scoffed: "Oh, you'll never do that;
    At least no one ever has done it";
But he took off his coat and he took off his hat,
    And the first thing we knew he'd begun it.
With a lift of his chin and a bit of a grin,
    Without any doubting or quiddit,
He started to sing as he tackled the thing
    That couldn't be done, and he did it.

There are thousands to tell you it cannot be done,
    There are thousands to prophesy failure;
There are thousands to point out to you, one by one,
    The dangers that wait to assail you.
But just buckle in with a bit of a grin,
    Just take off your coat and go to it;
Just start to sing as you tackle the thing
    That "cannot be done," and you'll do it.

                    EDGAR A. GUEST

OPPORTUNITY

THEY DO me wrong who say I come no more
    When once I knock and fail to find you in,
For every day I stand outside your door
    And bid you wake, and rise to fight and win.

Wail not for precious chances passed away,
    Weep not for golden ages on the wane!
Each night I burn the records of the day;
    At sunrise every soul is born again.

Laugh like a boy at splendors that have sped,
    To vanished joys be blind and deaf and dumb;
My judgments seal the dead past with its dead,
    But never bind a moment yet to come.

Tho' deep in mire, wring not your hands and weep;
    I lend my arm to all who say, "I can!"
No shamefaced outcast ever sank so deep
    But yet might rise and be again a man.

Dost thou behold thy lost youth all aghast?
    Dost reel from righteous retribution's blow?
Then turn from blotted archives of the past
    And find the future's pages white as snow.

Art thou a mourner? Rouse thee from thy spell;
    Art thou a sinner? Sins may be forgiven;
Each morning gives thee wings to flee from hell,
    Each night a star to guide thy feet to Heaven.

WALTER MALONE

THE HOUSE BY THE SIDE OF THE ROAD

"He was a friend to man, and lived in a house
by the side of the road"—Homer.

THERE ARE hermit souls that live withdrawn
    In the peace of their self-content;
There are souls, like stars, that dwell apart,
    In a fellowless firmament;
There are pioneer souls that blaze their paths
    Where highways never ran;
But let me live by the side of the road
    And be a friend to man.

Let me live in a house by the side of the road,
    Where the race of men go by—
The men who are good and the men who are bad,
    As good and as bad as I.
I would not sit in the scorner's seat,
    Or hurl the cynic's ban;
Let me live in a house by the side of the road
    And be a friend to man.

I see from my house by the side of the road,
    By the side of the highway of life,
The men who press with the ardor of hope,
    The men who are faint with the strife.
But I turn not away from their smiles nor their tears—
    Both parts of an infinite plan;
Let me live in my house by the side of the road
    And be a friend to man.

I know there are brook-gladdened meadows ahead,
    And mountains of wearisome height,
That the road passes on through the long afternoon
    And stretches away to the night.
But still I rejoice when the travelers rejoice,
    And weep with the strangers that moan,
Nor live in my house by the side of the road
    Like a man who dwells alone.

Let me live in my house by the side of the road
    Where the race of men go by—
They are good, they are bad, they are weak, they are strong,
    Wise, foolish—so am I.
Then why should I sit in the scorner's seat
    Or hurl the cynic's ban?—
Let me live in my house by the side of the road
    And be a friend to man.

SAM WALTER FOSS

LIVING

To TOUCH the cup with eager lips and taste, not drain it;
To woo and tempt and court a bliss—and not attain it;
To fondle and caress a joy, yet hold it lightly,
Lest it become necessity and cling too tightly;
To watch the sun set in the west without regretting;
To hail its advent in the east—the night forgetting;
To smother care in happiness and grief in laughter;
To hold the present close—not questioning hereafter;
To have enough to share—to know the joy of giving;
To thrill with all the sweets of life—is living.

ANONYMOUS

LIFE'S MIRROR

THERE ARE LOYAL HEARTS, there are spirits brave,
    There are souls that are pure and true;
Then give to the world the best you have,
    And the best will come back to you.

Give love, and love to your life will flow,
    A strength in your utmost need;
Have faith, and a score of hearts will show
    Their faith in your word and deed.

Give truth, and your gift will be paid in kind,
    And honor will honor meet;
And a smile that is sweet will surely find
    A smile that is just as sweet.

Give sorrow and pity to those who mourn;
    You will gather in flowers again
The scattered seeds of your thought outborne,
    Though the sowing seemed but vain.

For life is the mirror of king and slave—
    'Tis just what we are and do;
Then give to the world the best you have,
    And the best will come back to you.

                              "MADELINE BRIDGES"
                        (MARY AINGE DE VERE)

THE COMMON ROAD

I WANT TO TRAVEL the common road
With the great crowd surging by,
Where there's many a laugh and many a load,
And many a smile and sigh.
I want to be on the common way
With its endless tramping feet,
In the summer bright and winter gray,
In the noonday sun and heat.
In the cool of evening with shadows nigh,
At dawn, when the sun breaks clear,
I want the great crowd passing by,
To ken what they see and hear.
I want to be one of the common herd,
Not live in a sheltered way,
Want to be thrilled, want to be stirred
By the great crowd day by day;
To glimpse the restful valleys deep,
To toil up the rugged hill,
To see the brooks which shyly creep,
To have the torrents thrill.
I want to laugh with the common man
Wherever he chance to be,
I want to aid him when I can
Whenever there's need of me.
I want to lend a helping hand
Over the rough and steep
To a child too young to understand—

To comfort those who weep.
I want to live and work and plan
With the great crowd surging by,
To mingle with the common man,
No better or worse than I.

SILAS H. PERKINS

IF—

If YOU can keep your head when all about you
    Are losing theirs and blaming it on you;
If you can trust yourself when all men doubt you,
    But make allowance for their doubting too;
If you can wait and not be tired by waiting,
    Or, being lied about, don't deal in lies,
Or, being hated, don't give way to hating,
    And yet don't look too good, nor talk too wise;

If you can dream—and not make dreams your master;
    If you can think—and not make thoughts your aim;
If you can meet with triumph and disaster
    And treat those two impostors just the same;
If you can bear to hear the truth you've spoken
    Twisted by knaves to make a trap for fools,
Or watch the things you gave your life to broken,
    And stoop and build 'em up with wornout tools;

If you can make one heap of all your winnings
    And risk it on one turn of pitch-and-toss,
And lose, and start again at your beginnings
    And never breathe a word about your loss;
If you can force your heart and nerve and sinew
    To serve your turn long after they are gone,
And so hold on when there is nothing in you
    Except the Will which says to them: "Hold on";

If you can talk with crowds and keep your virtue,
    Or walk with kings—nor lose the common touch;
If neither foes nor loving friends can hurt you;
    If all men count with you, but none too much;
If you can fill the unforgiving minute
    With sixty seconds' worth of distance run—
Yours is the Earth and everything that's in it,
    And—which is more—you'll be a Man, my son!

RUDYARD KIPLING

OPTIMISM

TALK happiness. The world is sad enough
Without your woes. No path is wholly rough;
Look for the places that are smooth and clear,
And speak of those, to rest the weary ear
Of Earth, so hurt by one continuous strain
Of human discontent and grief and pain.

Talk faith. The world is better off without
Your uttered ignorance and morbid doubt.
If you have faith in God, or man, or self,
Say so. If not, push back upon the shelf
Of silence all your thoughts, till faith shall come;
No one will grieve because your lips are dumb.

Talk health. The dreary, never-changing tale
Of mortal maladies is worn and stale.
You cannot charm, or interest, or please
By harping on that minor chord, disease.
Say you are well, or all is well with you,
And God shall hear your words and make them true.

ELLA WHEELER WILCOX

THE LORD GOD PLANTED A GARDEN

THE Lord God planted a garden
    In the first white days of the world,
And he set there an angel warden
    In a garment of light enfurled.

So near to the peace of Heaven,
    That the hawk might nest with the wren,
For there in the cool of the even'
    God walked with the first of men.

The kiss of the sun for pardon,
    The song of the birds for mirth—
One is nearer God's heart in a garden
    Than anywhere else on earth.

DOROTHY FRANCES GURNEY

THE HIGHER GOOD

FATE, I will not ask for wealth or fame,
Though once they would have joyed my carnal sense:
I shudder not to bear a hated name,
Wanting all wealth, myself my sole defense.
But give me, Lord, eyes to behold the truth;
A seeing sense that knows the eternal right;
A heart with pity filled, and gentlest ruth;
A manly faith that makes all darkness light:
Give me the power to labor for mankind;
Make me the mouth of such as cannot speak;
Eyes let me be to groping men and blind;
A conscience to the base; and to the weak
Let me be hands and feet; and to the foolish, mind;
And lead still further on such as thy kingdom seek.

THEODORE PARKER

REWARD OF SERVICE

THE SWEETEST lives are those to duty wed,
Whose deeds both great and small
Are close-knit strands of an unbroken thread,
Where love ennobles all.
The world may sound no trumpets, ring no bells,
The Book of Life the slurring record tells.

Thy love shall chant its own beatitudes,
After its own like working. A child's kiss
Set on thy singing lips shall make thee glad;
A poor man served by thee shall make thee rich;
A sick man helped by thee shall make thee strong;
Thou shalt be served thyself by every sense
Of service which thou renderest.

ELIZABETH BARRETT BROWNING

LAST LINES

No COWARD soul is mine,
No trembler in the world's storm-troubled sphere:
I see Heaven's glories shine,
And faith shines equal, arming me from fear.

O God, within my breast,
Almighty, ever-present Deity!
    Life—that in me has rest,
As I—undying Life—have power in Thee!

    Vain are the thousand creeds
That move men's hearts: unutterably vain;
    Worthless as withered weeds,
Or idlest froth amid the boundless main,

    To waken doubt in one
Holding so fast by thine infinity;
    So surely anchored on
The steadfast rock of immortality.

    With wide-embracing love
Thy Spirit animates eternal years,
    Pervades and broods above,
Changes, sustains, dissolves, creates, and rears.

    Though earth and man were gone,
And suns and universes ceased to be,
    And Thou were left alone,
Every existence would exist in Thee.

    There is not room for Death,
Nor atom that his might could render void:
    Thou—Thou art Being and Breath,
And what Thou art may never be destroyed.
                                    EMILY BRONTË

SLEEP SWEET

Sleep sweet within this quiet room,
    O thou, whoe'er thou art,
And let no mournful yesterdays
    Disturb thy peaceful heart.

Nor let tomorrow mar thy rest
    With dreams of coming ill:
Thy Maker is thy changeless friend,
    His love surrounds thee still.

Forget thyself and all the world,
    Put out each garish light:
The stars are shining overhead—
    Sleep sweet! Good night! Good night!
                    ELLEN M. HUNTINGTON GATES

BE TRUE

THOU must be true thyself,
  If thou the truth wouldst teach;
Thy soul must overflow, if thou
  Another's soul wouldst reach!
It needs the overflow of heart
  To give the lips full speech.

Think truly, and thy thoughts
  Shall the world's famine feed;
Speak truly, and each word of thine
  Shall be a fruitful seed;
Live truly, and thy life shall be
  A great and noble creed.

HORATIUS BONAR

A LITTLE WORK

A LITTLE WORK, a little play
To keep us going—and so, good-day!
A little warmth, a little light
Of love's bestowing—and so, good-night!
A little fun, to match the sorrow
Of each day's growing—and so, good-morrow!
A little trust that when we die
We reap our sowing! And so—good-bye!

GEORGE DU MAURIER

INSPIRATION

IF WITH light head erect I sing
Though all the Muses lend their force,
From my poor love of anything,
The verse is weak and shallow as its source.

But if with bended neck I grope
Listening behind me for my wit,
With faith superior to hope,
More anxious to keep back than forward it,—

Making my soul accomplice there
Unto the flame my heart hath lit,
Then will the verse forever wear,—
Time cannot bend the line which God has writ.

I hearing get, who had but ears,
And sight, who had but eyes before;
I moments live, who lived but years,
And truth discern, who knew but learning's lore.

Now chiefly is my natal hour,
And only now my prime of life;
Of manhood's strength it is the flower,
'Tis peace's end, and war's beginning strife.

It comes in summer's broadest noon,
By a gray wall, or some chance place,
Unseasoning time, insulting June,
And vexing day with its presuming face.

I will not doubt the love untold
Which not my worth nor want hath bought,
Which wooed me young, and wooes me old,
And to this evening hath me brought.

HENRY DAVID THOREAU

HOPE AND FEAR

BENEATH the shadow of dawn's aerial cope,
With eyes enkindled as the sun's own sphere,
Hope from the front of youth in godlike cheer
Looks Godward, past the shades where blind men grope
Round the dark door that prayers nor dreams can ope,
And makes for joy the very darkness dear
That gives her wide wings play; nor dreams that Fear
At noon may rise and pierce the heart of Hope.
Then, when the soul leaves off to dream and yearn,
May Truth first purge her eyesight to discern
What once being known leaves time no power to appall;
Till youth at last, ere yet youth be not, learn
The kind wise word that falls from years that fall—
"Hope not thou much, and fear thou not at all."

ALGERNON CHARLES SWINBURNE

THE MINSTREL BOY

THE Minstrel Boy to the war is gone
    In the ranks of death you'll find him,
His father's sword he has girded on,
    And his wild harp slung behind him.

"Land of song!" said the warrior bard,
  "Tho' all the world betrays thee,
One sword, at least, thy rights shall guard,
  One faithful harp shall praise thee."

The minstrel fell! but the foeman's chain
  Could not bring that proud soul under;
The harp he loved ne'er spoke again,
  For he tore its chords asunder;
And said, "No chain shall sully thee,
  Thou soul of love and bravery.
Thy songs were made for the pure and free,
  They shall never sound in slavery."

THOMAS MOORE

THE VILLAGE BLACKSMITH

UNDER a spreading chestnut-tree
  The village smithy stands;
The smith, a mighty man is he,
  With large and sinewy hands;
And the muscles of his brawny arms
  Are strong as iron bands.

His hair is crisp, and black, and long,
  His face is like the tan;
His brow is wet with honest sweat,
  He earns whate'er he can,
And looks the whole world in the face,
  For he owes not any man.

Week in, week out, from morn till night,
  You can hear his bellows blow;
You can hear him swing his heavy sledge
  With measured beat and slow,
Like a sexton ringing the village bell,
  When the evening sun is low.

And children coming home from school
  Look in at the open door;
They love to see the flaming forge,
  And hear the bellows roar,
And catch the burning sparks that fly
  Like chaff from a threshing-floor.

He goes on Sunday to the church,
  And sits among his boys;

He hears the parson pray and preach,
  He hears his daughter's voice,
Singing in the village choir,
  And it makes his heart rejoice.

It sounds to him like her mother's voice,
  Singing in Paradise!
He needs must think of her once more,
  How in the grave she lies;
And with his hard, rough hand he wipes
  A tear out of his eyes.

Toiling,—rejoicing,—sorrowing,
  Onward through life he goes;
Each morning sees some task begin,
  Each evening sees its close;
Something attempted, something done,
  Has earned a night's repose.

Thanks, thanks to thee, my worthy friend,
  For the lesson thou hast taught!
Thus at the flaming forge of life
  Our fortunes must be wrought;
Thus on its sounding anvil shaped
  Each burning deed and thought!

      HENRY WADSWORTH LONGFELLOW

EVENING HYMN

SLOWLY by God's hand unfurled,
Down around the weary world
Falls the darkness; oh, how still
Is the working of Thy will!

Mighty Maker! Here am I,—
Work in me as silently,
Veil the day's distracting sights,
Show me heaven's eternal lights.

From the darkened sky come forth
Countless stars, a wondrous birth!
So may gleams of glory dart
Through the dim abyss, my heart;

Living worlds to view be brought,
In the boundless realms of thought,
High and infinite desires,
Burning like those upper fires.

Holy truth, eternal right,
Let them break upon my sight,
Let them shine unclouded, still,
And with light my being fill.

Thou art there. Oh, let me know,
Thou art here within me too;
Be the perfect peace of God
Here as there now shed abroad.

May my soul attunèd be
To that perfect harmony,
Which, beyond the power of sound,
Fills the universe around.

WILLIAM HENRY FURNESS

MY MIND TO ME A KINGDOM IS

My MIND to me a kingdom is,
    Such present joys therein I find,
That it excels all other bliss
    That earth affords or grows by kind:
Though much I want which most would have,
Yet still my mind forbids to crave.

No princely pomp, no wealthy store,
    No force to win the victory,
No wily wit to salve a sore,
    No shape to feed a loving eye;
To none of these I yield as thrall:
For why? My mind doth serve for all.

I see how plenty surfeits oft,
    And hasty climbers soon do fall;
I see that those which are aloft
    Mishap doth threaten most of all,
They get with toil, they keep with fear:
Such cares my mind could never bear.

Content to live, this is my stay;
    I seek no more than may suffice;
I press to bear no haughty sway;
    Look, what I lack my mind supplies:
Lo, thus I triumph like a king,
Content with that my mind doth bring.

Some have too much, yet still do crave;
    I little have, and seek no more.

They are but poor, though much they have,
    And I am rich with little store;
They poor, I rich; they beg, I give;
They lack, I leave; they pine, I live.

SIR EDWARD DYER

THE HUMAN TOUCH

'TIS the human touch in this world that counts,
    The touch of your hand and mine,
Which means far more to the fainting heart
    Than shelter and bread and wine;
For shelter is gone when the night is o'er,
    And bread lasts only a day,
But the touch of the hand and the sound of the voice
    Sing on in the soul alway.

SPENCER MICHAEL FREE

ALWAYS FINISH

IF A TASK is once begun
Never leave it till it's done.
Be the labor great or small,
Do it well or not at all.

ANONYMOUS

LOOK UP

LOOK UP and not down.
Look forward and not back.
Look out and not in.
Lend a hand.

EDWARD EVERETT HALE

SONNET ON HIS BLINDNESS

WHEN I consider how my light is spent
    Ere half my days, in this dark world and wide,
    And that one talent, which is death to hide,
Lodged with me useless, though my soul more bent
To serve therewith my Maker, and present
    My true account, lest He, returning chide;

"Doth God exact day labor, light denied?"
I fondly ask; but Patience, to prevent
   That murmur, soon replies, "God doth not need
     Either man's work, or His own gifts; who best
    Bear His mild yoke, they serve Him best.
      His state
Is kingly. Thousands at His bidding speed,
   And post o'er land and ocean without rest;
    They also serve who only stand and wait."

JOHN MILTON

THE LAMB

LITTLE lamb, who made thee?
Dost thou know who made thee,
Gave thee life and bade thee feed
By the stream and o'er the mead;
Gave thee clothing of delight,
Softest clothing, woolly, bright;
Gave thee such a tender voice,
Making all the vales rejoice?
    Little lamb, who made thee?
    Dost thou know who made thee?

Little lamb, I'll tell thee;
Little lamb, I'll tell thee.
He is callèd by thy name,
For He calls himself a Lamb;
He is meek and He is mild,
He became a little child.
I a child and thou a lamb,
We are callèd by His name.
    Little lamb, God bless thee!
    Little lamb, God bless thee!

WILLIAM BLAKE

A THANKSGIVING TO GOD FOR HIS HOUSE

LORD, thou hast given me a cell
   Wherein to dwell,
A little house, whose humble roof
   Is weather-proof;
Under the spars of which I lie
   Both soft and dry,
Where thou my chamber for to ward

Hast set a guard
Of harmless thoughts, to watch and keep
    Me while I sleep.
Low is my porch, as is my fate,
    Both void of state;
And yet the threshold of my door
    Is worn by the poor,
Who thither come and freely get
    Good words or meat;
Like as my parlor, so my hall
    And kitchen's small;
A little buttery, and therein
    A little bin
Which keeps my little loaf of bread
    Unchipped, unflead.
Some brittle sticks of thorn or briar
    Make me a fire,
Close by whose living coal I sit
    And glow like it.
Lord, I confess, too, when I dine,
    The pulse is thine,
And all those other bits that be
    There placed by thee:
The worts, the purslain, and the mess
    Of water-cress,
Which of thy kindness thou hast sent;
    And my content
Makes those, and my beloved beet,
    To be more sweet.
'Tis thou that crown'st my glittering hearth
    With guiltless mirth;
And giv'st me wassail bowls to drink,
    Spiced to the brink.
Lord, 'tis thy plenty-dropping hand
    That soils my land,
And giv'st me for my bushel sown
    Twice ten for one.
Thou mak'st my teeming hen to lay
    Her egg each day;
Besides my healthful ewes to bear
    Me twins each year,
The while the conduits of my kine
    Run cream for wine.
All these, and better, thou dost send
    Me to this end:
That I should render, for my part,

A thankful heart,
Which, fired with incense, I resign
    As wholly thine;
But the acceptance, that must be,
    My Christ, by thee.

ROBERT HERRICK

THE UNIVERSAL PRAYER

FATHER of all! in every age,
    In every clime adored,
By saint, by savage, and by sage,
    Jehovah, Jove, or Lord!

Thou great First Cause, least understood,
    Who all my sense confined
To know but this, that thou art good,
    And that myself am blind;

Yet gave me, in this dark estate,
    To see the good from ill;
And, binding nature fast in fate,
    Left free the human will:

What conscience dictates to be done,
    Or warns me not to do,
This, teach me more than hell to shun,
    That, more than heaven pursue.

What blessings thy free bounty gives
    Let me not cast away;
For God is paid when man receives,
    To enjoy is to obey.

Yet not to earth's contracted span
    Thy goodness let me bound,
Or think thee Lord alone of man,
    When thousand worlds are round:

Let not this weak, unknowing hand
    Presume thy bolts to throw,
And deal damnation round the land
    On each I judge thy foe.

If I am right, thy grace impart
    Still in the right to stay;
If I am wrong, O, teach my heart
    To find that better way!

Save me alike from foolish pride
   And impious discontent
At aught thy wisdom has denied,
   Or aught thy goodness lent.

Teach me to feel another's woe,
   To hide the fault I see;
That mercy I to others show,
   That mercy show to me.

Mean though I am, not wholly so,
   Since quickened by thy breath;
O, lead me wheresoe'er I go,
   Through this day's life or death!

This day be bread and peace my lot;
   All else beneath the sun,
Thou know'st if best bestowed or not,
   And let thy will be done.

To thee, whose temple is all space,
   Whose altar, earth, sea, skies,
One chorus let all Being raise,
   All Nature's incense rise!

                    ALEXANDER POPE

AD COELUM

AT THE MUEZZIN's call for prayer,
The kneeling faithful thronged the square,
And on Pushkara's lofty height
The dark priest chanted Brahma's might.
Amid a monastery's weeds
An old Franciscan told his beads,
While to the synagogue there came
A Jew, to praise Jehovah's name.
The one great God looked down and smiled
And counted each his loving child;
For Turk and Brahmin, monk and Jew
Had reached Him through the gods they knew.

                    HARRY ROMAINE

ABIDE WITH ME

ABIDE with me: fast falls the eventide;
The darkness deepens; Lord, with me abide:

When other helpers fail, and comforts flee,
Help of the helpless, O abide with me.

Swift to its close ebbs out life's little day;
Earth's joys grow dim, its glories pass away,
Change and decay in all around I see;
O thou who changest not, abide with me.

I need thy presence every passing hour;
What but thy grace can foil the tempter's power?
Who, like thyself, my guide and stay can be?
Through cloud and sunshine, Lord, abide with me.

I fear no foe, with thee at hand to bless:
Ills have no weight, and tears no bitterness.
Where is death's sting? where, grave, thy victory?
I triumph still, if thou abide with me.

Hold thou thy cross before my closing eyes:
Shine through the gloom, and point me to the skies:
Heaven's morning breaks, and earth's vain shadows flee:
In life, in death, O Lord, abide with me.

HENRY F. LYTE

THE TWENTY-THIRD PSALM

THE LORD is my shepherd; I shall not want.
He maketh me to lie down in green pastures:
He leadeth me beside the still waters.
He restoreth my soul:
He leadeth me in the paths of righteousness
        for his name's sake.
Yea, though I walk through the valley of the
        shadow of death, I will fear no evil:
For thou art with me; thy rod and thy staff
        they comfort me.
Thou preparest a table before me in the presence
        of mine enemies:
Thou anointest my head with oil; my cup
        runneth over.
Surely goodness and mercy shall follow me all
        the days of my life:
And I will dwell in the house of the Lord
        for ever.

Bible: Psalms, 23

LEAD, KINDLY LIGHT

LEAD, kindly Light, amid the encircling gloom,
     Lead thou me on!
The night is dark, and I am far from home,
     Lead thou me on!
Keep thou my feet! I do not ask to see
The distant scene; one step enough for me.

I was not ever thus, nor prayed that thou
     Shouldst lead me on;
I loved to choose and see my path; but now
     Lead thou me on!
I loved the garish day; and, spite of fears,
Pride ruled my will: remember not past years.

So long thy power hath blest me, sure it still
     Will lead me on
O'er moor and fen, o'er crag and torrent, till
     The night is gone;
And with the morn those angel faces smile,
Which I have loved long since, and lost awhile.

              JOHN HENRY NEWMAN

THE FIRST SNOWFALL

THE SNOW had begun in the gloaming,
     And busily all the night
Had been heaping field and highway
     With a silence deep and white.

Every pine and fir and hemlock
     Wore ermine too dear for an earl,
And the poorest twig on the elm-tree
     Was ridged inch deep with pearl.

From sheds new-roofed with Carrara
     Came Chanticleer's muffled crow,
The stiff rails were softened to swan's-down,
     And still fluttered down the snow.

I stood and watched by the window
     The noiseless work of the sky,
And the sudden flurries of snow-birds,
     Like brown leaves whirling by.

I thought of a mound in sweet Auburn
  Where a little headstone stood;
How the flakes were folding it gently,
  As did robins the babes in the wood.

Up spoke our own little Mabel,
  Saying, "Father, who makes it snow?"
And I told of the good All-father
  Who cares for us here below.

Again I looked at the snow-fall,
  And thought of the leaden sky
That arched o'er our first great sorrow,
  When that mound was heaped so high.

I remembered the gradual patience
  That fell from that cloud-like snow,
Flake by flake, healing and hiding
  The scar of our deep-plunged woe.

And again to the child I whispered,
  "The snow that husheth all,
Darling, the merciful Father
  Alone can make it fall!"

Then, with eyes that saw not, I kissed her;
  And she, kissing back, could not know
That *my* kiss was given to her sister,
  Folded close under deepening snow.
                  JAMES RUSSELL LOWELL

ROCKED IN THE CRADLE OF THE DEEP

ROCKED in the cradle of the deep
I lay me down in peace to sleep;
Secure I rest upon the wave,
For thou, O Lord, hast power to save.
I know thou wilt not slight my call,
For thou dost mark the sparrow's fall;
And calm and peaceful shall I sleep,
Rocked in the cradle of the deep.

When in the dead of night I lie
And gaze upon the trackless sky,
The star-bespangled heavenly scroll,
The boundless waters as they roll,—
I feel thy wondrous power to save
From perils of the stormy wave:

Rocked in the cradle of the deep
I calmly rest and soundly sleep.

And such the trust that still were mine,
Though stormy winds swept o'er the brine,
Or though the tempest's fiery breath
Roused me from sleep to wreck and death.
In ocean cave still safe with Thee
The gem of immortality!
And calm and peaceful shall I sleep
Rocked in the cradle of the deep.

EMMA WILLARD

NEARER, MY GOD, TO THEE

NEARER, my God, to thee,
   Nearer to thee,
E'en though it be a cross
   That raiseth me;
Still all my song would be,
Nearer, my God, to thee,
   Nearer to thee.

Though like the wanderer,
   The sun gone down,
Darkness be over me,
   My rest a stone;
Yet in my dreams I'd be
Nearer, my God, to thee,
   Nearer to thee.

There let the way appear
   Steps unto heaven;
All that thou sendest me
   In mercy given;
Angels to beckon me
Nearer, my God, to thee,
   Nearer to thee.

Then with my waking thoughts
   Bright with thy praise,
Out of my stony griefs
   Bethel I'll raise;
So by my woes to be
Nearer, my God, to thee,
   Nearer to thee.

Or if on joyful wing,
    Cleaving the sky,
Sun, moon, and stars forgot
    Upwards I fly,
Still all my song shall be,
Nearer, my God, to thee,
    Nearer to thee.

SARAH F. ADAMS

FROM "IN MEMORIAM"

O LIVING will that shalt endure
    When all that seems shall suffer shock,
    Rise in the spiritual rock,
Flow through our deeds and make them pure,

That we may lift from out of dust
    A voice as unto him that hears,
    A cry above the conquered years
To one that with us works, and trust,

With faith that comes of self-control,
    The truths that never can be proved
    Until we close with all we loved,
And all we flow from, soul in soul.

ALFRED TENNYSON

THERE IS NO DEATH

THERE IS no death! The stars go down
    To rise upon some other shore,
And bright in heaven's jeweled crown
    They shine forevermore.

There is no death! The forest leaves
    Convert to life the viewless air;
The rocks disorganize to feed
    The hungry moss they bear.

There is no death! The dust we tread
    Shall change, beneath the summer showers
To golden grain, or mellowed fruit,
    Or rainbow-tinted flowers.

There is no death! The leaves may fall,
    And flowers may fade and pass away—

They only wait, through wintry hours,
    The warm, sweet breath of May.

There is no death! The choicest gifts
    That heaven hath kindly lent to earth
Are ever first to seek again
    The country of their birth.

And all things that for growth or joy
    Are worthy of our love or care,
Whose loss has left us desolate,
    Are safely garnered there.

Though life become a desert waste,
    We know its fairest, sweetest flowers,
Transplanted into Paradise,
    Adorn immortal bowers.

The voice of birdlike melody
    That we have missed and mourned so long,
Now mingles with the angel choir
    In everlasting song.

There is no death! Although we grieve
    When beautiful, familiar forms
That we have learned to love are torn
    From our embracing arms—

Although with bowed and breaking heart,
    With sable garb and silent tread,
We bear their senseless dust to rest,
    And say that they are "dead,"

They are not dead! They have but passed
    Beyond the mists that blind us here
Into the new and larger life
    Of that serener sphere.

They have but dropped their robe of clay
    To put their shining raiment on;
They have not wandered far away—
    They are not "lost" nor "gone."

Though disenthralled and glorified
    They still are here and love us yet;
The dear ones they have left behind
    They never can forget.

And sometimes, when our hearts grow faint
    Amid temptations fierce and deep,

Or when the wildly raging waves
    Of grief or passion sweep,

We feel upon our fevered brow
    Their gentle touch, their breath of balm;
Their arms enfold us, and our hearts
    Grow comforted and calm.

And ever near us, though unseen,
    The dear, immortal spirits tread—
For all the boundless universe
    Is Life—there are no dead!

                                    J. L. MCCREERY

ONWARD, CHRISTIAN SOLDIERS

ONWARD, Christian soldiers,
    Marching as to war,
With the cross of Jesus
    Going on before!
Christ, the royal Master,
    Leads against the foe;
Forward into battle,
    See, his banners go.

Refrain:
Onward, Christian soldiers,
    Marching as to war,
With the cross of Jesus
    Going on before!

At the sign of triumph
    Satan's host doth flee;
On, then, Christian soldiers,
    On to victory!
Hell's foundations quiver
    At the shout of praise;
Brothers, lift your voices,
    Loud your anthems raise!

Like a mighty army
    Moves the Church of God:
Brothers, we are treading
    Where the saints have trod;
We are not divided,
    All one Body we,
One in hope and doctrine,
    One in charity.

Crowns and thrones may perish,
   Kingdoms rise and wane,
But the Church of Jesus
   Constant will remain;
Gates of hell can never
   'Gainst that Church prevail;
We have Christ's own promise,
   And that cannot fail.

Onward, then, ye people!
   Join our happy throng!
Blend with ours your voices
   In the triumph song!
Glory, laud, and honour,
   Unto Christ the King;
This through countless ages
   Men and angels sing.

            SABINE BARING-GOULD

GOD IS LOVE

GOD IS LOVE; his mercy brightens
   All the path in which we rove;
Bliss he wakes and woe he lightens;
   God is wisdom, God is love.

Chance and change are busy ever;
   Man decays, and ages move;
But his mercy waneth never;
   God is wisdom, God is love.

E'en the hour that darkest seemeth,
   Will his changeless goodness prove;
From the gloom his brightness streameth,
   God is wisdom, God is love.

He with earthly cares entwineth
   Hope and comfort from above;
Everywhere his glory shineth;
   God is wisdom, God is love.

            JOHN BOWRING

Favorite Poems About

AMERICA

THE STAR-SPANGLED BANNER

Oh, SAY, can you see, by the dawn's early light,
   What so proudly we hailed at the twilight's last gleaming,
Whose broad stripes and bright stars through the perilous fight,
   O'er the ramparts we watched were so gallantly streaming?
And the rocket's red glare, the bombs bursting in air,
Gave proof thro' the night that our flag was still there.
Oh, say, does that star-spangled banner yet wave
O'er the land of the free, and the home of the brave!

On the shore, dimly seen thro' the mists of the deep,
   Where the foe's haughty host in dread silence reposes,
What is that which the breeze o'er the towering steep,
   As it fitfully blows, half conceals, half discloses?
Now it catches the gleam of the morning's first beam,
In full glory reflected, now shines on the stream.
'Tis the star-spangled banner; oh, long may it wave
O'er the land of the free, and the home of the brave!

And where is that band who so vauntingly swore
   That the havoc of war and the battle's confusion
A home and a country should leave us no more?
   Their blood has washed out their foul footsteps' pollution.

No refuge could save the hireling and slave
From the terror of flight, or the gloom of the grave:
And the star-spangled banner in triumph doth wave
O'er the land of the free, and the home of the brave!

Oh, thus be it ever when freemen shall stand
    Between their loved homes and the war's desolation;
Blest with victory and peace, may the heaven-rescued land
    Praise the power that hath made and preserved us a nation!
Then conquer we must, when our cause it is just,
And this be our motto: "In God is our trust!"
And the star-spangled banner in triumph doth wave,
O'er the land of the free, and the home of the brave!

FRANCIS SCOTT KEY

COLUMBUS

Behind him lay the gray Azores,
Behind the Gates of Hercules;
Before him not the ghost of shores;
Before him only shoreless seas.
The good mate said: "Now must we pray,
For lo! the very stars are gone.
Brave Adm'r'l, speak! What shall I say?"
"Why, say: 'Sail on! sail on! and on!'"

"My men grow mutinous day by day;
My men grow ghastly, wan and weak."
The stout mate thought of home; a spray
Of salt wave washed his swarthy cheek.
"What shall I say, brave Adm'r'l, say,
If we sight naught but seas at dawn?"
"Why, you shall say at break of day:
'Sail on! sail on! sail on! and on!'"

They sailed and sailed, as winds might blow,
Until at last the blanched mate said:
"Why, now not even God would know
Should I and all my men fall dead.
These very winds forget their way,
For God from these dread seas is gone.
Now speak, brave Adm'r'l, speak and say——"
He said: "Sail on! sail on! and on!"

They sailed. They sailed. Then spake the mate:
"This mad sea shows his teeth tonight.
He curls his lip, he lies in wait,

He lifts his teeth as if to bite!
Brave Adm'r'l, say but one good word:
What shall we do when hope is gone?"
The words leapt like a leaping sword:
"Sail on! sail on! sail on! and on!"

Then pale and worn, he paced his deck,
And peered through darkness. Ah, that night
Of all dark nights! And then a speck—
A light! A light! At last a light!
It grew, a starlit flag unfurled!
It grew to be Time's burst of dawn.
He gained a world; he gave that world
Its grandest lesson: "On! sail on!"

JOAQUIN MILLER

THE MAYFLOWER

[DECEMBER 21, 1620]

Down in the bleak December bay
The ghostly vessel stands away;
Her spars and halyards white with ice,
Under the dark December skies.
A hundred souls, in company,
Have left the vessel pensively,—
Have reached the frosty desert there,
And touched it with the knees of prayer.
    And now the day begins to dip,
The night begins to lower
    Over the bay, and over the ship
        Mayflower.

Neither the desert nor the sea
Imposes rites: their prayers are free;
Danger and toil the wild imposes,
And thorns must grow before the roses.
And who are these?—and what distress
The savage-acred wilderness
On mother, maid, and child may bring,
Beseems them for a fearful thing;
    For now the day begins to dip,
The night begins to lower
    Over the bay, and over the ship
        Mayflower.

But Carver leads (in heart and health
A hero of the commonwealth)

The axes that the camp requires,
To build the lodge, and heap the fires.
And Standish from his warlike store
Arrays his men along the shore,
Distributes weapons resonant,
And dons his harness militant;
　　For now the day begins to dip,
The night begins to lower
　　　Over the bay, and over the ship
　　　　Mayflower;

And Rose, his wife, unlocks a chest—
She sees a Book, in vellum dressed,
She drops a tear, and kisses the tome,
Thinking of England and of home:
Might they—the Pilgrims, there and then
Ordained to do the work of men—
Have seen, in visions of the air,
While pillowed on the breast of prayer
　　(When now the day began to dip,
The night began to lower
　　　Over the bay, and over the ship
　　　　Mayflower),

The Canaan of their wilderness
A boundless empire of success;
And seen the years of future nights
Jewelled with myriad household lights;
And seen the honey fill the hive;
And seen a thousand ships arrive;
And heard the wheels of travel go;
It would have cheered a thought of woe,
　　When now the day began to dip,
The night began to lower
　　　Over the bay, and over the ship
　　　　Mayflower.

ERASTUS WOLCOTT ELLSWORTH

THE LANDING OF THE PILGRIM FATHERS

THE BREAKING WAVES dashed high
　　On a stern and rock-bound coast,
And the woods against a stormy sky
　　Their giant branches tossed;

And the heavy night hung dark
　　The hills and waters o'er,

When a band of exiles moored their bark
   On the wild New England shore.

Not as the conqueror comes,
   They, the true-hearted, came;
Not with the roll of the stirring drums,
   And the trumpet that sings of fame:

Not as the flying come,
   In silence and in fear;
They shook the depths of the desert gloom
   With their hymns of lofty cheer.

Amidst the storm they sang,
   And the stars heard, and the sea;
And the sounding aisles of the dim woods rang
   To the anthem of the free.

The ocean eagle soared
   From his nest by the white wave's foam,
And the rocking pines of the forest roared,—
   This was their welcome home.

There were men with hoary hair
   Amidst that pilgrim-band:
Why had they come to wither there,
   Away from their childhood's land?

There was woman's fearless eye,
   Lit by her deep love's truth;
There was manhood's brow serenely high,
   And the fiery heart of youth.

What sought they thus afar?
   Bright jewels of the mine?
The wealth of seas, the spoils of war?—
   They sought a faith's pure shrine!

Ay, call it holy ground,
   The soil where first they trod;
They have left unstained what there they found,—
   Freedom to worship God.

FELICIA D. HEMANS

PAUL REVERE'S RIDE

Listen, my children, and you shall hear
Of the midnight ride of Paul Revere,
On the eighteenth of April, in Seventy-five;

Hardly a man is now alive
Who remembers that famous day and year.

He said to his friend, "If the British march
By land or sea from the town to-night,
Hang a lantern aloft in the belfry arch
Of the North Church tower as a signal light,—
One, if by land, and two, if by sea;
And I on the opposite shore will be,
Ready to ride and spread the alarm
Through every Middlesex village and farm,
For the country folk to be up and to arm."

Then he said "Good-night," and with muffled oar
Silently row'd to the Charlestown shore,
Just as the moon rose over the bay,
Where swinging wide at her moorings lay
The Somerset, British man-of-war;
A phantom ship, with each mast and spar
Across the moon like a prison bar,
And a huge black hulk, that was magnified
By its own reflection in the tide.

Meanwhile his friend, through alley and street,
Wanders and watches with eager ears,
Till in the silence around him he hears
The muster of men at the barrack-door,
The sound of arms, and the tramp of feet,
And the measured tread of the grenadiers
Marching down to their boats on the shore.

Then he climb'd the tower of the Old North Church,
By the wooden stairs, with stealthy tread,
To the belfry-chamber overhead,
And started the pigeons from their perch
On the sombre rafters, that round him made
Masses of moving shapes of shade,—
By the trembling ladder, steep and tall,
To the highest window in the wall,
Where he paused to listen and look down
A moment on the roofs of the town,
And the moonlight flowing over all.

Beneath, in the churchyard, lay the dead,
In their night-encampment on the hill,
Wrapp'd in silence so deep and still
That he could hear, like a sentinel's tread,
The watchful night-wind, as it went

Creeping along from tent to tent,
And seeming to whisper, "All is well!"
A moment only he feels the spell
Of the place and the hour, and the secret dread
Of the lonely belfry and the dead;
For suddenly all his thoughts are bent
On a shadowy something far away,
Where the river widens to meet the bay,—
A line of black that bends and floats
On the rising tide like a bridge of boats.

Meanwhile, impatient to mount and ride,
Booted and spurr'd, with a heavy stride
On the opposite shore walk'd Paul Revere.
Now he patted his horse's side,
Now gazed at the landscape far and near,
Then, impetuous, stamp'd the earth,
And turn'd and tighten'd his saddle-girth;
But mostly he watch'd with eager search
The belfry-tower of the Old North Church,
As it rose above the graves on the hill,
Lonely and spectral and sombre and still.
And lo! as he looks, on the belfry's height
A glimmer, and then a gleam of light!
He springs to the saddle, the bridle he turns,
But lingers and gazes, till full on his sight
A second lamp in the belfry burns.

A hurry of hoofs in a village street,
A shape in the moonlight, a bulk in the dark,
And beneath, from the pebbles, in passing, a spark
Struck out by a steed flying fearless and fleet:
That was all; and yet, through the gloom and the light,
The fate of a nation was riding that night;
And the spark struck out by that steed in his flight
Kindled the land into flame with its heat.

He has left the village and mounted the steep,
And beneath him, tranquil and broad and deep,
Is the Mystic, meeting the ocean tides,
And under the alders that skirt its edge,
Now soft on the sand, now loud on the ledge,
Is heard the tramp of his steed as he rides.

It was twelve by the village clock
When he cross'd the bridge into Medford town.
He heard the crowing of the cock,

And the barking of the farmer's dog,
And felt the damp of the river fog,
That rises after the sun goes down.

It was one by the village clock
When he galloped into Lexington.
He saw the gilded weathercock
Swim in the moonlight as he pass'd,
And the meeting-house windows, blank and bare,
Gaze at him with a spectral glare,
As if they already stood aghast
At the bloody work they would look upon.

It was two by the village clock
When he came to the bridge in Concord town.
He heard the bleating of the flock,
And the twitter of birds among the trees,
And felt the breath of the morning breeze
Blowing over the meadows brown.
And one was safe and asleep in his bed
Who at the bridge would be first to fall,
Who that day would be lying dead,
Pierced by a British musket-ball.

You know the rest; in the books you have read,
How the British regulars fired and fled,—
How the farmers gave them ball for ball,
From behind each fence and farmyard wall,
Chasing the red-coats down the lane,
Then crossing the fields to emerge again
Under the trees at the turn of the road,
And only pausing to fire and load.
So through the night rode Paul Revere,
And so through the night went his cry of alarm
To every Middlesex village and farm,—
A cry of defiance, and not of fear,
A voice in the darkness, a knock at the door,
And a word that shall echo for evermore!
For, borne on the night-wind of the Past,
Through all our history, to the last,
In the hour of darkness, and peril, and need,
The people will waken and listen to hear
The hurrying hoof-beats of that steed,
And the midnight message of Paul Revere.

HENRY WADSWORTH LONGFELLOW

INDEPENDENCE BELL—JULY 4, 1776

THERE was a tumult in the city
In the quaint old Quaker town,
And the streets were rife with people
Pacing restless up and down—
People gathering at corners,
Where they whispered one to each,
And the sweat stood on their temples
With the earnestness of speech.

As the bleak Atlantic currents
Lash the wild Newfoundland shore,
So they beat against the State House,
So they surged against the door;
And the mingling of their voices
Made the harmony profound,
Till the quiet street of Chestnut
Was all turbulent with sound.

"Will they do it?" "Dare they do it?"
"Who is speaking?" "What's the news?"
"What of Adams?" "What of Sherman?"
"Oh, God grant they won't refuse!"
"Make some way there!" "Let me nearer!"
"I am stifling!" "Stifle then!
When a nation's life's at hazard,
We've no time to think of men!"

So they surged against the State House,
While all solemnly inside,
Sat the Continental Congress,
Truth and reason for their guide,
O'er a simple scroll debating,
Which, though simple it might be,
Yet should shake the cliffs of England
With the thunders of the free.

Far aloft in that high steeple
Sat the bellman, old and gray,
He was weary of the tyrant
And his iron-sceptered sway;
So he sat, with one hand ready
On the clapper of the bell,
When his eye could catch the signal,
The long-expected news to tell.

See! See! The dense crowd quivers
Through all its lengthy line,
As the boy beside the portal
Hastens forth to give the sign!
With his little hands uplifted,
Breezes dallying with his hair,
Hark! with deep, clear intonation,
Breaks his young voice on the air.

Hushed the people's swelling murmur,
Whilst the boy crys joyously;
"Ring!" he shouts, "Ring! Grandpapa,
Ring! oh, ring for Liberty!"
Quickly, at the given signal
The old bellman lifts his hand,
Forth he sends the good news, making
Iron music through the land.

How they shouted! What rejoicing!
How the old bell shook the air,
Till the clang of freedom ruffled,
The calmly gliding Delaware!
How the bonfires and the torches
Lighted up the night's repose,
And from the flames, like fabled Phoenix,
Our glorious liberty arose!

That old State House bell is silent,
Hushed is now its clamorous tongue;
But the spirit it awakened
Still is living—ever young;
And when we greet the smiling sunlight
On the fourth of each July,
We will ne'er forget the bellman
Who, betwixt the earth and sky,
Rung out, loudly, "Independence";
Which, please God, shall never die!

ANONYMOUS

BUNKER HILL

"NOT YET, not yet; steady, steady!"
On came the foe in even line,
Nearer and nearer to thrice paces nine.
We looked into their eyes. "Ready!"
A sheet of flame; a roll of death!

They fell by scores: we held our breath!
    Then nearer still they came.
    Another sheet of flame;
And brave men fled who never fled before.
    Immortal fight!
    Foreshadowing flight
Back to the astounded shore.

    Quickly they rallied, re-enforced,
'Mid louder roar of ships' artillery,
And bursting bombs and whistling musketry,
And shouts and groans anear, afar,
All the new din of dreadful war.
    Through their broad bosoms calmly coursed
The blood of those stout farmers, aiming
For freedom, manhood's birthright claiming.

Onward once more they came:
Another sheet of deathful flame!
    Another and another still.
      They broke, they fled;
      Again they sped
    Down the green, bloody hill.
Howe, Burgoyne, Clinton, Gage,
Stormed with commanders' rage.
Into each emptied barge
They crowd fresh men for a new charge
    Up that great hill.
    Again their gallant blood we spill.
That volley was the last:
    Our powder failed.
On three sides fast
    The foe pressed in, nor quailed
A man. Their barrels empty, with musket-stocks
They fought, and gave death-dealing knocks,
Till Prescott ordered the retreat.
Then Warren fell; and through a leaden sleet
From Bunker Hill and Breed,
Stark, Putnam, Pomeroy, Knowlton, Read,
Led off the remnant of those heroes true;
The foe too weakened to pursue.
    The ground they gained; but we
      The victory.

The tidings of that chosen band
    Flowed in a wave of power

Over the shaken, anxious land,
    To men, to man, a sudden dower.
History took a fresh, higher start
    From that stanch, beaming hour;
And when the speeding messenger that bare
    The news that strengthened every heart,
Met near the Delaware
    The leader who had just been named,
    Who was to be so famed,
The steadfast, earnest Washington,
    With hands uplifted, cries,
    His great soul flashing to his eyes,
"Our liberties are safe! the cause is won!"
A thankful look he cast to heaven, and then
His steed he spurred in haste to lead such noblemen.

GEORGE HENRY CALVERT

WARREN'S ADDRESS AT BUNKER HILL

[JUNE 16-17, 1775]

STAND! the ground's your own, my braves!
Will ye give it up to slaves?
Will ye look for greener graves?
    Hope ye mercy still?
What's the mercy despots feel?
Hear it in that battle-peal!
Read it on yon bristling steel!
    Ask it,—ye who will.

Fear ye foes who kill for hire?
Will ye to your homes retire?
Look behind you!—they're afire!
    And, before you, see
Who have done it! From the vale
On they come—and will ye quail?
Leaden rain and iron hail
    Let their welcome be!

In the God of battles trust!
Die we may,—and die we must:
But, O, where can dust to dust
    Be consigned so well,
As where heaven its dews shall shed
On the martyred patriot's bed,
And the rocks shall raise their head,
    Of his deeds to tell?

JOHN PIERPONT

THE SWAMP FOX

WE FOLLOW where the Swamp Fox guides,
　His friends and merry men are we;
And when the troop of Tarleton rides,
　We burrow in the cypress tree.
The turfy hammock is our bed,
　Our home is in the red deer's den,
Our roof, the tree-top overhead,
　For we are wild and hunted men.

We fly by day and shun its light,
　But, prompt to strike the sudden blow,
We mount and start with early night,
　And through the forest track our foe.
And soon he hears our charges leap,
　The flashing sabre blinds his eyes,
And ere he drives away his sleep,
　And rushes from his camp, he dies.

Free bridle-bit, good gallant steed,
　That will not ask a kind caress
To swim the Santee at our need,
　When on his heels the foemen press,—
The true heart and the ready hand,
　The spirit stubborn to be free
The twisted bore, the smiting brand,—
　And we are Marion's men, you see.

Now light the fire and cook the meal,
　The last perhaps that we shall taste;
I hear the Swamp Fox round us steal,
　And that's a sign we move in haste.
He whistles to the scouts, and hark!
　You hear his order calm and low.
Come, wave your torch across the dark,
　And let us see the boys that go.

We may not see their forms again,
　God help 'em, should they find the strife!
For they are strong and fearless men,
　And make no coward terms for life;
They'll fight as long as Marion bids,
　And when he speaks the word to shy,

Then, not till then, they turn their steeds,
    Through thickening shade and swamp to fly.

Now stir the fire and lie at ease,—
    The scouts are gone, and on the brush
I see the Colonel bend his knee,
    To take his slumbers too. But hush!
He's praying, comrades; 't is not strange;
    The man that's fighting day by day
May well, when night comes, take a change,
    And down upon his knees to pray.

Break up that hoe-cake, boys, and hand
    The sly and silent jug that's there;
I love not it should idly stand
    When Marion's men have need of cheer.
'T is seldom that our luck affords
    A stuff like this we just have quaffed,
And dry potatoes on our boards
    May always call for such a draught.

Now pile the brush and roll the log;
    Hard pillow, but a soldier's head
That's half the time in brake and bog
    Must never think of softer bed.
The owl is hooting to the night,
    The cooter crawling o'er the bank,
And in that pond the flashing light
    Tells where the alligator sank.

What! 't is the signal! start so soon,
    And through the Santee swamp so deep,
Without the aid of friendly moon,
    And we, Heaven help us! half asleep!
But courage, comrades! Marion leads,
    The Swamp Fox takes us out 'to-night;
So clear your swords and spur your steeds,
    There's goodly chance, I think, of fight.

We follow where the Swamp Fox guides,
    We leave the swamp and cypress-tree,
Our spurs are in our coursers' sides,
    And ready for the strife are we.
The Tory camp is now in sight,
    And there he cowers within his den;
He hears our shouts, he dreads the fight,
    He fears, and flies from Marion's men.

WILLIAM   GILMORE   SIMMS

HAIL, COLUMBIA!

Hail, Columbia, happy land! Hail, ye heroes, heaven-born band!
Who fought and bled in Freedom's cause, who fought and bled in Free-
dom's cause;
And when the storm of war was gone, enjoyed the peace your valor
won.
Let independence be our boast, ever mindful what it cost;
Ever grateful for the prize, let its altar reach the skies.

Refrain:
Firm, united, let us be, rallying round our liberty;
As a band of brothers joined, peace and safety we shall find.

Immortal patriots, rise once more! Defend your rights, defend your
shore;
Let no rude foe with impious hand, let no rude foe with impious hand,
Invade the shrine where sacred lies, of toil and blood, the well-earned
prize.
While offering peace, sincere and just, in heaven we place a manly
trust,
That truth and justice will prevail, and every scheme of bondage fail.

Sound, sound the trump of fame! Let Washington's great name
Ring through the world with loud applause, ring through the world
with loud applause;
Let every clime to freedom dear, listen with a joyful ear.
With equal skill, with God-like power, he governs in the fearful hour
Of horrid war; or guides with ease, the happier times of honest peace.

Behold the Chief who now commands, once more to serve his country
stands,
The rock on which the storm will beat, the rock on which the storm
will beat;
But armed in virtue, firm and true, his hopes are fixed on heaven and
you.
When hope was sinking in dismay, when gloom obscured Columbia's
day,
His steady mind, from changes free, resolved on death or liberty.

JOSEPH HOPKINSON

WASHINGTON

When dreaming kings, at odds with swift-paced time,
   Would strike that banner down,

A nobler knight than ever writ or rhyme
   With fame's bright wreath did crown
Through armed hosts bore it till it floated high
Beyond the clouds, a light that cannot die!
   Ah, hero of our younger race!
      Great ruler of a temple new!
   Ruler, who sought no lordly place!
      Warrior, who sheathed the sword he drew!
   Lover of men, who saw afar
   A world unmarred by want or war,
   Who knew the path, and yet forbore
   To tread, till all men should implore;
   Who saw the light, and led the way
   Where the gray world might greet the day;
   Father and leader, prophet sure,
   Whose will in vast works shall endure,
How shall we praise him on this day of days,
Great son of fame who has no need of praise?

How shall we praise him? Open wide the doors
   Of the fair temple whose broad base he laid.
    Through its white halls a shadowy cavalcade
Of heroes moves o'er unresounding floors—
Men whose brawned arms upraised these columns high,
And reared the towers that vanish in the sky,—
The strong who, having wrought, can never die.

HARRIET MONROE

From the "Commemoration Ode", World's Co-
lumbian Exposition, Chicago, October 21, 1892

OLD IRONSIDES

Ay, tear her tattered ensign down!
   Long has it waved on high,
And many an eye has danced to see
   That banner in the sky;
Beneath it rung the battle-shout,
   And burst the cannon's roar:
The meteor of the ocean air
   Shall sweep the clouds no more!

Her deck, once red with heroes' blood,
   Where knelt the vanquished foe,
When winds were hurrying o'er the flood
   And waves were white below,
No more shall feel the victor's tread,

Or know the conquered knee:
The harpies of the shore shall pluck
The eagle of the sea!

O better that her shattered hulk
Should sink beneath the wave!
Her thunders shook the mighty deep,
And there should be her grave:
Nail to the mast her holy flag,
Set every threadbare sail,
And give her to the god of storms,
The lightning and the gale!

OLIVER WENDELL HOLMES

THE YANKEE MAN-OF-WAR

'Tis of a gallant Yankee ship that flew the stripes and stars,
And the whistling wind from the west-nor'-west blew through the pitch-pine spars;
With her starboard tacks aboard, my boys, she hung upon the gale;
On an autumn night we raised the light on the old Head of Kinsale.

It was a clear and cloudless night, and the wind blew steady and strong,
As gayly over the sparkling deep our good ship bowled along;
With the foaming seas beneath her bow the fiery waves she spread,
And bending low her bosom of snow, she buried her lee cat-head.

There was no talk of short'ning sail by him who walked the poop,
And under the press of her pond'ring jib, the boom bent like a hoop!
And the groaning water-ways told the strain that held her stout main-tack,
But he only laughed as he glanced aloft at a white and silvery track.

The mid-tide meets in the Channel waves that flow from shore to shore,
And the mist hung heavy upon the land from Featherstone to Dunmore,
And that sterling light in Tusker Rock where the old bell tolls each hour,
And the beacon light that shone so bright was quenched on Waterford Tower.

What looms upon our starboard bow? What hangs upon the breeze?
'Tis time our good ship hauled her wind abreast the old Saltees,
For by her ponderous press of sail and by her consorts four
We saw our morning visitor was a British man-of-war.

Up spake our noble Captain then, as a shot ahead of us past—
"Haul snug your flowing courses! lay your topsail to the mast!"
Those Englishmen gave three loud hurrahs from the deck of their
    covered ark,
And we answered back by a solid broadside from the decks of our
    patriot bark.

"Out booms! out booms!" our skipper cried, "out booms and give her
    sheet,"
And the swiftest keel that was ever launched shot ahead of the British
    fleet,
And amidst a thundering shower of shot, with stun'-sails hoisting away,
Down the North Channel Paul Jones did steer just at the break of day.

ANONYMOUS

CONCORD HYMN

(SUNG AT THE COMPLETION OF THE CONCORD MONUMENT, APRIL 19, 1836)

By the RUDE BRIDGE that arched the flood,
    Their flag to April's breeze unfurled,
Here once the embattled farmers stood,
    And fired the shot heard round the world.

The foe long since in silence slept;
    Alike the conqueror silent sleeps;
And Time the ruined bridge has swept
    Down the dark stream which seaward creeps.

On this green bank, by this soft stream,
    We set to-day a votive stone;
That memory may their deed redeem,
    When, like our sires, our sons are gone.

Spirit, that made those heroes dare
    To die, and leave their children free,
Bid Time and Nature gently spare
    The shaft we raise to them and thee.

RALPH WALDO EMERSON

THE AMERICAN FLAG

When Freedom, from her mountain height,
    Unfurled her standard to the air,
She tore the azure robe of night,
    And set the stars of glory there!

She mingled with its gorgeous dyes
The milky baldric of the skies,
And striped its pure, celestial white
With streakings of the morning light;
Then, from his mansion in the sun,
She called her eagle-bearer down,
And gave into his mighty hand
The symbol of her chosen land!

Majestic monarch of the cloud!
    Who rear'st aloft thy regal form,
To hear the tempest trumping loud,
And see the lightning lances driven,
    When strive the warriors of the storm,
And rolls the thunder-drum of heaven,—
Child of the Sun! to thee 't is given
    To guard the banner of the free,
To hover in the sulphur smoke,
To ward away the battle-stroke,
And bid its blendings shine afar,
Like rainbows on the cloud of war,
    The harbingers of victory!

Flag of the brave! thy folds shall fly,
The sign of hope and triumph high!
When speaks the signal-trumpet tone,
And the long line comes gleaming on,
Ere yet the life-blood, warm and wet,
Has dimmed the glistening bayonet,
Each soldier's eye shall brightly turn
To where thy sky-born glories burn,
And, as his springing steps advance,
Catch war and vengeance from the glance.

And when the cannon-mouthings loud
Heave in wild wreaths the battle shroud,
And gory sabres rise and fall
Like shoots of flame on midnight's pall,
Then shall thy meteor glances glow,
    And cowering foes shall shrink beneath
Each gallant arm that strikes below
    That lovely messenger of death.

Flag of the seas! on ocean wave
Thy stars shall glitter o'er the brave;
When death, careering on the gale,
Sweeps darkly round the bellied sail,
And frighted waves rush wildly back

Before the broadside's reeling rack,
Each dying wanderer of the sea
Shall look at once to heaven and thee,
And smile to see thy splendors fly
In triumph o'er his closing eye.

Flag of the free heart's hope and home,
 By angel hands to valor given;
The stars have lit the welkin dome,
 And all thy hues were born in heaven.
Forever float that standard sheet!
 Where breathes the foe but falls before us,
With Freedom's soil beneath our feet,
 And Freedom's banner streaming o'er us?

JOSEPH RODMAN DRAKE

PIONEERS! O PIONEERS!

COME, my tan-faced children,
Follow well in order, get your weapons ready,
Have you your pistols? have you your sharp-edged axes?
 Pioneers! O pioneers!

For we cannot tarry here,
We must march my darlings, we must bear the brunt of danger,
We the youthful sinewy races, all the rest on us depend,
 Pioneers! O pioneers!

O you youths, Western youths,
So impatient, full of action, full of manly pride and friendship,
Plain I see you Western youths, see you tramping with the foremost,
 Pioneers! O pioneers!

Have the elder races halted?
Do they droop and end their lesson, wearied over there beyond the seas
We take up the task eternal, and the burden and the lesson,
 Pioneers! O pioneers!

All the past we leave behind,
We debouch upon a newer mightier world, varied world,
Fresh and strong the world we seize, world of labor and the march,
 Pioneers! O pioneers!

We detachments steady throwing,
Down the edges, through the passes, up the mountains steep,
Conquering, holding, daring, venturing as we go the unknown ways,
 Pioneers! O pioneers!

We primeval forests felling,
We the rivers stemming, vexing we and piercing deep the mines within,
We the surface broad surveying, we the virgin soil upheaving,
    Pioneers! O pioneers!

Colorado men are we,
From the peaks gigantic, from the great sierras and the high plateaus,
From the mine and from the gully, from the hunting trail we come,
    Pioneers! O pioneers!

From Nebraska, from Arkansas,
Central inland race are we, from Missouri, with the continental blood
    intervein'd,
All the hands of comrades clasping, all the Southern, all the Northern,
    Pioneers! O pioneers!

O resistless restless race!
O beloved race in all! O my breast aches with tender love for all!
O I mourn and yet exult, I am rapt with love for all,
    Pioneers! O pioneers!

Raise the mighty mother mistress,
Waving high the delicate mistress, over all the starry mistress, (bend
    your heads all,)
Raise the fang'd and warlike mistress, stern, impassive, weapon'd mis-
    tress,
    Pioneers! O pioneers!

See my children, resolute children,
By those swarms upon our rear we must never yield or falter,
Ages back in ghostly millions frowning there behind us urging,
    Pioneers! O pioneers!

On and on the compact ranks,
With accessions ever waiting, with the places of the dead quickly fill'd,
Through the battle, through defeat, moving yet and never stopping,
    Pioneers! O pioneers!

O to die advancing on!
Are there some of us to droop and die? has the hour come?
Then upon the march we fittest die, soon and sure the gap is fill'd,
    Pioneers! O pioneers!

All the pulses of the world,
Falling in they beat for us, with the Western movement beat,
Holding single or together, steady moving to the front, all for us,
    Pioneers! O pioneers!

Life's involv'd and varied pageants,
All the forms and shows, all the workmen at their work,

All the seamen and the landsmen, all the masters with their slaves,
　　　Pioneers! O pioneers!

　　　All the hapless silent lovers,
All the prisoners in the prisons, all the righteous and the wicked,
All the joyous, all the sorrowing, all the living, all the dying,
　　　Pioneers! O pioneers!

　　　I too with my soul and body,
We, a curious trio, picking, wandering on our way,
Through these shores amid the shadows, with the apparitions pressing,
　　　Pioneers! O pioneers!

　　　Lo, the darting bowling orb!
Lo, the brother orbs around, all the clustering suns and planets,
All the dazzling days, all the mystic nights with dreams,
　　　Pioneers! O pioneers!

　　　These are of us, they are with us,
All for primal needed work, while the followers there in embryo wait
　　　behind,
We to-day's procession heading, we the route for travel clearing,
　　　Pioneers! O pioneers!

　　　O you daughters of the West!
O you young and elder daughters! O you mothers and you wives!
Never must you be divided, in our ranks you move united,
　　　Pioneers! O pioneers!

　　　Minstrels latent on the prairies!
(Shrouded bards of other lands, you may rest, you have done your
　　　work,)
Soon I hear you coming warbling, soon you rise and tramp amid us,
　　　Pioneers! O pioneers!

　　　Not for delectations sweet,
Not the cushion and the slipper, not the peaceful and the studious,
Not the riches safe and palling, not for us the tame enjoyment,
　　　Pioneers! O pioneers!

　　　Do the feasters gluttonous feast?
Do the corpulent sleepers sleep? have they lock'd and bolted doors?
Still be ours the diet hard, and the blanket on the ground,
　　　Pioneers! O pioneers!

　　　Has the night descended?
Was the road of late so toilsome? did we stop discouraged nodding on
　　　our way?
Yet a passing hour I yield you in your tracks to pause oblivious,
　　　Pioneers! O pioneers!

Till with sound of trumpet,
Far, far off the daybreak call—hark! how loud and clear I hear it wind,
Swift! to the head of the army!—swift! spring to your places,
    Pioneers! O pioneers!

WALT WHITMAN

THE SETTLER

HIS ECHOING AXE the settler swung
    Amid the sea-like solitude,
And rushing, thundering, down were flung
    The Titans of the wood;
Loud shrieked the eagle as he dashed
From out his mossy nest, which crashed
    With its supporting bough,
And the first sunlight, leaping, flashed
    On the wolf's haunt below.

Rude was the garb, and strong the frame
    Of him who plied his ceaseless toil:
To form that garb, the wild-wood game
    Contributed their spoil;
The soul that warmed that frame disdained
The tinsel, gaud, and glare, that reigned
    Where men their crowds collect;
The simple fur, untrimmed, unstained,
    This forest-tamer decked.

The paths which wound mid gorgeous trees,
    The streams whose bright lips kissed their flowers,
The winds that swelled their harmonies
    Through those sun-hiding bowers,
The temple vast—the green arcade,
The nestling vale—the grassy glade,
    Dark cave and swampy lair,—
These scenes and sounds majestic, made
    His world and pleasures, there.

His roof adorned a lovely spot,
    Mid the black logs green glowed the grain,
And herbs and plants the woods knew not
    Throve in the sun and rain.
The smoke-wreath curling o'er the dell,
The low—the bleat—the tinkling bell,
    All made a landscape strange,
Which was the living chronicle
    Of deeds that wrought the change.

The violet sprung at spring's first tinge,
   The rose of summer spread its glow,
The maize hung on its autumn fringe,
   Rude winter brought its snow;
And still the settler labored there,
His shout and whistle woke the air,
   As cheerily he plied
His garden spade, or drove his share
   Along the hillock's side.

He marked the fire-storm's blazing flood
   Roaring and crackling on its path,
And scorching earth, and melting wood,
   Beneath its greedy wrath;
He marked the rapid whirlwind shoot
Trampling the pine-tree with its foot,
   And darkening thick the day
With streaming bough and severed root,
   Hurled whizzing on its way.

His gaunt hound yelled, his rifle flashed,
   The grim bear hushed its savage growl,
In blood and foam the panther gnashed
   Its fangs, with dying howl;
The fleet deer ceased its flying bound,
Its snarling wolf-foe bit the ground,
   And with its moaning cry
The beaver sank beneath the wound,
   Its pond-built Venice by.

Humble the lot, yet his the race,
   When Liberty sent forth her cry,
Who thronged in Conflict's deadliest place,
   To fight—to bleed—to die!
Who cumbered Bunker's height of red,
By hope through weary years were led,
   And witnessed Yorktown's sun
Blaze on a Nation's banner spread,
   A Nation's freedom won.

                ALFRED BILLINGS STREET

WESTWARD HO!

WHAT strength! what strife! what rude unrest!
What shocks! what half-shaped armies met!
A mighty nation moving west,
With all its steely sinews set

Against the living forests. Hear
The shouts, the shots of pioneer,
The rended forests, rolling wheels,
As if some half-checked army reels,
Recoils, redoubles, comes again,
Loud-sounding like a hurricane.

O bearded, stalwart, westmost men,
So tower-like, so Gothic built!
A kingdom won without the guilt
Of studied battle, that hath been
Your blood's inheritance. . . . Your heirs
Know not your tombs: the great plough shares
Cleave softly through the mellow loam
Where you have made eternal home,
And set no sign. Your epitaphs
Are writ in furrows. Beauty laughs
While through the green ways wandering
Beside her love, slow gathering
White, starry-hearted May-time blooms
Above your lowly levelled tombs;
And then below the spotted sky
She stops, she leans, she wonders why
The ground is heaved and broken so,
And why the grasses darker grow
And droop and trail like wounded wing.

Yea, Time, the grand old harvester,
Has gathered you from wood and plain.
We call to you again, again;
The rush and rumble of the car
Comes back in answer. Deep and wide
The wheels of progress have passed on;
The silent pioneer is gone.
His ghost is moving down the trees,
And now we push the memories
Of bluff, bold men who dared and died
In foremost battle, quite aside.

                              JOAQUIN MILLER

THE DEFENSE OF THE ALAMO

SANTA ANNA came storming, as a storm might come;
There was rumble of cannon; there was rattle of blade;
There was cavalry, infantry, bugle and drum—
Full seven proud thousand in pomp and parade,

The chivalry, flower of all Mexico;
And a gaunt two hundred in the Alamo!

And thirty lay sick, and some were shot through;
For the siege had been bitter, and bloody and long.
"Surrender, or die!"—"Men, what will you do?"
And Travis, great Travis, drew sword, quick and strong;
Drew a line at his feet . . . Will you come? Will you go?
I die with my wounded, in the Alamo."

Then Bowie gasped, "Guide me over that line!"
Then Crockett, one hand to the sick, one hand to his gun,
Crossed with him; then never a word or a sign,
Till all, sick or well, all, all, save but one,
One man. Then a woman stopped praying and slow
Across, to die with the heroes of the Alamo.

Then that one coward fled, in the night, in that night
When all men silently prayed and thought
Of home; of tomorrow; of God and the right,
Till dawn; then Travis sent his single last cannon-shot,
In answer to insolent Mexico,
From the old bell-tower of the Alamo.

Then came Santa Anna; a crescent of flame!
Then the red escalade; then the fight hand to hand;
Such an unequal fight as never had name
Since the Persian hordes butchered that doomed Spartan band.
All day—all day and all night, and the morning, so slow,
Through the battle smoke mantling the Alamo.

Then silence! Such silence! Two thousand lay dead
In a crescent outside! And within? Not a breath
Save the gasp of a woman, with gory, gashed head,
All alone, with her dead there, waiting for death;
And she but a nurse. Yet when shall we know
Another like this of the Alamo?

Shout "Victory, victory, victory ho!"
I say, 'tis not always with the hosts that win:
I say that the victory, high or low,
Is given the hero who grapples with sin,
Or legion or single; just asking to know
When duty fronts death in his Alamo.

JOAQUIN MILLER

MONTEREY

[SEPTEMBER 23, 1846]

WE WERE not many, we who stood
   Before the iron sleet that day:
Yet many a gallant spirit would
Give half his years if but he could
   Have been with us at Monterey.

Now here, now there, the shot it hailed
   In deadly drifts of fiery spray,
Yet not a single soldier quailed
When wounded comrades round them wailed
   Their dying shout at Monterey.

And on—still on our column kept
   Through walls of flame its withering way;
Where fell the dead, the living stepped,
Still charging on the guns which swept
   The slippery streets of Monterey.

The foe himself recoiled aghast,
   When, striking where he strongest lay,
We swooped his flanking batteries past,
And braving full their murderous blast,
   Stormed home the towers of Monterey.

Our banners on those turrets wave,
   And there our evening bugles play:
Where orange-boughs above their grave
Keep green the memory of the brave
   Who fought and fell at Monterey.

We are not many—we who pressed
   Beside the brave who fell that day—
But who of us has not confessed
He'd rather share their warrior rest
   Than not have been at Monterey?

                    CHARLES FENNO HOFFMAN

ALL QUIET ALONG THE POTOMAC

"ALL QUIET along the Potomac," they say,
   "Except, now and then, a stray picket
Is shot, as he walks on his beat to and fro,

By a rifleman hid in the thicket."
'Tis nothing—a private or two now and then
    Will not count in the news of the battle;
Not an officer lost—only one of the men
    Moaning out, all alone, the death-rattle.

All quiet along the Potomac to-night,
    Where the soldiers lie peacefully dreaming;
Their tents, in the rays of the clear autumn moon
    Or the light of the watch-fire, are gleaming.
A tremulous sigh of the gentle night-wind
    Through the forest-leaves softly is creeping,
While stars up above, with their glittering eyes,
    Keep guard, for the army is sleeping.

There's only the sound of the lone sentry's tread
    As he tramps from the rock to the fountain,
And thinks of the two in the low trundle-bed
    Far away in the cot on the mountain.
His musket falls slack; his face, dark and grim,
    Grows gentle with memories tender
As he mutters a prayer for the children asleep—
    For their mother; may Heaven defend her!

The moon seems to shine just as brightly as then,
    That night when the love yet unspoken
Leaped up to his lips—when low-murmured vows
    Were pledged to be ever unbroken.
Then, drawing his sleeve roughly over his eyes,
    He dashes off tears that are welling,
And gathers his gun closer up to its place,
    As if to keep down the heart-swelling.

He passes the fountain, the blasted pine tree,
    The footstep is lagging and weary;
Yet onward he goes through the broad belt of light,
    Toward the shade of the forest so dreary.
Hark! was it the night-wind that rustled the leaves?
    Was it moonlight so wondrously flashing?
It looked like a rifle—"Ha! Mary, good-bye!"
    The red life-blood is ebbing and plashing.

All quiet along the Potomac to-night,
    No sound save the rush of the river;
While soft falls the dew on the face of the dead—
    The picket's off duty for ever!

                                    ETHEL LYNN BEERS

SHERIDAN'S RIDE

Up FROM the south, at break of day,
Bringing to Winchester fresh dismay,
The affrighted air with a shudder bore,
Like a herald in haste to the chieftain's door,
The terrible grumble, and rumble, and roar,
Telling the battle was on once more,
    And Sheridan twenty miles away.

And wider still those billows of war
Thunder'd along the horizon's bar;
And louder yet into Winchester roll'd
The roar of that red sea uncontroll'd,
Making the blood of the listener cold,
As he thought of the stake in that fiery fray,
    And Sheridan twenty miles away.

But there is a road from Winchester town,
A good broad highway leading down;
And there, through the flush of the morning light,
A steed as black as the steeds of night
Was seen to pass, as with eagle flight,
As if he knew the terrible need;
He stretch'd away with his utmost speed;
Hills rose and fell; but his heart was gay,
    With Sheridan fifteen miles away.

Still sprang from those swift hoofs, thundering south,
The dust, like smoke from the cannon's mouth,
Or the trail of a comet, sweeping faster and faster,
Foreboding to traitors the doom of disaster.
The heart of the steed and the heart of the master
Were beating like prisoners assaulting their walls,
Impatient to be where the battle-field calls;
Every nerve of the charger was strain'd to full play,
    With Sheridan only ten miles away.

Under his spurning feet, the road
Like an arrowy Alpine river flow'd
And the landscape sped away behind
Like an ocean flying before the wind:
And the steed, like a bark fed with furnace ire.
Swept on, with his wild eye full of fire.
But, lo! he is nearing his heart's desire;

He is snuffing the smoke of the roaring fray,
   With Sheridan only five miles away.

The first that the general saw were the groups
Of stragglers, and then the retreating troops;
What was done? what to do? a glance told him both.
Then striking his spurs with a terrible oath,
He dash'd down the line, 'mid a storm of huzzas,
And the wave of retreat check'd its course there, because
The sight of the master compell'd it to pause.
With foam and with dust the black charger was gray;
By the flash of his eye, and the red nostril's play
He seem'd to the whole great army to say,
"I have brought you Sheridan all the way
   From Winchester down, to save the day."

Hurrah! hurrah for Sheridan!
Hurrah! hurrah for horse and man!
And when their statues are placed on high,
Under the dome of the Union sky,
The American soldier's Temple of Fame,
There with the glorious general's name
Be it said, in letters both bold and bright:
"Here is the steed that saved the day
By carrying Sheridan into the fight,
   From Winchester—twenty miles away!"

THOMAS BUCHANAN READ

BARBARA FRIETCHIE

UP FROM the meadows rich with corn,
Clear in the cool September morn,

The clustered spires of Frederick stand
Green-walled by the hills of Maryland.

Round about them orchards sweep,
Apple and peach tree fruited deep,

Fair as the garden of the Lord
To the eyes of the famished rebel horde,

On that pleasant morn of the early fall
When Lee marched over the mountain-wall,

Over the mountains winding down,
Horse and foot, into Frederick town.

Forty flags with their silver stars,
Forty flags with their crimson bars,

Flapped in the morning wind: the sun
Of noon looked down, and saw not one.

Up rose old Barbara Frietchie then,
Bowed with her fourscore years and ten,

Bravest of all in Frederick town,
She took up the flag the men hauled down.

In her attic window the staff she set,
To show that one heart was loyal yet.

Up the street came the rebel tread,
Stonewall Jackson riding ahead.

Under his slouched hat left and right
He glanced: the old flag met his sight.

"Halt!"—the dust-brown ranks stood fast.
"Fire!"—out blazed the rifle-blast.

It shivered the window, pane and sash;
It rent the banner with seam and gash.

Quick, as it fell, from the broken staff
Dame Barbara snatched the silken scarf.

She leaned far out on the window-sill,
And shook it forth with a royal will.

"Shoot, if you must, this old gray head,
But spare your country's flag," she said.

A shade of sadness, a blush of shame,
Over the face of the leader came;

The nobler nature within him stirred
To life at that woman's deed and word;

"Who touches a hair of yon gray head
Dies like a dog! March on!" he said.

All day long through Frederick street
Sounded the tread of marching feet:

All day long that free flag tossed
Over the heads of the rebel host.

Ever its torn folds rose and fell
On the loyal winds that loved it well;

And through the hill-gaps sunset light
Shone over it with a warm good-night.

Barbara Frietchie's work is o'er,
And the Rebel rides on his raids no more.

Honor to her! and let a tear
Fall, for her sake, on Stonewall's bier.

Over Barbara Frietchie's grave,
Flag of Freedom and Union, wave!

Peace and order and beauty draw
Round thy symbol of light and law;

And ever the stars above look down
On thy stars below in Frederick town!

JOHN GREENLEAF WHITTIER

THE HIGH TIDE AT GETTYSBURG

[JULY 3, 1863]

A CLOUD possessed the hollow field,
The gathering battle's smoky shield:
   Athwart the gloom the lightning flashed,
   And through the cloud some horsemen dashed,
And from the heights the thunder pealed.

Then, at the brief command of Lee,
Moved out that matchless infantry,
   With Picket leading grandly down,
   To rush against the roaring crown
Of those dread heights of destiny.

Far heard above the angry guns,
A cry across the tumult runs:
   The voice that rang through Shiloh's woods,
   And Chickamauga's solitudes:
The fierce South cheering on her sons!

Ah, how the withering tempest blew
Against the front of Pettigrew!
   A Khamsin wind that scorched and singed,
   Like that infernal flame that fringed
The British squares at Waterloo!

A thousand fell where Kemper led;
A thousand died where Garnett bled;

In blinding flame and strangling smoke,
The remnant through the batteries broke,
And crossed the works with Armistead.

"Once more in Glory's van with me!"
Virginia cried to Tennessee:
  "We two together, come what may,
  Shall stand upon those works today!"
The reddest day in history.

Brave Tennessee! In reckless way
Virginia heard her comrade say:
  "Close round this rent and riddled rag!"
  What time she set her battle flag
Amid the guns of Doubleday.

But who shall break the guards that wait
Before the awful face of Fate?
  The tattered standards of the South
  Were shriveled at the cannon's mouth,
And all her hopes were desolate.

In vain the Tennesseean set
His breast against the bayonet;
  In vain Virginia charged and raged,
  A tigress in her wrath uncaged,
Till all the hill was red and wet!

Above the bayonets, mixed and crossed,
Men saw a gray, gigantic ghost
  Receding through the battle cloud,
  And heard across the tempest loud
The death cry of a nation lost!

The brave went down! Without disgrace
They leaped to Ruin's red embrace;
  They only heard Fame's thunders wake,
  And saw the dazzling sunburst break
In smiles on Glory's bloody face!

They fell, who lifted up a hand
And bade the sun in heaven to stand;
  They smote and fell, who set the bars
  Against the progress of the stars,
And stayed the march of Motherland!

They stood, who saw the future come
On through the fight's delirium;
  They smote and stood, who held the hope

Of nations on that slippery slope,
Amid the cheers of Christendom!

God lives! He forged the iron will
That clutched and held that trembling hill!
   God lives and reigns! He built and lent
   The heights for Freedom's battlement,
Where floats her flag in triumph still!

Fold up the banners! Smelt the guns!
Love rules. Her gentler purpose runs.
   A mighty mother turns in tears
   The pages of her battle years,
Lamenting all her fallen sons!

WILL HENRY THOMPSON

FARRAGUT

[MOBILE BAY, AUGUST 5, 1864]

FARRAGUT, Farragut,
   Old Heart of Oak,
Daring Dave Farragut,
   Thunderbolt stroke,
Watches the hoary mist
   Lift from the bay,
Till his flag, glory-kissed,
   Greets the young day.

Far, by gray Morgan's walls,
   Looms the black fleet.
Hark, deck to rampart calls
   With the drums' beat!
Buoy your chains overboard,
   While the steam hums;
Men! to the battlement,
   Farragut comes.

See, as the hurricane
   Hurtles in wrath
Squadrons of clouds amain
   Back from its path!
Back to the parapet,
   To the guns' lips,
Thunderbolt Farragut
   Hurls the black ships.

Now through the battle's roor
    Clear the boy sings,
"By the mark fathoms four,"
    While his lead swings.
Steady the wheelmen five
    "Nor' by East keep her,"
"Steady," but two alive:
    How the shells sweep her!

Lashed to the mast that sways
    Over red decks,
Over the flame that plays
    Round the torn wrecks,
Over the dying lips
    Framed for a cheer,
Farragut leads his ships,
    Guides the line clear.

On by heights cannon-browed,
    While the spars quiver;
Onward still flames the cloud
    Where the hulks shiver.
See, yon fort's star is set,
    Storm and fire past.
Cheer him, lads—Farragut,
    Lashed to the mast!

Oh! while Atlantic's breast
    Bears a white sail,
While the Gulf's towering crest
    Tops a green vale,
Men thy bold deeds shall tell,
    Old Heart of Oak,
Daring Dave Farragut,
    Thunderbolt stroke!
        WILLIAM TUCKEY MEREDITH

MY MARYLAND

The despot's heel is on thy shore,
        Maryland!
His torch is at thy temple door,
        Maryland!
Avenge the patriotic gore
That flecked the streets of Baltimore,
And be the battle-queen of yore,
        Maryland, my Maryland!

Hark to an exiled son's appeal,
    Maryland!
My Mother State, to thee I kneel,
    Maryland!
For life and death, for woe and weal,
Thy peerless chivalry reveal,
And gird thy beauteous limbs with steel,
    Maryland, my Maryland!

Thou wilt not cower in the dust,
    Maryland!
Thy beaming sword shall never rust,
    Maryland!
Remember Carroll's sacred trust,
Remember Howard's warlike thrust,
And all thy slumberers with the just,
    Maryland, my Maryland!

Come! 'tis the red dawn of the day,
    Maryland!
Come with thy panoplied array,
    Maryland!
With Ringgold's spirit for the fray,
With Watson's blood at Monterey,
With fearless Lowe and dashing May,
    Maryland, my Maryland!

Dear Mother, burst the tyrant's chain,
    Maryland!
Virginia should not call in vain,
    Maryland!
She meets her sisters on the plain,—
"*Sic semper!*" 'tis the proud refrain
That baffles minions back amain,
    Maryland!
Arise in majesty again,
    Maryland, my Maryland!

Come! for thy shield is bright and strong,
    Maryland!
Come! for thy dalliance does thee wrong,
    Maryland!
Come to thine own heroic throng
Stalking with Liberty along,
And chant thy dauntless slogan-song,
    Maryland, my Maryland!

I see the blush upon thy cheek,
    Maryland!
For thou wast ever bravely meek,
    Maryland!
But lo! there surges forth a shriek,
From hill to hill, from creek to creek,
Potomac calls to Chesapeake,
    Maryland, my Maryland!

Thou wilt not yield the Vandal toll,
    Maryland!
Thou wilt not crook to his control,
    Maryland!
Better the fire upon thee roll,
Better the shot, the blade, the bowl,
Than crucifixion of the soul,
    Maryland, my Maryland!

I hear the distant thunder hum,
    Maryland!
The Old Line's bugle, fife, and drum,
    Maryland!
She is not dead, nor deaf, nor dumb;
Huzza! She spurns the Northern scum!
She breathes! She burns! She'll come!
    She'll come!
    Maryland, my Maryland!
        JAMES RYDER RANDALL

BATTLE-HYMN OF THE REPUBLIC

MINE EYES have seen the glory of the coming of the Lord:
He is trampling out the vintage where the grapes of wrath are stored;
He hath loosed the fateful lightning of his terrible swift sword:
    His truth is marching on.

I have seen him in the watch-fires of a hundred circling camps;
They have builded him an altar in the evening dews and damps;
I can read his righteous sentence by the dim and flaring lamps:
    His day is marching on.

I have read a fiery gospel, writ in burnished rows of steel:
"As ye deal with my contemners, so with you my grace shall deal;
Let the Hero, born of woman, crush the serpent with his heel,
    Since God is marching on."

He has sounded forth the trumpet that shall never call retreat;
He is sifting out the hearts of men before his judgment-seat:

O, be swift, my soul, to answer him! be jubilant, my feet!
   Our God is marching on.

In the beauty of the lilies Christ was born across the sea,
With a glory in his bosom that transfigures you and me;
As he died to make men holy, let us die to make men free,
   While God is marching on.

He is coming like the glory of the morning on the wave,
He is wisdom to the mighty, he is honor to the brave,
So the world shall be his footstool, and the soul of wrong his slave,
   Our God is marching on!

JULIA WARD HOWE

THE BLUE AND THE GRAY

(The women of Columbus, Mississippi, scattered flowers alike on the graves of the Confederate and the Union Soldiers.)

BY THE FLOW of the inland river,
   Whence the fleets of iron have fled,
Where the blades of the grave grass quiver,
   Asleep are the ranks of the dead;—
      Under the sod and the dew,
         Waiting the judgment day;—
      Under the one, the Blue;
         Under the other, the Gray.

These in the robings of glory,
   Those in the gloom of defeat,
All with the battle blood gory,
   In the dusk of eternity meet;—
      Under the sod and the dew,
         Waiting the judgment day;—
      Under the laurel, the Blue;
         Under the willow, the Gray.

From the silence of sorrowful hours
   The desolate mourners go,
Lovingly laden with flowers
   Alike for the friend and the foe,—
      Under the sod and the dew,
         Waiting the judgment day;—
      Under the roses, the Blue;
         Under the lilies, the Gray.

So with an equal splendor
   The morning sun rays fall,

With a touch, impartially tender,
   On the blossoms blooming for all;—
      Under the sod and the dew,
         Waiting the judgment day;—
      'Broidered with gold, the Blue;
         Mellowed with gold, the Gray.

So, when the summer calleth,
   On forest and field of grain
With an equal murmur falleth
   The cooling drip of the rain;—
      Under the sod and the dew,
         Waiting the judgment day;—
      Wet with the rain, the Blue;
         Wet with the rain, the Gray.

Sadly, but not with upbraiding,
   The generous deed was done;
In the storm of the years that are fading,
   No braver battle was won;—
      Under the sod and the dew,
         Waiting the judgment day;—
      Under the blossoms, the Blue;
         Under the garlands, the Gray.

No more shall the war cry sever,
   Or the winding rivers be red;
They banish our anger forever
   When they laurel the graves of our dead!
      Under the sod and the dew,
         Waiting the judgment day;—
      Love and tears for the Blue,
         Tears and love for the Gray.

                    FRANCIS MILES FINCH

O CAPTAIN! MY CAPTAIN!

O CAPTAIN! My Captain! our fearful trip is done,
The ship has weathered every rack, the prize we sought is won;
The port is near, the bells I hear, the people all exulting,
While follow eyes the steady keel, the vessel grim and daring;

   But O heart! heart! heart!
      O the bleeding drops of red,
   Where on the deck my Captain lies,
      Fallen cold and dead.

O Captain! My Captain! rise up and hear the bells;
Rise up—for you the flag is flung—for you the bugle trills,
For you bouquets and ribboned wreaths—for you the shores acrowd-
       ing,
For you they call, the swaying mass, their eager faces turning;

   Here Captain! dear father!
     This arm beneath your head!
   It is some dream that on the deck
     You've fallen cold and dead.

My Captain does not answer, his lips are pale and still,
My father does not feel my arm, he has no pulse nor will,
The ship is anchored safe and sound, its voyage closed and done,
From fearful trip the victor ship comes in with object won;

   Exult, O shores, and ring, O bells!
     But I, with mournful tread,
   Walk the deck my Captain lies,
     Fallen cold and dead.

                  WALT   WHITMAN

FROM AN "ODE FOR DECORATION DAY"

   O GALLANT brothers of the generous South,
     Foes for a day and brothers for all time!
   I charge you by the memories of our youth,
     By Yorktown's field and Montezuma's clime,
   Hold our dead sacred—let them quietly rest
   In your unnumbered vales, where God thought best.
   Your vines and flowers learned long since to forgive,
   And o'er their graves a broidered mantle weave:
   Be you as kind as they are, and the word
   Shall reach the Northland with each summer bird,
   And thoughts as sweet as summer shall awake
   Responsive to your kindness, and shall make
   Our peace the peace of brothers once again,
   And banish utterly the days of pain.

   And ye, O Northmen! be ye not outdone
     In generous thought and deed.
   We all do need forgiveness, every one;
     And they that give shall find it in their need.
   Spare of your flowers to deck the stranger's grave,
     Who died for a lost cause:—
   A soul more daring, resolute, and brave,
     Ne'r won a world's applause.

A brave man's hatred pauses at the tomb.
For him some Southern home was robed in gloom,
Some wife or mother looked with longing eyes
Through the sad days and nights with tears and sighs,
Hope slowly hardening into gaunt Despair.
Then let your foeman's grave remembrance share:
Pity a higher charm to Valor lends,
And in the realms of Sorrow all our friends.

HENRY PETERSON

ABRAHAM LINCOLN

Not as when some great Captain falls
In battle, where his Country calls,
    Beyond the struggling lines
    That push his dread designs

To doom, by some stray ball struck dead:
Or, in the last charge, at the head
    Of his determined men,
    Who *must* be victors then.

Nor as when sink the civic great,
The safer pillars of the State,
    Whose calm, mature, wise words
    Suppress the need of swords.

With no such tears as e'er were shed
Above the noblest of our dead
    Do we to-day deplore
    The Man that is no more.

Our sorrow hath a wider scope,
Too strange for fear, too vast for hope,
    A wonder, blind and dumb,
    That waits—what is to come!

Not more astounded had we been
If Madness, that dark night, unseen,
    Had in our chambers crept,
    And murdered while we slept!

We woke to find a mourning earth,
Our Lares shivered on the hearth,
    The roof-tree fallen, all
    That could affright, appall!

Such thunderbolts, in other lands,
Have smitten the rod from royal hands,
     But spared, with us, till now,
     Each laurelled Cæsar's brow.

No Cæsar he whom we lament,
A Man without a precedent,
     Sent, it would seem, to do
     His work, and perish, too.

Not by the weary cares of State,
The endless tasks, which will not wait,
     Which, often done in vain,
     Must yet be done again:

Not in the dark, wild tide of war,
Which rose so high, and rolled so far,
     Sweeping from sea to sea
     In awful anarchy:

Four fateful years of mortal strife,
Which slowly drained the nation's life,
     (Yet for each drop that ran
     There sprang an armëd man!)

Not then; but when, by measures meet,
By victory, and by defeat,
     By courage, patience, skill,
     The people's fixed "*We will!*"

Had pierced, had crushed Rebellion dead,
Without a hand, without a head,
     At last, when all was well,
     He fell, O how he fell!

The time, the place, the stealing shape,
The coward shot, the swift escape,
     The wife—the widow's scream,—
     It is a hideous Dream!

A dream? What means this pageant, then?
These multitudes of solemn men,
     Who speak not when they meet,
     But throng the silent street?

The flag half-mast that late so high
Flaunted at each new victory?
     (The stars no brightness shed,
     But bloody looks the red!)

The black festoons that stretch for miles,
And turn the streets to funeral aisles?
    (No house too poor to show
    The nation's badge of woe.)

The cannon's sudden, sullen boom,
The bells that toll of death and doom,
    The rolling of the drums,
    The dreadful car that comes?

Cursed be the hand that fired the shot,
The frenzied brain that hatched the plot,
    Thy country's Father slain
    By thee, thou worse than Cain!

Tyrants have fallen by such as thou,
And good hath followed—may it now!
    (God lets bad instruments
    Produce the best events.)

But he, the man we mourn to-day,
No tyrant was: so mild a sway
    In one such weight who bore
    Was never known before.

Cool should he be, of balanced powers,
The ruler of a race like ours,
    Impatient, headstrong, wild,
    The Man to guide the Child.

And this *he* was, who most unfit
(So hard the sense of God to hit,)
    Did seem to fill his place;
    With such a homely face,

Such rustic manners, speech uncouth,
(That somehow blundered out the truth,)
    Untried, untrained to bear
    The more than kingly care.

Ah! And his genius put to scorn
The proudest in the purple born,
    Whose wisdom never grew
    To what, untaught, he knew,

The People, of whom he was one:
No gentleman, like Washington,
    (Whose bones, methinks, make room,
    To have him in their tomb!)

A laboring man, with horny hands,
Who swung the axe, who tilled his lands,
    Who shrank from nothing new,
    But did as poor men do.

One of the People! Born to be
Their curious epitome;
    To share yet rise above
    Their shifting hate and love.

Common his mind (it seemed so then,)
His thoughts the thoughts of other men:
    Plain were his words, and poor,
    But now they will endure!

No hasty fool, of stubborn will,
But prudent, cautious, pliant still;
    Who since his work was good
    Would do it as he could.

Doubting, was not ashamed to doubt,
And, lacking prescience, went without:
    Often appeared to halt,
    And was, of course, at fault;

Heard all opinions, nothing loath,
And, loving both sides, angered both:
    Was—*not* like Justice, blind,
    But watchful, clement, kind.

No hero this of Roman mould,
Nor like our stately sires of old:
    Perhaps he was not great,
    But he preserved the State!

O honest face, which all men knew!
O tender heart, but known to few!
    O wonder of the age,
    Cut off by tragic rage!

Peace! Let the long procession come,
For hark, the mournful, muffled drum,
    The trumpet's wail afar,
    And see, the awful car!

Peace! Let the sad procession go,
While cannon boom and bells toll slow.
    And go, thou sacred car,
    Bearing our woe afar!

Go, darkly borne, from State to State,
Whose loyal, sorrowing cities wait
    To honor all they can
    The dust of that good man.

Go, grandly borne, with such a train
As greatest kings might die to gain.
    The just, the wise, the brave,
    Attend thee to the grave.

And you, the soldiers of our wars,
Bronzed veterans, grim with noble scars,
    Salute him once again,
    Your late commander—slain!

Yes, let your tears indignant fall,
But leave your muskets on the wall;
    Your country needs you now
    Beside the forge—the plough.

(When Justice shall unsheathe her brand,—
If Mercy may not stay her hand,
    Nor would we have it so,—
    She must direct the blow.)

And you, amid the master-race,
Who seem so strangely out of place,
    Know ye who cometh? He
    Who hath declared ye free.

Bow while the body passes—nay,
Fall on your knees, and weep, and pray!
    Weep, weep—I would ye might—
    Your poor black faces white!

And, children, you must come in bands,
With garlands in your little hands,
    Of blue and white and red,
    To strew before the dead.

So sweetly, sadly, sternly goes
The Fallen to his last repose.
    Beneath no mighty dome,
    But in his modest home;

The churchyard where his children rest,
The quiet spot that suits him best,
    There shall his grave be made,
    And there his bones be laid.

And there his countrymen shall come,
With memory proud, with pity dumb,
    And strangers far and near,
    For many and many a year.

For many a year and many an age,
While History on her ample page
    The virtues shall enroll
    Of that Paternal Soul.

RICHARD HENRY STODDARD

THE SHIP OF STATE

Thou, too, sail on, O ship of State!
Sail on, O Union, strong and great!
Humanity with all its fears,
With all its hopes of future years,
Is hanging breathless on thy fate!
We know what Master laid thy keel,
What workmen wrought thy ribs of steel,
Who made each mast, and sail, and rope,
What anvils rang, what hammers beat,
In what a forge and what a heat
Were shaped the anchors of thy hope!
Fear not each sudden sound and shock,
'Tis of the wave and not the rock;
'Tis but the flapping of the sail,
And not a rent made by the gale!
In spite of rock and tempest's roar,
In spite of false lights on the shore,
Sail on, nor fear to breast the sea!
Our hearts, our hopes, are all with thee,
Our hearts, our hopes, our prayers, our tears,
Our faith, triumphant o'er our fears,
Are all with thee,—are all with thee!

HENRY WADSWORTH LONGFELLOW
From "The Building of the Ship"

THE FLAG GOES BY

Hats off!
Along the streets there comes
A blare of bugles, a ruffle of drums,
A flash of colour beneath the sky:

                    Hats off!
        The flag is passing by!

        Blue and crimson and white it shines
        Over the steel-tipped, ordered lines.
                    Hats off!
        The colours before us fly;
        But more than the flag is passing by.

        Sea-fights and land-fights, grim and great,
        Fought to make and to save the State:
        Weary marches and sinking ships;
        Cheers of victory on dying lips;

        Days of plenty and years of peace;
        March of a strong land's swift increase;
        Equal justice, right and law,
        Stately honour and reverend awe;

        Sign of a nation, great and strong
        Toward her people from foreign wrong:
        Pride and glory and honour,—all
        Live in the colours to stand or fall.

                    Hats off!
        Along the street there comes
        A blare of bugles, a ruffle of drums;
        And loyal hearts are beating high:
                    Hats off!
        The flag is passing by!
                    HENRY HOLCOMB BENNETT

THE BATTLE CRY OF FREEDOM

YES, we'll rally round the flag, boys, we'll rally once again,
    Shouting the battle cry of Freedom;
We will rally from the hillside, we'll gather from the plain,
    Shouting the battle cry of Freedom.

Refrain:
    The Union forever, hurrah, boys, hurrah!
    Down with the traitor, up with the star;
    While we rally round the flag, boys, rally once again,
    Shouting the battle cry of Freedom.

We are springing to the call of our brothers gone before,
    Shouting the battle cry of Freedom;

And we'll fill the vacant ranks with a million free men more,
Shouting the battle cry of Freedom.

We will welcome to our numbers the loyal, true, and brave,
Shouting the battle cry of Freedom;
And although they may be poor, not a man shall be a slave,
Shouting the battle cry of Freedom.

So we're springing to the call from the East and from the West,
Shouting the battle cry of Freedom;
And we'll prove a loyal crew for the land we love the best,
Shouting the battle cry of Freedom.

GEORGE F. ROOT

OUT WHERE THE WEST BEGINS

OUT WHERE the handclasp's a little stronger,
Out where the smile dwells a little longer,
That's where the West begins;
Out where the sun is a little brighter,
Where the snows that fall are a trifle whiter,
Where the bonds of home are a wee bit tighter,—
That's where the West begins.

Out where the skies are a trifle bluer,
Out where friendship's a little truer,
That's where the West begins;
Out where a fresher breeze is blowing,
Where there's laughter in every streamlet flowing,
Where there's more of reaping and less of sowing,—
That's where the West begins.

Out where the world is in the making,
Where fewer hearts in despair are aching,
That's where the West begins;
Where there's more of singing and less of sighing,
Where there's more of giving and less of buying,
And a man makes friends without half trying—
That's where the West begins.

ARTHUR CHAPMAN

PIONEERS

A BROKEN wagon wheel that rots away beside the river,
A sunken grave that dimples on the bluff above the trail;
The larks call, the wind sweeps, the prairie grasses quiver

And sing a wistful roving song of hoof and wheel and sail,
Pioneers, pioneers, you trailed it on to glory,
    Across the circling deserts to the mountains blue and dim.
New England was a night camp; Old England was a story,
    The new home, the true home, lay beyond the rim.

You fretted at the old hearth, the kettle and the cricket,
    The fathers' little acres, the wood lot and the pond.
Aye, better storm and famine and the arrow from the thicket,
    Along the trail to wider lands that glimmered out beyond.
Pioneers, pioneers, the quicksands where you wallowed,
    The rocky hills and thirsty plains—they hardly won your heed.
You snatched the thorny chance, broke the trail that others followed,
    For sheer joy, for dear joy of marching in the lead.

Your wagon track is laid with steel; your tired dust is sleeping.
    Your spirit stalks the valleys where a restive nation teems.
Your soul has never left them in their sowing, in their reaping.
    The children of the outward trail, their eyes are full of dreams.
Pioneers, pioneers, your children will not reckon
    The dangers on the dusky ways no man has ever gone.
They look beyond the sunset where the better countries beckon,
    With old faith, with bold faith to find a wider dawn.

                                        BADGER CLARK

I HEAR AMERICA SINGING

I HEAR America singing, the varied carols I hear,
Those of mechanics, each one singing his as it should be blithe and
        strong,
The carpenter singing his as he measures his plank or beam,
The mason singing his as he makes ready for work, or leaves off work,
The boatman singing what belongs to him in his boat, the deckhand
        singing on the steamboat deck,
The shoemaker singing as he sits on his bench, the hatter singing as
        he stands,
The wood-cutter's song, the ploughboy's on his way in the morning, or
        at noon intermission or at sundown,
The delicious singing of the mother, or of the young wife at work, or
        of the girl sewing or washing,
Each singing what belongs to him or her and to none else,
The day what belongs to the day—at night the party of young fellows,
        robust, friendly,
Singing with open mouths their strong melodious songs.

                                    WALT   WHITMAN

THE MEN BEHIND THE GUNS

A CHEER and salute for the Admiral, and here's to the Captain bold,
And never forget the Commodore's debt when the deeds of might are
told!
They stand to the deck through the battle's wreck when the great shells
roar and screech—
And never they fear when the foe is near to practice what they preach:
But off with your hat and three times three for Columbia's true-blue
sons,
The men below who batter the foe—the men behind the guns!

Oh, light and merry of heart are they when they swing into port once
more,
When, with more than enough of the "green-backed stuff," they start
for their leave-o'-shore;
And you'd think, perhaps, that the blue-bloused chaps who loll along
the street
Are a tender bit, with salt on it, for some fierce "mustache" to eat—
Some warrior bold, with straps of gold, who dazzles and fairly stuns
The modest worth of the sailor boys—the lads who serve the guns.

But say not a word till the shot is heard that tells that the fight is on,
Till the long, deep roar grows more and more from the ships of "Yank"
and "Don,"
Till over the deep the tempests sweep of fire and bursting shell,
And the very air is a mad Despair in the throes of a living hell;
Then down, deep down, in the mighty ship, unseen by the midday
suns,
You'll find the chaps who are giving the raps—the men behind the
guns!

Oh, well they know how the cyclones blow that they loose from their
cloud of death,
And they know is heard the thunder-word their fierce ten-incher saith!
The steel decks rock with the lightning shock, and shake with the great
recoil,
And the sea grows red with the blood of the dead and reaches for
his spoil—
But not till the foe has gone below or turns his prow and runs,
Shall the voice of peace bring sweet release to the men behind the
guns!

JOHN JEROME ROONEY

WHEN THE GREAT GRAY SHIPS COME IN

[NEW YORK HARBOR, AUGUST 20, 1898]

To EASTWARD ringing, to westward winging, o'er mapless miles of sea,
On winds and tides the gospel rides that the furthermost isles are free,
And the furthermost isles make answer, harbor, and height, and hill,
Breaker and beach cry each to each, " 'Tis the Mother who calls! Be
    still!"
Mother! new-found, belovèd, and strong to hold from harm,
Stretching to these across the seas the shield of her sovereign arm,
Who summoned the guns of her sailor sons, who bade her navies roam,
Who calls again to the leagues of main, and who calls them this time
    Home!

And the great gray ships are silent, and the weary watchers rest,
The black cloud dies in the August skies, and deep in the golden west
Invisible hands are limning a glory of crimson bars,
And far above is the wonder of a myriad wakened stars!
Peace! As the tidings silence the strenuous cannonade,
Peace at last! is the bugle blast the length of the long blockade,
And eyes of vigil weary are lit with the glad release,
From ship to ship and from lip to lip it is "Peace! Thank God for
    peace."

Ah, in the sweet hereafter Columbia still shall show
The sons of those who swept the seas how she bade them rise and go,—
How, when the stirring summons smote on her children's ear,
South and North at the call stood forth, and the whole land answered,
    "Here!"
For the soul of the soldier's story and the heart of the sailor's song
Are all of those who meet their foes as right should meet with wrong,
Who fight their guns till the foeman runs, and then, on the decks they
    trod,
Brave faces raise, and give the praise to the grace of their country's
    God!

Yes, it is good to battle, and good to be strong and free,
To carry the hearts of a people to the uttermost ends of the sea,
To see the day steal up the bay where the enemy lies in wait,
To run your ship to the harbor's lip and sink her across the strait:—
But better the golden evening when the ships round heads for home,
And the long gray miles slip swiftly past in a whirl of seething foam,
And the people wait at the haven's gate to greet the men who win!
Thank God for peace! Thank God for peace, when the great gray
    ships come in!

GUY WETMORE CARRYL

THE COMING AMERICAN

BRING me men to match my mountains,
Bring me men to match my plains,
Men with empires in their purpose,
And new eras in their brains.
Bring me men to match my prairies,
Men to match my inland seas,
Men whose thoughts shall pave a highway
Up to ampler destinies,
Pioneers to cleanse thought's marshlands,
    And to cleanse old error's fen;
Bring me men to match my mountains—
    Bring me men!

Bring me men to match my forests,
Strong to fight the storm and beast,
Branching toward the skyey future,
Rooted on the futile past.
Bring me men to match my valleys,
    Tolerant of rain and snow,
Men within whose fruitful purpose
    Time's consummate blooms shall grow,
Men to tame the tigerish instincts
    Of the lair and cave and den,
Cleanse the dragon slime of nature—
    Bring me men!

Bring me men to match my rivers,
    Continent cleansers, flowing free,
Drawn by eternal madness,
    To be mingled with the sea—
Men of oceanic impulse,
    Men whose moral currents sweep
Toward the wide, infolding ocean
    Of an undiscovered deep—
Men who feel the strong pulsation
    Of the central sea, and then
Time their currents by its earth throbs—
    Bring me Men.

                                    SAM WALTER FOSS

COLUMBIA, THE GEM OF THE OCEAN

O COLUMBIA, the gem of the ocean,
The home of the brave and the free,
The shrine of each patriot's devotion,
A world offers homage to thee.
Thy mandates make heroes assemble,
When Liberty's form stands in view;
Thy banners make tyranny tremble,
When borne by the red, white, and blue!
   When borne by the red, white, and blue!
   When borne by the red, white, and blue!
Thy banners make tyranny tremble,
   When borne by the red, white, and blue!

When war winged its wide desolation,
And threatened the land to deform,
The ark then of freedom's foundation,
Columbia rode safe through the storm;
With her garlands of vict'ry around her,
When so proudly she bore her brave crew;
With her flag proudly floating before her,
The boast of the red, white, and blue!
   The boast of the red, white, and blue!
   The boast of the red, white, and blue!
With her flag proudly floating before her,
   The boast of the red, white, and blue!

The star-spangled banner bring hither,
O'er Columbia's true sons let it wave;
May the wreaths they have won never wither,
Nor its stars cease to shine on the brave.
May the service, united, ne'er sever,
But hold to their colors so true;
The army and navy forever,
Three cheers for the red, white, and blue!
   Three cheers for the red, white, and blue!
   Three cheers for the red, white, and blue!
The army and navy forever,
   Three cheers for the red, white, and blue!

DAVID T. SHAW

OH MOTHER OF A MIGHTY RACE

Oh mother of a mighty race,
Yet lovely in thy youthful grace!
The elder dames, thy haughty peers,
Admire and hate thy blooming years.
    With words of shame
And taunts of scorn they join thy name.

For on thy cheeks the glow is spread
That tints thy morning hills with red;
Thy step—the wild deer's rustling feet
Within thy woods are not more fleet;
    Thy hopeful eye
Is bright as thine own sunny sky.

Ay, let them rail—those haughty ones,
While safe thou dwellest with thy sons.
They do not know how loved thou art,
How many a fond and fearless heart
    Would rise to throw
Its life between thee and the foe.

They know not, in their hate and pride,
What virtues with thy children bide;
How true, how good, thy graceful maids
Make bright, like flowers, the valley-shades;
    What generous men
Spring, like thine oaks, by hill and glen;—

What cordial welcomes greet the guest
By thy lone rivers of the West;
How faith is kept, and truth revered,
And man is loved, and God is feared,
    In woodland homes,
And where the ocean border foams.

There's freedom at thy gates and rest
For Earth's down-trodden and oppressed,
A shelter for the hunted head,
For the starved laborer toil and bread.
    Power, at thy bounds,
Stops and calls back his baffled hounds.

Oh, fair young mother! on thy brow
Shall sit a nobler grace than now.
Deep in the brightness of the skies

The thronging years in glory rise,
    And, as they fleet,
Drop strength and riches at thy feet.

WILLIAM CULLEN BRYANT

AMERICA, THE BEAUTIFUL

O BEAUTIFUL for spacious skies,
    For amber waves of grain,
For purple mountain majesties
    Above the fruited plain!
            America! America!
    God shed His grace on thee,
And crown thy good with brotherhood
    From sea to shining sea!

O beautiful for pilgrim feet,
    Whose stern, impassioned stress
A thoroughfare for freedom beat
    Across the wilderness!
            America! America!
    God mend thine every flaw,
Confirm thy soul in self-control,
    Thy liberty in law!

O beautiful for heroes proved
    In liberating strife,
Who more than self their country loved,
    And mercy more than life!
            America! America!
    May God thy gold refine
Till all success be nobleness
    And every gain divine!

O beautiful for patriot dream
    That sees beyond the years
Thine alabaster cities gleam
    Undimmed by human tears!
            America! America!
    God shed His grace on thee
And crown thy good with brotherhood
    From sea to shining sea!

KATHARINE LEE BATES

AMERICA

MY COUNTRY, 'tis of thee,
Sweet land of liberty,
  Of thee I sing;
Land where my fathers died,
Land of the pilgrims' pride,
From every mountain side
  Let freedom ring.

My native country, thee,
Land of the noble free,
  Thy name I love;
I love thy rocks and rills,
Thy woods and templed hills;
My heart with rapture thrills
  Like that above.

Let music swell the breeze,
And ring from all the trees
  Sweet freedom's song:
Let mortal tongues awake;
Let all that breathe partake;
Let rocks their silence break,
  The sound prolong.

Our fathers' God, to thee,
Author of liberty,
  To thee we sing:
Long may our land be bright
With freedom's holy light;
Protect us by thy might,
  Great God, our King.

SAMUEL F. SMITH

Favorite Poems Of
HOME AND FIRESIDE

MY LOST YOUTH

Often I think of the beautiful town
     That is seated by the sea;
Often in thought go up and down
The pleasant streets of that dear old town,
     And my youth comes back to me.
          And a verse of a Lapland song
          Is haunting my memory still:
          "A boy's will is the wind's will,
And the thoughts of youth, are long, long thoughts."

I can see the shadowy lines of its trees,
     And catch, in sudden gleams,
The sheen of the far-surrounding seas,
And islands that were the Hesperides
     Of all my boyish dreams.
          And the burden of that old song,
          It murmurs and whispers still:
          "A boy's will is the wind's will,
And the thoughts of youth are long, long thoughts."

I remember the black wharves and the slips,
     And the sea-tides tossing free;

And Spanish sailors with bearded lips,
And the beauty and mystery of the ships,
    And the magic of the sea.
        And the voice of that wayward song
        Is singing and saying still:
        "A boy's will is the wind's will,
And the thoughts of youth are long, long thoughts."

I remember the bulwarks by the shore,
    And the fort upon the hill;
The sunrise gun, with its hollow roar,
The drum-beat repeated o'er and o'er,
    And the bugle wild and shrill.
        And the music of that old song
        Throbs in my memory still:
        "A boy's will is the wind's will,
And the thoughts of youth are long, long thoughts."

I remember the sea-fight far away,
    How it thundered o'er the tide!
And the dead captains, as they lay
In their graves, o'erlooking the tranquil bay
    Where they in battle died.
        And the sound of that mournful song
        Goes through me with a thrill:
        "A boy's will is the wind's will,
And the thoughts of youth are long, long thoughts."

I can see the breezy dome of groves,
    The shadows of Deering's Woods;
And the friendships old and the early loves
Come back with a Sabbath sound, as of doves
    In quiet neighborhoods.
        And the verse of that sweet old song,
        It flutters and murmurs still:
        "A boy's will is the wind's will,
And the thoughts of youth are long, long thoughts."

I remember the gleams and glooms that dart
    Across the school-boy's brain;
The song and the silence in the heart,
That in part are prophecies, and in part
    Are longings wild and vain.
        And the voice of that fitful song
        Sings on, and is never still:
        "A boy's will is the wind's will,
And the thoughts of youth are long, long thoughts."

There are things of which I may not speak;
   There are dreams that cannot die;
There are thoughts that make the strong heart weak,
And bring a pallor into the cheek,
   And a mist before the eye.
     And the words of that fatal song
     Come over me like a chill:
     "A boy's will is the wind's will,
And the thoughts of youth are long, long thoughts."

Strange to me now are the forms I meet
   When I visit the dear old town;
But the native air is pure and sweet,
And the trees that o'ershadow each well-known street,
   As they balance up and down,
     Are singing the beautiful song,
     Are sighing and whispering still:
     "A boy's will is the wind's will,
And the thoughts of youth are long, long thoughts."

And Deering's Woods are fresh and fair,
   And with joy that is almost pain
My heart goes back to wander there,
And among the dreams of the days that were,
   I find my lost youth again.
     And the strange and beautiful song,
     The groves are repeating it still:
     "A boy's will is the wind's will,
And the thoughts of youth are long, long thoughts."
              HENRY WADSWORTH LONGFELLOW

SWEET AND LOW

SWEET and low, sweet and low,
   Wind of the western sea,
Low, low, breathe and blow,
   Wind of the western sea!
Over the rolling waters go,
Come from the dying moon, and blow,
   Blow him again to me;
While my little one, while my pretty one, sleeps.

Sleep and rest, sleep and rest,
   Father will come to thee soon;
Rest, rest, on mother's breast,
   Father will come to thee soon;
Father will come to his babe in the nest,

Silver sails all out of the west
   Under the silver moon:
Sleep, my little one, sleep, my pretty one, sleep.
ALFRED TENNYSON

THE CHILDREN'S HOUR

BETWEEN the dark and the daylight,
   When the night is beginning to lower,
Comes a pause in the day's occupations,
   That is known as the Children's Hour.

I hear in the chamber above me
   The patter of little feet,
The sound of a door that is opened,
   And voices soft and sweet.

From my study I see in the lamplight,
   Descending the broad hall stair,
Grave Alice, and laughing Allegra,
   And Edith with golden hair.

A whisper, and then a silence:
   Yet I know by their merry eyes
They are plotting and planning together
   To take me by surprise.

A sudden rush from the stairway,
   A sudden raid from the hall!
By three doors left unguarded
   They enter my castle wall!

They climb up into my turret
   O'er the arms and back of my chair;
If I try to escape, they surround me;
   They seem to be everywhere.

They almost devour me with kisses,
   Their arms about me entwine,
Till I think of the Bishop of Bingen
   In his Mouse-Tower on the Rhine!

Do you think, O blue-eyed banditti,
   Because you have scaled the wall,
Such an old mustache as I am
   Is not a match for you all!

I have you fast in my fortress,
   And will not let you depart,

But put you down into the dungeon
   In the round-tower of my heart.

And there will I keep you forever,
   Yes, forever and a day,
Till the walls shall crumble to ruin,
   And moulder in dust away.
          HENRY WADSWORTH LONGFELLOW

THE BAREFOOT BOY

BLESSINGS on thee, little man,
Barefoot boy, with cheek of tan!
With thy turned-up pantaloons,
And thy merry whistled tunes;
With thy red lip, redder still
Kissed by strawberries on the hill;
With the sunshine on thy face,
Through thy torn brim's jaunty grace;
From my heart I give thee joy,—
I was once a barefoot boy!

Prince thou art,—the grown-up man
Only is republican.
Let the million-dollared ride!
Barefoot, trudging at his side,
Thou hast more than he can buy
In the reach of ear and eye,—
Outward sunshine, inward joy:
Blessings on thee, barefoot boy!

Oh for boyhood's painless play,
Sleep that wakes in laughing day,
Health that mocks the doctor's rules,
Knowledge never learned of schools,
Of the wild bee's morning chase,
Of the wild-flower's time and place,
Flight of fowl and habitude
Of the tenants of the wood;
How the tortoise bears his shell,
How the woodchuck digs his cell,
And the ground-mole sinks his well;
How the robin feeds her young,
How the oriole's nest is hung;
Where the whitest lilies blow,
Where the freshest berries grow,

Where the ground-nut trails its vine,
Where the wood-grape's clusters shine;
Of the black wasp's cunning way,
Mason of his walls of clay,
And the architectural plans
Of gray hornet artisans!
For, eschewing books and tasks,
Nature answers all he asks;
Hand in hand with her he walks,
Face to face with her he talks,
Part and parcel of her joy,—
Blessings on the barefoot boy!

Oh for boyhood's time of June,
Crowding years in one brief moon,
When all things I heard or saw,
Me, their master, waited for.
I was rich in flowers and trees,
Humming-birds and honey-bees;
For my sport the squirrel played,
Plied the snouted mole his spade;
For my taste the blackberry cone
Purpled over hedge and stone;
Laughed the brook for my delight
Through the day and through the night,
Whispering at the garden wall,
Talked with me from fall to fall;
Mine the sand-rimmed pickerel pond,
Mine the walnut slopes beyond,
Mine, on bending orchard trees,
Apples of Hesperides!
Still as my horizon grew,
Larger grew my riches too;
All the world I saw or knew
Seemed a complex Chinese toy,
Fashioned for a barefoot boy!

Oh for festal dainties spread,
Like my bowl of milk and bread;
Pewter spoon and bowl of wood,
On the door-stone, gray and rude!
O'er me, like a regal tent,
Cloudy-ribbed, the sunset bent,
Purple-curtained, fringed with gold,
Looped in many a wind-swung fold;
While for music came the play
Of the pied frogs' orchestra;

And, to light the noisy choir,
Lit the fly his lamp of fire.
I was monarch: pomp and joy
Waited on the barefoot boy!

Cheerily, then, my little man,
Live and laugh, as boyhood can!
Though the flinty slopes be hard,
Stubble-speared the new-mown sward,
Every morn shall lead thee through
Fresh baptisms of the dew;
Every evening from thy feet
Shall the cool wind kiss the heat:
All too soon these feet must hide
In the prison cells of pride,
Lose the freedom of the sod,
Like a colt's for work be shod,
Made to tread the mills of toil,
Up and down in ceaseless moil:
Happy if their track be found
Never on forbidden ground;
Happy if they sink not in
Quick and treacherous sands of sin.
Ah! that thou couldst know thy joy,
Ere it passes, barefoot boy!

JOHN GREENLEAF WHITTIER

HOME

It TAKES a heap o' livin' in a house t' make it home,
A heap o' sun an' shadder, an' ye sometimes have t' roam
Afore ye really 'preciate the things ye lef' behind,
An' hunger fer 'em somehow, with 'em allus on yer mind.
It don't make any differunce how rich ye get t' be,
How much yer chairs an' tables cost, how great yer luxury;
It ain't home t' ye, though it be the palace of a king,
Until somehow yer soul is sort o' wrapped round everything.

Home ain't a place that gold can buy or get up in a minute;
Afore it's home there's got t' be a heap o' livin' in it;
Within the walls there's got t' be some babies born, and then
Right there ye've got t' bring 'em up t' women good, an' men;
And gradjerly, as time goes on, ye find ye wouldn't part
With anything they ever used—they've grown into yer heart;
The old high chairs, the playthings, too, the little shoes they wore
Ye hoard; an' if ye could ye'd keep the thumb-marks on the door.

Ye've got t' weep t' make it home, ye've got t' sit an' sigh
An' watch beside a loved one's bed, an' know that Death is nigh;
An' in the stillness o' the night t' see Death's angel come,
An' close the eyes o' her that smiled, an' leave her sweet voice dumb.
For these are scenes that grip the heart, an' when yer tears are dried,
Ye find the home is dearer than it was, an' sanctified;
An' tuggin' at ye always are the pleasant memories
O' her that was an' is no more—ye can't escape from these.

Ye've got to sing an' dance fer years, ye've got t' romp an' play,
An' learn t' love the things ye have by usin' 'em each day;
Even the roses round the porch must blossom year by year
Afore they 'come a part o' ye, suggestin' someone dear
Who used t' love 'em long ago, and trained 'em just t' run
The way they do, so's they would get the early mornin' sun;
Ye've got to love each brick an' stone from cellar up t' dome:
It takes a heap o' livin' in a house t' make it home.

EDGAR A. GUEST

HOME, SWEET HOME

'MID PLEASURES and palaces though we may roam,
Be it ever so humble, there's no place like home;
A charm from the sky seems to hallow us there,
Which, seek through the world, is ne'er met with elsewhere.
    Home, home, sweet, sweet home!
There's no place like home, oh, there's no place like home!

An exile from home, splendor dazzles in vain;
Oh, give me my lowly thatched cottage again!
The birds singing gayly, that came at my call—
Give me them—and the peace of mind, dearer than all!
    Home, home, sweet, sweet home!
There's no place like home, oh, there's no place like home!

I gaze on the moon as I tread the drear wild,
And feel that my mother now thinks of her child,
As she looks on that moon from our own cottage door
Thro' the woodbine, whose fragrance shall cheer me no more.
    Home, home, sweet, sweet home!
There's no place like home, oh, there's no place like home!

How sweet 'tis to sit 'neath a fond father's smile,
And the caress of a mother to soothe and beguile!
Let others delight 'mid new pleasure to roam,
But give me, oh, give me, the pleasures of home,
    Home, home, sweet, sweet home!
There's no place like home, oh, there's no place like home!

To thee I'll return, overburdened with care;
The heart's dearest solace will smile on me there;
No more from that cottage again will I roam;
Be it ever so humble, there's no place like home.
   Home, home, sweet, sweet home!
There's no place like home, oh, there's no place like home!

JOHN HOWARD PAYNE

ROCK ME TO SLEEP

BACKWARD, turn backward, O time, in your flight,
Make me a child again just for to-night!
Mother, come back from the echoless shore,
Take me again to your heart as of yore;
Kiss from my forehead the furrows of care,
Smooth the few silver threads out of my hair;
Over my slumbers your loving watch keep;—
Rock me to sleep, Mother—rock me to sleep!

Backward, flow backward, oh, tide of the years!
I am so weary of toil and of tears—
Toil without recompense, tears all in vain—
Take them, and give me my childhood again!
I have grown weary of dust and decay—
Weary of flinging my soul-wealth away;
Weary of sowing for others to reap;—
Rock me to sleep, Mother—rock me to sleep!

Tired of the hollow, the base, the untrue,
Mother, O Mother, my heart calls for you!
Many a summer the grass has grown green,
Blossomed and faded, our faces between:
Yet, with strong yearning and passionate pain,
Long I to-night for your presence again.
Come from the silence so long and so deep;—
Rock me to sleep, Mother—rock me to sleep!

Over my heart, in the days that are flown,
No love like mother-love ever has shone;
No other worship abides and endures—
Faithful, unselfish, and patient like yours:
None like a mother can charm away pain
From the sick soul and the world-weary brain.
Slumber's soft calms o'er my heavy lids creep;—
Rock me to sleep, Mother—rock me to sleep!

Come, let your brown hair, just lighted with gold,
Fall on your shoulders again as of old;

Let it drop over my forehead to-night,
Shading my faint eyes away from the light;
For with its sunny-edged shadows once more
Haply will throng the sweet visions of yore;
Lovingly, softly, its bright billows sweep:—
Rock me to sleep, Mother—rock me to sleep!

Mother, dear Mother, the years have been long
Since I last listened your lullaby song:
Sing, then, and unto my soul it shall seem
Womanhood's years have been only a dream.
Clasped to your heart in a loving embrace,
With your light lashes just sweeping my face,
Never hereafter to wake or to weep;—
Rock me to sleep, Mother—rock me to sleep!

ELIZABETH AKERS ALLEN

THE BLUE BOWL

REWARD

ALL DAY I did the little things,
The little things that do not show;
I brought the kindling for the fire
I set the candles in a row,
I filled a bowl with marigolds,
The shallow bowl you love the best—
And made the house a pleasant place
Where weariness might take its rest.

The hours sped on, my eager feet
Could not keep pace with my desire.
So much to do, so little time!
I could not let my body tire;
Yet, when the coming of the night
Blotted the garden from my sight,
And on the narrow, graveled walks
Between the guarding flower stalks
I heard your step: I was not through
With services I meant for you.

You came into the quiet room
That glowed enchanted with the bloom
Of yellow flame. I saw your face,
Illumined by the firelit space,
Slowly grow still and comforted—
"It's good to be at home," you said.

BLANCHE BANE KUDER

MILK FOR THE CAT

When the tea is brought at five o'clock,
And all the neat curtains are drawn with care,
The little black cat with bright green eyes
Is suddenly purring there.

At first she pretends, having nothing to do,
She has come in merely to blink by the grate,
But, though tea may be late or the milk may be sour,
She is never late.

And presently her agate eyes
Take a soft large milky haze,
And her independent casual glance
Becomes a stiff hard gaze.

Then she stamps her claws or lifts her ears
Or twists her tail and begins to stir.
Till suddenly all her lithe body becomes
One breathing, trembling purr.

The children eat and wriggle and laugh;
The two old ladies stroke their silk:
But the cat is grown small and thin with desire,
Transformed to a creeping lust for milk.

The white saucer like some full moon descends
At last from the clouds of the table above;
She sighs and dreams and thrills and glows,
Transfigured with love.

She nestles over the shining rim,
Buries her chin in the creamy sea;
Her tail hangs loose; each drowsy paw
Is doubled under each bending knee.

A long dim ecstasy holds her life;
Her world is an infinite shapeless white,
Till her tongue has curled the last holy drop,
Then she sinks back into the night,

Draws and dips her body to heap
Her sleepy nerves in the great arm-chair,
Lies defeated and buried deep
Three or four hours unconscious there.

HAROLD MONRO

MY MOTHER'S GARDEN

HER HEART is like her garden,
Old-fashioned, quaint and sweet,
With here a wealth of blossoms,
And there a still retreat.
Sweet violets are hiding,
We know as we pass by,
And lilies, pure as angel thoughts,
Are opening somewhere nigh.

Forget-me-nots there linger,
To full perfection brought,
And there bloom purple pansies
In many a tender thought.
There love's own roses blossom,
As from enchanted ground,
And lavish perfume exquisite
The whole glad year around.

And in that quiet garden—
The garden of her heart—
Songbirds are always singing
Their songs of cheer apart.
And from it floats forever,
O'ercoming sin and strife,
Sweet as the breath of roses blown,
The fragrance of her life.

ALICE E. ALLEN

AN OLD WOMAN OF THE ROADS

O TO have a little house!
To own the hearth and stool and all!
The heaped up sods upon the fire,
The pile of turf against the wall!

To have a clock with weights and chains
And pendulum, swinging up and down!
A dresser filled with shining delph,
Speckled and white and blue and brown!

I could be busy all the day
Clearing and sweeping hearth and floor,
And fixing on their shelf again
My white and blue and speckled store!

I could be quiet there at night
Beside the fire and by myself,
Sure of a bed and loth to leave
The ticking clock and the shining delph!

Och! but I'm weary of mist and dark,
And roads where there's never a house nor bush,
And tired I am of bog and road
And the crying wind and the lonesome hush!

And I am praying to God on high,
And I am praying Him night and day,
For a little house—a house of my own—
Out of the wind's and the rain's way.

PADRAIC COLUM

TREE AT MY WINDOW

TREE at my window, window tree,
My sash is lowered when night comes on;
But let there never be curtain drawn
Between you and me.

Vague dream-head lifted out of the ground,
And thing next most diffuse to cloud,
Not all your light tongues talking aloud
Could be profound.

But tree, I have seen you taken and tossed,
And if you have seen me when I slept,
You have seen me when I was taken and swept
And all but lost.

That day she put our heads together,
Fate had her imagination about her—
Your head so much concerned with outer,
Mine with inner, weather.

ROBERT FROST

A PRAYER FOR A LITTLE HOME

GOD SEND us a little home,
To come back to, when we roam.

Low walls and fluted tiles,
Wide windows, a view for miles.

Red firelight and deep chairs,
Small white beds upstairs—

Great talk in little nooks,
Dim colors, rows of books.

One picture on each wall,
Not many things at all.

God send us a little ground,
Tall trees stand round.

Homely flowers in brown sod,
Overhead, thy stars, O God.

God bless thee, when winds blow,
Our home, and all we know.

FLORENCE BONE

HOME IS WHERE THERE IS ONE TO LOVE US

HOME's not merely four square walls,
Though with pictures hung and gilded;
Home is where Affection calls—
Filled with shrines the Hearth had builded!
Home! Go watch the faithful dove,
Sailing 'neath the heaven above us.
Home is where there's one to love!
Home is where there's one to love us.

Home's not merely roof and room,
It needs something to endear it;
Home is where the heart can bloom,
Where there's some kind lip to cheer it!
What is home with none to meet,
None to welcome, none to greet us?
Home is sweet, and only sweet,
Where there's one we love to meet us!

CHARLES SWAIN

A HOME ON THE RANGE

OH GIVE me a home where the buffalo roam,
    Where the deer and the antelope play;
Where never is heard a discouraging word
    And the skies are not cloudy all day.

Refrain:
Home, home on the range, where the deer and the antelope play;
Where never is heard a discouraging word
And the skies are not cloudy all day.

Where the air is so pure and the zephyrs so free,
    And the breezes so balmy and light;
That I would not exchange my home on the range
    For all of the cities so bright.

How often at night, when the heavens are bright,
    With the light from the glittering stars,
Have I stood there amazed, and asked as I gazed
    If their glory exceeds that of ours.

ANONYMOUS

THE OLD OAKEN BUCKET

How DEAR to my heart are the scenes of my childhood,
    When fond recollection presents them to view!
The orchard, the meadow, the deep tangled wildwood,
    And every loved spot which my infancy knew,
The wide-spreading pond and the mill that stood by it,
    The bridge and the rock where the cataract fell;
The cot of my father, the dairy house nigh it,
    And e'en the rude bucket that hung in the well.

That moss-covered bucket I hailed as a treasure,
    For often at noon, when returned from the field,
I found it the source of an exquisite pleasure,
    The purest and sweetest that nature can yield.
How ardent I seized it, with hands that were glowing,
    And quick to the white-pebbled bottom it fell.
Then soon, with the emblem of truth overflowing,
    And dripping with coolness, it rose from the well.

How sweet from the green, mossy brim to receive it,
    As, poised on the curb, it inclined to my lips!
Not a full, blushing goblet could tempt me to leave it,
    Tho' filled with the nectar that Jupiter sips.
And now, far removed from the loved habitation,
    The tear of regret will intrusively swell,
As fancy reverts to my father's plantation,
    And sighs for the bucket that hung in the well.

SAMUEL WOODWORTH

MY DOG

I HAVE no dog, but it must be
Somewhere there's one belongs to me—
A little chap with wagging tail,
And dark brown eyes that never quail,
But look you through, and through, and through,
With love unspeakable and true.

Somewhere it must be, I opine,
There is a little dog of mine
With cold black nose that sniffs around
In search of what things may be found
In pocket or some nook hard by
Where I have hid them from his eye.

Somewhere my doggie pulls and tugs
The fringes of rebellious rugs,
Or with the mischief of the pup
Chews all my shoes and slippers up,
And when he's done it to the core,
With eyes all eager, pleads for more.

Somewhere upon his hinder legs
My little doggie sits and begs,
And in a wistful minor tone
Pleads for the pleasures of the bone—
I pray it be his owner's whim
To yield, and grant the same to him.

Somewhere a little dog doth wait;
It may be by some garden gate.
With eyes alert and tail attent—
You know the kind of tail that's meant—
With stores of yelps of glad delight
To bid me welcome home at night.

Somewhere a little dog is seen,
His nose two shaggy paws between,
Flat on his stomach, one eye shut
Held fast in dreamy slumber, but
The other open, ready for
His master coming through the door.

JOHN KENDRICK BANGS

WOODMAN, SPARE THAT TREE

WOODMAN, spare that tree!
   Touch not a single bough!
In youth it sheltered me,
   And I'll protect it now.
'Twas my forefather's hand
   That placed it near his cot;
There, woodman, let it stand,
   Thy axe shall harm it not!

That old familiar tree,
   Whose glory and renown
Are spread o'er land and sea,
   And wouldst thou hew it down?
Woodman, forbear thy stroke!
   Cut not its earth-bound ties;
O, spare that aged oak,
   Now towering to the skies!

When but an idle boy
   I sought its grateful shade;
In all their gushing joy
   Here too my sisters played.
My mother kissed me here;
   My father pressed my hand—
Forgive this foolish tear,
   But let that old oak stand!

My heart-strings round thee cling,
   Close as thy bark, old friend!
Here shall the wild-bird sing,
   And still thy branches bend.
Old tree! the storm still brave!
   And, woodman, leave the spot;
While I've a hand to save,
   Thy axe shall hurt it not.

              GEORGE POPE MORRIS

I REMEMBER, I REMEMBER

I REMEMBER, I remember,
   The house where I was born,
The little window where the sun
   Came peeping in at morn:

He never came a wink too soon,
    Nor brought too long a day;
But now, I often wish the night
    Had borne my breath away.

I remember, I remember,
    The roses, red and white;
The violets and the lily-cups,
    Those flowers made of light!
The lilacs where the robin built,
    And where my brother set
The laburnum on his birthday,—
    The tree is living yet!

I remember, I remember,
    Where I was used to swing;
And thought the air must rush as fresh
    To swallows on the wing:
My spirit flew in feathers then,
    That is so heavy now,
And summer pools could hardly cool
    The fever on my brow!

I remember, I remember,
    The fir trees dark and high;
I used to think their slender tops
    Were close against the sky:
It was a childish ignorance,
    But now 'tis little joy
To know I'm farther off from heaven
    Than when I was a boy.

THOMAS HOOD

MY TRUNDLE BED

As I RUMMAGED thro' the attic,
    List'ning to the falling rain
As it patter'd on the shingles
    And against the windowpane,
Peeping over chests and boxes
    Which with dust were thickly spread,
Saw I in the farthest corner
    What was once—my trundle bed.
So I drew it from the recess
    Where it had remained so long,
Hearing all the while the music
    Of my mother's voice in song,

As she sang in sweetest accents
    What I since have often read:
"Hush, my dear, lie still and slumber;
    Holy angels guard thy bed."

As I listen'd, recollections
    That I thought had been forgot
Came, with all the gush of mem'ry,
    Rushing, thronging to the spot;
And I wander'd back to childhood,
    To those merry days of yore,
Where I knelt beside my mother
    By this bed, upon the floor.
Then it was, with hands so gently
    Placed upon my infant head,
That she taught my lips to utter
    Carefully the words she said;
Never can they be forgotten,
    Deep are they in memory riven:

"Hallowed be thy name, O, Father,
    Father! Thou who art in Heaven."
Years have pass'd, and that dear mother
    Long hast moulder'd 'neath the sod,
And I trust her sainted spirit
    Revels in the home of God;
But that scene at summer twilight
    Never has from mem'ry fled,
And it comes in all its freshness
    When I see my trundle bed.

This she taught me, then she told me
    Of its import, great and deep,
After which I learned to utter
    "Now I lay me down to sleep";
Then it was, with hands uplifted
    And in accents soft and mild,
That my mother asked Our Father:
    "Father, do Thou bless my child."

J. G. BAKER

HOME-THOUGHTS, FROM ABROAD

Oh, to be in England
Now that April's there,
And whoever wakes in England
Sees, some morning, unaware,

That the lowest boughs and the brush-wood sheaf
Round the elm-tree bole are in tiny leaf,
While the chaffinch sings on the orchard bough
In England—now!

And after April, when May follows,
And the whitethroat builds, and all the swallows!
Hark, where my blossomed pear-tree in the hedge
Leans to the field and scatters on the clover
Blossoms and dewdrops—at the bent spray's edge—
That's the wise thrush; he sings each song twice over,

Lest you should think he never could recapture
The first fine careless rapture!
And though the fields look rough with hoary dew,
All will be gay when noontide wakes anew
The buttercups, the little children's dower
—Far brighter than this gaudy melon-flower!

ROBERT BROWNING

MY HEART'S IN THE HIGHLANDS

My HEART's in the Highlands, my heart is not here;
My heart's in the Highlands a-chasing the deer;
A-chasing the wild deer, and following the roe,
My heart's in the Highlands, wherever I go.
Farewell to the Highlands, farewell to the North,
The birth place of Valour, the country of Worth,
Wherever I wander, wherever I rove,
The hills of the Highlands for ever I love.

Farewell to the mountains high cover'd with snow;
Farewell to the straths and green vallies below:
Farewell to the forests and wild hanging woods;
Farewell to the torrents and loud pouring floods.
My heart's in the Highlands, my heart is not here,
My heart's in the Highlands a-chasing the deer;
Chasing the wild deer, and following the roe;
My heart's in the Highlands, wherever I go.

ROBERT BURNS

THE OLD FAMILIAR FACES

I HAVE HAD playmates, I have had companions,
In my days of childhood, in my joyful school-days;
All, all are gone, the old familiar faces.

I have been laughing, I have been carousing,
Drinking late, sitting late, with my bosom cronies;
All, all are gone, the old familiar faces.

I loved a Love once, fairest among women:
Closed are her doors on me, I must not see her,—
All, all are gone, the old familiar faces.

I have a friend, a kinder friend has no man,
Like an ingrate, I left my friend abruptly;
Left him, to muse on the old familiar faces.

Ghost-like I paced round the haunts of my childhood,
Earth seemed a desert I was bound to traverse,
Seeking to find the old familiar faces.

Friend of my bosom, thou more than a brother,
Why wert not thou born in my father's dwelling?
So might we talk of the old familiar faces.

How some they have died, and some they have left me,
And some are taken from me; all are departed;
All, all are gone, the old familiar faces.

                                        CHARLES LAMB

MEMORY

My CHILDHOOD'S HOME I see again,
    And sadden with the view;
And still, as memory crowds my brain,
    There's pleasure in it, too.

O memory! thou midway world
    'Twixt earth and paradise,
Where things decayed and loved ones lost
    In dreamy shadows rise,

And, freed from all that's earthly, vile,
    Seem hallowed, pure and bright,
Like scenes in some enchanted isle
    All bathed in liquid light.

As dusky mountains please the eye
    When twilight chases day;
As bugle notes that, passing by,
    In distance die away;

As, leaving some grand waterfall,
    We, lingering, list its roar—

So memory will hallow all
　　We've known but know no more.

Near twenty years have passed away
　　Since here I bid farewell
To woods and fields, and scenes of play,
　　And playmates loved so well.

Where many were, but few remain
　　Of old familiar things,
But seeing them to mind again
　　The lost and absent brings.

The friends I left that parting day,
　　How changed, as time has sped!
Young childhood grown, strong manhood gray;
　　And half of all are dead.

I hear the loved survivors tell
　　How nought from death could save,
Till every sound appears a knell
　　And every spot a grave.

I range the fields with pensive tread,
　　And pace the hollow rooms,
And feel (companion of the dead)
　　I'm living in the tombs.

ABRAHAM LINCOLN
(*when thirty-seven years old*)

MY MOTHER'S PRAYER

As I WANDERED round the homestead,
　　Many a dear, familiar spot
Brought within my recollection
　　Scenes I'd seemingly forgot.
There the orchard meadow yonder,
　　Here the deep, old-fashioned well,
With its old moss-covered bucket,
　　Sent a thrill no tongue can tell.

Though the house was held by strangers,
　　All remained the same within,
Just as when a child I rambled
　　Up and down and out and in.
To the garret dark, ascending,
　　Once a source of childish dread,
Peering through the misty cobwebs,
　　Lo, I saw my trundle bed.

Quick, I drew it from the rubbish,
    Covered o'er with dust so long,
When, behold, I heard, in fancy,
    Strains of one familiar song,
Often sung by my dear mother
    To me in that trundle bed:
"Hush, my dear, lie still and slumber,
    Holy angels guard thy bed."

As I listened to the music,
    Stealing on in gentle strain,
I am carried back to childhood,
    I am now a child again.
'Tis the hour of my retiring,
    At the dusky eventide,
Near my trundle bed I'm kneeling,
    As of yore, by Mother's side.

Hands are on my head so loving,
    As they were in childhood's days;
I with weary tones am trying
    To repeat the words she says.
'Tis a prayer in language simple
    As a mother's lips can frame,
"Father, Thou who art in Heaven,
    Hallowed ever be Thy name."

Prayer is over, to my pillow,
    With a good-night kiss, I creep,
Scarcely waking while I whisper,
    "Now I lay me down to sleep."
Then my mother over me bending,
    Prays in earnest words but mild,
"Hear my prayer, O Heavenly Father,
    Bless, O bless, my precious child."

Yet I am but only dreaming,
    Ne'er I'll be a child again,
Many years has that dear mother
    In the quiet churchyard lain.
But the memory of her counsels
    O'er my path a light has spread,
Daily calling me to heaven,
    Even from my trundle bed.

                              T. C. O'KANE

OFT IN THE STILLY NIGHT

OFT in the stilly night,
    Ere Slumber's chain has bound me,
Fond Memory brings the light
    Of other days around me;
            The smiles, the tears,
            Of boyhood's years,
        The words of love then spoken;
            The eyes that shone,
            Now dimmed and gone,
        The cheerful hearts now broken!
Thus in the stilly night,
    Ere Slumber's chain has bound me,
Sad Memory brings the light
    Of other days around me.

When I remember all
    The friends, so linked together,
I've seen around me fall,
    Like leaves in wintry weather;
            I feel like one
            Who treads alone
        Some banquet-hall deserted,
            Whose lights are fled,
            Whose garlands dead,
        And all but he departed!
Thus in the stilly night,
    Ere Slumber's chain has bound me,
Sad Memory brings the light
    Of other days around me.

                                    THOMAS MOORE

MOTHER, HOME, HEAVEN

THREE words fall sweetly on my soul,
    As music from an angel's lyre,
That bid my spirit spurn control,
    And upward to its source aspire;
The sweetest sounds to mortals given
Are heard in Mother, Home, and Heaven.

Dear Mother!—ne'er shall I forget
    Thy brow, thine eye, thy pleasant smile;

Though in the sea of death hath set
　　Thy star of life, my guide awhile,
Oh, never shall thy form depart
From the bright pictures in my heart.

And like a bird that from the flowers,
　　Wing-weary seeks her wonted nest,
My spirit, e'en in manhood's hours,
　　Turns back in childhood's Home to rest;
The cottage, garden, hill, and stream,
Still linger like a pleasant dream.

And while to one engulfing grave
　　By Time's swift tide we're driven,
How sweet the thought that every wave
　　But bears us nearer Heaven!
There we shall meet, when life is o'er,
In that blest Home, to part no more.

WILLIAM GOLDSMITH BROWN

MY AIN FIRESIDE

I HAE seen great anes and sat in great ha's,
'Mang lords and fine ladies a' covered wi' braws,
At feasts made for princes wi' princes I've been,
When the grand shine o' splendor has dazzled my een;
But a sight sae delightfu' I trow I ne'er spied
As the bonny blithe blink o' my ain fireside.
My ain fireside, my ain fireside,
O, cheery's the blink o' my ain fireside;
　　My ain fireside, my ain fireside,
　　O, there's naught to compare wi' ane's ain fireside.

Ance mair, Gude be thankit, round my ain heartsome ingle
Wi' the friends o' my youth I cordially mingle;
Nae forms to compel me to seem wae or glad,
I may laugh when I'm merry, and sigh when I'm sad.
Nae falsehood to dread, and nae malice to fear,
But truth to delight me, and friendship to cheer;
Of a' roads to happiness ever were tried,
There's nane half so sure as ane's ain fireside.
　　My ain fireside, my ain fireside,
　　O, there's naught to compare wi' ane's ain fireside.

When I draw in my stool on my cozy hearthstane,
My heart loups sae light I scarce ken 't for my ain;
Care's down on the wind, it is clean out o' sight,

Past troubles they seem but as dreams o' the night.
I hear but kend voices, kend faces I see,
And mark saft affection glent fond frae ilk ee;
Nae fleechings o' flattery, nae boastings o' pride,
'Tis heart speaks to heart at ane's ain fireside.
    My ain fireside, my ain fireside,
      O, there's naught to compare wi' ane's ain fireside.
ELIZABETH HAMILTON

CARRY ME BACK TO OLD VIRGINNY

CARRY me back to old Virginny,
There's where the cotton and the corn and taters grow,
There's where the birds warble sweet in the spring-time,
There's where the old darkey's heart am longed to go.
There's where I labored so hard for old Massa,
Day after day in the field of yellow corn,
No place on earth do I love more sincerely
Than old Virginny, the state where I was born.

Refrain:
Carry me back to old Virginny,
There's where the cotton and the corn and taters grow,
There's where the birds warble sweet in the spring-time,
There's where the old darkey's heart am longed to go.

Carry me back to old Virginny,
There let me live till I wither and decay,
Long by the old dismal swamp have I wandered,
There's where this old darkey's life will pass away.
Massa and Missis have long gone before,
Soon we will meet on that bright and golden shore,
There we'll be happy and free from all sorrow,
There's where we'll meet and we'll never part no more.
JAMES A. BLAND

MY OLD KENTUCKY HOME

THE SUN shines bright in the old Kentucky home,
    'Tis summer, the darkies are gay;
The corn-top's ripe and the meadow's in the bloom,
    While the birds make music all the day.
The young folks roll on the little cabin floor,
    All merry, all happy and bright;

By'n-by hard times comes a-knocking at the door,
   Then my old Kentucky home, good night!

Refrain:
Weep no more, my lady, O weep no more today!
We will sing one song for the old Kentucky home,
   For the old Kentucky home, far away.

They hunt no more for the possum and the coon,
   On the meadow, the hill, and the shore;
They sing no more by the glimmer of the moon,
   On the bench by the old cabin door;
The day goes by like a shadow o'er the heart,
   With sorrow where all was delight;
The time has come when the darkies have to part,
   Then my old Kentucky home, good night!

The head must bow and the back will have to bend,
   Wherever the darkey may go;
A few more days, and the trouble all will end,
   In the field where the sugar-canes grow;
A few more days for to tote the weary load,
   No matter, 'twill never be light;
A few more days till we totter on the road,
   Then my old Kentucky home, good night!

STEPHEN C. FOSTER

OLD FOLKS AT HOME

'WAY down upon de Swanee River,
   Far, far away,
Dere's wha my heart is turning ever,
   Dere's wha de old folks stay.
All up and down de whole creation,
   Sadly I roam,
Still longing for de old plantation,
   And for de old folks at home.

Refrain:
All de world am sad and dreary,
   Ev'rywhere I roam;
Oh! darkies, how my heart grows weary,
   Far from de old folks at home.

All roun' de little farm I wandered,
   When I was young;
Den many happy days I squandered,
   Many de songs I sung.

When I was playing wid my brother,
    Happy was I;
Oh! take me to my kind old mother,
    There let me live and die.

One little hut among de bushes,
    One that I love,
Still sadly to my mem'ry rushes,
    No matter where I rove.
When will I see de bees ahumming
    All round de comb?
When will I hear de banjo tumming,
    Down in my good old home?

STEPHEN C. FOSTER

THE COTTER'S SATURDAY NIGHT

MY LOVED, my honored, much-respected friend,
    No mercenary bard his homage pays:
With honest pride I scorn each selfish end;
    My dearest meed, a friend's esteem and praise.
To you I sing, in simple Scottish lays,
    The lowly train in life's sequestered scene;
The native feelings strong, the guileless ways;
    What Aiken in a cottage would have been;
Ah! though his worth unknown, far happier there, I ween.

November chill blaws loud wi' angry sugh;
    The shortening winter-day is near a close;
The miry beasts retreating frae the pleugh,
    The blackening trains o' craws to their repose;
The toilworn cotter frae his labor goes,—
    This night his weekly moil is at an end,—
Collects his spades, his mattocks, and his hoes,
    Hoping the morn in ease and rest to spend,
And weary, o'er the moor, his course does hameward bend.

At length his lonely cot appears in view,
    Beneath the shelter of an aged tree;
Th' expectant wee things, toddlin', stacher through
    To meet their dad, wi' flichterin' noise an' glee.
His wee bit ingle, blinking bonnily,
    His clean hearthstane, his thriftie wifie's smile,
The lisping infant prattling on his knee,
    Does a' his weary carking cares beguile,
And makes him quite forget his labor and his toil.

Belyve the elder bairns come drapping in,
　　At service out amang the farmers roun;
Some ca' the pleugh, some herd, some tentie rin
　　A cannie errand to a neibor town;
Their eldest hope, their Jenny, woman grown,
　　In youthfu' bloom, love sparkling in her e'e,
Comes hame, perhaps, to shew a bra' new gown,
　　Or deposit her sair-won penny-fee,
To help her parents dear, if they in hardship be.

Wi' joy unfeigned brothers and sisters meet,
　　An' each for other's weelfare kindly spiers:
The social hours, swift-winged, unnoticed fleet;
　　Each tells the uncos that he sees or hears;
The parents, partial, eye their hopeful years;
　　Anticipation forward points the view:
The mother, wi' her needle an' her shears,
　　Gars auld claes look amaist as weel's the new;
The father mixes a' wi' admonition due.

Their master's an' their mistress's command,
　　The younkers a' are warnèd to obey;
And mind their labors wi' an eydent hand,
　　And ne'er, though out o' sight, to jauk or play;
"An' O, be sure to fear the Lord alway!
　　An' mind your duty, duly, morn an' night!
Lest in temptation's path ye gang astray,
　　Implore his counsel and assisting might;
They never sought in vain that sought the Lord aright!"

But, hark! a rap comes gently to the door.
　　Jenny, wha kens the meaning o' the same,
Tells how a neibor lad cam o'er the moor,
　　To do some errands and convoy her hame.
The wily mother sees the conscious flame
　　Sparkle in Jenny's e'e, and flush her cheek;
Wi' heart-struck anxious care inquires his name,
　　While Jenny hafflins is afraid to speak;
Weel pleased the mother hears it's nae wild, worthless rake.

Wi' kindly welcome, Jenny brings him ben;
　　A strappin' youth; he taks the mother's e'e;
Blithe Jenny sees the visit's no ill ta'en;
　　The father cracks of horses, pleughs, and kye.
The youngster's artless heart o'erflows wi' joy,
　　But blate and lathefu', scarce can weel behave;

The mother, wi' a woman's wiles, can spy
    What makes the youth sae bashfu' an' sae grave;
Weel pleased to think her bairn's respected like the lave.

O happy love! where love like this is found!
    O heartfelt raptures! bliss beyond compare!
I've pacèd much this weary mortal round,
    And sage experience bids me this declare:—
If Heaven a draught of heavenly pleasure spare,
    One cordial in this melancholy vale,
'T is when a youthful, loving, modest pair
    In other's arms breathe out the tender tale,
Beneath the milk-white thorn that scents the evening gale.

Is there, in human form, that bears a heart,
    A wretch, a villain, lost to love and truth,
That can, with studied, sly, ensnaring art,
    Betray sweet Jenny's unsuspecting youth?
Curse on his perjured arts! dissembling smooth!
    Are honor, virtue, conscience, all exiled?
Is there no pity, no relenting ruth,
    Points to the parents fondling o'er their child,
Then paints the ruined maid, and their distraction wild?

But now the supper crowns their simple board,
    The halesome parritch, chief o' Scotia's food;
The soupe their only hawkie does afford,
    That 'yont the hallan snugly chows her cood;
The dame brings forth, in complimental mood,
    To grace the lad, her weel-hained kebbuck fell,
An' aft he's prest, an' aft he ca's it guid;
    The frugal wifie, garrulous, will tell,
How 't was a towmond auld, sin' lint was i' the bell.

The cheerfu' supper done, wi' serious face,
    They, round the ingle, form a circle wide;
The sire turns o'er, wi' patriarchal grace,
    The big ha'-Bible, ance his father's pride:
His bonnet reverently is laid aside,
    His lyart haffets wearing thin an' bare:
Those strains that once did sweet in Zion glide,
    He wales a portion with judicious care;
And "Let us worship God!" he says with solemn air.

They chant their artless notes in simple guise;
    They tune their hearts, by far the noblest aim:
Perhaps "Dundee's" wild-warbling measures rise,
    Or plaintive "Martyrs," worthy of the name;

Or noble "Elgin" beets the heavenward flame,
    The sweetest far of Scotia's holy lays:
Compared with these, Italian trills are tame;
    The tickled ears no heartfelt raptures raise;
Nae unison hae they with our Creator's praise.

The priest-like father reads the sacred page,—
    How Abram was the friend of God on high;
Or Moses bade eternal warfare wage
    With Amalek's ungracious progeny;
Or how the royal bard did groaning lie
    Beneath the stroke of Heaven's avenging ire;
Or Job's pathetic plaint, and wailing cry;
    Or rapt Isaiah's wild, seraphic fire;
Or other holy seers that tune the sacred lyre.

Perhaps the Christian volume is the theme,—
    How guiltless blood for guilty man was shed;
How He, who bore in heaven the second name,
    Had not on earth whereon to lay his head:
How his first followers and servants sped;
    The precepts sage they wrote to many a land;
How he, who lone in Patmos banishèd,
    Saw in the sun a mighty angel stand,
And heard great Bab'lon's doom pronounced by Heaven's command.

Then, kneeling down, to heaven's eternal King,
    The saint, the father, and the husband prays:
Hope "springs exulting on triumphant wing,"
    That thus they all shall meet in future days;
There ever bask in uncreated rays,
    No more to sigh, or shed the bitter tear,
Together hymning their Creator's praise,
    In such society, yet still more dear;
While circling Time moves round in an eternal sphere.

Compared with this, how poor Religion's pride,
    In all the pomp of method and of art,
When men display to congregations wide,
    Devotion's every grace, except the heart!
The Power, incensed, the pageant will desert,
    The pompous strain, the sacerdotal stole;
But, haply, in some cottage far apart,
    May hear, well pleased, the language of the soul;
And in his Book of Life the inmates poor enroll.

Then homeward all take off their several way;
    The youngling cottagers retire to rest:

The parent-pair their secret homage pay,
  And proffer up to Heaven the warm request,
That He who stills the raven's clamorous nest,
  And decks the lily fair in flowery pride,
Would, in the way his wisdom sees the best,
  For them and for their little ones provide;
But, chiefly, in their hearts with grace divine preside.

From scenes like these old Scotia's grandeur springs,
  That makes her loved at home, revered abroad;
Princes and lords are but the breath of kings,
  "An honest man's the noblest work of God!"
And certes, in fair Virtue's heavenly road,
  The cottage leaves the palace far behind:
What is a lordling's pomp?—a cumbrous load,
  Disguising oft the wretch of humankind,
Studied in arts of hell, in wickedness refined!

O Scotia! my dear, my native soil!
  For whom my warmest wish to Heaven is sent,
Long may thy hardy sons of rustic toil
  Be blest with health, and peace, and sweet content!
And, O, may Heaven their simple lives prevent
  From luxury's contagion, weak and vile!
Then, howe'er crowns and coronets be rent,
  A virtuous populace may rise the while,
And stand a wall of fire around their much-loved isle.

O Thou! who poured the patriotic tide,
  That streamed through Wallace's undaunted heart;
Who dared to nobly stem tyrannic pride,
  Or nobly die, the second glorious part,
(The patriot's God peculiarly thou art,
  His friend, inspirer, guardian, and reward!)
O, never, never Scotia's realm desert;
  But still the patriot and the patriot bard
In bright succession raise, her ornament and guard!

ROBERT BURNS

"NOW I LAY ME DOWN TO SLEEP"

"Now I lay me down to sleep:
I pray the Lord my soul to keep,"
Was my childhood's early prayer
Taught by my mother's love and care.
Many years since then have fled;

Mother slumbers with the dead;
Yet methinks I see her now,
With love-lit eye and holy brow,
As, kneeling by her side to pray,
She gently taught me how to say,
"Now I lay me down to sleep:
I pray the Lord my soul to keep."

Oh!could the faith of childhood's days,
Oh!could its little hymns of praise,
Oh!could its simple, joyous trust
Be recreated from the dust
That lies around a wasted life,
The fruit of many a bitter strife!
Oh! then at night in prayer I'd bend,
And call my God, my Father, Friend,
And pray with childlike faith once more
The prayer my mother taught of yore,—
"Now I lay me down to sleep:
I pray the Lord my soul to keep."

EUGENE HENRY PULLEN

NURSE'S SONG

When the voices of children are heard on the green
   And laughing is heard on the hill,
My heart is at rest within my breast,
   And everything else is still.

"Then come home, my children, the sun is gone down,
   And the dews of the night arise;
Come, come, leave off play, and let us away
   Till the morning appears in the skies."

"No, no, let us play, for it is yet day,
   And we cannot go to sleep;
Besides in the sky the little birds fly,
   And the hills are all covered with sheep."

"Well, well, go and play till the light fades away,
   And then go home to bed."
The little ones leaped and shouted and laughed;
   And all the hills echoèd.

WILLIAM BLAKE

THE LAST LEAF

I saw him once before,
As he passed by the door,
    And again
The pavement stones resound,
As he totters o'er the ground
    With his cane.

They say that in his prime,
Ere the pruning-knife of Time
    Cut him down,
Not a better man was found
By the Crier on his round
    Through the town.

But now he walks the streets,
And he looks at all he meets
    Sad and wan,
And he shakes his feeble head,
That it seems as if he said,
    "They are gone."

The mossy marbles rest
On the lips that he has pressed
    In their bloom,
And the names he loved to hear
Have been carved for many a year
    On the tomb.

My grandmamma has said,—
Poor old lady, she is dead
    Long ago,—
That he had a Roman nose,
And his cheek was like a rose
    In the snow:

But now his nose is thin,
And it rests upon his chin
    Like a staff,
And a crook is in his back,
And a melancholy crack
    In his laugh.

I know it is a sin
For me to sit and grin
   At him here;
But the old three-cornered hat,
And the breeches, and all that,
   Are so queer!

And if I should live to be
The last leaf upon the tree
   In the spring,
Let them smile, as I do now,
At the old forsaken bough
   Where I cling.

OLIVER WENDELL HOLMES

LONG, LONG BE MY HEART WITH SUCH MEMORIES FILLED

FAREWELL!—but whenever you welcome the hour
That awakens the night-song of mirth in your bower,
Then think of the friend who once welcomed it too,
And forgot his own griefs, to be happy with you.
His griefs may return,—not a hope may remain
Of the few that have brightened his pathway of pain,—
But he ne'er will forget the short vision that threw
Its enchantment around him, while ling'ring with you!

And still on that evening, when Pleasure fills up
To the highest top sparkle each heart and each cup,
Where'er my path lies, be it gloomy or bright,
My soul, happy friends, shall be with you that night;
Shall join in your revels, your sports, and your wiles,
And return to me, beaming all o'er with your smiles,—
Too blest if it tell me that, 'mid the gay cheer,
Some kind voice had murmured, "I wish he were here!"

Let fate do her worst, there are relics of joy,
Bright dreams of the past, which she cannot destroy;
Which come, in the night-time of sorrow and care,
And bring back the features that joy used to wear.
Long, long be my heart with such memories filled!
Like the vase in which roses have once been distilled,—
You may break, you may shatter the vase, if you will,
But the scent of the roses will hang 'round it still.

THOMAS MOORE

DO THEY THINK OF ME AT HOME

Do THEY think of me at home,
     Do they ever think of me?
I who shared their every grief,
     I who mingled in their glee?
Have their hearts grown cold and strange,
     To the one now doomed to roam?
I would give the world to know,
     Do they think of me at home?
I would give the world to know,
     Do they think of me at home?

Do they think of me at eve,
     Of the songs I used to sing?
Is the harp I struck untouched,
     Does a stranger wake the string?
Will no kind, forgiving word
     Come across the raging foam?
Shall I never cease to sigh,
     "Do they think of me at home?"
Shall I never cease to sigh,
     "Do they think of me at home?"

Do they think of how I loved
     In my happy, early days?
Do they think of him who came
     But could never win their praise?
I am happy by his side,
     And from mine he'll never roam,
But my heart will sadly ask,
     "Do they think of me at home?"
But my heart will sadly ask,
     "Do they think of me at home?"

                              J. E. CARPENTER

THE DEAREST SPOT ON EARTH

THE dearest spot on earth to me
     Is home, sweet home;
The fairy-land I long to see
     Is home, sweet home;
There how charmed the sense of hearing,
There, where love is so endearing!

All the world is not so cheering
  As home, sweet home.

I've taught my heart the way to prize
  My home, sweet home;
I've learned to look with lover's eyes
  On home, sweet home;
There, where vows were truly plighted,
There, where hearts are so united!
All the world beside I've slighted
  For home, sweet home.

               W. T. WRIGHTON

YOUNG AND OLD

WHEN all the world is young, lad,
  And all the trees are green;
And every goose a swan, lad,
  And every lass a queen;
Then hey for boot and horse, lad,
  And round the world away;
Young blood must have its course, lad,
  And every dog his day.

When all the world is old, lad,
  And all the trees are brown;
And all the sport is stale, lad,
  And all the wheels run down:
Creep home, and take your place there,
  The spent and maimed among:
God grant you find one face there
  You loved when all was young.

               CHARLES KINGSLEY
               From "The Water Babies"

LOVE'S OLD SWEET SONG

ONCE in the dear dead days beyond recall,
When on the world the mists began to fall,
Out of the dreams that rose in happy throng,
Low to our hearts love sang an old sweet song;
And in the dusk, where fell the firelight gleam,
Softly it wove itself into our dream.

Refrain:
Just a song at twilight, when the lights are low,
And the flick'ring shadows, softly come and go;
Though the heart be weary, sad the day and long,
Still to us at twilight, comes love's old song,
    Comes love's old sweet song.

Even today we hear love's song of yore,
Deep in our hearts it dwells forevermore,
Footsteps may falter, weary grow the way,
Still we can hear it at the close of day;
So till the end, when life's dim shadows fall,
Love will be found the sweetest song of all.

G. CLIFTON BINGHAM

Favorite Poems For

CHILDREN

THE GARDEN YEAR

JANUARY brings the snow,
Makes our feet and fingers glow.

February brings the rain,
Thaws the frozen lake again.

March brings breezes, loud and shrill,
To stir the dancing daffodil.

April brings the primrose sweet,
Scatters daisies at our feet.

May brings flocks of pretty lambs
Skipping by their fleecy dams.

June brings tulips, lilies, roses,
Fills the children's hands with posies.

Hot July brings cooling showers,
Apricots, and gillyflowers.

August brings the sheaves of corn,
Then the harvest home is borne.

Warm September brings the fruit;
Sportsmen then begin to shoot.

Fresh October brings the pheasant;
Then to gather nuts is pleasant.

Dull November brings the blast;
Then the leaves are whirling fast.

Chill December brings the sleet,
Blazing fire, and Christmas treat.

SARA COLERIDGE

THE STAR

TWINKLE, twinkle, little star,
How I wonder what you are,
Up above the world so high,
Like a diamond in the sky.

When the blazing sun is set,
And the grass with dew is wet,
Then you show your little light,
Twinkle, twinkle, all the night.

Then the traveler in the dark
Thanks you for your tiny spark,
He could not see where to go
If you did not twinkle so.

In the dark blue sky you keep,
And often through my curtains peep,
For you never shut your eye
Till the sun is in the sky.

As your bright and tiny spark
Lights the traveler in the dark,
Though I know not what you are,
Twinkle, twinkle, little star.

JANE TAYLOR

MARY'S LAMB

MARY had a little lamb,
  Its fleece was white as snow,
And every where that Mary went
  The lamb was sure to go;

He followed her to school one day—
    That was against the rule,
It made the children laugh and play,
    To see a lamb at school.

And so the teacher turned him out,
    But still he lingered near,
And waited patiently about,
    Till Mary did appear;
And then he ran to her, and laid
    His head upon her arm,
As if he said—"I'm not afraid—
    You'll keep me from all harm."

"What makes the lamb love Mary so?"
    The eager children cry—
"O, Mary loves the lamb, you know,"
    The Teacher did reply;—
"And you each gentle animal
    In confidence may bind,
And make them follow at your call,
    If you are always *kind*."

SARA JOSEPHA HALE

I LIKE LITTLE PUSSY

I LIKE little Pussy, her coat is so warm;
And if I don't hurt her she'll do me no harm.
So I'll not pull her tail, nor drive her away,
But Pussy and I very gently will play.

She shall sit by my side, and I'll give her some food;
And she'll love me because I am gentle and good.
I'll pat little Pussy and then she will purr,
And thus show her thanks for my kindness to her.

I'll not pinch her ears, nor tread on her paw,
Lest I should provoke her to use her sharp claw;
I never will vex her, nor make her displeased,
For Pussy can't bear to be worried or teased.

JANE TAYLOR

THE CITY MOUSE AND THE GARDEN MOUSE

THE city mouse lives in a house;—
    The garden mouse lives in a bower,

He's friendly with the frogs and toads,
And sees the pretty plants in flower.

The city mouse eats bread and cheese;—
The garden mouse eats what he can;
We will not grudge him seeds and stocks,
Poor little timid furry man.

CHRISTINA GEORGINA ROSSETTI

MISS T.

It's a very odd thing—
As odd as can be—
That whatever Miss T. eats
Turns into Miss T.;
Porridge and apples,
Mince, muffins and mutton,
Jam, junket, jumbles—
Not a rap, not a button
It matters; the moment
They're out of her plate,
Though shared by Miss Butcher
And sour Mr. Bate;
Tiny and cheerful,
And neat as can be,
Whatever Miss T. eats
Turns into Miss T.

WALTER DE LA MARE

A PLEASANT SHIP

I saw a ship a-sailing,
A-sailing on the sea,
And oh! it was all laden
With pretty things for thee!

There were comfits in the cabin,
And apples in the hold;
The sails were made of silk,
And the masts were made of gold.

The four-and-twenty sailors
That stood between the decks
Were four-and-twenty white mice,
With chains about their necks.

The captain was a duck,
With a packet on his back,
And when the ship began to move,
The captain said "Quack! Quack!"
                    ANONYMOUS

THE DUEL

THE GINGHAM DOG and the calico cat
Side by side on the table sat;
'Twas half-past twelve, and (what do you think?)
Nor one nor t'other had slept a wink!
    The old Dutch clock and the Chinese plate
    Appeared to know as sure as fate
There was going to be a terrible spat.
    (*I wasn't there; I simply state*
    What was told me by the Chinese plate!)

The gingham dog went "bow-wow-wow!"
And the calico cat replied "mee-ow!"
The air was littered, an hour or so,
With bits of gingham and calico,
    While the old Dutch clock in the chimney-place
    Up with its hands before its face,
For it always dreaded a family row!
    (*Now mind: I'm only telling you*
    What the old Dutch clock declares is true!)

The Chinese plate looked very blue,
And wailed, "Oh, dear! what shall we do?"
But the gingham dog and the calico cat
Wallowed this way and tumbled that,
    Employing every tooth and claw
    In the awfullest way you ever saw—
And, oh! how the gingham and calico flew!
    (*Don't fancy I exaggerate!*
    I got my news from the Chinese plate!)

Next morning, where the two had sat,
They found no trace of dog or cat;
And some folks think unto this day
That burglars stole that pair away!
    But the truth about the cat and pup
    Is this: They ate each other up!

Now what do you really think of that!
(*The old Dutch clock it told me so,*
And that is how I came to know.)

EUGENE FIELD

THE LITTLE ELF

I MET a little Elf-man, once,
    Down where the lilies blow.
I asked him why he was so small
    And why he didn't grow.

He slightly frowned, and with his eye
    He looked me through and through.
"I'm quite as big for me," said he,
    "As you are big for you."

JOHN KENDRICK BANGS

THE ELF AND THE DORMOUSE

UNDER a toadstool crept a wee Elf,
Out of the rain, to shelter himself.

Under the toadstool sound asleep,
Sat a big Dormouse all in a heap.

Trembled the wee Elf, frightened, and yet
Fearing to fly away lest he get wet.

To the next shelter—maybe a mile!
Sudden the wee Elf smiled a wee smile,

Tugged till the toadstool toppled in two.
Holding it over him, gayly he flew.

Soon he was safe home, dry as could be.
Soon woke the Dormouse—"Good gracious me!

"Where is my toadstool?" loud he lamented.
—And that's how umbrellas first were invented.

OLIVER HERFORD

ANGER

ANGER in its time and place
May assume a kind of grace.
It must have some reason in it,

And not last beyond a minute.
If to further lengths it go,
It does into malice grow.
'Tis the difference that we see
'Twixt the serpent and the bee.
If the latter you provoke,
It inflicts a hasty stroke,
Puts you to some little pain,
But it never stings again.
Close in tufted bush or brake
Lurks the poison-swellèd snake
Nursing up his cherished wrath;
In the purlieus of his path,
In the cold, or in the warm,
Mean him good, or mean him harm,
Wheresoever fate may bring you,
The vile snake will always sting you.

CHARLES AND MARY LAMB

THE WORLD'S MUSIC

THE world's a very happy place,
    Where every child should dance and sing,
And always have a smiling face,
    And never sulk for anything.

I waken when the morning's come,
    And feel the air and light alive
With strange sweet music like the hum
    Of bees about their busy hive.

The linnets play among the leaves
    At hide-and-seek, and chirp and sing;
While, flashing to and from the eaves,
    The swallows twitter on the wing.

The twigs that shake, and boughs that sway;
    And tall old trees you could not climb;
And winds that come, but cannot stay,
    Are gaily singing all the time.

From dawn to dark the old mill-wheel
    Makes music, going round and round;
And dusty-white with flour and meal,
    The miller whistles to its sound.

And if you listen to the rain
　　When leaves and birds and bees are dumb,
You hear it pattering on the pane
　　Like Andrew beating on his drum.

The coals beneath the kettle croon,
　　And clap their hands and dance in glee;
And even the kettle hums a tune
　　To tell you when it's time for tea.

The world is such a happy place,
　　That children, whether big or small,
Should always have a smiling face,
　　And never, never sulk at all.

GABRIEL SETOUN

HAPPY THOUGHT

THE world is so full of a number of things,
I'm sure we should all be as happy as kings.

ROBERT LOUIS STEVENSON

MY SHADOW

I HAVE a little shadow that goes in and out with me,
And what can be the use of him is more than I can see.
He is very, very like me from the heels up to the head;
And I see him jump before me, when I jump into my bed.

The funniest thing about him is the way he likes to grow—
Not at all like proper children, which is always very slow;
For he sometimes shoots up taller like an india-rubber ball,
And he sometimes gets so little that there's none of him at all.

He hasn't got a notion of how children ought to play,
And can only make a fool of me in every sort of way.
He stays so close beside me, he's a coward, you can see;
I'd think shame to stick to nursie as that shadow sticks to me!

One morning, very early, before the sun was up,
I rose and found the shining dew on every buttercup;
But my lazy little shadow, like an arrant sleepy-head,
Had stayed at home behind me and was fast asleep in bed.

ROBERT LOUIS STEVENSON

THE LAND OF COUNTERPANE

When I was sick and lay a-bed,
I had two pillows at my head,
And all my toys beside me lay
To keep me happy all the day.

And sometimes for an hour or so
I watched my leaden soldiers go,
With different uniforms and drills,
Among the bed-clothes, through the hills.

And sometimes sent my ships in fleets
All up and down among the sheets;
Or brought my trees and houses out,
And planted cities all about.

I was the giant great and still
That sits upon the pillow-hill,
And sees before him, dale and plain,
The pleasant land of Counterpane.

ROBERT LOUIS STEVENSON

THE SWING

How do you like to go up in a swing,
    Up in the air so blue?
"Oh, I do think it the pleasantest thing
    Ever a child can do!"

"Up in the air and over the wall,
    Till I can see so wide,
Rivers and trees and cattle and all
    Over the countryside—

"Till I look down on the garden green
    Down on the roof so brown—
Up in the air I go flying again,
    Up in the air and down!"

ROBERT LOUIS STEVENSON

WHERE GO THE BOATS?

Dark brown is the river,
    Golden is the sand,

It flows along for ever,
　　With trees on either hand,

Green leaves a-floating,
　　Castles of the foam,
Boats of mine a-boating—
　　Where will all come home?

On goes the river
　　And out past the mill,
Away down the valley,
　　Away down the hill.

Away down the river,
　　A hundred miles or more,
Other little children
　　Shall bring my boats ashore.
　　　　　ROBERT LOUIS STEVENSON

THE LAND OF STORY-BOOKS

At EVENING when the lamp is lit,
Around the fire my parents sit;
They sit at home and talk and sing
And do not play at anything.

Now, with my little gun, I crawl
All in the dark along the wall,
And follow round the forest track
Away behind the sofa back.

There, in the night, where none can spy,
All in my hunter's camp I lie,
And play at books that I have read
Till it is time to go to bed.

These are the hills, these are the woods,
These are my starry solitudes;
And there the river by whose brink
The roaring lions come to drink.

I see the others far away
As if in firelit camp they lay,
And I, like to an Indian scout,
Around their party prowled about.

So, when my nurse comes in for me,
Home I return across the sea,

And go to bed with backward looks
At my dear Land of Story-books.

ROBERT LOUIS STEVENSON

THE OWL AND THE PUSSY-CAT

THE OWL and the Pussy-cat went to sea
   In a beautiful pea-green boat:
They took some honey, and plenty of money
   Wrapped up in a five-pound note.
The Owl looked up to the stars above,
   And sang to a small guitar,
"O lovely Pussy, O Pussy, my love,
   What a beautiful Pussy you are,
         You are,
         You are!
   What a beautiful Pussy you are!"

Pussy said to the Owl, "You elegant fowl,
   How charmingly sweet you sing!
Oh! let us be married; too long we have tarried:
   But what shall we do for a ring?"
They sailed away, for a year and a day,
   To the land where the bong-tree grows;
And there in a wood a Piggy-wig stood,
   With a ring at the end of his nose,
         His nose,
         His nose,
   With a ring at the end of his nose.

"Dear Pig, are you willing to sell for one shilling
   Your ring?" Said the Piggy, "I will."
So they took it away, and were married next day
   By the turkey who lives on the hill.
They dined on mince and slices of quince,
   Which they ate with a runcible spoon;
And hand in hand, on the edge of the sand,
   They danced by the light of the moon,
         The moon,
         The moon,
   They danced by the light of the moon.

EDWARD LEAR

LITTLE THINGS

LITTLE drops of water,
  Little grains of sand,
Make the mighty ocean
  And the pleasant land.

Thus the little minutes,
  Humble though they be,
Make the mighty ages
  Of eternity.

JULIA A. FLETCHER

A VISIT FROM ST. NICHOLAS

'TWAS THE NIGHT before Christmas, when all through the house
Not a creature was stirring, not even a mouse;
The stockings were hung by the chimney with care,
In hopes that St. Nicholas soon would be there;
The children were nestled all snug in their beds,
While visions of sugar-plums danced in their heads;
And mamma in her kerchief, and I in my cap,
Had just settled our brains for a long winter's nap,—
When out on the lawn there arose such a clatter,
I sprang from my bed to see what was the matter.
Away to the window I flew like a flash,
Tore open the shutters and threw up the sash.
The moon on the breast of the new-fallen snow
Gave a lustre of midday to objects below;
When what to my wondering eyes should appear,
But a miniature sleigh and eight tiny reindeer,
With a little old driver, so lively and quick
I knew in a moment it must be St. Nick.
More rapid than eagles his coursers they came,
And he whistled and shouted, and called them by name:
"Now, Dasher! now, Dancer! now, Prancer and Vixen!
On, Comet! on, Cupid! on, Donder and Blitzen!
To the top of the porch, to the top of the wall!
Now dash away, dash away, dash away all!"
As dry leaves that before the wild hurricane fly,
When they meet with an obstacle, mount to the sky,
So up to the house-top the coursers they flew,
With the sleigh full of toys,—and St. Nicholas too.
And then in a twinkling I heard on the roof

The prancing and pawing of each little hoof.
As I drew in my head, and was turning around,
Down the chimney St. Nicholas came with a bound.
He was dressed all in fur from his head to his foot,
And his clothes were all tarnished with ashes and soot;
A bundle of toys he had flung on his back,
And he looked like a pedlar just opening his pack.
His eyes, how they twinkled! his dimples, how merry!
His cheeks were like roses, his nose like a cherry;
His droll little mouth was drawn up like a bow,
And the beard on his chin was as white as the snow.
The stump of a pipe he held tight in his teeth,
And the smoke it encircled his head like a wreath.
He had a broad face and a little round belly
That shook, when he laughed, like a bowl full of jelly.
He was chubby and plump,—a right jolly old elf;
And I laughed, when I saw him, in spite of myself.
A wink of his eye and a twist of his head
Soon gave me to know I had nothing to dread.
He spoke not a word, but went straight to his work,
And filled all the stockings; then turned with a jerk,
And laying his finger aside of his nose,
And giving a nod, up the chimney he rose.
He sprang to his sleigh, to his team gave a whistle,
And away they all flew like the down of a thistle;
But I heard him exclaim, ere he drove out of sight,
"Happy Christmas to all, and to all a good-night!"

                              CLEMENT CLARKE MOORE

WYNKEN, BLYNKEN, AND NOD

Wynken, Blynken, and Nod one night
    Sailed off in a wooden shoe—
Sailed on a river of crystal light
    Into a sea of dew.
"Where are you going, and what do you wish?"
    The old moon asked the three.
"We have come to fish for the herring-fish
    That live in this beautiful sea;
    Nets of silver and gold have we,"
                Said Wynken,
                Blynken,
                And Nod.

The old moon laughed and sang a song,
    As they rocked in the wooden shoe;

And the wind that sped them all night long
    Ruffled the waves of dew;
The little stars were the herring-fish
    That lived in the beautiful sea.
"Now cast your nets wherever you wish—
    Never afeard are we!"
    So cried the stars to the fishermen three,
        Wynken,
        Blynken,
        And Nod.

All night long their nets they threw
    To the stars in the twinkling foam—
Then down from the skies came the wooden shoe,
    Bringing the fishermen home:
'Twas all so pretty a sail, it seemed
    As if it could not be;
And some folk thought 'twas a dream they'd dreamed
    Of sailing that beautiful sea;
    But I shall name you the fishermen three:
        Wynken,
        Blynken,
        And Nod.

Wynken and Blynken are two little eyes,
    And Nod is a little head,
And the wooden shoe that sailed the skies
    Is a wee one's trundle-bed;
So shut your eyes while Mother sings
    Of wonderful sights that be,
And you shall see the beautiful things
    As you rock on the misty sea
    Where the old shoe rocked the fishermen three,—
        Wynken,
        Blynken,
        And Nod.

                    EUGENE FIELD

FAVORITE MOTHER GOOSE RHYMES

      HEY, diddle, diddle,
      The cat and the fiddle,
    The cow jumped over the moon;
      The little dog laughed
      To see such sport,
    And the dish ran away with the spoon.

Sing a song of sixpence, a pocket full of rye,
Four and twenty blackbirds, baked in a pie;
When the pie was opened, the birds began to sing;
Wasn't that a dainty dish to set before a king?

The king was in his counting-house, counting out his money,
The queen was in the parlor, eating bread and honey,
The maid was in the garden, hanging out the clothes,
Along came a blackbird and pecked off her nose.

Humpty Dumpty sat on a wall,
Humpty Dumpty had a great fall;
All the king's horses and all the king's men
Couldn't put Humpty Dumpty together again.

Old King Cole was a merry old soul,
And a merry old soul was he;
He called for his pipe, and he called for his bowl,
And he called for his fiddlers three.

Pussy-cat, pussy-cat, where have you been?
I've been to London to look at the Queen,
Pussy-cat, pussy-cat, what did you there?
I frightened a little mouse under the chair.

Higgledy, piggledy, my black hen,
She lays eggs for gentlemen;
Sometimes nine, and sometimes ten,
Higgledy, piggledy, my black hen.

Baa, baa, black sheep, have you any wool?
Yes, sir; yes, sir, three bags full.
One for my master, one for my dame,
And one for the little boy that lives in the lane.

To market, to market, to buy a fat pig,
Home again, home again, jiggety-jig;
To market, to market, to buy a fat hog,
Home again, home again, jiggety-jog.

Hickory, dickory, dock,
The mouse ran up the clock;

The clock struck one,
The mouse ran down,
Hickory, dickory, dock.

SIMPLE Simon met a pieman
    Going to the fair;
Says Simple Simon to the pieman,
    "Let me taste your ware."

Says the pieman to Simple Simon,
    "Show me first your penny";
Says Simple Simon to the pieman.
    "Indeed I have not any."

Simple Simon went a-fishing
    For to catch a whale;
All the water he had got
    Was in his mother's pail.

Simple Simon went to look
    If plums grew on a thistle;
He pricked his fingers very much,
    Which made poor Simon whistle.

LITTLE Jack Horner sat in the corner
    Eating a Christmas pie;
He put in his thumb, and pulled out a plum,
    And said, "What a good boy am I!"

    LITTLE Miss Muffet,
      Sat on a tuffet,
Eating of curds and whey;
      There came a great spider
      That sat down beside her,
And frightened Miss Muffet away.

RIDE a cock-horse to Banbury Cross,
To see a fine lady ride on a white horse,
Rings on her fingers, and bells on her toes,
She shall have music wherever she goes.

JACK and Jill went up the hill,
    To fetch a pail of water;
Jack fell down and broke his crown
    And Jill came tumbling after.

Up Jack got and home did trot
 As fast as he could caper,
And went to bed to mend his head
 With vinegar and brown paper.

LITTLE Bo-Peep has lost her sheep,
And can't tell where to find them;
Leave them alone and they'll come home,
Wagging their tails behind them.

LITTLE Boy Blue, come blow your horn,
The sheep's in the meadow, the cow's in the corn;
But where is the boy that looks after the sheep?
He's under the haystack, fast asleep.

 A DILLAR, a dollar,
 A ten o'clock scholar,
 What makes you come so soon?
 You used to come at ten o'clock
 But now you come at noon.

 OLD Mother Hubbard
 Went to the cupboard,
To get her poor dog a bone:
 But when she got there
 The cupboard was bare,
And so the poor dog had none.

THERE was an old woman who lived in a shoe,
She had so many children she didn't know what to do;
She gave them some broth without any bread;
Then whipped them all soundly and put them to bed.

 MISTRESS MARY, quite contrary,
 How does your garden grow?
 With cockle-shells, and silver bells,
 And pretty maids all in a row.

 PETER, Peter, pumpkin eater,
 Had a wife and couldn't keep her;
 He put her in a pumpkin shell
 And there he kept her very well.

JACK SPRAT could eat no fat,
His wife could eat no lean,
And so, betwixt them both, you see,
They licked the platter clean.

THE Queen of Hearts
She made some tarts,
All on a summer's day;
The Knave of Hearts
He stole those tarts,
And with them ran away.

The King of Hearts
Called for the tarts,
And beat the Knave full sore;
The Knave of Hearts
Brought back the tarts,
And vowed he'd *steal* no more!

ONE misty, moisty morning,
When cloudy was the weather,
I met a little old man
Clothed all in leather;
He began to compliment,
And I began to grin,—
How do you do, and how do you do,
And how do you do again?

THERE was a crooked man, and he went a crooked mile.
He found a crooked sixpence against a crooked stile:
He bought a crooked cat, which caught a crooked mouse,
And they all lived together in a little crooked house.

PETER PIPER picked a peck of pickled peppers;
A peck of pickled peppers Peter Piper picked;
If Peter Piper picked a peck of pickled peppers,
Where's the peck of pickled peppers Peter Piper picked?

RHYMES ABOUT MONTHS AND DAYS

THIRTY days hath September,
April, June, and November;
All the rest have thirty-one;

February twenty-eight alone,—
Except in leap year, at which time
February's days are twenty-nine.

MONDAY's child is fair of face,
Tuesday's child is full of grace,
Wednesday's child is full of woe,
Thursday's child has far to go,
Friday's child is loving and giving,
Saturday's child works hard for its living,
And a child that's born on the Sabbath day
Is fair and wise and good and gay.

THEY that wash on Monday
Have all the week to dry;
They that wash on Tuesday
Are not so much awry;
They that wash on Wednesday
Are not so much to blame;
They that wash on Thursday,
Wash for shame;
They that wash on Friday,
Wash in need;
And they that wash on Saturday,
Oh, they are slovens, indeed.

A SWARM of bees in May
Is worth a load of hay;
A swarm of bees in June
Is worth a silver spoon;
A swarm of bees in July
Is not worth a fly.

RHYMES ABOUT THE WEATHER

RAIN before seven,
Fair by eleven.

A SUNSHINY shower
Won't last half an hour.

EVENING red and morning gray
Set the traveller on his way,
But evening gray and morning red,
Bring the rain upon his head.

RAINBOW at night
Is the sailor's delight;

Rainbow at morning,
Sailors, take warning.

MARCH winds and April showers
Bring forth May flowers.

SOME PROVERBS IN VERSE

Early to bed
Early to rise
Makes a man healthy, wealthy and wise.

If wishes were horses,
Beggars would ride.

A man of words, and not of deeds,
Is like a garden full of weeds.

Needles and pins, needles and pins,
When a man marries his trouble begins.

If "ifs" and "ands"
Were pots and pans,
There would be no need for tinkers!

See a pin and pick it up,
All the day you'll have good luck.

For want of a nail, the shoe was lost;
For want of a shoe, the horse was lost;
For want of a horse, the rider was lost;
For want of the rider, the battle was lost;
For want of the battle, the kingdom was lost;
And all from the want of a horseshoe nail.

THE HOUSE THAT JACK BUILT

This is the house that Jack built.

This is the malt
That lay in the house that Jack built.

This is the rat
That ate the malt
That lay in the house that Jack built.

This is the cat
That killed the rat
That ate the malt
That lay in the house that Jack built.

This is the cow with the crumpled horn
That tossed the dog
That worried the cat
That killed the rat
That ate the malt
That lay in the house that Jack built.

This is the maiden all forlorn
That milked the cow with the crumpled horn
That tossed the dog
That worried the cat
That killed the rat
That ate the malt
That lay in the house that Jack built.

This is the man all tattered and torn
That kissed the maiden all forlorn
That milked the cow with the crumpled horn
That tossed the dog
That worried the cat
That killed the rat
That ate the malt
That lay in the house that Jack built.

This is the priest all shaven and shorn
That married the man all tattered and torn
That kissed the maiden all forlorn
That milked the cow with the crumpled horn
That tossed the dog
That worried the cat
That killed the rat
That ate the malt
That lay in the house that Jack built.

This is the cock that crowed in the morn
That waked the priest all shaven and shorn
That married the man all tattered and torn
That kissed the maiden all forlorn
That milked the cow with the crumpled horn
That tossed the dog
That worried the cat
That killed the rat
That ate the malt
That lay in the house that Jack built.

This is the farmer sowing his corn
That kept the cock that crowed in the morn
That waked the priest all shaven and shorn
That married the man all tattered and torn
That kissed the maiden all forlorn
That milked the cow with the crumpled horn
    That tossed the dog
    That worried the cat
    That killed the rat
    That ate the malt
That lay in the house that Jack built.

ANONYMOUS

DAME WIGGINS OF LEE
AND
HER SEVEN WONDERFUL CATS

DAME Wiggins of Lee
    Was a worthy old soul
As e'er threaded a needle
    Or washed in a bowl.

She held mice and rats
    In such antipathee,
That seven fine cats
    Kept Dame Wiggins of Lee.

The rats and mice scared
    By this fierce-whiskered crew,
The seven poor cats
    Soon had nothing to do;

So, as anyone idle
    She ne'er loved to see,
She sent them to school,
    Did Dame Wiggins of Lee.

The master soon wrote
    That they all of them knew
How to read the word "milk"
    And to spell the word "mew,"

And they all washed their faces
    Before they took tea.
"Were there ever such dears?"
    Said Dame Wiggins of Lee.

He had also thought well
    To comply with their wish

To spend all their play time
  In learning to fish—

For titlings; they sent her
  A present of three,
Which fried were a feast
  For Dame Wiggins of Lee.

But the Dame soon grew tired
  Of living alone;
So she sent for her cats
  From school to come home.

Each rowing a wherry,
  Returning you see:
The frolic made merry
  Dame Wiggins of Lee.

The Dame was quite pleas'd,
  And ran out to market;
And when she came back
  They were mending the carpet.

The needle each handled
  As brisk as a bee.
"Well done, my good cats!"
  Said Dame Wiggins of Lee.

To give them a treat,
  She ran out for some rice;
When she came back,
  They were skating on ice.

"I shall soon see one down,
  Aye, perhaps, two or three,
I'll bet half a crown,"
  Said Dame Wiggins of Lee.

When springtime came back,
  They had breakfast of curds
And were greatly afraid
  Of disturbing the birds.

"If you sit like good cats,
  All the seven in a tree,
They will teach you to sing,"
  Said Dame Wiggins of Lee.

So they sat in a tree
  And said "Beautiful! Hark!"

And they listened and looked
　　In the clouds for a lark.

Then sang by the fireside
　　Sym-pho-ni-ous-ly
A song without words
　　To Dame Wiggins of Lee.

They called the next day
　　On the tomtit and sparrow
And wheeled a poor sick lamb
　　Home in a barrow.

"You shall all have some sprats
　　For your humanitee,
My seven good cats,"
　　Said Dame Wiggins of Lee.

While she ran to the field
　　To look for its dam,
They were warming the bed
　　For the poor sick lamb:

They turned up the clothes
　　All as neat as could be.
"I shall ne'er want a nurse,"
　　Said Dame Wiggins of Lee.

She wished them good-night
　　And went up to bed:
When, lo! in the morning,
　　The cats were all fled.

But soon—what a fuss!
　　"Where can they all be?
Here, pussy, puss, puss!"
　　Cried Dame Wiggins of Lee.

The Dame's heart was nigh broke,
　　So she sat down to weep,
When she saw them come back
　　Each riding a sheep:

She fondled and patted
　　Each purring Tommee:
"Ah! welcome, my dears,"
　　Said Dame Wiggins of Lee.

The Dame was unable
　　Her pleasure to smother

To see the sick lamb
   Jump up to its mother.

In spite of the gout
   And the pain in her knee,
She went dancing about,
   Did Dame Wiggins of Lee.

The farmer soon heard
   Where his sheep went astray
And arrived at Dame's door
   With his faithful dog Tray.

He knocked with his crook,
   And the stranger to see,
Out of window did look
   Dame Wiggins of Lee.

For their kindness he had them
   All drawn by the team,
And gave them some field-mice
   And raspberry cream.

Said he, "All my stock
   You shall presently see,
For I *know* the cats
   Of Dame Wiggins of Lee."

He sent his maid out
   For some muffins and crumpets;
And when he turned round
   They were blowing of trumpets.

Said he, "I suppose
   She's as deaf as can be,
Or this ne'er could be borne
   By Dame Wiggins of Lee."

To show them his poultry,
   He turned them all loose,
When each nimbly leap'd
   On the back of a goose,

Which frighten'd them so
   That they ran to the sea
And half-drown'd the poor cats
   Of Dame Wiggins of Lee.

For the care of his lamb
   And their comical pranks

He gave them a ham
   And abundance of thanks.

"I wish you good-day,
   My fine fellows," said he.
"My compliments, pray,
   To Dame Wiggins of Lee."

You see them arrived
   At their Dame's welcome door;
They show her their presents
   And all their good store.

"Now come in to supper
   And sit down with me,
All welcome once more,"
   Cried Dame Wiggins of Lee.

ANONYMOUS

THREE WISE MEN OF GOTHAM

THREE wise men of Gotham
Went to sea in a bowl:
If the bowl had been stronger,
My song had been longer.

ANONYMOUS

Favorite Poems About

NATURE

THE YEAR'S AT THE SPRING

THE YEAR'S at the spring
And the day's at the morn;
Morning's at seven;
The hillside's dew-pearled;
The lark's on the wing;
The snail's on the thorn:
God's in his heaven—
All's right with the world!

ROBERT BROWNING

DAFFODILS

I WANDERED lonely as a cloud
　That floats on high o'er vales and hills,
When all at once I saw a crowd,—
　A host of golden daffodils
Beside the lake, beneath the trees,
Fluttering and dancing in the breeze.

Continuous as the stars that shine
   And twinkle on the Milky Way,
They stretched in never-ending line
   Along the margin of a bay:
Ten thousand saw I, at a glance,
Tossing their heads in sprightly dance.

The waves beside them danced, but they
   Outdid the sparkling waves in glee;
A poet could not but be gay
   In such a jocund company;
I gazed—and gazed—but little thought
What wealth the show to me had brought.

For oft, when on my couch I lie,
   In vacant or in pensive mood,
They flash upon that inward eye
   Which is the bliss of solitude;
And then my heart with pleasure fills,
And dances with the daffodils.

           WILLIAM WORDSWORTH

WHEN DAFFODILS BEGIN TO PEER

WHEN daffodils begin to peer,
   With heigh! the doxy, over the dale,
Why, then comes in the sweet o' the year;
   For the red blood reigns in the winter's pale.

The white sheet bleaching on the hedge,
   With heigh! the sweet birds, O, how they sing!
Doth set my pugging tooth on edge;
   For a quart of ale is a dish for a king.

The lark, that tirra-lirra chants,
   With heigh! with heigh! the thrush and the jay,
Are summer songs for me and my aunts,
   While we lie tumbling in the hay.

           WILLIAM SHAKESPEARE
           From "The Winter's Tale"

ROBERT OF LINCOLN

MERRILY swinging on brier and weed,
   Near to the nest of his little dame,
Over the mountain-side or mead,

Robert of Lincoln is telling his name:
 Bob-o'-link, bob-o'-link,
 Spink, spank, spink;
Snug and safe is that nest of ours,
Hidden among the summer flowers.
      Chee, chee, chee.

Robert of Lincoln is gayly dressed,
 Wearing a bright black wedding-coat;
White are his shoulders and white his crest.
 Hear him call in his merry note:
  Bob-o'-link, bob-o'-link,
  Spink, spank, spink;
Look, what a nice new coat is mine,
Sure there was never a bird so fine.
      Chee, chee, chee.

Robert of Lincoln's Quaker wife,
 Pretty and quiet, with plain brown wings,
Passing at home a patient life,
 Broods in the grass while her husband sings:
  Bob-o'-link, bob-o'-link,
  Spink, spank, spink;
Brood, kind creature; you need not fear
Thieves and robbers while I am here.
      Chee, chee, chee.

Modest and shy as a nun is she;
 One weak chirp is her only note.
Braggart and prince of braggarts is he,
 Pouring boasts from his little throat:
  Bob-o'-link, bob-o'-link,
  Spink, spank, spink;
Never was I afraid of man;
Catch me, cowardly knaves, if you can!
      Chee, chee, chee.

Six white eggs on a bed of hay,
 Flecked with purple, a pretty sight!
There as the mother sits all day,
 Robert is singing with all his might:
  Bob-o'-link, bob-o'-link,
  Spink, spank, spink;
Nice good wife, that never goes out,
Keeping house while I frolic about.
      Chee, chee, chee.

Soon as the little ones chip the shell,
   Six wide mouths are open for food;
Robert of Lincoln bestirs him well,
   Gathering seeds for the hungry brood.
     Bob-o'-link, bob-o'-link,
     Spink, spank, spink;
This new life is likely to be
Hard for a gay young fellow like me.
               Chee, chee, chee.

Robert of Lincoln at length is made
   Sober with work, and silent with care;
Off is his holiday garment laid,
   Half forgotten that merry air:
     Bob-o'-link, bob-o'-link,
     Spink, spank, spink;
Nobody knows but my mate and I
Where our nest and our nestlings lie.
               Chee, chee, chee.

Summer wanes; the children are grown;
   Fun and frolic no more he knows;
Robert of Lincoln's a humdrum crone;
   Off he flies, and we sing as he goes:
     Bob-o'-link, bob-o'-link,
     Spink, spank, spink;
When you can pipe that merry old strain,
Robert of Lincoln, come back again.
               Chee, chee, chee.
         WILLIAM CULLEN BRYANT

LOVELIEST OF TREES

LOVELIEST of trees, the cherry now
Is hung with bloom along the bough,
And stands about the woodland ride
Wearing white for Eastertide.

Now, of my threescore years and ten,
Twenty will not come again,
And take from seventy springs a score,
It only leaves me fifty more.

And since to look at things in bloom
Fifty springs are little room,
About the woodlands I will go
To see the cherry hung with snow.
        A. E. HOUSMAN

WHAT IS SO RARE AS A DAY IN JUNE

AND what is so rare as a day in June?
   Then, if ever, come perfect days;
Then Heaven tries the earth if it be in tune,
   And over it softly her warm ear lays:
Whether we look, or whether we listen,
We hear life murmur, or see it glisten;
Every clod feels a stir of might,
   An instinct within it that reaches and towers,
And, groping blindly above it for light,
   Climbs to a soul in grass and flowers;
The flush of life may well be seen
   Thrilling back over hills and valleys;
The cowslip startles in meadows green,
   The buttercup catches the sun in its chalice,
And there's never a leaf nor a blade too mean
   To be some happy creature's palace;
The little bird sits at his door in the sun,
   Atilt like a blossom among the leaves,
And lets his illumined being o'errun
   With the deluge of summer it receives;
His mate feels the eggs beneath her wings,
And the heart in her dumb breast flutters and sings;
He sings to the wide world, and she to her nest,—
In the nice ear of Nature which song is the best?

Now is the high tide of the year,
   And whatever of life hath ebbed away
Comes flooding back, with a ripply cheer,
   Into every bare inlet and creek and bay;
Now the heart is so full that a drop overfills it,
We are happy now because God wills it;
No matter how barren the past may have been,
'T is enough for us now that the leaves are green;
We sit in the warm shade and feel right well
How the sap creeps up and the blossoms swell;
We may shut our eyes, but we cannot help knowing
That skies are clear and grass is growing;
The breeze comes whispering in our ear,
That dandelions are blossoming near,
That maize has sprouted, that streams are flowing,
That the river is bluer than the sky,
That the robin is plastering his house hard by;
And if the breeze kept the good news back,

For other couriers we should not lack;
   We could guess it all by yon heifer's lowing,
And hark! how clear bold chanticleer,
Warmed with the new wine of the year,
   Tells all in his lusty crowing!

JAMES RUSSELL LOWELL
From "The Vision of Sir Launfal"

TO A SKYLARK

HAIL to thee, blithe spirit!
   Bird thou never wert,
That from heaven, or near it,
   Pourest thy full heart
In profuse strains of unpremeditated art.

Higher still and higher
   From the earth thou springest,
Like a cloud of fire;
   The blue deep thou wingest,
And singing still dost soar, and soaring ever singest.

In the golden lightning
   Of the setting sun,
O'er which clouds are brightening,
   Thou dost float and run;   .
Like an unbodied joy whose race is just begun.

The pale purple even
   Melts around thy flight;
Like a star of heaven,
   In the broad daylight
Thou art unseen, but yet I hear thy shrill delight.

Keen as are the arrows
   Of that silver sphere,
Whose intense lamp narrows
   In the white dawn clear,
Until we hardly see, we feel that it is there.

All the earth and air
   With thy voice is loud,
As, when night is bare,
   From one lonely cloud
The moon rains out her beams, and heaven is overflowed.

What thou art we know not;
   What is most like thee?

From rainbow clouds there flow not
   Drops so bright to see,
As from thy presence showers a rain of melody.

Like a poet hidden
   In the light of thought,
Singing hymns unbidden,
   Till the world is wrought
To sympathy with hopes and fears it heeded not;

Like a high-born maiden
   In a palace tower,
Soothing her love-laden
   Soul in secret hour
With music sweet as love, which overflows her bower;

Like a glow-worm golden,
   In a dell of dew,
Scattering unbeholden
   Its aerial hue
Among the flowers and grass which screen it from the view;

Like a rose embowered
   In its own green leaves,
By warm winds deflowered,
   Till the scent it gives
Makes faint with too much sweet these heavy-wingèd thieves.

Sound of vernal showers
   On the twinkling grass,
Rain-awakened flowers,
   All that ever was
Joyous and fresh and clear thy music doth surpass.

Teach us, sprite or bird,
   What sweet thoughts are thine;
I have never heard
   Praise of love or wine
That panted forth a flood of rapture so divine.

Chorus Hymeneal,
   Or triumphal chaunt,
Matched with thine would be all
   But an empty vaunt,
A thing wherein we feel there is some hidden want.

What objects are the fountains
   Of thy happy strain?
What fields, or waves, or mountains?
   What shapes of sky or plain?
What love of thine own kind? what ignorance of pain?

With thy clear keen joyance
   Languor cannot be:
Shadow of annoyance
   Never came near thee:
Thou lovest; but ne'er knew love's sad satiety.

Waking or asleep,
   Thou of death must deem
Things more true and deep
   Than we mortals dream,
Or how could thy notes flow in such a crystal stream?

We look before and after,
   And pine for what is not:
Our sincerest laughter
   With some pain is fraught;
Our sweetest songs are those that tell of saddest thought.

Yet if we could scorn
   Hate, and pride, and fear:
If we were things born
   Not to shed a tear,
I know not how thy joy we ever should come near.

Better than all measures
   Of delightful sound,
Better than all treasures
   That in books are found,
Thy skill to poet were, thou scorner of the ground!

Teach me half the gladness
   That thy brain must know,
Such harmonious madness
   From my lips would flow,
The world should listen then, as I am listening now.

                PERCY BYSSHE SHELLEY

MY GARDEN IS A PLEASANT PLACE

My GARDEN is a pleasant place
Of sun glory and leaf grace.
There is an ancient cherry tree
Where yellow warblers sing to me,
And an old grape arbor, where.
A robin builds her nest, and there
Above the lima beans and peas
She croons her little melodies,

Her blue eggs hidden in the green
Fastness of that leafy screen.
Here are striped zinnias that bees
Fly far to visit; and sweet peas,
Like little butterflies newborn,
And over by the tasseled corn
Are sunflowers and hollyhocks,
And pink and yellow four-o'clocks.
Here are hummingbirds that come
To seek the tall delphinium—
Songless bird and scentless flower
Communing in a golden hour.

There is no blue like the blue cup
The tall delphinium holds up,
Not sky, nor distant hill, nor sea,
Sapphire, nor lapis lazuli.

My lilac trees are old and tall;
I cannot reach their bloom at all.
They send their perfume over trees
And roofs and streets, to find the bees.

I wish some power would touch my ear
With magic touch, and make me hear
What all the blossoms say, and so
I might know what the winged things know.
I'd hear the sunflower's mellow pipe,
"Goldfinch, goldfinch, my seeds are ripe!"
I'd hear the pale wistaria sing,
"Moon moth, moon moth, I'm blossoming!"

I'd hear the evening primrose cry,
"Oh, firefly! come, firefly!"
And I would learn the jeweled word
The ruby-throated hummingbird
Drops into cups of larkspur blue,
And I would sing them all for you!

My garden is a pleasant place
Of moon glory and wind grace.
O friend, wherever you may be,
Will you not come to visit me?
Over fields and streams and hills,
I'll pipe like yellow daffodils,
And every little wind that blows
Shall take my message as it goes.
A heart may travel very far
To come where its desires are,

Oh, may some power touch my ear,
And grant me grace, and make you hear!

LOUISE DRISCOLL

TREES

I THINK that I shall never see
A poem lovely as a tree.

A tree whose hungry mouth is prest
Against the earth's sweet flowing breast;

A tree that looks at God all day,
And lifts her leafy arms to pray;

A tree that may in Summer wear
A nest of robins in her hair;

Upon whose bosom snow has lain;
Who intimately lives with rain.

Poems are made by fools like me,
But only God can make a tree.

JOYCE KILMER

SEA-BIRDS

O LONESOME sea-gull, floating far
  Over the ocean's icy waste,
Aimless and wide thy wanderings are,
    Forever vainly seeking rest:—
    Where is thy mate, and where thy nest?

'Twixt wintry sea and wintry sky,
  Cleaving the keen air with thy breast,
Thou sailest slowly, solemnly;
    No fetter on thy wing is pressed:—
    Where is thy mate, and where thy nest?

O restless, homeless human soul,
  Following for aye thy nameless quest,
The gulls float, and the billows roll;
    Thou watchest still, and questionest:—
    Where is *thy* mate, and where thy nest?

ELIZABETH AKERS ALLEN

QUIET WORK

ONE LESSON, Nature, let me learn from thee,
One lesson which in every wind is blown,
One lesson of two duties kept at one
Though the loud world proclaim their enmity—
Of toil unsevered from tranquillity;
Of labor, that in lasting fruit outgrows
Far noisier schemes, accomplished in repose,
Too great for haste, too high for rivalry.

Yes, while on earth a thousand discords ring,
Man's fitful uproar mingling with his toil,
Still do thy sleepless ministers move on,
Their glorious tasks in silence perfecting;
Still working, blaming still our vain turmoil;
Laborers that shall not fail, when man is gone.

MATTHEW ARNOLD

GOD'S WORLD

O WORLD, I cannot hold thee close enough!
  Thy winds, thy wide grey skies!
  Thy mists, that roll and rise!
Thy woods, this autumn day, that ache and sag
And all but cry with colour! That gaunt crag
To crush! To lift the lean of that black bluff!
World, World, I cannot get thee close enough!

Long have I known a glory in it all,
  But never knew I this;
  Here such a passion is
As stretcheth me apart,—Lord, I do fear
Thou'st made the world too beautiful this year;
My soul is all but out of me,—let fall
No burning leaf; prithee, let no bird call.

EDNA ST. VINCENT MILLAY

THE WIND

WHO HAS SEEN the wind?
  Neither I nor you.
But when the leaves hang trembling,
  The wind is passing through.

Who has seen the wind?
 Neither you nor I.
But when the trees bow down their heads,
 The wind is passing by.
    CHRISTINA GEORGINA ROSSETTI

FAR FROM THE MADDING CROWD

IT SEEMS to me I'd like to go
Where bells ne'er ring or whistles blow;
Where clocks ne'er strike and gongs ne'er sound,
But where there's stillness all around.

Not real still stillness—just the trees'
Low whisperings or the croon of bees;
The drowsy tinkling of the rill,
Or twilight song of whippoorwill.

'Twould be a joy could I behold
The dappled fields of green and gold,
Or in the cool, sweet clover lie
And watch the cloud-ships drifting by.

I'd like to find some quaint old boat,
And fold its oars, and with it float
Along the lazy, limpid stream
Where water-lilies drowse and dream.

Sometimes it seems to me I must
Just quit the city's din and dust,
For fields of green and skies of blue;
And, say! how does it seem to you?
    NIXON WATERMAN

SONNET

To ONE who has been long in city pent,
 'Tis very sweet to look into the fair
 And open face of heaven,—to breathe a prayer
Full in the smile of the blue firmament.
Who is more happy, when, with heart content,
 Fatigued he sinks into some pleasant lair
 Of wavy grass, and reads a debonair
And gentle tale of love and languishment?
 Returning home at evening, with an ear
Catching the notes of Philomel,—an eye

Watching the sailing cloudlet's bright career,
He mourns that day so soon has glided by:
E'en like the passage of an angel's tear
That falls through the clear ether silently.

JOHN KEATS

THE BROOK'S SONG

I COME from haunts of coot and hern,
   I make a sudden sally,
And sparkle out among the fern,
   To bicker down a valley.

By thirty hills I hurry down,
   Or slip between the ridges,
By twenty thorps, a little town,
   And half a hundred bridges.

Till last by Philip's farm I flow
   To join the brimming river,
For men may come and men may go,
   But I go on for ever.

I chatter over stony ways,
   In little sharps and trebles,
I bubble into eddying bays,
   I babble on the pebbles.

With many a curve my banks I fret
   By many a field and fallow,
And many a fairy foreland set
   With willow-weed and mallow.

I chatter, chatter, as I flow
   To join the brimming river,
For men may come and men may go,
   But I go on for ever.

I wind about, and in and out,
   With here a blossom sailing,
And here and there a lusty trout,
   And here and there a grayling,

And here and there a foamy flake
   Upon me, as I travel
With many a silvery water-break
   Above the golden gravel,

And draw them all along, and flow
   To join the brimming river,
For men may come and men may go,
   But I go on for ever.

I steal by lawns and grassy plots,
   I slide by hazel covers;
I move the sweet forget-me-nots
   That grow for happy lovers.

I slip, I slide, I gloom, I glance,
   Among my skimming swallows;
I make the netted sunbeam dance
   Against my sandy shallows.

I murmur under moon and stars
   In brambly wildernesses;
I linger by my shingly bars;
   I loiter round my cresses;

And out again I curve and flow
   To join the brimming river,
For men may come and men may go,
   But I go on for ever.

                    ALFRED TENNYSON

                    From "The Brook"

FLOW GENTLY, SWEET AFTON

Flow gently, sweet Afton, amang thy green braes;
   Flow gently, I'll sing thee a song in thy praise;
My Mary's asleep by thy murmuring stream,
   Flow gently, sweet Afton, disturb not her dream.
Thou stock-dove, whose echo resounds from the hill,
   Ye wild whistling blackbirds in yon thorny dell,
Thou green-crested lapwing, thy screaming forbear,
   I charge you, disturb not my slumbering fair.

How lofty, sweet Afton, thy neighboring hills,
   Far marked with the courses of clear-winding rills!
There daily I wander, as morn rises high,
   My flocks and my Mary's sweet cot in my eye.
How pleasant thy banks and green valleys below,
   Where wild in the woodlands the primroses blow!
There oft, as mild evening creeps over the lea,
   The sweet-scented birk shades my Mary and me.

Thy crystal stream, Afton, how lovely it glides,
  And winds by the cot where my Mary resides!
How wanton thy waters her snowy feet lave,
  As, gath'ring sweet flow'rets, she stems thy clear wave!
Flow gently, sweet Afton, amang thy green braes,
  Flow gently, sweet river, the theme of my lays;
My Mary's asleep by thy murmuring stream,
  Flow gently, sweet Afton, disturb not her dream.

ROBERT BURNS

SONG OF THE CHATTAHOOCHEE

Out of the hills of Habersham,
  Down the valleys of Hall,
I hurry amain to reach the plain,
Run the rapid and leap the fall,
Split at the rock and together again,
Accept my bed, or narrow or wide,
And flee from folly on every side
With a lover's pain to attain the plain
  Far from the hills of Habersham,
  Far from the valleys of Hall.

All down the hills of Habersham,
  All through the valleys of Hall,
The rushes cried *Abide, abide,*
The wilful waterweeds held me thrall,
The laving laurel turned my tide,
The ferns and the fondling grass said *Stay,*
The dewberry dipped for to work delay,
And the little reeds sighed *Abide, abide.*
  Here in the hills of Habersham,
  Here in the valleys of Hall.

High o'er the hills of Habersham,
  Veiling the valleys of Hall,
The hickory told me manifold
Fair tales of shade, the poplar tall
Wrought me her shadowy self to hold,
The chestnut, the oak, the walnut, the pine,
Overleaning, with flickering meaning and sign,
Said, *Pass not, so cold, these manifold*
  Deep shades of the hills of Habersham,
  These glades in the valleys of Hall.

And oft in the hills of Habersham,
  And oft in the valleys of Hall,

The white quartz shone, and the smooth brook-stone
Did bar me of passage with friendly brawl,
And many a luminous jewel lone
—Crystals clear or a-cloud with mist,
Ruby, garnet and amethyst—
Made lures with the lights of streaming stone
    In the clefts of the hills of Habersham,
    In the beds of the valleys of Hall.

    But oh, not the hills of Habersham,
    And oh, not the valleys of Hall
Avail: I am fain for to water the plain.
Downward the voices of Duty call—
Downward, to toil and be mixed with the main.
The dry fields burn, and the mills are to turn,
And a myriad flowers mortally yearn,
And the lordly main from beyond the plain
    Calls o'er the hills of Habersham,
    Calls through the valleys of Hall.

                SIDNEY LANIER

NATURE

O NATURE! I do not aspire
To be the highest in thy choir,—
To be a meteor in thy sky,
Or comet that may range on high;
Only a zephyr that may blow
Among the reeds by the river low;
Give me thy most privy place
Where to run my airy race.

In some withdrawn, unpublic mead
Let me sigh upon a reed,
Or in the woods, with leafy din,
Whisper the still evening in:
Some still work give me to do,—
Only—be it near to you!

For I'd rather be thy child
And pupil, in the forest wild,
Than be the king of men elsewhere,
And most sovereign slave of care;
To have one moment of thy dawn,
Than share the city's year forlorn.

            HENRY DAVID THOREAU

ODE TO A BUTTERFLY

Thou spark of life that wavest wings of gold,
Thou songless wanderer mid the songful birds,
With Nature's secrets in thy tints unrolled
Through gorgeous cipher, past the reach of words,
    Yet dear to every child
    In glad pursuit beguiled,
Living his unspoiled days mid flowers and flocks and herds!

Thou wingèd blossom, liberated thing,
What secret tie binds thee to other flowers,
Still held within the garden's fostering?
Will they too soar with the completed hours,
    Take flight, and be like thee
    Irrevocably free,
Hovering at will o'er their parental bowers?

Or is thy luster drawn from heavenly hues,—
A sumptuous drifting fragment of the sky,
Caught when the sunset its last glance imbues
With sudden splendor, and the tree-tops high
    Grasp that swift blazonry,
    Then lend those tints to thee,
On thee to float a few short hours, and die?

Birds have their nests; they rear their eager young,
And flit on errands all the livelong day;
Each fieldmouse keeps the homestead whence it sprung;
But thou art Nature's freeman,—free to stray
    Unfettered through the wood,
    Seeking thine airy food,
The sweetness spiced on every blossomed spray.

The garden one wide banquet spreads for thee,
O daintiest reveller of the joyous earth!
One drop of honey gives satiety;
A second draught would drug thee past all mirth.
    Thy feast no orgy shows;
    Thy calm eyes never close,
Thou soberest sprite to which the sun gives birth.

And yet the soul of man upon thy wings
Forever soars in aspiration; thou
His emblem of the new career that springs
When death's arrest bids all his spirit bow.

He seeks his hope in thee
Of immortality,
Symbol of life, me with such faith endow!

THOMAS WENTWORTH HIGGINSON

THE SANDPIPER

Across the narrow beach we flit,
    One little sandpiper and I,
And fast I gather, bit by bit,
    The scattered driftwood bleached and dry.
The wild waves reach their hands for it,
    The wild wind raves, the tide runs high,
As up and down the beach we flit,—
    One little sandpiper and I.

Above our heads the sullen clouds
    Scud black and swift across the sky;
Like silent ghosts in misty shrouds
    Stand out the white lighthouses high.
Almost as far as eye can reach
    I see the close-reefed vessels fly,
As fast we flit along the beach,—
    One little sandpiper and I.

I watch him as he skims along,
    Uttering his sweet and mournful cry.
He starts not at my fitful song,
    Or flash of fluttering drapery.
He has no thought of any wrong;
    He scans me with a fearless eye:
Staunch friends are we, well tried and strong,
    The little sandpiper and I.

Comrade, where wilt thou be to-night
    When the loosed storm breaks furiously?
My driftwood fire will burn so bright!
    To what warm shelter canst thou fly?
I do not fear for thee, though wroth
    The tempest rushes through the sky:
For are we not God's children both,
    Thou, little sandpiper, and I?

CELIA THAXTER

TO THE MAN-OF-WAR-BIRD

Thou who hast slept all night upon the storm,
Waking renewed on thy prodigious pinions,
(Burst the wild storm? above it thou ascended'st,
And rested on the sky, thy slave that cradled thee,)
Now a blue point, far, far in heaven floating,
As to the light emerging here on deck I watch thee,
(Myself a speck, a point on the world's floating vast.)

Far, far at sea,
After the night's fierce drifts have strewn the shore with
        wrecks,
With re-appearing day as now so happy and serene,
The rosy and elastic dawn, the flashing sun,
The limpid spread of air cerulean,
Thou also re-appearest.

Thou born to match the gale, (thou art all wings,)
To cope with heaven and earth and sea and hurricane,
Thou ship of air that never furl'st thy sails,
Days, even weeks untired and onward, through spaces,
        realms gyrating,
At dusk that look'st on Senegal, at morn America,
That sport'st amid the lightning-flash and thunder-cloud,
In them, in thy experiences, hadst thou my soul,
What joys! what joys were thine!

                              WALT WHITMAN

ODE TO A NIGHTINGALE

My heart aches, and a drowsy numbness pains
    My sense, as though of hemlock I had drunk,
Or emptied some dull opiate to the drains
        One minute past, and Lethe-wards had sunk:
'Tis not through envy of thy happy lot,
    But being too happy in thine happiness,—
        That thou, light-wingèd Dryad of the trees,
            In some melodious plot
Of beechen green, and shadows numberless,
    Singest of summer in full-throated ease.

O, for a draught of vintage! that hath been
    Cool'd a long age in the deep-delvèd earth,
Tasting of Flora and the country green,
    Dance, and Provençal song, and sunburnt mirth!

O for a beaker full of the warm South,
   Full of the true, the blushful Hippocrene,
     With beaded bubbles winking at the brim,
       And purple-stained mouth;
   That I might drink, and leave the world unseen,
     And with thee fade away into the forest dim:

Fade far away, dissolve, and quite forget
   What thou among the leaves has never known,
The weariness, the fever, and the fret
   Here, where men sit and hear each other groan;
Where palsy shakes a few, sad, last gray hairs,
     Where youth grows pale, and spectre-thin, and dies;
       Where but to think is to be full of sorrow
       And leaden-eyed despairs,
   Where Beauty cannot keep her lustrous eyes,
     Or new Love pine at them beyond to-morrow.

Away! away! for I will fly to thee,
   Not charioted by Bacchus and his pards,
But on the viewless wings of Poesy,
   Though the dull brain perplexes and retards:
Already with thee! tender is the night,
   And haply the Queen-Moon is on her throne,
     Cluster'd around by all her starry Fays;
       But here there is no light,
   Save what from heaven is with the breezes blown
     Through verdurous glooms and winding mossy ways.

I cannot see what flowers are at my feet,
   Nor what soft incense hangs upon the boughs,
But, in embalmed darkness, guess each sweet
   Wherewith the seasonable month endows
The grass, the thicket, and the fruit-tree wild;
     White hawthorn, and the pastoral eglantine;
       Fast fading violets cover'd up in leaves;
       And mid-May's eldest child,
   The coming musk-rose, full of dewy wine,
     The murmurous haunt of flies on summer eves.

Darkling I listen; and for many a time
   I have been half in love with easeful Death,
Call'd him soft names in many a muséd rhyme,
   To take into the air my quiet breath;
Now more than ever seems it rich to die,
   To cease upon the midnight with no pain,
     While thou art pouring forth thy soul abroad

In such an ecstasy!
  Still wouldst thou sing, and I have ears in vain—
    To thy high requiem become a sod.

Thou wast not born for death, immortal Bird!
  No hungry generations tread thee down;
The voice I hear this passing night was heard
  In ancient days by emperor and clown:
Perhaps the self-same song that found a path
    Through the sad heart of Ruth, when, sick for home,
      She stood in tears amid the alien corn;
        The same that oft-times hath
    Charm'd magic casements, opening on the foam
      Of perilous seas, in faery lands forlorn.

Forlorn! the very word is like a bell
  To toll me back from thee to my sole self!
Adieu! the fancy cannot cheat so well
  As she is famed to do, deceiving elf.
Adieu! adieu! thy plaintive anthem fades
    Past the near meadows, over the still stream,
      Up the hill-side; and now 'tis buried deep
        In the next valley-glades:
    Was it a vision, or a waking dream?
    Fled is that music:—do I wake or sleep?

JOHN KEATS

ODE TO EVENING

IF AUGHT of oaten stop or pastoral song
May hope, chaste Eve, to soothe thy modest ear
    Like thy own solemn springs,
    Thy springs, and dying gales;

O Nymph reserved,—while now the bright-hair'd sun
Sits in yon western tent, whose cloudy skirts
    With brede ethereal wove,
    O'erhang his wavy bed,

Now air is hush'd, save where the weak-eyed bat
With short shrill shriek flits by on leathern wing,
    Or where the beetle winds
    His small but sullen horn,

As oft he rises midst the twilight path,
Against the pilgrim borne in heedless hum,—
    Now teach me, maid composed,
    To breathe some soften'd strain

Whose numbers, stealing through thy dark'ning vale,
May not unseemly with its stillness suit;
　　　As musing slow I hail
　　　Thy genial loved return.

For when thy folding star arising shows
His paly circlet, at his warning lamp
　　　The fragrant Hours, and Elves
　　　Who slept in flowers the day.

And many a Nymph who wreathes her brows with sedge,
And sheds the freshening dew, and, lovelier still,
　　　The pensive Pleasures sweet,
　　　Prepare thy shadowy car.

Then let me rove some wild and heathy scene;
Or find some ruin, 'midst its dreary dells,
　　　Whose walls more awful nod
　　　By thy religious gleams.

Or, if chill blustering winds, or driving rain,
Prevent my willing feet, be mine the hut
　　　That, from the mountain's side,
　　　Views wilds, and swelling floods,

And hamlets brown, and dim-discovered spires;
And hears their simple bell; and marks o'er all
　　　Thy dewy fingers draw
　　　The gradual dusky veil,

While Spring shall pour his showers, as oft he wont,
And bathe thy breathing tresses, meekest Eve!
　　　While Summer loves to sport
　　　Beneath thy lingering light;

While sallow Autumn fills thy lap with leaves;
Or Winter, yelling through the troublous air,
　　　Affrights thy shrinking train,
　　　And rudely rends thy robes;

So long, sure-found beneath the sylvan shed,
Shall Fancy, Friendship, Science, smiling Peace,
　　　Thy gentlest influence own,
　　　And love thy favorite name!

WILLIAM COLLINS

THE LAST ROSE OF SUMMER

'Tis the last rose of summer,
   Left blooming alone;
All her lovely companions
   Are faded and gone;
No flower of her kindred,
   No rosebud is nigh,
To reflect back her blushes,
   Or give sigh for sigh!

I'll not leave thee, thou lone one,
   To pine on the stem;
Since the lovely are sleeping,
   Go sleep thou with them.
Thus kindly I scatter
   Thy leaves o'er the bed
Where thy mates of the garden
   Lie scentless and dead.

So soon may I follow,
   When friendships decay,
And from Love's shining circle
   The gems drop away!
When true hearts lie withered,
   And fond ones are flown,
Oh! who would inhabit
   This bleak world alone?

THOMAS MOORE

ROBIN REDBREAST

Good-by, good-by to Summer!
   For Summer's nearly done;
The garden smiling faintly,
   Cool breezes in the sun;
Our thrushes now are silent,
   Our swallows flown away,—
But Robin's here in coat of brown,
   And scarlet breast-knot gay.
     Robin, Robin Redbreast,
      O Robin dear!
     Robin sings so sweetly
      In the falling of the year.

Bright yellow, red, and orange,
    The leaves come down in hosts;
The trees are Indian princes,
    But soon they'll turn to ghosts;
The scanty pears and apples
    Hang russet on the bough;
It's Autumn, Autumn, Autumn late,
    'Twill soon be Winter now.
      Robin, Robin Redbreast,
        O Robin dear!
      And what will this poor Robin do?
        For pinching days are near.

The fireside for the cricket,
    The wheat-stack for the mouse,
When trembling night-winds whistle
    And moan all round the house.
The frosty ways like iron,
    The branches plumed with snow,—
Alas! in Winter dead and dark,
    Where can poor Robin go?
      Robin, Robin Redbreast,
        O Robin dear!
      And a crumb of bread for Robin,
        His little heart to cheer!

              WILLIAM ALLINGHAM

TO THE FRINGED GENTIAN

THOU blossom bright with autumn dew,
And colored with the heaven's own blue,
That openest when the quiet light
Succeeds the keen and frosty night,

Thou comest not when violets lean
O'er wandering brooks and springs unseen,
Or columbines, in purple dressed,
Nod o'er the ground-bird's hidden nest.

Thou waitest late and com'st alone,
When woods are bare and birds are flown,
And frosts and shortening days portend
The aged year is near his end.

Then doth thy sweet and quiet eye
Look through its fringes to the sky,

Blue—blue—as if that sky let fall
A flower from its cerulean wall.

I would that thus, when I shall see
The hour of death draw near to me,
Hope, blossoming within my heart,
May look to heaven as I depart.

WILLIAM CULLEN BRYANT

OCTOBER'S BRIGHT BLUE WEATHER

O suns and skies and clouds of June,
   And flowers of June together,
Ye cannot rival for one hour
   October's bright blue weather.

When loud the humblebee makes haste,
   Belated, thriftless vagrant,
And Golden Rod is dying fast,
   And lanes with grapes are fragrant;

When Gentians roll their fringes tight,
   To save them for the morning,
And chestnuts fall from satin burrs
   Without a sound of warning;

When on the ground red apples lie
   In piles like jewels shining,
And redder still on old stone walls
   Are leaves of woodbine twining;

When all the lovely wayside things
   Their white-winged seeds are sowing,
And in the fields, still green and fair,
   Late aftermaths are growing;

When springs run low, and on the brooks,
   In idle golden freighting,
Bright leaves sink noiseless in the hush
   Of woods, for winter waiting;

When comrades seek sweet country haunts,
   By twos and twos together,
And count like misers, hour by hour,
   October's bright blue weather.

O suns and skies and flowers of June,
   Count all your boasts together,
Love loveth best of all the year
   October's bright blue weather.

HELEN HUNT JACKSON

ODE TO THE WEST WIND

I

O WILD West Wind, thou breath of Autumn's being,
Thou, from whose unseen presence the leaves dead
Are driven, like ghosts from an enchanter fleeing,

Yellow, and black, and pale, and hectic red,
Pestilence-stricken multitudes: O thou
Who chariotest to their dark wintry bed

The wingèd seeds, where they lie cold and low,
Each like a corpse within its grave, until
Thine azure sister of the Spring shall blow

Her clarion o'er the dreaming earth, and fill
(Driving sweet buds like flocks to feed in air)
With living hues and odours plain and hill:

Wild Spirit, which art moving everywhere;
Destroyer and preserver; hear, oh, hear!

II

Thou on whose stream, mid the steep sky's commotion,
Loose clouds like earth's decaying leaves are shed,
Shook from the tangled boughs of Heaven and Ocean,

Angels of rain and lightning: there are spread
On the blue surface of thine airy surge,
Like the bright hair uplifted from the head

Of some fierce Maenad, even from the dim verge
Of the horizon to the zenith's height,
The locks of the approaching storm. Thou dirge

Of the dying year, to which this closing night
Will be the dome of a vast sepulchre,
Vaulted with all thy congregated might

Of vapours, from whose solid atmosphere
Black rain, and fire, and hail will burst: oh, hear!

III

Thou who didst waken from his summer dreams
The blue Mediterranean, where he lay,
Lulled by the coil of his crystàlline streams,

Beside a pumice isle in Baiae's bay,
And saw in sleep old palaces and towers
Quivering within the wave's intenser day,

All overgrown with azure moss and flowers
So sweet, the sense faints picturing them! Thou
For whose path the Atlantic's level powers

Cleave themselves into chasms, while far below
The sea-blooms and the oozy woods which wear
The sapless foliage of the ocean, know

Thy voice, and suddenly grow gray with fear,
And tremble and despoil themselves: oh, hear!

IV

If I were a dead leaf thou mightest bear;
If I were a swift cloud to fly with thee;
A wave to pant beneath thy power, and share

The impulse of thy strength, only less free
Than thou, O uncontrollable! If even
I were as in my boyhood, and could be

The comrade of thy wanderings over heaven,
As then, when to outstrip thy skyey speed
Scarce seemed a vision; I would ne'er have striven

As thus with thee in prayer in my sore need.
Oh, lift me as a wave, a leaf, a cloud!
I fall upon the thorns of life! I bleed!

A heavy weight of hours has chained and bowed
One too like thee: tameless, and swift, and proud.

V

Make me thy lyre, even as the forest is:
What if my leaves are falling like its own!
The tumult of thy mighty harmonies

Will take from both a deep, autumnal tone,
Sweet though in sadness. Be thou, Spirit fierce,
My spirit! Be thou me, impetuous one!

Drive my dead thoughts over the universe
Like withered leaves to quicken a new birth!
And, by the incantation of this verse,

Scatter, as from an unextinguished hearth
Ashes and sparks, my words among mankind!
Be through my lips to unawakened earth

The trumpet of a prophecy! O, wind,
If Winter comes, can Spring be far behind?

PERCY BYSSHE SHELLEY

WHEN THE FROST IS ON THE PUNKIN

WHEN the frost is on the punkin and the fodder's in the shock,
And you hear the kyouck and gobble of the struttin' turkey-cock,
And the clackin' of the guineys, and the cluckin' of the hens,
And the rooster's hallylooyer as he tiptoes on the fence;
Oh, it's then's the times a feller is a-feelin' at his best,
With the risin' sun to greet him from a night of peaceful rest,
As he leaves the house, bareheaded, and goes out to feed the stock,
When the frost is on the punkin and the fodder's in the shock.

They's something kind o'harty-like about the atmusfere
When the heat of summer's over and the coolin' fall is here.—
Of course we miss the flowers, and the blossums on the trees,
And the mumble of the hummin'-birds and buzzin' of the bees;
But the air's so appetizin', and the landscape through the haze
Of a crisp and sunny morning of the airly autumn days
Is a pictur' that no painter has the colorin' to mock,—
When the frost is on the punkin and the fodder's in the shock.

The husky, rusty russel of the tossels of the corn,
And the raspin' of the tangled leaves, as golden as the morn;
The stubble in the furries—kind o' lonesome-like, but still
A-preachin' sermuns to us of the barns they growed to fill;
The straw-stack in the medder, and the reaper in the shed;
The hosses in theyr stalls below, the clover overhead,—
Oh, it sets my hart a-clickin' like the tickin' of a clock,
When the frost is on the punkin and the fodder's in the shock!

Then your apples all is gethered, and the ones a feller keeps
Is poured around the celler-floor in red and yeller heaps;
And your cider-makin' 's over, and your wimmern-folks is through
With their mince and apple butter, and theyr souse and saussage, too! . . .
I don't know how to tell it—but ef sich a thing could be
As the Angels wantin' boardin', and they'd call around on *me*—
I'd want to 'commodate 'em—all the whole-indurin' flock—
When the frost is on the punkin and the fodder's in the shock!

JAMES WHITCOMB RILEY

THE BRAVE OLD OAK

A SONG to the oak, the brave old oak,
  Who hath ruled in the greenwood long;
Here's health and renown to his broad green crown,
  And his fifty arms so strong.
There's fear in his frown when the sun goes down,
  And the fire in the west fades out;
And he showeth his might on a wild midnight,
  When the storms through his branches shout.

        Then here's to the oak, the brave old oak,
          Who stands in his pride alone;
        And still flourish he, a hale green tree,
          When a hundred years are gone!

In the days of old, when the spring with cold
  Had brightened his branches gray,
Through the grass at his feet crept maidens sweet,
  To gather the dew of May.
And on that day to the rebeck gay
  They frolicked with lovesome swains;
They are gone, they are dead, in the churchyard laid,
  But the tree it still remains.

He saw the rare times when the Christmas chimes
  Were a merry sound to hear,
When the squire's wide hall and the cottage small
  Were filled with good English cheer.
Now gold hath sway we all obey,
  And a ruthless king is he;
But he never shall send our ancient friend
  To be tossed on the stormy sea.

                    HENRY FOTHERGILL CHORLEY

WHEN THE HOUNDS OF SPRING ARE ON WINTER'S TRACES

WHEN the hounds of spring are on winter's traces,
  The mother of months in meadow or plain
Fills the shadows and windy places
  With lisp of leaves and ripple of rain;
And the brown bright nightingale amorous
Is half assuaged for Itylus,

For the Thracian ships and the foreign faces,
    The tongueless vigil, and all the pain.

Come with bows bent and with emptying of quivers,
    Maiden most perfect, lady of light,
With a noise of winds and many rivers,
    With a clamour of waters, and with might;
Bind on thy sandals, O thou most fleet,
Over the splendour and speed of thy feet;
For the faint east quickens, the wan west shivers,
    Round the feet of the day and the feet of the night.

Where shall we find her, how shall we sing to her,
    Fold our hands round her knees, and cling?
O that man's heart were as fire and could spring to her,
    Fire, or the strength of the streams that spring!
For the stars and the winds are unto her
As raiment, as songs of the harp-player;
For the risen stars and the fallen cling to her,
    And the southwest-wind and the west-wind sing.

For winter's rains and ruins are over,
    And all the season of snows and sins;
The days dividing lover and lover,
    The light that loses, the night that wins;
And time remembered is grief forgotten,
And frosts are slain and flowers begotten,
And in green underwood and cover
    Blossom by blossom the spring begins.

The full streams feed on flower of rushes,
    Ripe grasses trammel a travelling foot,
The faint fresh flame of the young year flushes
    From leaf to flower and flower to fruit;
And fruit and leaf are as gold and fire,
And the oat is heard above the lyre,
And the hoofèd heel of a satyr crushes
    The chestnut-husk at the chestnut-root.

And Pan by noon and Bacchus by night,
    Fleeter of foot than the fleet-foot kid,
Follows with dancing and fills with delight
    The Mænad and the Bassarid;
And soft as lips that laugh and hide
The laughing leaves of the trees divide,
And screen from seeing and leave in sight
    The god pursuing, the maiden hid.

The ivy falls with the Bacchanal's hair
  Over her eyebrows hiding her eyes;
The wild vine slipping down leaves bare
  Her bright breast shortening into sighs;
The wild vine slips with the weight of its leaves,
But the berried ivy catches and cleaves
To the limbs that glitter, the feet that scare,
  The wolf that follows, the fawn that flies.

ALGERNON CHARLES SWINBURNE

UNDER THE GREENWOOD TREE

    UNDER the greenwood tree
    Who loves to lie with me,
    And tune his merry note
    Unto the sweet bird's throat—
Come hither, come hither, come hither!
      Here shall he see
      No enemy
But winter and rough weather.

    Who doth ambition shun
    And loves to live i' the sun,
    Seeking the food he eats
    And pleased with what he gets—
Come hither, come hither, come hither!
      Here shall he see
      No enemy
But winter and rough weather.

WILLIAM SHAKESPEARE

THE SNOW-STORM

ANNOUNCED by all the trumpets of the sky,
Arrives the snow, and, driving o'er the fields,
Seems nowhere to alight: the whited air
Hides hills and woods, the river, and the heaven,
And veils the farm-house at the garden's end.
The sled and traveller stopped, the courier's feet
Delayed, all friends shut out, the housemates sit
Around the radiant fireplace, enclosed
In a tumultuous privacy of storm.

  Come see the north wind's masonry.
Out of an unseen quarry evermore

Furnished with tile, the fierce artificer
Curves his white bastions with projected roof
Round every windward stake, or tree, or door.
Speeding, the myriad-handed, his wild work
So fanciful, so savage, naught cares he
For number or proportion. Mockingly,
On coop or kennel he hangs Parian wreaths;
A swan-like form invests the hidden thorn;
Fills up the farmer's lane from wall to wall,
Maugre the farmer's sighs; and at the gate
A tapering turret overtops the work.
And when his hours are numbered, and the world
Is all his own, retiring, as he were not,
Leaves, when the sun appears, astonished Art
To mimic in slow structures, stone by stone,
Built in an age, the mad wind's night-work,
The frolic architecture of the snow.

RALPH WALDO EMERSON

Favorite Poems Of

CONTEMPLATION

THE DAY IS DONE

THE DAY is done, and the darkness
    Falls from the wings of Night,
As a feather is wafted downward
    From an eagle in his flight.

I see the lights of the village
    Gleam through the rain and the mist:
And a feeling of sadness comes o'er me,
    That my soul cannot resist:

A feeling of sadness and longing,
    That is not akin to pain,
And resembles sorrow only
    As the mist resembles the rain.

Come, read to me some poem,
    Some simple and heartfelt lay,
That shall soothe this restless feeling,
    And banish the thoughts of day.

Not from the grand old masters,
    Not from the bards sublime,

Whose distant footsteps echo
   Through the corridors of Time.

For, like strains of martial music,
   Their mighty thoughts suggest
Life's endless toil and endeavor;
   And to-night I long for rest.

Read from some humbler poet,
   Whose songs gush'd from his heart,
As showers from the clouds of summer,
   Or tears from the eyelids start;

Who, through long days of labor,
   And nights devoid of ease,
Still heard in his soul the music
   Of wonderful melodies.

Such songs have power to quiet
   The restless pulse of care,
And come like the benediction
   That follows after prayer.

Then read from the treasured volume
   The poem of thy choice;
And lend to the rhyme of the poet
   The beauty of thy voice.

And the night shall be fill'd with music,
   And the cares that infest the day
Shall fold their tents like the Arabs,
   And as silently steal away.

           HENRY WADSWORTH LONGFELLOW

THANATOPSIS

To HIM who in the love of Nature holds
Communion with her visible forms, she speaks
A various language; for his gayer hours
She has a voice of gladness, and a smile
And eloquence of beauty, and she glides
Into his darker musings, with a mild
And healing sympathy, that steals away
Their sharpness, ere he is aware. When thoughts
Of the last bitter hour come like a blight
Over thy spirit, and sad images
Of the stern agony, and shroud, and pall,
And breathless darkness, and the narrow house,

Make thee to shudder and grow sick at heart;—
Go forth, under the open sky, and list
To Nature's teachings, while from all around—
Earth and her waters, and the depths of air—
Comes a still voice:—
                           Yet a few days, and thee
The all-beholding sun shall see no more
In all his course; nor yet in the cold ground,
Where thy pale form was laid, with many tears,
Nor in the embrace of ocean, shall exist
Thy image. Earth, that nourished thee, shall claim
Thy growth, to be resolved to earth again,
And, lost each human trace, surrendering up
Thine individual being, shalt thou go
To mix forever with the elements,
To be a brother to the insensible rock
And to the sluggish clod, which the rude swain
Turns with his share, and treads upon. The oak
Shall send his roots abroad, and pierce thy mould.

    Yet not to thine eternal resting-place
Shalt thou retire alone, nor couldst thou wish
Couch more magnificent. Thou shalt lie down
With patriarchs of the infant world—with kings,
The powerful of the earth—the wise, the good,
Fair forms, and hoary seers of ages past,
All in one mighty sepulchre. The hills
Rock-ribbed and ancient as the sun,—the vales
Stretching in pensive quietness between;
The venerable woods—rivers that move
In majesty, and the complaining brooks
That make the meadows green; and, poured round all,
Old Ocean's gray and melancholy waste,—
Are but the solemn decorations all
Of the great tomb of man. The golden sun,
The planets, all the infinite host of heaven,
Are shining on the sad abodes of death
Through the still lapse of ages. All that tread
The globe are but a handful to the tribes
That slumber in its bosom.—Take the wings
Of morning, pierce the Barcan wilderness,
Or lose thyself in the continuous woods
Where rolls the Oregon, and hears no sound,
Save his own dashings—yet the dead are there:
And millions in those solitudes, since first
The flight of years began, have laid them down
In their last sleep—the dead reign there alone.

So shalt thou rest, and what if thou withdraw
In silence from the living, and no friend
Take note of thy departure? All that breathe
Will share thy destiny. The gay will laugh
When thou art gone, the solemn brood of care
Plod on, and each one as before will chase
His favorite phantom; yet all these shall leave
Their mirth and their employments, and shall come
And make their bed with thee. As the long train
Of ages glides away, the sons of men—
The youth in life's fresh spring, and he who goes
In the full strength of years, matron and maid,
The speechless babe, and the gray-headed man—
Shall one by one be gathered to thy side,
By those, who in their turn shall follow them.

So live, that when thy summons comes to join
The innumerable caravan, which moves
To that mysterious realm, where each shall take
His chamber in the silent halls of death,
Thou go not, like the quarry-slave at night,
Scourged to his dungeon, but, sustained and soothed
By an unfaltering trust, approach thy grave
Like one who wraps the drapery of his couch
About him, and lies down to pleasant dreams.

WILLIAM CULLEN BRYANT

FOR A' THAT AND A' THAT

Is THERE, for honest poverty,
  That hangs his head, and a' that;
The coward-slave, we pass him by,
  We dare be poor for a' that!
    For a' that, and a' that,
      Our toils obscure, and a' that,
      The rank is but the guinea's stamp,
        The man's the gowd for a' that.

What though on hamely fare we dine,
  Wear hoddin gray, and a' that;
Gie fools their silks, and knaves their wine,
  A man's a man for a' that:
    For a' that, and a' that,
      Their tinsel show, and a' that;
      The honest man, though e'er sae poor,
        Is king o' men for a' that.

Ye see yon birkie, ca'd a lord,
   Wha struts, and stares, and a' that;
Though hundreds worship at his word,
   He's but a coof for a' that:
     For a' that, and a' that:
      His riband, star, and a' that,
      The man of independent mind,
       He looks and laughs at a' that.

A prince can make a belted knight,
   A marquis, duke, and a' that;
But an honest man's aboon his might,
   Guid faith, he maunna fa' that!
     For a' that, and a' that,
      Their dignities, and a' that,
      The pith o' sense and pride o' worth,
      Are higher ranks than a' that.

Then let us pray that come it may,
   As come it will for a' that,
That sense and worth, o'er a' the earth,
   May bear the gree, and a' that.
     For a' that, and a' that,
      It's comin' yet for a' that,
      That man to man, the warld o'er,
      Shall brothers be for a' that.

                ROBERT BURNS

IN SCHOOL-DAYS

STILL SITS the school-house by the road,
   A ragged beggar sunning;
Around it still the sumachs grow,
   And blackberry-vines are running.

Within, the master's desk is seen,
   Deep scarred by raps official;
The warping floor, the battered seats,
   The jack-knife's carved initial;

The charcoal frescoes on its wall;
   Its door's worn sill, betraying
The feet that, creeping slow to school,
   Went storming out to playing!

Long years ago a winter sun
   Shone over it at setting;

Lit up its western window-panes,
　　And low eaves' icy fretting.

It touched the tangled golden curls,
　　And brown eyes full of grieving,
Of one who still her steps delayed
　　When all the school were leaving.

For near her stood the little boy
　　Her childish favor singled;
His cap pulled low upon a face
　　Where pride and shame were mingled.

Pushing with restless feet the snow
　　To right and left, he lingered;—
As restlessly her tiny hands
　　The blue-checked apron fingered.

He saw her lift her eyes; he felt
　　The soft hand's light caressing,
And heard the tremble of her voice,
　　As if a fault confessing.

"I'm sorry that I spelt the word:
　　I hate to go above you,
Because,"—the brown eyes lower fell,—
　　"Because, you see, I love you!"

Still memory to a gray-haired man
　　That sweet child-face is showing.
Dear girl! the grasses on her grave
　　Have forty years been growing!

He lives to learn, in life's hard school,
　　How few who pass above him
Lament their triumph and his loss,
　　Like her,—because they love him.

JOHN GREENLEAF WHITTIER

A PSALM OF LIFE

TELL ME NOT, in mournful numbers,
　　Life is but an empty dream!—
For the soul is dead that slumbers,
　　And things are not what they seem.

Life is real! Life is earnest!
　　And the grave is not its goal;
Dust thou art, to dust returnest,
　　Was not spoken of the soul.

Not enjoyment, and not sorrow,
   Is our destined end or way;
But to act, that each to-morrow
   Find us farther than to-day.

Art is long, and Time is fleeting,
   And our hearts, though stout and brave,
Still, like muffled drums, are beating
   Funeral marches to the grave.

In the world's broad field of battle,
   In the bivouac of Life,
Be not like dumb, driven cattle!
   Be a hero in the strife!

Trust no Future, howe'er pleasant!
   Let the dead Past bury its dead!
Act,—act in the living Present!
   Heart within, and God o'erhead!

Lives of great men all remind us
   We can make our lives sublime,
And, departing, leave behind us
   Footprints on the sands of time;

Footprints, that perhaps another,
   Sailing o'er life's solemn main,
A forlorn and shipwrecked brother,
   Seeing, shall take heart again.

Let us then, be up and doing,
   With a heart for any fate;
Still achieving, still pursuing,
   Learn to labor and to wait.

       HENRY WADSWORTH LONGFELLOW

CHARACTER OF THE HAPPY WARRIOR

WHO IS the happy Warrior? Who is he
That every man in arms should wish to be?

It is the generous spirit, who, when brought
Among the tasks of real life, hath wrought
Upon the plan that pleased his boyish thought:
Whose high endeavors are an inward light
That makes the path before him always bright:
Who, with a natural instinct to discern
What knowledge can perform, is diligent to learn;

Abides by this resolve, and stops not there,
But makes his moral being his prime care;
Who, doomed to go in company with pain,
And fear, and bloodshed, miserable train!
Turns his necessity to glorious gain;
In face of these doth exercise a power
Which is our human nature's highest dower;
Controls them and subdues, transmutes, bereaves
Of their bad influence, and their good receives:
By objects, which might force the soul to abate
Her feeling, rendered more compassionate;
Is placable—because occasions rise
So often that demand such sacrifice;
More skilful in self-knowledge, even more pure,
As tempted more; more able to endure,
As more exposed to suffering and distress;
Thence, also, more alive to tenderness.

'Tis he whose law is reason; who depends
Upon that law as on the best of friends;
Whence, in a state where men are tempted still
To evil for a guard against worse ill,
And what in act or quality is best
Doth seldom on a right foundation rest,
He labors good on good to fix, and owes
To virtue every triumph that he knows:
Who, if he rise to station of command,
Rises by open means; and there will stand
On honorable terms, or else retire,
And in himself possess his own desire;
Who comprehends his trust, and to the same
Keeps faithful with a singleness of aim;
And therefore does not stoop, nor lie in wait
For wealth, or honors, or for worldly state;
Whom they must follow; on whose head must fall,
Like showers of manna, if they come at all:
Whose powers shed round him in the common strife,
Or mild concerns of ordinary life,
A constant influence, a peculiar grace;
But who, if he be called upon to face
Some awful moment to which Heaven has joined
Great issues, good or bad for human kind,
Is happy as a lover; and attired
With sudden brightness, like a man inspired;
And, through the heat of conflict, keeps the law
In calmness made, and sees what he foresaw;
Or if an unexpected call succeed,

Come when it will, is equal to the need:
He who, though thus endued as with a sense
And faculty for storm and turbulence,
Is yet a soul whose master-bias leans
To homefelt pleasures and to gentle scenes;
Sweet images! which, wheresoe'er he be,
Are at his heart; and such fidelity
It is his darling passion to approve;
More brave for this, that he hath much to love.
'Tis, finally, the Man, who, lifted high,
Conspicuous object in a Nation's eye,
Or left unthought-of in obscurity,—
Who, with a toward or untoward lot,
Prosperous or adverse, to his wish or not—
Plays, in the many games of life, that one
Where what he most doth value must be won:
Whom neither shape of danger can dismay,
Nor thought of tender happiness betray;
Who, not content that former worth stand fast,
Looks forward, persevering to the last,
From well to better, daily self-surpassed:
Who, whether praise of him must walk the earth
For ever, and to noble deeds give birth,
Or he must fall, to sleep without his fame,
And leave a dead unprofitable name—
Finds comfort in himself and in his cause;
And, while the mortal mist is gathering, draws
His breath in confidence of Heaven's applause.

This is the happy Warrior; this is he
That every man in arms should wish to be.

WILLIAM WORDSWORTH

FREEDOM FOR THE MIND

High walls and huge the body may confine,
And iron grates obstruct the prisoner's gaze,
And massive bolts may baffle his design,
And vigilant keepers watch his devious ways:
Yet scorns the immortal mind this base control!
No chains can bind it, and no cell enclose:
Swifter than light, it flies from pole to pole,
And, in a flash, from earth to heaven it goes!
It leaps from mount to mount—from vale to vale
It wanders, plucking honeyed fruits and flowers;
It visits home, to hear the fireside tale,

Or in sweet converse pass the joyous hours.
'Tis up before the sun, roaming afar,
And, in its watches, wearies every star!

WILLIAM LLOYD GARRISON

ELEGY WRITTEN IN A COUNTRY
CHURCHYARD

THE curfew tolls the knell of parting day,
    The lowing herd winds slowly o'er the lea,
The plowman homeward plods his weary way,
    And leaves the world to darkness and to me.

Now fades the glimmering landscape on the sight,
    And all the air a solemn stillness holds,
Save where the beetle wheels his droning flight,
    And drowsy tinklings lull the distant folds:

Save that from yonder ivy-mantled tower
    The moping owl does to the moon complain
Of such as, wandering near her secret bower,
    Molest her ancient solitary reign.

Beneath those rugged elms, that yew-tree's shade,
    Where heaves the turf in many a moldering heap,
Each in his narrow cell for ever laid,
    The rude forefathers of the hamlet sleep.

The breezy call of incense-breathing morn,
    The swallow twittering from the straw-built shed,
The cock's shrill clarion, or the echoing horn,
    No more shall rouse them from their lowly bed.

For them no more the blazing hearth shall burn,
    Or busy housewife ply her evening care:
No children run to lisp their sire's return,
    Or climb his knees the envied kiss to share.

Oft did the harvest to their sickle yield,
    Their furrow oft the stubborn glebe has broke;
How jocund did they drive their team afield!
    How bowed the woods beneath their sturdy stroke!

Let not ambition mock their useful toil,
    Their homely joys, and destiny obscure;
Nor grandeur hear with a disdainful smile
    The short and simple annals of the poor.

The boast of heraldry, the pomp of power,
    And all that beauty, all that wealth e'er gave,
Awaits alike the inevitable hour.
    The paths of glory lead but to the grave.

Nor you, ye proud, impute to these the fault,
    If Memory o'er their tomb no trophies raise,
Where, through the long-drawn aisle and fretted vault
    The pealing anthem swells the note of praise.

Can storied urn or animated bust
    Back to its mansion call the fleeting breath?
Can honor's voice provoke the silent dust,
    Or flattery soothe the dull, cold ear of death?

Perhaps in this neglected spot is laid
    Some heart once pregnant with celestial fire;
Hands, that the rod of empire might have swayed,
    Or waked to ecstasy the living lyre:

But knowledge to their eyes her ample page,
    Rich with the spoils of time, did ne'er unroll;
Chill penury repressed their noble rage,
    And froze the genial current of the soul.

Full many a gem of purest ray serene
    The dark, unfathomed caves of ocean bear;
Full many a flower is born to blush unseen,
    And waste its sweetness on the desert air.

Some village Hampden, that, with dauntless breast,
    The little tyrant of his fields withstood,
Some mute, inglorious Milton here may rest,
    Some Cromwell, guiltless of his country's blood.

Th' applause of listening senates to command,
    The threats of pain and ruin to despise,
To scatter plenty o'er a smiling land,
    And read their history in a nation's eyes,

Their lot forbade: nor circumscribed alone
    Their growing virtues, but their crimes confined;
Forbade to wade through slaughter to a throne,
    And shut the gates of mercy on mankind,

The struggling pangs of conscious truth to hide,
    To quench the blushes of ingenuous shame,
Or heap the shrine of luxury and pride
    With incense kindled at the muse's flame.

Far from the madding crowd's ignoble strife,
    Their sober wishes never learned to stray;
Along the cool, sequestered vale of life
    They kept the noiseless tenor of their way.

Yet even these bones from insult to protect
    Some frail memorial still erected nigh,
With uncouth rhymes and shapeless sculpture decked,
    Implores the passing tribute of a sigh.

Their name, their years, spelt by the unlettered Muse,
    The place of fame and elegy supply:
And many a holy text around she strews,
    That teach the rustic moralist to die.

For who, to dumb Forgetfulness a prey,
    This pleasing anxious being e'er resigned,
Left the warm precincts of the cheerful day,
    Nor cast one longing lingering look behind?

On some fond breast the parting soul relies,
    Some pious drops the closing eye requires;
E'en from the tomb the voice of Nature cries,
    E'en in our ashes live their wonted fires.

For thee, who, mindful of the unhonored dead,
    Dost in these lines their artless tale relate;
If chance, by lonely contemplation led,
    Some kindred spirit shall inquire thy fate,—

Haply some hoary-headed swain may say,
    "Oft have we seen him at the peep of dawn
Brushing with hasty steps the dews away
    To meet the sun upon the upland lawn.

"There at the foot of yonder nodding beech
    That wreathes its old fantastic roots so high,
His listless length at noontide would he stretch,
    And pore upon the brook that babbles by.

"Hard by yon wood, now smiling as in scorn,
    Muttering his wayward fancies he would rove,
Now drooping, woeful-wan, like one forlorn,
    Or crazed with care, or crossed in hopeless love.

"One morn I missed him on the 'customed hill,
    Along the heath, and near his favorite tree;
Another came; nor yet beside the rill,
    Nor up the lawn, nor at the wood was he:

"The next, with dirges due in sad array,
    Slow through the church-way path we saw him borne.
Approach and read (for thou canst read) the lay
    Graved on the stone beneath yon aged thorn:"

THE EPITAPH

Here rests his head upon the lap of Earth
    A youth to Fortune and to Fame unknown;
Fair Science frowned not on his humble birth,
    And Melancholy marked him for her own.

Large was his bounty, and his soul sincere,
    Heaven did a recompense as largely send;
He gave to Misery all he had, a tear,
    He gained from Heaven ('t was all he wished) a friend.

No farther seek his merits to disclose,
    Or draw his frailties from their dread abode,
(There they alike in trembling hope repose)
    The bosom of his Father and his God.

THOMAS GRAY

LOCKSLEY HALL

COMRADES, leave me here a little, while as yet 'tis early morn,—
Leave me here, and when you want me, sound upon the bugle horn.

'T is the place, and all around it, as of old, the curlews call,
Dreary gleams about the moorland, flying over Locksley Hall:

Locksley Hall, that in the distance overlooks the sandy tracts,
And the hollow ocean-ridges roaring into cataracts.

Many a night from yonder ivied casement, ere I went to rest,
Did I look on great Orion sloping slowly to the west.

Many a night I saw the Pleiads, rising through the mellow shade,
Glitter like a swarm of fire-flies tangled in a silver braid.

Here about the beach I wandered, nourishing a youth sublime
With the fairy tales of science, and the long result of time;

When the centuries behind me like a fruitful land reposed;
When I clung to all the present for the promise that it closed;

When I dipt into the future far as human eye could see,—
Saw the vision of the world, and all the wonder that would be.

In the spring a fuller crimson comes upon the robin's breast;
In the spring the wanton lapwing gets himself another crest;

In the spring a livelier iris changes on the burnished dove;
In the spring a young man's fancy lightly turns to thoughts of love.

Then her cheek was pale and thinner than should be for one so young,
And her eyes on all my motions with a mute observance hung.

And I said, "My cousin Amy, speak, and speak the truth to me;
Trust me, cousin, all the current of my being sets to thee."

On her pallid cheek and forehead came a color and a light,
As I have seen the rosy red flushing in the northern night.

And she turned,—her bosom shaken with a sudden storm of sighs;
All the spirit deeply dawning in the dark of hazel eyes,—

Saying, "I have hid my feelings, fearing they should do me wrong;"
Saying, "Dost thou love me, cousin?" weeping, "I have loved thee
    long."

Love took up the glass of time, and turned it in his glowing hands;
Every moment, lightly shaken, ran itself in golden sands.

Love took up the harp of life, and smote on all the chords with might;
Smote the chord of self, that, trembling, passed in music out of sight.

Many a morning on the moorland did we hear the copses ring,
And her whisper thronged my pulses with the fulness of the spring.

Many an evening by the waters did we watch the stately ships,
And our spirits rushed together at the touching of the lips.

O my cousin, shallow-hearted! O my Amy, mine no more!
O the dreary, dreary moorland! O the barren, barren shore!

Falser than all fancy fathoms, falser than all songs have sung,—
Puppet to a father's threat, and servile to a shrewish tongue!

Is it well to wish thee happy?—having known me; to decline
On a range of lower feelings and a narrower heart than mine!

Yet it shall be: thou shalt lower to his level day by day,
What is fine within thee growing coarse to sympathize with clay.

As the husband is, the wife is; thou art mated with a clown,
And the grossness of his nature will have weight to drag thee down.

He will hold thee, when his passion shall have spent its novel force,
Something better than his dog, a little dearer than his horse.

What is this? his eyes are heavy,—think not they are glazed with wine.
Go to him; it is thy duty,—kiss him; take his hand in thine.

It may be my lord is weary, that his brain is overwrought,—
Soothe him with thy finer fancies, touch him with thy lighter thought.

He will answer to the purpose, easy things to understand,—
Better thou wert dead before me, though I slew thee with my hand.

Better thou and I were lying, hidden from the heart's disgrace,
Rolled in one another's arms, and silent in a last embrace.

Cursed be the social wants that sin against the strength of youth!
Cursed be the social lies that warp us from the living truth!

Cursed be the sickly forms that err from honest Nature's rule!
Cursed be the gold that gilds the straitened forehead of the fool!

Well—'tis well that I should bluster!—Hadst thou less unworthy proved,
Would to God—for I have loved thee more than ever wife was loved.

Am I mad, that I should cherish that which bears but bitter fruit?
I will pluck it from my bosom, though my heart be at the root.

Never! though my mortal summers to such length of years should come
As the many-wintered crow that leads the clanging rookery home.

Where is comfort? in division of the records of the mind?
Can I part her from herself, and love her, as I knew her, kind?

I remember one that perished; sweetly did she speak and move;
Such a one do I remember, whom to look at was to love.

Can I think of her as dead, and love her for the love she bore?
No,—she never loved me truly; love is love for evermore.

Comfort? comfort scorned of devils! this is truth the poet sings,
That a sorrow's crown of sorrow is remembering happier things.

Drug thy memories, lest thou learn it, lest thy heart be put to proof,
In the dead, unhappy night, and when the rain is on the roof.

Like a dog, he hunts in dreams; and thou art staring at the wall,
Where the dying night-lamp flickers, and the shadows rise and fall.

Then a hand shall pass before thee, pointing to his drunken sleep,
To thy widowed marriage-pillows, to the tears that thou wilt weep.

Thou shalt hear the "Never, never," whispered by the phantom years,
And a song from out the distance in the ringing of thine ears.

And an eye shall vex thee, looking ancient kindness on thy pain.
Turn thee, turn thee on thy pillow; get thee to thy rest again.

Nay, but Nature brings thee solace; for a tender voice will cry;
'Tis a purer life than thine, a lip to drain thy trouble dry.

Baby lips will laugh me down; my latest rival brings thee rest,—
Baby fingers, waxen touches, press me from the mother's breast.

O, the child too clothes the father with a dearness not his due.
Half is thine and half is his; it will be worthy of the two.

O, I see thee old and formal, fitted to thy petty part,
With a little hoard of maxims preaching down a daughter's heart.

"They were dangerous guides, the feelings—she herself was not
       exempt—
Truly, she herself had suffered"—Perish in thy self-contempt!

Overlive it—lower yet—be happy! wherefore should I care?
I myself must mix with action, lest I wither by despair.

What is that which I should turn to, lighting upon days like these?
Every door is barred with gold, and opens but to golden keys.

Every gate is thronged with suitors, all the markets overflow.
I have but an angry fancy: what is that which I should do?

I had been content to perish, falling on the foeman's ground,
When the ranks are rolled in vapor, and the winds are laid with sound.

But the jingling of the guinea helps the hurt that honor feels,
And the nations do but murmur, snarling at each other's heels.

Can I but relive in sadness? I will turn that earlier page.
Hide me from my deep emotion, O thou wondrous mother-age!

Make me feel the wild pulsation that I felt before the strife,
When I heard my days before me, and the tumult of my life;

Yearning for the large excitement that the coming years would yield,
Eager-hearted as a boy when first he leaves his father's field,

And at night along the dusky highway near and nearer drawn,
Sees in heaven the light of London flaring like a dreary dawn;

And his spirit leaps within him to be gone before him then,
Underneath the light he looks at, in among the throngs of men;

Men, my brothers, men the workers, ever reaping something new:
That which they have done but earnest of the things that they shall do:

For I dipt into the future, far as human eye could see,
Saw the vision of the world, and all the wonder that would be;

Saw the heavens fill with commerce, argosies of magic sails,
Pilots of the purple twilight, dropping down with costly bales;

Heard the heavens fill with shouting, and there rained a ghastly dew
From the nations' airy navies grappling in the central blue;

Knowledge comes, but wisdom lingers; and I linger on the shore,
And the individual withers, and the world is more and more.

Knowledge comes, but wisdom lingers, and he bears a laden breast,
Full of sad experience moving toward the stillness of his rest.

Hark! my merry comrades call me, sounding on the bugle horn,—
They to whom my foolish passion were a target for their scorn;

Shall it not be scorn to me to harp on such a mouldered string?
I am shamed through all my nature to have loved so slight a thing.

Weakness to be wroth with weakness! woman's pleasure, woman's
   pain—
Nature made them blinder motions bounded in a shallower brain;

Woman is the lesser man, and all thy passions, matched with mine,
Are as moonlight unto sunlight, and as water unto wine—

Here at least, where nature sickens, nothing. Ah for some retreat
Deep in yonder shining Orient, where my life began to beat!

Where in wild Mahratta-battle fell my father, evil-starred;
I was left a trampled orphan, and a selfish uncle's ward.

Or to burst all links of habit,—there to wander far away,
On from island unto island at the gateways of the day,—

Larger constellations burning, mellow moons and happy skies,
Breadths of tropic shade and palms in cluster, knots of Paradise.

Never comes the trader, never floats an European flag,—
Slides the bird o'er lustrous woodland, swings the trailer from the
   crag,—

Droops the heavy-blossomed bower, hangs the heavy-fruited tree,—
Summer isles of Eden lying in dark-purple spheres of sea.

There, methinks, would be enjoyment more than in this march of
   mind—
In the steamship, in the railway, in the thoughts that shake mankind.

There the passions, cramped no longer, shall have scope and breathing-
   space;

I will take some savage woman, she shall rear my dusky race.

Iron-jointed, supple-sinewed, they shall dive, and they shall run,
Catch the wild goat by the hair, and hurl their lances in the sun,

Whistle back the parrot's call, and leap the rainbows of the brooks,
Not with blinded eyesight poring over miserable books—

Fool, again the dream, the fancy! but I *know* my words are wild,
But I count the gray barbarian lower than the Christian child.

I, to herd with narrow foreheads, vacant of our glorious gains,
Like a beast with lower pleasures, like a beast with lower pains!

Mated with a squalid savage,—what to me were sun or clime?
I, the heir of all the ages, in the foremost files of time,—

I, that rather held it better men should perish one by one,
Than that earth should stand at gaze like Joshua's moon in Ajalon!

Not in vain the distance beacons. Forward, forward let us range;
Let the great world spin for ever down the ringing grooves of change.

Through the shadow of the globe we sweep into the younger day;
Better fifty years of Europe than a cycle of Cathay.

Mother-Age,—for mine I knew not,—help me as when life begun,—
Rift the hills, and roll the waters, flash the lightnings, weigh the sun.

O, I see the crescent promise of my spirit hath not set;
Ancient founts of inspiration well through all my fancy yet.

Howsoever these things be, a long farewell to Locksley Hall!
Now for me the woods may wither, now for me the roof-tree fall.

Comes a vapor from the margin, blackening over heath and holt,
Cramming all the blast before it, in its breast a thunderbolt.

Let it fall on Locksley Hall, with rain or hail, or fire or snow;
For the mighty wind arises, roaring seaward, and I go.

ALFRED TENNYSON

MYSELF

I CELEBRATE myself, and sing myself,
And what I assume you shall assume,
For every atom belonging to me as good belongs to you.
I loaf and invite my soul,
I lean and loaf at my ease observing a spear of summer grass.

My tongue, every atom of my blood, formed from this soil, this air,
Born here of parents born here from parents the same, and their par-
    ents the same,
I, now thirty-seven years old in perfect health begin,
Hoping to cease not till death.

Creeds and schools in abeyance,
Retiring back awhile sufficed at what they are, but never forgotten,
I harbor for good or bad, I permit to speak at every hazard,
Nature without check for original energy.

WALT WHITMAN

THE CHAMBERED NAUTILUS

This is the ship of pearl, which, poets feign,
    Sails the unshadowed main,—
    The venturous bark that flings
On the sweet summer wind its purpled wings
In gulfs enchanted, where the Siren sings,
    And coral reefs lie bare,
Where the cold sea-maids rise to sun their streaming hair.

Its webs of living gauze no more unfurl;
    Wrecked is the ship of pearl!
    And every chambered cell,
Where its dim dreaming life was wont to dwell,
As the frail tenant shaped his growing shell,
    Before thee lies revealed,—
Its irised ceiling rent, its sunless crypt unsealed!

Year after year beheld the silent toil
    That spread his lustrous coil;
    Still, as the spiral grew,
He left the past year's dwelling for the new,
Stole with soft step its shining archway through,
    Built up its idle door,
Stretched in his last-found home, and knew the old no more.

Thanks for the heavenly message brought by thee,
    Child of the wandering sea,
    Cast from her lap, forlorn!
From thy dead lips a clearer note is born
Than ever Triton blew from wreathed horn!
    While on mine ear it rings,
Through the deep caves of thought I hear a voice that sings,—

Build thee more stately mansions, O my soul,
   As the swift seasons roll!
   Leave thy low-vaulted past!
Let each new temple, nobler than the last,
Shut thee from heaven with a dome more vast,
   Till thou at length art free,
Leaving thine outgrown shell by life's unresting sea!

OLIVER WENDELL HOLMES

DOVER BEACH

THE SEA is calm to-night.
The tide is full, the moon lies fair
Upon the straits;—on the French coast the light
Gleams and is gone; the cliffs of England stand,
Glimmering and vast, out in the tranquil bay.
Come to the window, sweet is the night-air!
Only, from the long line of spray
Where the sea meets the moon-blanch'd sand,
Listen! you hear the grating roar
Of pebbles which the waves draw back, and fling,
At their return, up the high strand,
Begin, and cease, and then again begin,
With tremulous cadence slow, and bring
The eternal note of sadness in.

Sophocles long ago
Heard it on the Ægean, and it brought
Into his mind the turbid ebb and flow
Of human misery; we
Find also in the sound a thought,
Hearing it by this distant northern sea.

The sea of faith
Was once, too, at the full, and round earth's shore
Lay like the folds of a bright girdle furl'd.
But now I only hear
Its melancholy, long, withdrawing roar,
Retreating, to the breath
Of the night-wind, down the vast edges drear
And naked shingles of the world.

Ah, love, let us be true
To one another! for the world, which seems
To lie before us like a land of dreams,
So various, so beautiful, so new,

Hath really neither joy, nor love, nor light,
Nor certitude, nor peace, nor help for pain;
And we are here as on a darkling plain
Swept with confused alarms of struggle and flight,
Where ignorant armies clash by night.

MATTHEW ARNOLD

LEISURE

WHAT is this life if, full of care,
We have no time to stand and stare.

No time to stand beneath the boughs
And stare as long as sheep or cows.

No time to see, when woods we pass,
Where squirrels hide their nuts in grass.

No time to see, in broad daylight,
Streams full of stars, like stars at night.

No time to turn at Beauty's glance,
And watch her feet, how they can dance.

No time to wait till her mouth can
Enrich that smile her eyes began.

A poor life this if, full of care,
We have no time to stand and stare.

W. H. DAVIES

THE RUBAIYAT OF OMAR KHAYYAM

I

WAKE! For the Sun, who scatter'd into flight
The Stars before him from the Field of Night,
   Drives Night along with them from Heav'n, and strikes
The Sultan's Turret with a Shaft of Light.

II

Before the phantom of False morning died,
Methought a Voice within the Tavern cried,
   "When all the Temple is prepared within,
"Why nods the drowsy Worshipper outside?"

III

And, as the Cock crew, those who stood before
The Tavern shouted—"Open then the Door!
    "You know how little while we have to stay,
"And, once departed, may return no more."

IV

Now the New Year reviving old Desires,
The thoughtful Soul to Solitude retires,
    Where the WHITE HAND OF MOSES on the Bough
Puts out, and Jesus from the Ground suspires.

V

Iram indeed is gone with all his Rose,
And Jamshyd's sev'n-ringed Cup where no one knows:
    But still a Ruby kindles in the Vine,
And many a Garden by the Water blows.

VI

And David's lips are lockt; but in divine
High-piping Pehlevi, with "Wine! Wine! Wine!
    "Red Wine!"—the Nightingale cries to the Rose
That sallow cheek of hers to' incardine.

VII

Come, fill the Cup, and in the fire of Spring
Your Winter-garment of Repentance fling:
    The Bird of Time has but a little way
To flutter—and the Bird is on the Wing.

VIII

Whether at Naishapur or Babylon,
Whether the Cup with sweet or bitter run,
    The wine of Life keeps oozing drop by drop,
The Leaves of Life keep falling one by one.

IX

Each morn a thousand Roses brings, you say;
Yes, but where leaves the Rose of Yesterday?
    And this first Summer month that brings the Rose
Shall take Jamshyd and Kaikobád away.

X

Well, let it take them! What have we to do
With Kaikobád the Great, or Kaikhosrú?
    Let Zál and Rustum bluster as they will,
Or Hátim call to Supper—heed not you.

XI

With me along the strip of Herbage strown
That just divides the desert from the sown,
    Where name of Slave and Sultán is forgot—
And Peace to Mahmúd on his golden Throne!

XII

A Book of Verses underneath the Bough,
A Jug of Wine, a Loaf of Bread—and Thou
    Beside me singing in the Wilderness—
Oh, Wilderness were Paradise enow!

XIII

Some for the Glories of This World; and some
Sigh for the Prophet's Paradise to come;
    Ah, take the Cash, and let the Credit go,
Nor heed the rumble of a distant Drum!

XIV

Look to the blowing Rose about us—"Lo,
Laughing," she says, "into the world I blow,
    At once the silken tassel of my Purse
Tear, and its Treasure on the garden throw."

XV

And those who husbanded the Golden Grain,
And those who flung it to the winds like Rain,
    Alike to no such aureate Earth are turn'd
As, buried once, Men want dug up again.

XVI

The Worldly Hope men set their Hearts upon
Turns Ashes—or it prospers; and anon,
    Like Snow upon the Desert's dusty Face,
Lighting a little hour or two—is gone.

XVII

Think, in this batter'd Caravanserai
Whose Portals are alternate Night and Day,
    How Sultan after Sultan with his Pomp
Abode his destined Hour, and went his way.

XVIII

They say the Lion and the Lizard keep
The Courts where Jamshyd gloried and drank deep:
    And Bahram, that great Hunter—the Wild Ass
Stamps o'er his Head, but cannot break his Sleep.

XIX

I sometimes think that never blows so red
The Rose as where some buried Cæsar bled;
    That every Hyacinth the Garden wears
Dropt in her Lap from some once lovely Head.

XX

And this reviving Herb whose tender Green
Fledges the River-Lip on which we lean—
    Ah, lean upon it lightly! for who knows
From what once lovely Lip it springs unseen!

XXI

Ah, my Belovèd, fill the Cup that clears
To-DAY of past Regrets and future Fears:
    To-morrow!—Why, To-morrow I may be
Myself with Yesterday's Sev'n thousand Years.

XXII

For some we loved, the loveliest and the best
That from his Vintage rolling Time hath prest,
    Have drunk their Cup a Round or two before.
And one by one crept silently to rest.

XXIII

And we that now make merry in the Room
They left, and Summer dresses in new bloom,
    Ourselves must we beneath the Couch of Earth
Descend—ourselves to make a couch—for whom?

XXIV

Ah, make the most of what we yet may spend,
Before we too into the Dust descend;
   Dust into Dust, and under Dust to lie,
Sans Wine, sans Song, sans Singer, and—sans End!

XXV

Alike for those who for To-DAY prepare,
And those that after some To-MORROW stare,
   A Muezzín from the Tower of Darkness cries,
"Fools! your Reward is neither Here nor There."

XXVI

Why, all the Saints and Sages who discuss'd
Of the Two Worlds so wisely—they art thrust
   Like foolish Prophets forth; their Words to Scorn
Are scatter'd, and their Mouths are stopt with Dust.

XXVII

Myself when young did eagerly frequent
Doctor and Saint, and heard great argument
   About it and about: but evermore
Came out by the same door where in I went.

XXVIII

With them the seed of Wisdom did I sow,
And with mine own hand wrought to make it grow;
   And this was all the Harvest that I reap'd—
"I came like Water, and like Wind I go."

XXIX

Into this Universe, and *Why* not knowing
Nor *Whence*, like Water willy-nilly flowing;
   And out of it, as Wind along the Waste,
I know not *Whither*, willy-nilly blowing.

XXX

What, without asking, hither hurried *Whence?*
And, without asking, *whither* hurried hence!
   Oh, many a Cup of this forbidden Wine
Must drown the memory of that insolence!

XXXI

Up from Earth's Centre through the Seventh Gate
I rose, and on the Throne of Saturn sate,
   And many a Knot unravel'd by the Road;
But not the Master-knot of Human Fate.

XXXII

There was the Door to which I found no Key;
There was the Veil through which I might not see:
   Some little talk a while of ME and THEE
There was—and then no more of THEE and ME.

XXXIII

Earth could not answer, nor the Seas that mourn
In flowing Purple, of their Lord forlorn;
   Nor rolling Heaven, with all his Signs reveal'd
And hidden by the sleeve of Night and Morn.

XXXIV

Then of the THEE in ME who works behind
The Veil, I lifted up my hands to find
   A Lamp amid the Darkness; and I heard,
As from Without—"THE ME WITHIN THEE BLIND!"

XXXV

Then to the Lip of this poor earthern Urn
I lean'd, the Secret of my Life to learn:
   And Lip to Lip it murmur'd—"While you live,
Drink!—for, once dead, you never shall return."

XXXVI

I think the Vessel, that with fugitive
Articulation answer'd, once did live,
   And drink; and Ah! the passive Lip I kiss'd,
How many Kisses might it take—and give!

XXXVII

For I remember stopping by the way
To watch a Potter thumping his wet Clay:
   And with its all-obliterated Tongue
It murmur'd—"Gently, Brother, gently, pray!"

XXXVIII

And has not such a Story from of Old
Down Man's successive generations roll'd
   Of such a clod of saturated Earth
Cast by the Maker into Human mould?

XXXIX

And not a drop that from our Cups we throw
For Earth to drink of, but may steal below
   To quench the fire of Anguish in some Eye
There hidden—far beneath, and long ago.

XL

As then the Tulip for her morning sup
Of Heav'nly Vintage from the soil looks up,
   Do you devoutly do the like, till Heav'n
To Earth invert you—like an empty Cup.

XLI

Perplext no more with Human or Divine,
To-morrow's tangle to the winds resign,
   And lose your fingers in the tresses of
The Cypress-slender Minister of Wine.

XLII

And if the Wine you drink, the Lip you press,
End in what All begins and ends in—Yes;
   Think then you are To-day what YESTERDAY
You were—To-morrow you shall not be less.

XLIII

So when that Angel of the darker Drink
At last shall find you by the river-brink,
   And, offering his Cup, invite your Soul
Forth to your Lips to quaff—you shall not shrink.

XLIV

Why, if the Soul can fling the Dust aside,
And naked on the Air of Heaven ride,
   Were't not a Shame—were't not a Shame for him
In this clay carcase crippled to abide?

XLV

'Tis but a Tent where takes his one day's rest
A Sultan to the realm of Death addrest;
    The Sultan rises, and the dark Ferrash
Strikes, and prepares it for another Guest.

XLVI

And fear not lest Existence closing your
Account, and mine, should know the like no more;
    The Eternal Saki from that Bowl has pour'd
Millions of Bubbles like us, and will pour.

XLVII

When You and I behind the Veil are past,
Oh, but the long, long while the World shall last
    Which of our Coming and Departure heeds
As the Sea's self should heed a pebble-cast.

XLVIII

A Moment's Halt—a momentary taste
Of BEING from the Well amid the Waste—
    And Lo!—the phantom Caravan has reach'd
The NOTHING it set out from—Oh, make haste!

XLIX

Would you that spangle of Existence spend
About THE SECRET—quick about it, Friend!
    A Hair perhaps divides the False and True—
And upon what, prithee, does life depend?

L

A Hair perhaps divides the False and True;
Yes; and a single Alif were the clue—
    Could you but find it—to the Treasure-house,
And peradventure to THE MASTER too;

LI

Whose secret Presence, through Creation's veins
Running Quicksilver-like eludes your pains;
    Taking all shapes from Máh to Máhi; and
They change and perish all—but He remains;

LII

A moment guess'd—then back behind the Fold
Immerst of Darkness round the Drama roll'd
   Which, for the Pastime of Eternity,
He doth Himself contrive, enact, behold.

LIII

But if in vain, down on the stubborn floor
Of Earth, and up to Heav'n's unopening Door,
   You gaze TO-DAY, while You are You—how then
TO-MORROW, You when shall be You no more?

LIV

Waste not your Hour, nor in the vain pursuit
Of This and That endeavor and dispute;
   Better be jocund with the fruitful Grape
Than sadden after none, or bitter, Fruit.

LV

You know, my Friends, with what a brave Carouse
I made a Second Marriage in my house;
   Divorced old barren Reason from my Bed,
And took the Daughter of the Vine to Spouse.

LVI

For "Is" and "Is-NOT" though with Rule and Line
And "UP-AND-DOWN" by Logic I define,
   Of all that one should care to fathom, I
Was never deep in anything but—Wine.

LVII

Ah, but my Computations, People say,
Reduced the Year to better reckoning?—Nay,
   'Twas only striking from the Calendar
Unborn To-morrow, and dead Yesterday.

LVIII

And lately, by the Tavern Door agape,
Came shining through the Dusk an Angel Shape
   Bearing a Vessel on his Shoulder; and
He bid me taste of it; and 'twas—the Grape!

LIX

The Grape that can with Logic absolute
The Two-and-Seventy jarring Sects confute:
    The sovereign Alchemist that in a trice
Life's leaden metal into Gold transmute:

LX

The mighty Mahmúd, Allah-breathing Lord,
That all the misbelieving and black Horde
    Of Fears and Sorrows that infest the Soul
Scatters before him with his whirlwind Sword.

LXI

Why, be this Juice the growth of God, who dare
Blaspheme the twisted tendril as a Snare?
    A Blessing, we should use it, should we not?
And if a Curse—why, then, Who set it there?

LXII

I must abjure the Balm of Life, I must,
Scared by some After-reckoning ta'en on trust,
    Or lured with Hope of some Diviner Drink,
To fill the Cup—when crumbled into Dust!

LXIII

Oh, threats of Hell and Hopes of Paradise!
One thing at least is certain—*This* Life flies;
    One thing is certain and the rest is Lies;
The Flower that once has blown for ever dies.

LXIV

Strange, is it not? that of the myriads who
Before us pass'd the door of Darkness through,
    Not one returns to tell us of the Road,
Which to discover we must travel too.

LXV

The Revelations of Devout and Learn'd
Who rose before us, and as Prophets burn'd,
    Are all but Stories, which, awoke from Sleep
They told their comrades, and to Sleep return'd.

LXVI

I sent my Soul through the Invisible,
Some letter of that After-life to spell:
   And by and by my Soul return'd to me,
And answered "I Myself am Heav'n and Hell:"

LXVII

Heav'n but the Vision of fulfill'd Desire,
And Hell the Shadow from a Soul on fire,
   Cast on the Darkness into which Ourselves,
So late emerged from, shall so soon expire.

LXVIII

We are no other than a moving row
Of Magic Shadow-shapes that come and go
   Round with the Sun-illumined Lantern held
In Midnight by the Master of the Show;

LXIX

But helpless Pieces of the Game He plays
Upon his Chequer-board of Nights and Days;
   Hither and thither moves, and checks, and slays,
And one by one back in the Closet lays.

LXX

The Ball no question makes of Ayes and Noes,
But Here or There as strikes the Player goes;
   And He that toss'd you down into the Field,
He knows about it all—HE knows—HE knows!

LXXI

The Moving Finger writes; and, having writ,
Moves on: nor all your Piety nor Wit
   Shall lure it back to cancel half a Line,
Nor all your Tears wash out a Word of it.

LXXII

And that inverted Bowl they call the Sky,
Whereunder crawling coop'd we live and die,
   Lift not your hands to *It* for help—for It
As impotently moves as you or I.

LXXIII

With Earth's first Clay They did the Last Man knead,
And there of the Last Harvest sow'd the Seed:
   And the first Morning of Creation wrote
What the Last Dawn of Reckoning shall read.

LXXIV

YESTERDAY *This* Day's Madness did prepare;
To-MORROW's Silence, Triumph, or Despair:
   Drink! for you know not whence you came, nor why:
Drink! for you know not why you go, nor where.

LXXV

I tell you this—When, started from the Goal,
Over the flaming shoulders of the Foal
   Of Heav'n Parwín and Mushtarí they flung,
In my predestined Plot of Dust and Soul.

LXXVI

The Vine had struck a fibre: which about
If clings my Being—let the Dervish flout;
   Of my Base metal may be filed a Key,
That shall unlock the Door he howls without.

LXXVII

And this I know: whether the one True Light
Kindle to Love, or Wrath consume me quite,
   One Flash of It within the Tavern caught
Better than in the Temple lost outright.

LXXVIII

What! out of senseless Nothing to provoke
A conscious Something to resent the yoke
   Of unpermitted Pleasure, under pain
Of Everlasting Penalties, if broke!

LXXIX

What! from his helpless Creature be repaid
Pure Gold for what he lent him dross-allay'd—
   Sue for a Debt he never did contract,
And cannot answer—Oh the sorry trade!

LXXX

Oh Thou, who didst with pitfall and with gin
Beset the Road I was to wander in,
    Thou wilt not with Predestined Evil round
Enmesh, and then impute my Fall to Sin!

LXXXI

Oh Thou, who Man of baser Earth didst make,
And ev'n with Paradise devise the Snake:
    For all the Sin wherewith the Face of Man
Is blacken'd—Man's forgiveness give—and take!

LXXXII

As under cover of departing Day
Slunk hunger-stricken Ramazan away,
    Once more within the Potter's house alone
I stood, surrounded by the Shapes of Clay.

LXXXIII

Shapes of all Sorts and Sizes, great and small,
That stood along the floor and by the wall;
    And some loquacious Vessels were; and some
Listen'd perhaps, but never talk'd at all.

LXXXIV

Said one among them—"Surely not in vain
My substance of the common Earth was ta'en
    And to this Figure moulded, to be broke,
Or trampled back to shapeless Earth again."

LXXXV

Then said a Second—"Ne'er a peevish Boy
Would break the Bowl from which he drank in joy;
    And He that with his hand the Vessel made
Will surely not in after Wrath destroy."

LXXXVI

After a momentary silence spake
Some Vessel of a more ungainly Make:
    "They sneer at me for leaning all awry:
What! did the Hand then of the Potter shake?"

LXXXVII

Whereat some of the loquacious Lot—
I think a Sufi pipkin—waxing hot—
   "All this of Pot and Potter—Tell me then,
Who is the Potter, pray, and who the Pot?"

LXXXVIII

"Why," said another, "Some there are who tell
Of one who threatens he will toss to Hell
   The luckless Pots he marr'd in making—Pish!
He's a Good Fellow, and 'twill all be well."

LXXXIX

"Well," murmur'd one, "Let whoso make or buy,
"My Clay with long Oblivion is gone dry:
   "But fill me with the old familiar Juice,
"Methinks I might recover by and by."

XC

So while the Vessels one by one were speaking,
The little Moon look'd in that all were seeking:
   And then they jogg'd each other, "Brother! Brother!
"Now for the Porter's shoulder-knot a-creaking!"

XCI

Ah, with the Grape my fading Life provide,
And wash the Body whence the Life has died,
   And lay me, shrouded in the living Leaf,
By some not unfrequented Garden-side.

XCII

That ev'n my buried Ashes such as snare
Of Vintage shall fling up into the Air
   As not a True-believer passing by
But shall be overtaken unaware.

XCIII

Indeed the Idols I have loved so long
Have done my credit in this World much wrong:
   Have drown'd my Glory in a shallow Cup,
And sold my Reputation for a Song.

XCIV

Indeed, indeed, Repentance oft before
I swore—but was I sober when I swore?
   And then and then came Spring, and Rose-in-hand
My thread-bare Penitence apieces tore.

XCV

And much as Wine has play'd the Infidel,
And robb'd me of my Robe of Honor—Well,
   I wonder often what the Vintners buy
One half so precious as the stuff they sell.

XCVI

Yet Ah, that Spring should vanish with the Rose!
That Youth's sweet-scented manuscript should close!
   The Nightingale that in the branches sang,
Ah whence, and whither flown again, who knows!

XCVII

Would but the Desert of the Fountain yield
One glimpse—if dimly, yet indeed, reveal'd,
   To which the fainting Traveller might spring,
As springs the trampled herbage of the field.

XCVIII

Would but some wingèd Angel ere too late
Arrest the yet unfolded Roll of Fate,
   And make the stern Recorder otherwise
Enregister, or quite obliterate!

XCIX

Ah Love! could you and I with Him conspire
To grasp this sorry Scheme of Things Entire,
   Would not we shatter it to bits—and then
Re-mould it nearer to the Heart's desire! . . .

C

Yon rising Moon that looks for us again—
How oft hereafter will she wax and wane;
   How oft hereafter rising look for us
Through this same Garden—and for *one* in vain!

CI

And when like her, oh Saki, you shall pass
Among the Guests Star-scatter'd on the Grass,
   And in your joyous errand reach the spot
Where I made One—turn down an empty Glass!
                    Translated by EDWARD FITZGERALD

A MUSICAL INSTRUMENT

WHAT was he doing, the great god Pan,
   Down in the reeds by the river?
Spreading ruin and scattering ban,
Splashing and paddling with hoofs of a goat,
And breaking the golden lilies afloat
   With the dragon-fly on the river.

He tore out a reed, the great god Pan,
   From the deep cool bed of the river:
The limpid water turbidly ran,
And the broken lilies a-dying lay,
And the dragon-fly had fled away,
   Ere he brought it out of the river.

High on the shore sat the great god Pan,
   While turbidly flowed the river;
And hacked and hewed as a great god can,
With his hard bleak steel at the patient reed,
Till there was not a sign of a leaf indeed
   To prove it fresh from the river.

He cut it short, did the great god Pan,
   (How tall it stood in the river!)
Then drew the pith, like the heart of a man,
Steadily from the outside ring,
And notched the poor dry empty thing
   In holes, as he sat by the river.

"This is the way," laughed the great god Pan,
   (Laughed while he sat by the river,)
"The only way, since gods began
To make sweet music, they could succeed."
Then, dropping his mouth to a hole in the reed,
   He blew in power by the river.

Sweet, sweet, sweet, O Pan!
   Piercing sweet by the river!
Blinding sweet, O great god Pan!

The sun on the hill forgot to die,
And the lilies revived, and the dragon-fly
    Came back to dream on the river.

Yet half a beast is the great god Pan,
    To laugh as he sits by the river,
Making a poet out of a man:
The true gods sigh for the cost and pain,—
For the reed which grows nevermore again
    As a reed with the reeds in the river.

ELIZABETH BARRETT BROWNING

BEN BOLT

Don't you remember sweet Alice, Ben Bolt,—
    Sweet Alice whose hair was so brown,
Who wept with delight when you gave her a smile,
    And trembled with fear at your frown?
In the old churchyard in the valley, Ben Bolt,
    In a corner obscure and alone,
They have fitted a slab of the granite so gray,
    And Alice lies under the stone.

Under the hickory tree, Ben Bolt,
    Which stood at the foot of the hill,
Together we've lain in the noonday shade,
    And listened to Appleton's mill.
The mill-wheel has fallen to pieces, Ben Bolt,
    The rafters have tumbled in,
And a quiet which crawls round the walls as you gaze
    Has followed the olden din.

Do you mind of the cabin of logs, Ben Bolt,
    At the edge of the pathless wood,
And the button-ball tree with its motley limbs,
    Which nigh by the doorstep stood?
The cabin to ruin has gone, Ben Bolt,
    The tree you would seek for in vain;
And where once the lords of the forest waved
    Are grass and the golden grain.

And don't you remember the school, Ben Bolt,
    With the master so cruel and grim,
And the shaded nook in the running brook
    Where the children went to swim?
Grass grows on the master's grave, Ben Bolt,

The spring of the brook is dry,
And of all the boys who were schoolmates then
        There are only you and I.

There is change in the things I loved, Ben Bolt,
        They have changed from the old to the new;
But I feel in the deeps of my spirit the truth,
        There never was change in you.
Twelvemonths twenty have passed, Ben Bolt,
        Since first we were friends—yet I hail
Your presence a blessing, your friendship a truth,
        Ben Bolt of the salt-sea gale.

                                   THOMAS DUNN ENGLISH

BISHOP DOANE ON HIS DOG

I AM QUITE SURE he thinks that I am God—
Since he is God on whom each one depends
For life, and all things that His bounty sends—
My dear old dog, most constant of all friends;
Not quick to mind, but quicker far than I
To Him whom God I know and own; his eye,
Deep brown and liquid, watches for my nod;
He is more patient underneath the rod
Than I, when God His wise corrections sends.

He looks love at me, deep as words e'er spake;
And from me never crumb nor sup will take
But he wags thanks with his most vocal tail;
And when some crashing noise wakes all his fear,
He is content and quiet, if I am near,
Secure that my protection will prevail.
So, faithful, mindful, thankful, trustful, he
Tells me what I unto my God should be.

                              GEORGE WASHINGTON DOANE

OZYMANDIAS

I MET a traveler from an antique land
Who said: Two vast and trunkless legs of stone
Stand in the desert. Near them, on the sand,
Half sunk, a shattered visage lies, whose frown
And wrinkled lip and sneer of cold command
Tell that its sculptor well those passions read
Which yet survive, stamped on these lifeless things,

The hand that mocked them and the heart that fed;
And on the pedestal these words appear:
"My name is Ozymandias, king of kings:
Look on my works, ye Mighty, and despair!"
Nothing beside remains. Round the decay
Of that colossal wreck, boundless and bare,
The lone and level sands stretch far away.

PERCY BYSSHE SHELLEY

INTRODUCTION TO "SONGS OF INNOCENCE"

PIPING down the valleys wild,
Piping songs of pleasant glee,
On a cloud I saw a child,
And he laughing said to me:

"Pipe a song about a Lamb!"
So I piped with merry cheer.
"Piper, pipe that song again;"
So I piped: he wept to hear.

"Drop thy pipe, thy happy pipe;
"Sing thy songs of happy cheer:"
So I sang the same again,
While he wept with joy to hear.

"Piper, sit thee down and write
"In a book, that all may read."
So he vanish'd from my sight,
And I pluck'd a hollow reed,

And I made a rural pen,
And I stain'd the water clear,
And I wrote my happy songs
Every child may joy to hear.

WILLIAM BLAKE

THE TIGER

TIGER! TIGER! burning bright
In the forests of the night,
What immortal hand or eye
Could frame thy fearful symmetry?

In what distant deeps or skies
Burnt the fire of thine eyes?
On what wings dare he aspire?
What the hand dare seize the fire?

And what shoulder, and what art,
Could twist the sinews of thy heart?
And when thy heart began to beat,
What dread hand? and what dread feet?

What the hammer? what the chain?
In what furnace was thy brain?
What the anvil? what dread grasp
Dare its deadly terrors clasp?

When the stars threw down their spears,
And watered heaven with their tears,
Did he smile his work to see?
Did he who made the Lamb make thee?

Tiger! Tiger! burning bright
In the forests of the night,
What immortal hand or eye
Dare frame thy fearful symmetry?

WILLIAM BLAKE

NIGHT

THE sun descending in the West,
The evening star does shine;
The birds are silent in their nest,
And I must seek for mine.

The moon, like a flower
In heaven's high bower,
With silent delight
Sits and smiles on the night.

Farewell, green fields and happy grove,
Where flocks have ta'en delight;
Where lambs have nibbled, silent move
The feet of angels bright:
Unseen, they pour blessing,
And joy without ceasing,
On each bud and blossom,
On each sleeping bosom.

They look in every thoughtless nest,
Where birds are covered warm;
They visit caves of every beast,
To keep them all from harm.
If they see any weeping
That should have been sleeping,

They pour sleep on their head,
And sit down by their bed.

When wolves and tigers howl for prey
They pitying stand and weep,
Seeking to drive their thirst away,
And keep them from the sheep.
But, if they rush dreadful,
The angels, most heedful,
Receive each mild spirit
New worlds to inherit.

And there the lion's ruddy eyes
Shall flow with tears of gold:
And pitying the tender cries,
And walking round the fold,
Saying: "Wrath by His meekness,
And by His health, sickness,
Are driven away
From our immortal day.

"And now beside thee, bleating lamb,
I can lie down and sleep.
Or think on Him who bore thy name,
Graze after thee, and weep.
For, washed in life's river,
My bright mane for ever
Shall shine like the gold,
As I guard o'er the fold."

WILLIAM BLAKE

ON FIRST LOOKING INTO CHAPMAN'S HOMER

MUCH have I travelled in the realms of gold,
And many goodly states and kingdoms seen;
Round many western islands have I been
Which bards in fealty to Apollo hold.
Oft of one wide expanse had I been told
That deep-browed Homer ruled as his demesne:
Yet did I never breathe its pure serene
Till I heard Chapman speak out loud and bold:
Then felt I like some watcher of the skies
When a new planet swims into his ken;
Or like stout Cortez, when with eagle eyes
He stared at the Pacific—and all his men
Looked at each other with a wild surmise—
Silent, upon a peak in Darien.

JOHN KEATS

ODE ON A GRECIAN URN

Thou still unravish'd bride of quietness,
  Thou foster-child of silence and slow time,
Sylvan historian, who canst thus express
  A flowery tale more sweetly than our rhyme:
What leaf-fring'd legend haunts about thy shape
  Of deities or mortals, or of both,
    In Tempe or the dales of Arcady?
What men or gods are these? What maidens loth?
  What mad pursuit? What struggle to escape?
    What pipes and timbrels? What wild ecstasy?

Heard melodies are sweet, but those unheard
  Are sweeter; therefore, ye soft pipes, play on;
Not to the sensual ear, but, more endear'd,
  Pipe to the spirit ditties of no tone:
Fair youth, beneath the trees, thou canst not leave
  Thy song, nor ever can those trees be bare;
    Bold Lover, never, never canst thou kiss
Though winning near the goal—yet, do not grieve;
  She cannot fade, though thou hast not thy bliss,
    For ever wilt thou love, and she be fair!

Ah, happy, happy boughs! that cannot shed
  Your leaves, nor ever bid the Spring adieu;
And, happy melodist, unwearied,
  For ever piping songs for ever new;
More happy love! more happy, happy love!
  For ever warm and still to be enjoy'd,
    For ever panting, and for ever young;
All breathing human passion far above,
  That leaves a heart high-sorrowful and cloy'd,
    A burning forehead, and a parching tongue.

Who are these coming to the sacrifice?
  To what green altar, O mysterious priest,
Lead'st thou that heifer lowing at the skies,
  And all her silken flanks with garlands dressed?
What little town by river or sea shore,
  Or mountain-built with peaceful citadel,
    Is emptied of this folk, this pious morn?
And, little town, thy streets for evermore
  Will silent be; and not a soul to tell
    Why thou art desolate, can e'er return.

O Attic shape! Fair attitude! with brede
  Of marble men and maidens over wrought,
With forest branches and the trodden weed;
  Thou, silent form, dost tease us out of thought
As doth eternity: Cold Pastoral!
  When old age shall this generation waste,
    Thou shalt remain, in midst of other woe
Than ours, a friend to man, to whom thou say'st,
  "Beauty is truth, truth beauty,"—that is all
    Ye know on earth, and all ye need to know.

JOHN KEATS

THE MERMAID TAVERN

Souls of Poets dead and gone,
What Elysium have ye known,
Happy field or mossy cavern,
Choicer than the Mermaid Tavern,
Have ye tippled drink more fine
Than mine host's Canary wine?
Or are fruits of Paradise
Sweeter than those dainty pies
Of venison? O generous food!
Dressed as though bold Robin Hood
Would, with his maid Marian,
Sup and browse from horn and can.

I have heard that on a day
Mine host's sign-board flew away,
Nobody knew whither, till
An astrologer's old quill
To a sheepskin gave the story,
Said he saw you in your glory,
Underneath a new old sign
Sipping beverage divine,
And pledging with contented smack
The Mermaid in the Zodiac!
Souls of Poets dead and gone,
What Elysium have ye known,
Happy field or mossy cavern,
Choicer than the Mermaid Tavern?

JOHN KEATS

HYACINTHS TO FEED THY SOUL

IF OF THY MORTAL GOODS thou art bereft,
And from thy slender store two loaves alone to thee are left,
Sell one, and with the dole
Buy hyacinths to feed thy soul.

SAADI

DREAM-PEDLARY

IF THERE were dreams to sell,
  What would you buy?
Some cost a passing bell;
  Some a light sigh,
That shakes from Life's fresh crown
Only a rose-leaf down.
If there were dreams to sell,
Merry and sad to tell,
And the crier rang the bell,
  What would you buy?

A cottage lone and still,
  With bowers nigh,
Shadowy, my woes to still,
  Until I die.
Such pearl from Life's fresh crown
Fain would I shake me down.
Were dreams to have at will,
This would best heal my ill,
  This would I buy.

THOMAS L. BEDDOES

IN EARLIEST SPRING

TOSSING HIS mane of snows in wildest eddies and tangles,
  Lion-like, March cometh in, hoarse, with tempestuous breath,
Through all the moaning chimneys, and thwart all the hollows and
    angles
  Round the shuddering house, threating of winter and death.

But in my heart I feel the life of the wood and the meadow
  Thrilling the pulses that own kindred with fibres that lift
Bud and blade to the sunward, within the inscrutable shadow,
  Deep in the oak's chill core, under the gathering drift.

Nay, to earth's life in mine some prescience, or dream, or desire
  (How shall I name it aright?) comes for a moment and goes,—
Rapture of life ineffable, perfect—as if in the brier,
  Leafless there by my door, trembled a sense of the rose.

WILLIAM DEAN HOWELLS

ON THE GRASSHOPPER AND CRICKET

THE poetry of earth is never dead:
When all the birds are faint with the hot sun,
And hide in cooling trees, a voice will run
From hedge to hedge about the new-mown mead:
That is the Grasshopper's—he takes the lead
In summer luxury,—he has never done
With his delights, for when tired out with fun,
He rests at ease beneath some pleasant weed.
The poetry of earth is ceasing never:
On a lone winter evening, when the frost
Has wrought a silence, from the stove there shrills
The Cricket's song, in warmth increasing ever,
And seems to one in drowsiness half-lost,
The Grasshopper's among the grassy hills.

JOHN KEATS

NATURE

As A fond mother, when the day is o'er,
Leads by the hand her little child to bed,
Half willing, half reluctant to be led,
And leave his broken playthings on the floor,
Still gazing at them through the open door,
Nor wholly reassured and comforted
By promises of others in their stead,
Which, though more splendid, may not please him more;
So Nature deals with us, and takes away
Our playthings one by one, and by the hand
Leads us to rest so gently, that we go
Scarce knowing if we wish to go or stay,
Being too full of sleep to understand
How far the unknown transcends the what we know.

HENRY WADSWORTH LONGFELLOW

BREAK, BREAK, BREAK

BREAK, break, break,
    On thy cold grey stones, O Sea!
And I would that my tongue could utter
    The thoughts that arise in me.

O well for the fisherman's boy,
    That he shouts with his sister at play!
O well for the sailor lad,
    That he sings in his boat on the bay!

And the stately ships go on
    To their haven under the hill;
But O for the touch of a vanish'd hand,
    And the sound of a voice that is still!

Break, break, break,
    At the foot of thy crags, O Sea!
But the tender grace of a day that is dead
    Will never come back to me.

                                        ALFRED TENNYSON

LET ME GROW LOVELY

LET ME grow lovely, growing old—
    So many fine things do;
Laces, and ivory, and gold,
    And silks need not be new;

And there is healing in old trees,
    Old streets a glamour hold;
Why may not I, as well as these,
    Grow lovely, growing old?

                                    KARLE WILSON BAKER

Favorite Poems Of

ADVENTURE
ON LAND AND SEA

SEA-FEVER

I MUST go down to the seas again, to the lonely sea and the sky,
And all I ask is a tall ship and a star to steer her by;
And the wheel's kick and the wind's song and the white sail's shaking,
And a gray mist on the sea's face, and a gray dawn breaking.

I must go down to the seas again, for the call of the running tide
Is a wild call and a clear call that may not be denied;
And all I ask is a windy day with the white clouds flying,
And the flung spray and the blown spume, and the sea-gulls crying.

I must go down to the seas again, to the vagrant gypsy life,
To the gull's way and the whale's way, where the wind's like a
    whetted knife;
And all I ask is a merry yarn from a laughing fellow-rover,
And quiet sleep and a sweet dream when the long trick's over.

JOHN MASEFIELD

A LIFE ON THE OCEAN WAVE

A LIFE on the ocean wave,
     A home on the rolling deep,
Where the scattered waters rave,
     And the winds their revels keep!
Like an eagle caged, I pine
     On this dull, unchanging shore:
Oh! give me the flashing brine,
     The spray and the tempest's roar!

Once more on the deck I stand
     Of my own swift-gliding craft:
Set sail! farewell to the land!
     The gale follows fair abaft.
We shoot through the sparkling foam
     Like an ocean-bird set free;—
Like the ocean-bird, our home
     We'll find far out on the sea.

The land is no longer in view,
     The clouds have begun to frown;
But with a stout vessel and crew,
     We'll say, Let the storm come down!
And the song of our hearts shall be,
     While the wind and the waters rave,
A home on the rolling sea!
     A life on the ocean wave!

                              EPES SARGENT

THE BALLAD OF EAST AND WEST

Oh East is East, and West is West, and never the twain shall meet,
Till Earth and Sky stand presently at God's great Judgment Seat;
But there is neither East nor West, Border, nor Breed, nor Birth,
When two strong men stand face to face, tho' they come from the
     ends of the earth!

Kamal is out with twenty men to raise the Border side,
And he has lifted the Colonel's mare that is the Colonel's pride:
He has lifted her out of the stable-door between the dawn and the day,
And turned the calkins upon her feet, and ridden her far away.
Then up and spoke the Colonel's son that led a troop of the Guides:
"Is there never a man of all my men can say where Kamal hides?"
Then up and spoke Mahommed Khan, the son of the Ressaldar,

"If ye know the track of the morning-mist, ye know where his pickets
are.
"At dusk he harries the Abazai—at dawn he is into Bonair,
"But he must go by Fort Bukloh to his own place to fare,
"So if ye gallop to Fort Bukloh as fast as a bird can fly,
"By the favor of God ye may cut him off, ere he win to the Tongue of
Jagai,
"But if he be passed the Tongue of Jagai, right swiftly turn ye then,
"For the length and the breadth of that grisly plain is sown with
Kamal's men.
"There is rock to the left, and rock to the right, and low, lean thorn
between,
"And ye may hear a breech bolt snick where never a man is seen."
The Colonel's son has taken a horse, and a raw rough dun was he,
With the mouth of a bell and the heart of Hell, and the head of the
gallows-tree.
The Colonel's son to the Fort has won, they bid him stay to eat—
Who rides at the tail of a Border thief, he sits not long at his meat.
He's up and away from Fort Bukloh as fast as he can fly,
Till he was aware of his father's mare in the gut of the Tongue of
Jagai,
Till he was aware of his father's mare with Kamal upon her back,
And when he could spy the white of her eye, he made the pistol crack.
He has fired once, he has fired twice, but the whistling ball went wide.
"Ye shoot like a soldier," Kamal said. "Show now if ye can ride."
It's up and over the Tongue of Jagai, as blown dust-devils go,
The dun he fled like a stag of ten, but the mare like a barren doe.
The dun he leaned against the bit and slugged his head above,
But the red mare played with the snaffle-bars, as a maiden plays with
a glove.
There was rock to the left and rock to the right, and low lean thorn be-
tween,
And thrice he heard a breech-bolt snick tho' never a man was seen.
They have ridden the low moon out of the sky, their hoofs drum up the
dawn,
The dun he went like a wounded bull, but the mare like a new-roused
fawn.
The dun he fell at a water-course—in a woful heap fell he,
And Kamal has turned the red mare back, and pulled the rider free.
He has knocked the pistol out of his hand—small room was there to
strive,
" 'Twas only by favor of mine," quoth he, "ye rode so long alive:
"There was not a rock for twenty miles, there was not a clump of tree,
"But covered a man of my own men with his rifle cocked on his knee.
"If I had raised my bridle-hand, as I have held it low,
"The little jackals that flee so fast, were feasting all in a row:

"If I had bowed my head on my breast, as I have held it high,
"The kite that whistles above us now were gorged till she could not
    fly."
Lightly answered the Colonel's son: "Do good to bird and beast,
"But count who come for the broken meats before thou makest a feast.
"If there should follow a thousand swords to carry my bones away,
"Belike the price of a jackal's meal were more than a thief could pay.
"They will feed their horse on the standing crop, their men on the
    garnered grain,
"The thatch of the byres will serve their fires when all the cattle are
    slain.
"But if thou thinkest the price be fair,—thy brethren wait to sup,
"The hound is kin to the jackal-spawn,—howl, dog, and call them up!
"And if thou thinkest the price be high, in steer and gear and stack,
"Give me my father's mare again, and I'll fight my own way back!"
Kamal has gripped him by the hand and set him upon his feet.
"No talk shall be of dogs," said he, "when wolf and gray wolf meet.
"May I eat dirt if thou hast hurt of me in deed or breath;
"What dam of lances brought thee forth to jest at the dawn with
    Death?"
Lightly answered the Colonel's son: "I hold by the blood of my clan:
"Take up the mare for my father's gift—by God, she has carried a
    man!"
The red mare ran to the Colonel's son, and nuzzled against his breast;
"We be two strong men," said Kamal then, "but she loveth the younger
    best.
"So she shall go with a lifter's dower, my turquoise-studded rein,
"My broidered saddle and saddle-cloth, and silver stirrups twain."
The Colonel's son a pistol drew and held it muzzle-end,
"Ye have taken the one from a foe," said he; "will ye take the mate
    from a friend?"
"A gift for a gift," said Kamal straight; "a limb for the risk of a limb.
"Thy father has sent his son to me, I'll send my son to him!"
With that he whistled his only son, that dropped from a mountain-
    crest—
He trod the ling like a buck in spring, and he looked like a lance in rest.
"Now here is thy master," Kamal said, "who leads a troop of the
    Guides,
"And thou must ride at his left side as shield on shoulder rides.
"Till Death or I cut loose the tie, at camp and board and bed,
"Thy life is his—thy fate is to guard him with thy head.
"So thou must eat the White Queen's meat, and all her foes are thine,
"And thou must harry thy father's hold for the peace of the Border-
    line,
"And thou must make a trooper tough and hack thy way to power—
"Belike they will raise thee to Ressaldar when I am hanged in Pesha-
    wur."

They have looked each other between the eyes, and there they have
    found no fault,
They have taken the Oath of the Brother-in-Blood on leavened bread
    and salt;
They have taken the Oath of the Brother-in-Blood on fire and fresh-cut
    sod,
On the hilt and the haft of the Khyber knife, and the Wondrous
    Names of God.
The Colonel's son he rides the mare and Kamal's boy the dun,
And two have come back to Fort Bukloh where there went forth but
    one.
And when they drew to the Quarter-Guard, full twenty swords flew
    clear—
There was not a man but carried his feud with the blood of the moun-
    taineer.
"Ha' done! ha' done!" said the Colonel's son. "Put up the steel at
    your sides!
"Last night ye had struck at a Border thief—tonight 'tis a man of the
    Guides!"

Oh East is East and West is West, and never the twain shall meet,
Till Earth and Sky stand presently at God's great Judgment Seat;
But there is neither East nor West, Border, nor Breed, nor Birth,
When two strong men stand face to face, tho' they come from the ends
    of the earth.

RUDYARD KIPLING

TACKING SHIP OFF SHORE

The weather-leech of the topsail shivers,
    The bowlines strain, and the lee-shrouds slacken,
The braces are taut, the lithe boom quivers,
    And the waves with the coming squall-cloud blacken.

Open one point on the weather-bow,
    Is the lighthouse tall on Fire Island Head.
There's a shade of doubt on the captain's brow,
    And the pilot watches the heaving lead.

I stand at the wheel, and with eager eye
    To sea and to sky and to shore I gaze,
Till the muttered order of "Full and by!"
    Is suddenly changed for "Full for stays!"

The ship bends lower before the breeze,
    As her broadside fair to the blast she lays;
And she swifter springs to the rising seas,
    As the pilot calls, "Stand by for stays!"

It is silence all, as each in his place,
    With the gathered coil in his hardened hands,
By tack and bowline, by sheet and brace,
    Waiting the watchword impatient stands.

And the light on Fire Island Head draws near,
    As, trumpet-winged, the pilot's shout
From his post on the bowsprit's heel I hear,
    With the welcome call of "Ready! About!"

No time to spare! It is touch and go;
    And the captain growls, "Down helm! hard down!"
As my weight on the whirling spokes I throw,
    While heaven grows black with the storm-cloud's frown.

High o'er the knight-heads flies the spray,
    As we meet the shock of plunging sea;
And my shoulder stiff to the wheel I lay,
    As I answer, "Ay, ay, sir! Ha-a-rd a-lee!"

With the swerving leap of a startled steed
    The ship flies fast in the eye of the wind,
The dangerous shoals on the lee recede,
    And the headland white we have left behind.

The topsails flutter, the jibs collapse,
    And belly and tug at the groaning cleats;
The spanker slats, and the mainsail flaps;
    And thunders the order, "Tacks and sheets!"

Mid the rattle of blocks and the tramp of the crew,
    Hisses the rain of the rushing squall:
The sails are aback from clew to clew,
    And now is the moment for "Mainsail, haul!"

And the heavy yards, like a baby's toy,
    By fifty strong arms are swiftly swung:
She holds her way, and I look with joy
    For the first white spray o'er the bulwarks flung.

"Let go, and haul!" 'Tis the last command,
    And the head-sails fill to the blast once more:
Astern and to leeward lies the land,
    With its breakers white on the shingly shore.

What matters the reef, or the rain, or the squall?
    I steady the helm for the open sea;
The first mate clamors, "Belay, there, all!"
    And the captain's breath once more comes free.

And so off shore let the good ship fly;
  Little care I how the gusts may blow,
In my fo'castle bunk, in a jacket dry.
  Eight bells have struck, and my watch is below.

WALTER MITCHELL

A SEA-SONG

A WET SHEET and a flowing sea,
  A wind that follows fast,
And fills the white and rustling sail
  And bends the gallant mast;
And bends the gallant mast, my boys,
  While, like the eagle free,
Away the good ship flies, and leaves
  Old England on the lee.

"O for a soft and gentle wind!"
  I heard a fair one cry;
But give to me the snoring breeze
  And white waves heaving high;
And white waves heaving high, my lads,
  The good ship tight and free,—
The world of waters is our home,
  And merry men are we.

There's tempest in yon hornèd moon,
  And lightning in yon cloud;
But hark the music, mariners!
  The wind is piping loud;
The wind is piping loud, my boys,
  The lightning flashes free,—
While the hollow oak our palace is,
  Our heritage the sea.

ALLAN CUNNINGHAM

DERELICT

"FIFTEEN men on the Dead Man's Chest—
  Yo-ho-ho and a bottle of rum!
Drink and the devil had done for the rest—
  Yo-ho-ho and a bottle of rum!"
The mate was fixed by the bos'n's pike,
The bos'n brained with a marlinspike,
And Cookey's throat was marked belike

It had been gripped
By fingers ten;
And there they lay,
All good dead men,
Like break-o'-day in a boozing-ken—
Yo-ho-ho and a bottle of rum!

Fifteen men of a whole ship's list—
Yo-ho-ho and a bottle of rum!
Dead and bedamned and the rest gone whist!—
Yo-ho-ho and a bottle of rum!
The skipper lay with his nob in gore
Where the scullion's ax his cheek had shore—
And the scullion he was stabbed times four.
And there they lay,
And the soggy skies
Dripped all day long
In upstaring eyes—
At murk sunset and at foul sunrise—
Yo-ho-ho and a bottle of rum!

Fifteen men of 'em stiff and stark—
Yo-ho-ho and a bottle of rum!
Ten of the crew had the Murder mark—
Yo-ho-ho and a bottle of rum!
'Twas a cutlass swipe, or an ounce of lead,
Or a yawing hole in a battered head—
And the scuppers glut with a rotting red.
And there they lay—
Aye, damn my eyes!—
All lookouts clapped
On paradise—
All souls bound just contrariwise—
Yo-ho-ho and a bottle of rum!

Fifteen men of 'em good and true—
Yo-ho-ho and a bottle of rum!
Every man jack could ha' sailed with Old Pew—
Yo-ho-ho and a bottle of rum!
There was chest on chest full of Spanish gold,
With a ton of plate in the middle hold,
And the cabins riot of stuff untold.
And they lay there,
That had took the plum,
With sightless glare
And their eyes struck dumb,
While we shared all by the rule of thumb—
Yo-ho-ho and a bottle of rum!

More was seen through the sternlight screen—
  Yo-ho-ho and a bottle of rum!
Chartings ondoubt where a woman had been!—
  Yo-ho-ho and a bottle of rum!
A flimsy shift on a bunker cot,
With a thin dirk slot through the bosom spot
And the lace stiff-dry in a purplish blot.
      Or was she wench . . .
        Or some shuddering maid . . . ?
      That dared the knife—
        And that took the blade!
By God! she was stuff for a plucky jade—
  Yo-ho-ho and a bottle of rum!

Fifteen men on the Dead Man's Chest—
  Yo-ho-ho and a bottle of rum!
Drink and the devil had done for the rest—
  Yo-ho-ho and a bottle of rum!
We wrapped 'em all in a mains'l tight,
With twice ten turns of a hawser's bight,
And we heaved 'em over and out of sight—
      With a yo-heave-ho!
      And a fare-you-well!
    And a sullen plunge
    In the sullen swell,
Ten fathoms deep on the road to hell!
  Yo-ho-ho and a bottle of rum!

YOUNG E. ALLISON

THE "JULIE PLANTE"

ON WAN DARK NIGHT on Lac St. Pierre
De wind, she blow, blow, blow,
An' de crew of de wood-scow *Julie Plante*
Got scairt and run below.
For de wind she blow lak hurricane;
Bimeby she blow some more,
An' de scow bust up on Lac St. Pierre
Wan arpent from de shore.

De captain walk on de fronte deck,
An' walk on the hin' deck too.
He call de crew from up de hole;
He call de cook also.
De cook she's name was Rosie,
She come from Montreal,

Was chambermaid on lumber barge
On de Grande Lachine Canal.

De wind she blow from nor'-eas'-wes'—
De sout' wind she blow too.
Rosie cry, "Mon cher Captain;
Mon cher, what I shall do?"
Den de captain throw the big ankerre,
But still de skow she dreef;
De crew he can't pass on de shore
Becos he lose hees skeef.

De night was dark lak wan black cat,
De wave run high an' fas'
When de captain tak de Rosie girl
An' tie her to de mas'.
Den he also tak de life preserve
An' jump off on de lac,
An' say, "Good-bye, my Rosie dear,
I go drown for your sak."

Next morning very early
Bout half-past two, three, four,
De captain, scow, and de poor Rosie
Was corpses on de shore.
For de wind she blow lak hurricane,
Bimeby she blow some more,
An' de scow bust up on Lac St. Pierre,
Wan arpent from de shore.

Now all good wood-scow sailorman
Tak warning from dat storm,
An' go an' marry some nice French girl
An' live on wan beeg farm.
De wind can blow lak hurricane,
An' spose she blow some more,
You can't get drown on Lac St. Pierre
So long you stay on shore.

WILLIAM HENRY DRUMMOND

THE SEA

THERE is a pleasure in the pathless woods,
There is a rapture on the lonely shore,
There is society where none intrudes
By the deep sea, and music in its roar:
I love not man the less, but nature more,

From these our interviews, in which I steal
From all I may be, or have been before,
To mingle with the universe, and feel
What I can ne'er express, yet cannot all conceal.

Roll on, thou deep and dark blue Ocean,—roll!
Ten thousand fleets sweep over thee in vain;
Man marks the earth with ruin,—his control
Stops with the shore;—upon the watery plain
The wrecks are all thy deed, nor doth remain
A shadow of man's ravage, save his own,
When, for a moment, like a drop of rain,
He sinks into thy depths with bubbling groan,
Without a grave, unknelled, uncoffined, and unknown.

His steps are not upon thy paths,—thy fields
Are not a spoil for him,—thou dost arise
And shake him from thee; the vile strength he wields
For earth's destruction thou dost all despise,
Spurning him from thy bosom to the skies,
And send'st him, shivering in thy playful spray
And howling, to his gods, where haply lies
His petty hope in some near port or bay,
And dashest him again to earth:—there let him lay.

The armaments which thunderstrike the walls
Of rock-built cities, bidding nations quake
And monarchs tremble in their capitals,
The oak leviathans, whose huge ribs make
Their clay creator the vain title take
Of lord of thee and arbiter of war,—
These are thy toys, and, as the snowy flake,
They melt into thy yeast of waves, which mar
Alike the Armada's pride or spoils of Trafalgar.

Thy shores are empires, changed in all save thee;—
Assyria, Greece, Rome, Carthage, what are they?
Thy waters washed them power while they were free,
And many a tyrant since; their shores obey
The stranger, slave, or savage; their decay
Has dried up realms to deserts:—not so thou;
Unchangeable save to thy wild waves' play,
Time writes no wrinkle on thine azure brow;
Such as creation's dawn beheld, thou rollest now.

Thou glorious mirror, where the Almighty's form
Glasses itself in tempests; in all time,
Calm or convulsed,—in breeze, or gale, or storm,
Icing the pole, or in the torrid clime

Dark-heaving;—boundless, endless, and sublime,—
The image of Eternity,—the throne
Of the Invisible; even from out thy slime
The monsters of the deep are made; each zone
Obeys thee; thou goest forth, dread, fathomless, alone.

And I have loved thee, Ocean! and my joy
Of youthful sports was on thy breast to be
Borne, like thy bubbles, onward. From a boy
I wantoned with thy breakers,—they to me
Were a delight; and if the freshening sea
Made them a terror, 'twas a pleasing fear;
For I was as it were a child of thee,
And trusted to thy billows far and near,
And laid my hand upon thy mane,—as I do here.

GEORGE GORDON BYRON

WHERE LIES THE LAND

WHERE lies the land to which the ship would go?
Far, far ahead, is all her seamen know.
And where the land she travels from? Away,
Far, far behind, is all that they can say.

On sunny noons upon the deck's smooth face,
Linked arm in arm, how pleasant here to pace;
Or, o'er the stern reclining, watch below
The foaming wake far widening as we go.

On stormy nights, when wild north-westers rave,
How proud a thing to fight with wind and wave!
The dripping sailor on the reeling mast
Exults to bear, and scorns to wish it past.

Where lies the land to which the ship would go?
Far, far ahead, is all her seamen know.
And where the land she travels from? Away,
Far, far behind, is all that they can say.

ARTHUR HUGH CLOUGH

THE BRAVE OLD SHIP, THE ORIENT

WOE for the brave ship Orient!
Woe for the old ship Orient!
For in broad, broad light, and with land in sight,
Where the waters bubbled white,

One great sharp shriek! One shudder of affright!—
And—
       down went the brave old ship, the Orient!

It was the fairest day in the merry month of May,
And sleepiness had settled on the seas;
And we had our white sail set, high up, and higher yet,
And our flag flashed and fluttered at its ease;
The cross of St. George, that in mountain and in gorge,—
On the hot and dusty plain,—
On the tiresome, trackless main,—
Conquering out,—conquering home again,—
Had flamed, the world over, on the breeze.
Ours was the far-famed Albion,
And she had her best look of might and beauty on,
As she swept across the seas that day.
The wind was fair and soft, both alow and aloft,
And we wore the even hours away.
The steadying sun heaved up as day drew on,
And there grew a long swell of the sea.
And, first in upper air, then under, everywhere,
From the topmost towering sail
Down, down to quarter-rail,
The wind began to breathe more free.
It was soon to breathe its last,
For a wild and bitter blast
Was the master of that stormy day to be.

"Ho! Hilloa! A sail!" was the top-man's hail:
"A sail, hull-down upon our lee!"
Then with sea-glass to his eye,
And his gray locks blowing by,
The Admiral sought what she might be.
And from top, and from deck,
Was it ship? Was it wreck? A far-off, far-off speck,
Of a sudden we found upon our lee.

On the round waters wide, floated no thing beside,
But we and the stranger sail;
And a hazy sky, that threatened storm,
Came coating the heaven so blue and warm,
And ahead hung the portent of a gale:
A black bank hanging there
When the order came, to wear,
Was remembered, ever after, in the tale.

Across the long, slow swell
That scarcely rose and fell,

The wind began to blow out of the cloud;
And scarce an hour was gone ere the gale was fairly on,
And through our strained rigging howled aloud.
Before the stormy wind, that was maddening behind,
We gathered in our canvas farthest spread.
Black clouds had started out
From the heavens all about,
And the welkin grew all black overhead.
But though stronger and more strong
The fierce gale rushed along,
The stranger brought her old wind in her breast.
Up came the ship from the far-off sea
And on with the strong wind's breath rushed we.
She grew to the eye, against the clouded sky,
And eagerly her points and gear we guessed.
As we made her out, at last,
She was maimed in spar and mast
And she hugged the easy breeze for rest.

We could see the old wind fail
At the nearing of our gale;
We could see them lay their course with the wind:
Still we neared and neared her fast,
Hurled on by our fierce blast,
With the seas tumbling headlong behind.
She had come out of some storm, and, in many a busy swarm,
Her crew were refitting as they might,
The wreck of upper spars
That had left their ugly scars,
As if the ship had come out of a fight.
We scanned her well, as we drifted by,—
A strange old ship, with her poop built high,
And with quarter-galleries wide,
And a huge beaked prow, as no ships are builded now,
And carvings all strange, beside.
A Byzantine bark, and a ship of name and mark
Long years and generations ago;
Ere any mast or yard of ours was growing hard
With the seasoning of long Norwegian snow.
She was the brave old Orient,
The old imperial Orient,
Brought down from times afar,
Not such as our ships are,
But unchanged in hull and unchanged in spar,
Since mighty ships of war were builded so.

Down her old black side poured the water in a tide,
As they toiled to get the better of a leak.
We had got a signal set in the shrouds,
And our men through the storm looked on in crowds:—
But for wind, we were near enough to speak.
It seemed her sea and sky were in times long, long gone by,
That we read in winter-evens about;
As if to other stars
She had reared her old-world spars,
And her hull had kept an old-time ocean out.
We saw no signal fly, and her men scarce lifted eye,
But toiled at the work that was to do:
It warmed our English blood
When across the stormy flood
We saw the old ship and her crew.
The glories and the memories of other days agone
Seemed clinging to the old ship, as in storm she labored on.
The old ship Orient!
The brave, imperial Orient!

All that stormy night through, our ship was lying-to
Whenever we could keep her to the wind;
But late in the next day we gained a quiet bay,
For the tempest had left us far behind.
So before the sunny town
Went our anchors splashing down;
Our sails we hung all out to the sun;
While airs from off the steep
Came playing at bo-peep
With our canvas, hour by hour, in their fun.
We leaned on boom or rail with many a lazy tale
Of the work of the storm that had died;
And watched, with idle eyes,
Our floats, like summer flies,
Riding lazily about the ship's side.
Suddenly they cried, from the other deck,
That the Orient was gone to wreck!
That her hull lay high on a broken shore,
And the brave old ship would float no more.
But we heard a sadder tale, ere the night came on,
And a truer tale, of the ship that was gone.
They had seen from the height,
As she came from yester-night,
While the storm had not gone by, and the sea was running high,
A ship driving heavily to land;
A strange great ship (so she seemed to be

While she tumbled and rolled on the far-off sea,
And strange when she toiled, near at hand),
But some ship of mark and fame,
Though crippled, then, and lame,
And that must have been gallantly manned.
So she came, driving fast;
They could tell her men, at last;
There were harbors down the coast on her lee;
When, strangely, she broached to,—
Then, with her gallant crew,
Went headlong down into the sea.

That was the Orient,
The brave old Orient,—
Such a ship as nevermore will be.

ROBERT TRAILL SPENCE LOWELL

BALLAD OF THE TEMPEST

WE WERE crowded in the cabin,
    Not a soul would dare to sleep,—
It was midnight on the waters,
    And a storm was on the deep.

'Tis a fearful thing in Winter
    To be shattered in the blast,
And to hear the rattling trumpet
    Thunder: "Cut away the mast!"

So we shuddered there in silence,—
    For the stoutest held his breath,
While the hungry sea was roaring,
    And the breakers talked with Death.

As thus we sat in darkness,
    Each one busy in his prayers,
"We are lost!" the captain shouted
    As he staggered down the stairs.

But his little daughter whispered,
    As she took his icy hand:
"Isn't God upon the ocean
    Just the same as on the land?"

Then we kissed the little maiden,
    And we spoke in better cheer,
And we anchored safe in harbor
    When the morn was shining clear.

JAMES T. FIELDS

SPANISH WATERS

SPANISH WATERS, Spanish waters, you are ringing in my ears,
Like a slow sweet piece of music from the gray forgotten years;
Telling tales, and beating tunes, and bringing weary thoughts to me
Of the sandy beach at Muertos, where I would that I could be.

There's a surf breaks on Los Muertos, and it never stops to roar,
And it's there we came to anchor, and it's there we went ashore,
Where the blue lagoon is silent amid snags of rotting trees,
Dropping like the clothes of corpses cast up by the seas.

We anchored at Los Muertos when the dipping sun was red,
We left her half-a-mile to sea, to west of Nigger Head;
And before the mist was on the Cay, before the day was done,
We were all ashore on Muertos with the gold that we had won.

We bore it through the marshes in a half-score battered chest,
Sinking, in the sucking quagmires to the sunburn on our breasts,
Heaving over tree-trunks, gasping, damning at the flies and heat,
Longing for a long drink, out of silver, in the ship's cool lazareet.

The moon came white and ghostly as we laid the treasure down,
There was gear there'd make a beggarman as rich as Lima Town,
Copper charms and silver trinkets from the chests of Spanish crews,
Gold doubloons and double moydores, louis d'ors and ortagues,

Clumsy yellow-metal earrings from the Indians of Brazil,
Uncut emeralds out of Rio, bezoar stones from Guayaquil,
Silver, in the crude and fashioned, pots of old Arica bronze,
Jewels from the bones of Incas desecrated by the Dons.

We smoothed the place with mattocks, and we took and blazed the
tree,
Which marks yon where the gear is hid that none will ever see,
And we laid aboard the ship again, and south away we steers,
Through the loud surf of Los Muertos which is beating in my ears.

I'm the last alive that knows it. All the rest have gone their ways
Killed, or died, or come to anchor in the old Mulatas Cays,
And I go singing, fiddling, old and starved and in despair,
And I know where all that gold is hid, if I were only there.

It's not the way to end it all. I'm old and nearly blind,
And an old man's past's a strange thing, for it never leaves his mind.
And I see in dreams, awhiles, the beach, the sun's disc dipping red,
And the tall ship, under topsails, swaying in past Nigger Head.

I'd be glad to step ashore there. Glad to take a pick and go
To the lone blazed coco-palm tree in the place no others know,
And lift the gold and silver that has mouldered there for years
By the loud surf of Los Muertos which is beating in my ears.

JOHN MASEFIELD

LOCHINVAR

Oh, young Lochinvar is come out of the West,—
Through all the wide Border his steed was the best,
And saved his good broadsword he weapons had none,—
He rode all unarm'd and he rode all alone.
So faithful in love, and so dauntless in war,
There never was knight like the young Lochinvar.

He stay'd not for brake, and he stopp'd not for stone,
He swam the Eske river where ford there was none,
But ere he alighted at Netherby gate,
The bride had consented, the gallant came late;
For a laggard in love and a dastard in war
Was to wed the fair Ellen of brave Lochinvar.

So boldly he enter'd the Netherby hall,
'Mong bridesmen and kinsmen and brothers and all.
Then spoke the bride's father, his hand on his sword
(For the poor craven bridegroom said never a word),
"Oh, come ye in peace here, or come ye in war,
Or to dance at our bridal, young Lord Lochinvar?"

"I long woo'd your daughter,—my suit you denied;
Love swells like the Solway, but ebbs like its tide;
And now am I come, with this lost love of mine
To lead but one measure, drink one cup of wine.
There are maidens in Scotland more lovely, by far,
That would gladly be bride to the young Lochinvar."

The bride kiss'd the goblet, the knight took it up,
He quaff'd off the wine and he threw down the cup.
She look'd down to blush, and she look'd up to sigh,
With a smile on her lips and a tear in her eye.
He took her soft hand ere her mother could bar:
"Now tread we a measure," said young Lochinvar.

So stately his form, and so lovely her face,
That never a hall such a galliard did grace,
While her mother did fret, and her father did fume,
And the bridegroom stood dangling his bonnet and plume,

And the bridemaidens whisper'd, " 'Twere better by far
To have match'd our fair cousin with young Lochinvar."

One touch to her hand, and one word in her ear,
When they reach'd the hall-door, and the charger stood near;
So light to the croupe the fair lady he swung,
So light to the saddle before her he sprung!
"She is won! we are gone, over bank, bush, and scaur;
They'll have fleet steeds that follow," quoth young Lochinvar.

There was mounting 'mong Græmes of the Netherby clan;
Forsters, Fenwicks, and Musgraves, they rode and they ran;
There was racing and chasing on Cannobie Lee,
But the lost bride of Netherby ne'er did they see.
So daring in love, and so dauntless in war,
Have ye e'er heard of gallant like young Lochinvar?

SIR WALTER SCOTT

THE WRECK OF THE HESPERUS

IT WAS the schooner Hesperus,
    That sailed the wintry sea;
And the skipper had taken his little daughter,
    To bear him company.

Blue were her eyes as the fairy-flax,
    Her cheeks like the dawn of day,
And her bosom white as the hawthorn buds,
    That ope in the month of May.

The skipper he stood beside the helm,
    His pipe was in his mouth,
And he watched how the veering flaw did blow
    The smoke now West, now South.

Then up spake an old Sailòr,
    Had sailed to the Spanish Main,
"I pray thee, put into yonder port,
    For I fear a hurricane.

"Last night, the moon had a golden ring,
    And to-night no moon we see!"
The skipper, he blew a whiff from his pipe,
    And a scornful laugh laughed he.

Colder and louder blew the wind,
    A gale from the Northeast,
The snow fell hissing in the brine,
    And the billows frothed like yeast.

Down came the storm, and smote amain
    The vessel in its strength;
She shuddered and paused, like a frighted steed,
    Then leaped her cable's length.

"Come hither! come hither! my little daughter,
    And do not tremble so;
For I can weather the roughest gale
    That ever wind did blow."

He wrapped her warm in his seaman's coat
    Against the stinging blast;
He cut a rope from a broken spar,
    And bound her to the mast.

"O father! I hear the church-bells ring,
    Oh say, what may it be?"
" 'Tis a fog-bell on a rock-bound coast!"—
    And he steered for the open sea.

"O father! I hear the sound of guns,
    Oh say, what may it be?"
"Some ship in distress, that cannot live
    In such an angry sea!"

"O father! I see a gleaming light,
    Oh say, what may it be?"
But the father answered never a word,
    A frozen corpse was he.

Lashed to the helm, all stiff and stark,
    With his face turned to the skies,
The lantern gleamed through the gleaming snow
    On his fixed and glassy eyes.

Then the maiden clasped her hands and prayed
    That savèd she might be;
And she thought of Christ, who stilled the wave,
    On the Lake of Galilee.

And fast through the midnight dark and drear,
    Through the whistling sleet and snow,
Like a sheeted ghost, the vessel swept
    Tow'rds the reef of Norman's Woe.

And ever the fitful gusts between
    A sound came from the land;
It was the sound of the trampling surf
    On the rocks and the hard sea-sand.

The breakers were right beneath her bows,
 She drifted a dreary wreck,
And a whooping billow swept the crew
 Like icicles from her deck.

She struck where the white and fleecy waves
 Looked soft as carded wool,
But the cruel rocks, they gored her side
 Like the horns of an angry bull.

Her rattling shrouds, all sheathed in ice,
 With the masts went by the board;
Like a vessel of glass, she stove and sank,
 Ho! ho! the breakers roared!

At daybreak, on the bleak sea-beach,
 A fisherman stood aghast,
To see the form of a maiden fair,
 Lashed close to a drifting mast.

The salt sea was frozen on her breast,
 The salt tears in her eyes;
And he saw her hair, like the brown seaweed,
 On the billows fall and rise.

Such was the wreck of the Hesperus,
 In the midnight and the snow!
Christ save us all from a death like this,
 On the reef of Norman's Woe!
    HENRY WADSWORTH LONGFELLOW

JOHN MAYNARD

'TWAS ON Lake Erie's broad expanse
 One bright midsummer day,
The gallant steamer *Ocean Queen*
 Swept proudly on her way.
Bright faces clustered on the deck
 Or, leaning o'er the side,
Watched carelessly the feathery foam
 That flecked the rippling tide.

Ah, who beneath that cloudless sky,
 That, smiling, bends serene,
Could dream that danger, awful, vast,
 Impended o'er the scene—
Could dream that ere an hour had sped
 That frame of sturdy oak

Would sink beneath the lake's blue waves,
    Blackened with fire and smoke?

A seaman sought the captain's side,
    A moment whispered low;
The captain's swarthy face grew pale;
    He hurried down below.
Alas, too late! Though quick and sharp
    And clear his orders came,
No human efforts could avail
    To quench the insidious flame.

The bad news quickly reached the deck,
    It sped from lip to lip,
And ghastly faces everywhere
    Looked from the doomed ship.
"Is there no hope, no chance of life?"
    A hundred lips implore;
"But one," the captain made reply,
    "To run the ship on shore."

A sailor whose heroic soul
    That hour should yet reveal,
By name John Maynard, Eastern born,
    Stood calmly at the wheel.
"Head her southeast!" the captain shouts
    Above the smothered roar,
"Head her southeast without delay!
    Make for the nearest shore!"

No terror pales the helmsman's cheeks,
    Or clouds his dauntless eye,
As, in a sailor's measured tone
    His voice responds "Ay! ay!"
Three hundred souls, the steamer's freight,
    Crowd forward, wild with fear,
While at the stern the dreaded flames
    Above the deck appear.

John Maynard watched the nearing flames,
    But still with steady hand
He grasped the wheel and steadfastly
    He steered the ship to land.
"John Maynard, can you still hold out?"
    He heard the captain cry;
A voice from out the stifling smoke
    Faintly responds, "Ay! ay!"

But half a mile, a hundred hands
   Stretch eagerly to shore;
But half a mile that distance sped,
   Peril shall all be o'er.
But half a mile! Yet stay, the flames
   No longer slowly creep,
But gather round that helmsman bold
   With fierce, impetuous sweep.

"John Maynard!" with an anxious voice
   The captain cries once more,
"Stand by the wheel five minutes yet,
   And we shall reach the shore."
Through flame and smoke that dauntless heart
   Responded firmly still,
Unawed, though face to face with death,
   "With God's good help I will!"

The flames approach with giant strides,
   They scorch his hand and brow;
One arm, disabled, seeks his side,
   Ah! he is conquered now.
But no, his teeth are firmly set,
   He crushes down his pain;
His knee upon the stanchion pressed,
   He guides the ship again.

One moment yet! one moment yet!
   Brave heart, thy task is o'er;
The pebbles grate beneath the keel
   The steamer touches shore.
Three hundred grateful voices rise
   In praise to God that he
Hath saved them from the fearful fire,
   And from the engulfing sea.

But where is he, that helmsman bold?
   The captain saw him reel;
His nerveless hands released their task;
   He sank beside the wheel.
The wave received his lifeless corse,
   Blackened with smoke and fire.
God rest him! Never hero had
   A nobler funeral pyre!

                    HORATIO ALGER, JR.

THE LAST HUNT

OH, it's twenty gallant gentlemen
   Rode out to hunt the deer,
With mirth upon the silver horn
   And gleam upon the spear;
They galloped through the meadow-grass,
   They sought the forest's gloom,
And loudest rang Sir Morven's laugh,
   And lightest tossed his plume.
      There's no delight by day or night
        Like hunting in the morn;
      So busk ye, gallant gentlemen,
        And sound the silver horn!

They rode into the dark greenwood
   By ferny dell and glade,—
And now and then upon their cloaks
   The yellow sunshine played;
They heard the timid forest-birds
   Break off amid their glee,
They saw the startled leveret,
   But not a stag did see.
      Wind, wind the horn, on summer morn!
        Though ne'er a buck appear,
      There's health for horse and gentleman
        A-hunting of the deer!

They panted up Ben Lomond's side
   Where thick the leafage grew,
And when they bent the branches back
   The sunbeams darted through;
Sir Morven in his saddle turned,
   And to his comrades spake,
"Now quiet! we shall find a stag
   Beside the Brownies' Lake."
      Then sound not on the bugle-horn,
        Bend bush and do not break,
      Lest ye should start the timid hart
        A-drinking at the lake.

Now they have reached the Brownies' Lake,—
   A blue eye in the wood,—
And on its brink a moment's space
   All motionless they stood:
When, suddenly, the silence broke

With fifty bowstrings' twang,
And hurtling through the drowsy air
    Full fifty arrows sang.
        Ah, better for those gentlemen,
            Than horn and slender spear,
        Were morion and buckler true,
            A-hunting of the deer.

Not one of that brave company
    Shall hunt the deer again;
Some fell beside the Brownies' Pool,
    Some dropped in dell or glen;
An arrow pierced Sir Morven's breast,
    His horse plunged in the lake,
And swimming to the farther bank
    He left a bloody wake.
        Ah, what avails the silver horn,
            And what the slender spear?
        There's other quarry in the wood
            Beside the fallow deer!

O'er ridge and hollow sped the horse
    Besprent with blood and foam,
Nor slackened pace until at eve
    He brought his master home.
How tenderly the Lady Ruth
    The cruel dart withdrew!
"False Tirrell shot the bolt," she said,
    "That my Sir Morven slew!"
        Deep in the forest lurks the foe,
            While gayly shines the morn:
        Hang up the broken spear, and blow
            A dirge upon the horn.

WILLIAM ROSCOE THAYER

THE LAST FIGHT

THAT night I think that no one slept;
    No bells were struck, no whistle blew,
And when the watch was changed I crept
    From man to man of all the crew
With whispered orders. Though we swept
    Through roaring seas, we hushed the clock,
    And muffled every clanking block.

So when one fool, unheeding, cried
    Some petty order, straight I ran

And threw him sprawling o'er the side.
   All life is but a narrow span:
It little matters that one bide
   A moment longer here, for all
   Fare the same road, whate'er befall.

But vain my care; for when the day
   Broke gray and wet, we saw the foe
But half a stormy league away.
   By noon we saw his black bows throw
Five fathoms high a wall of spray;
   A little more, we heard the drum,
   And knew that our last hour had come.

All day our crew had lined the side
   With grim, set faces, muttering;
And once a boy (the first that died)
   One of our wild songs tried to sing:
But when the first shot missed us wide,
   A dozen sprang aboard our rail,
   Shook fists, and roared a cursing hail.

Thereon, all hot for war, they bound
   Their heads with cool, wet bands, and drew
Their belts close, and their keen blades ground;
   Then, at the next gun's puff of blue,
We set the grog-cup on its round,
   And pledged for life or pledged for death
   Our last sigh of expiring breath.

Laughing, our brown young singer fell
   As their next shot crashed through our rail;
Then 'twixt us flashed the fire of hell,
   That shattered spar and riddled sail.
What ill we wrought we could not tell;
   But blood-red all their scuppers dripped
   When their black hull to starboard dipped.

Nine times I saw our helmsman fall,
   And nine times sent new men, who took
The whirling wheel as at death's call;
   But when I saw the last one look
From sky to deck, then, reeling, crawl
   Under the shattered rail to die,
   I knew where I should surely lie.

I could not send more men to stand
   And turn in idleness the wheel
Until they took death's beckoning hand,

While others, melting steel with steel,
Flamed out their lives—an eager band,
    Cheers on their lips, and in their eyes
    The goal-rapt look of high emprise.

So to the wheel I went. Like bees
    I heard the shot go darting by;
There came a trembling in my knees,
    And black spots whirled about the sky.
I thought of things beyond the seas—
    The little town where I was born,
    And swallows twittering in the morn.

A wounded creature drew him where
    I grasped the wheel, and begged to steer.
It mattered not how he might fare
    The little time he had for fear;
So if I left this to his care
    He too might serve us yet, he said.
    He died there while I shook my head.

I would not fall so like a dog,
    My helpless back turned to the foe;
So when his great hulk, like a log,
    Came surging past our quarter, lo!
With helm hard down, straight through the fog
    Of battle smoke, and luffing wide,
    I sent our sharp bow through his side.

The willing waves came rushing in
    The ragged entrance that we gave;
Like snakes I heard their green coils spin
    Up, up around our floating grave;
But dauntless still, amid a din
    Of clashing steel and battle-shout,
    We rushed to drive their boarders out.

Around me in a closing ring
    My grim-faced foemen darkly drew;
Then, sweeter than the lark in spring,
    Loud rang our blades; the red sparks flew.
Twice, thrice, I felt the sudden sting
    Of some keen stroke; then, swinging fair,
    My own clave more than empty air.

The fight went raging past me when
    My good blade cleared a silent place;
Then in a ring of fallen men
    I paused to breathe a little space.

Elsewhere the deck roared like a glen
　　When mountain torrents meet; the fray
　　A moment then seemed far away.

The barren sea swept to the sky;
　　The empty sky dipped to the sea;
Such utter waste could scarcely lie
　　Beyond death's starved periphery.
Only one living thing went by:
　　Far overhead an ominous bird
　　Rode down the gale with wings unstirred.

Windward I saw the billows swing
　　Dark crests to beckon others on
To see our end; then, hurrying
　　To reach us ere we should be gone,
They came, like tigers mad to fling
　　Their jostling bodies on our ships,
　　And snarl at us with foaming lips.

There was no time to spare: a wave
　　E'en then broke growling at my feet;
One last look to the sky I gave,
　　Then sprang my eager foes to meet.
Loud rang the fray above our grave—
　　I felt the vessel downward reel
　　As my last thrust met thrusting steel.

I heard a roaring in my ears;
　　A green wall pressed against my eyes;
Down, down I passed; the vanished years
　　I saw in mimicry arise.
Yet even then I felt no fears,
　　And with my last expiring breath
　　My past rose up and mocked at death.

LEWIS FRANK TOOKER

THE LAST BUCCANEER

OH, England is a pleasant place for them that's rich and high;
But England is a cruel place for such poor folks as I;
And such a port for mariners I ne'er shall see again
As the pleasant Isle of Avès, beside the Spanish main.

There were forty craft in Avès that were both swift and stout,
All furnish'd well with small-arms and cannons round about;
And a thousand men in Avès made laws so fair and free
To choose their valiant captains and obey them loyally.

Thence we sail'd against the Spaniard with his hoards of plate and gold,
Which he wrung with cruel tortures from the Indian folk of old;
Likewise the merchant captains, with hearts as hard as stone,
Who flog men and keel-haul them and starve them to the bone.

Oh the palms grew high in Avès and fruits that shone like gold,
And the colibris and parrots they were gorgeous to behold;
And the negro maids to Avès from bondage fast did flee,
To welcome gallant sailors a-sweeping in from sea.

Oh sweet it was in Avès to hear the landward breeze
A-swing with good tobacco in a net between the trees,
With a negro lass to fan you while you listen'd to the roar
Of the breakers on the reef outside that never touch'd the shore.

But Scripture saith, an ending to all fine things must be,
So the King's ships sail'd on Avès, and quite put down were we.
All day we fought like bulldogs, but they burst the booms at night;
And I fled in a piragua sore wounded from the fight.

Nine days I floated starving, and a negro lass beside,
Till for all I tried to cheer her, the poor young thing she died;
But as I lay a-gasping a Bristol sail came by,
And brought me home to England here to beg until I die.

And now I'm old and going—I'm sure I can't tell where;
One comfort is, this world's so hard I can't be worse off there:
If I might but be a sea-dove I'd fly across the main,
To the pleasant Isle of Avès, to look at it once again.

CHARLES KINGSLEY

THE CAVALIER'S ESCAPE

TRAMPLE! trample! went the roan,
　　Trap! trap! went the gray;
But pad! *pad!* PAD! like a thing that was mad,
　　My chestnut broke away.
It was just five miles from Salisbury town,
　　And but one hour to day.

Thud! THUD! came on the heavy roan,
　　Rap! RAP! the mettled gray;
But my chestnut mare was of blood so rare,
　　That she showed them all the way.
Spur on! spur on!—I doffed my hat,
　　And wished them all good-day.

They splashed through miry rut and pool,—
    Splintered through fence and rail;
But chestnut Kate switched over the gate,—
    I saw them droop and trail.
To Salisbury town—but a mile of down,
    Once over this brook and rail.

Trap! trap! I heard their echoing hoofs
    Past the walls of mossy stone;
The roan flew on at a staggering pace,
    But blood is better than bone.
I patted old Kate, and gave her the spur,
    For I knew it was all my own.

But trample! trample! came their steeds,
    And I saw their wolf's eyes burn;
I felt like a royal hart at bay,
    And made me ready to turn.
I looked where highest grew the may,
    And deepest arched the fern.

I flew at the first knave's sallow throat;
    One blow, and he was down.
The second rogue fired twice, and missed;
    I sliced the villain's crown,—
Clove through the rest, and flogged brave Kate,
    Fast, fast to Salisbury town!

Pad! pad! they came on the level sward,
    Thud! thud! upon the sand,—
With a gleam of swords and a burning match,
    And a shaking of flag and hand;
But one long bound, and I passed the gate,
    Safe from the canting band.

                              WALTER THORNBURY

ROBIN HOOD AND ALLEN-A-DALE

COME listen to me, you gallants so free,
    All you that love mirth for to hear,
And I will tell you of a bold outláw,
    That lived in Nottinghamshire.

As Robin Hood in the forest stood,
    All under the greenwood tree,
There was he aware of a brave young man,
    As fine as fine might be.

The youngster was clad in scarlet red,
    In scarlet fine and gay;
And he did frisk it over the plain,
    And chanted a roundelay.

As Robin Hood next morning stood
    Amongst the leaves so gay,
There did he espy the same young man
    Come drooping along the way.

The scarlet he wore the day before
    It was clean cast away;
And at every step he fetched a sigh,
    "Alas! and well-a-day!"

Then steppèd forth brave Little John,
    And Midge, the miller's son;
Which made the young man bend his bow
    When as he see them come.

"Stand off! stand off!" the young man said,
    "What is your will with me?"
"You must come before our master straight,
    Under yon greenwood tree."

And when he came bold Robin before,
    Robin asked him courteously,
"O, hast thou any money to spare,
    For my merry men and me?"

"I have no money," the young man said,
    "But five shillings and a ring;
And that I have kept these seven long years,
    To have at my wedding.

"Yesterday I should have married a maid,
    But she was from me ta'en,
And chosen to be an old knight's delight,
    Whereby my poor heart is slain."

"What is thy name?" then said Robin Hood,
    "Come tell me, without any fail."
"By the faith of my body," then said the young man,
    "My name it is Allen-a-Dale."

"What wilt thou give me," said Robin Hood,
    "In ready gold or fee,
To help thee to thy true-love again,
    And deliver her unto thee?"

"I have no money," then quoth the young man,
  "No ready gold nor fee,
But I will swear upon a book
  Thy true servant for to be."

"How many miles is it to thy true-love?
  Come tell me without guile."
"By the faith of my body," then said the young man,
  "It is but five little mile."

Then Robin he hasted over the plain;
  He did neither stint nor lin,
Until he came unto the church
  Where Allen should keep his weddin'.

"What dost thou here?" the bishop then said;
  "I prithee now tell unto me."
"I am a bold harper," quoth Robin Hood,
  "And the best in the north country."

"Oh welcome, oh welcome," the bishop he said;
  "That music best pleaseth me."
"You shall have no music," quoth Robin Hood,
  "Till the bride and the bridegroom I see."

With that came in a wealthy knight,
  Which was both grave and old;
And after him a finikin lass,
  Did shine like glistering gold.

"This is no fit match," quoth Robin Hood,
  "That you do seem to make here;
For since we are come into the church,
  The bride shall chuse her own dear."

Then Robin Hood put his horn to his mouth,
  And blew blasts two or three;
When four-and-twenty yeomen bold
  Came leaping over the lea.

And when they came into the church-yard,
  Marching all in a row,
The first man was Allen-a-Dale,
  To give bold Robin his bow.

"This is thy true love," Robin he said.
  "Young Allen, as I hear say:
And you shall be married at this same time,
  Before we depart away."

"That shall not be," the bishop he cried,
   "For thy word it shall not stand;
They shall be three times asked in the church,
   As the law is of our land."

Robin Hood pulled off the bishop's coat,
   And put it upon Little John;
"By the faith of my body," then Robin said,
   "This cloth doth make thee a man."

When Little John went into the quire,
   The people began to laugh;
He asked them seven times into church,
   Lest three times should not be enough.

"Who gives me this maid?" then said Little John,
   Quoth Robin Hood, "That do I;
And he that takes her from Allen-a-Dale,
   Full dearly he shall her buy."

And then having ended this merry wedding,
   The bride looked as fresh as a queen;
And so they returned to the merry greenwood,
   Amongst the leaves so green.

                        ANONYMOUS

HOW THEY BROUGHT THE GOOD NEWS FROM GHENT TO AIX

I sprang to the stirrup, and Joris, and he;
I gallop'd, Dirck gallop'd, we gallop'd all three;
"Good speed!" cried the watch, as the gate-bolts undrew;
"Speed!" echo'd the wall to us galloping through;
Behind shut the postern, the lights sank to rest,
And into the midnight we gallop'd abreast.

Not a word to each other; we kept the great pace
Neck by neck, stride by stride, never changing our place;
I turn'd in my saddle and made its girths tight,
Then shorten'd each stirrup, and set the pique right,
Rebuckled the check-strap, chain'd slacker the bit,
Nor gallop'd less steadily Roland a whit.

'Twas moonset at starting; but while we drew near
Lokeren, the cocks crew and twilight dawn'd clear;
At Boom, a great yellow star came out to see;
At Düffeld, 'twas morning as plain as could be;

And from Mecheln church-steeple we heard the half-chime,
So Joris broke silence with, "Yet there is time!"

At Aerschot, up leap'd of a sudden the sun,
And against him the cattle stood black every one,
To stare through the mist at us galloping past,
And I saw my stout galloper Roland at last,
With resolute shoulders, each butting away
The haze, as some bluff river headland its spray.

And his low head and crest, just one sharp ear bent back
For my voice, and the other prick'd out on his track;
And one eye's black intelligence,—ever that glance
O'er its white edge at me, his own master, askance!
And the thick heavy spume flakes which aye and anon
His fierce lips shook upward in galloping on.

By Hasselt, Dirck groan'd; and cried Joris, "Stay spur!
Your Roos gallop'd bravely, the fault's not in her;
We'll remember at Aix—" for one heard the quick wheeze
Of her chest, saw the stretch'd neck, and staggering knees,
And sunk tail, and horrible heave of the flank,
As down on her haunches she shudder'd and sank.

So we were left galloping, Joris and I,
Past Looz and past Tongres, no cloud in the sky;
The broad sun above laugh'd a pitiless laugh,
'Neath our feet broke the brittle bright stubble like chaff;
Till over by Dalhem a dome-spire sprang white,
And "Gallop," gasp'd Joris, "for Aix is in sight!

"How they'll greet us!"—and all in a moment his roan
Roll'd neck and croup over, lay dead as a stone;
And there was my Roland to bear the whole weight
Of the news which alone could save Aix from her fate,
With his nostrils like pits full of blood to the brim,
And with circles of red for his eye-sockets' rim.

Then I cast loose my buff coat, each holster let fall,
Shook off both my jack-boots, let go belt and all,
Stood up in the stirrup, lean'd, patted his ear,
Call'd my Roland his pet-name, my horse without peer;
Clapp'd my hands, laugh'd and sang, any noise, bad or good,
Till at length into Aix Roland gallop'd and stood.

And all I remember is, friends flocking round
As I sate with his head 'twixt my knees on the ground,
And no voice but was praising this Roland of mine,
As I pour'd down his throat our last measure of wine,

Which (the burgesses voted by common consent)
Was no more than his due who brought good news from Ghent.

ROBERT BROWNING

THE CHARGE OF THE LIGHT BRIGADE

HALF a league, half a league,
   Half a league onward,
All in the valley of Death
   Rode the six hundred.
"Forward, the Light Brigade!
Charge for the guns!" he said:
Into the valley of Death
   Rode the six hundred.

"Forward, the Light Brigade!"
Was there a man dismay'd?
Not though the soldier knew
   Some one had blunder'd:
Their's not to make reply,
Their's not to reason why,
Their's but to do and die:
Into the valley of Death
   Rode the six hundred.

Cannon to right of them,
Cannon to left of them,
Cannon in front of them
   Volley'd and thunder'd;
Storm'd at with shot and shell,
Boldly they rode and well,
Into the jaws of Death,
Into the mouth of Hell
   Rode the six hundred:

Flash'd all their sabres bare,
Flash'd as they turn'd in air,
Sabring the gunners there,
Charging an army, while
   All the world wonder'd:
Plunged in the battery-smoke,
Right through the line they broke;
   Cossack and Russian
Reel'd from the sabre-stroke
   Shatter'd and sunder'd.
Then they rode back, but not—
   Not the six hundred.

Cannon to right of them,
Cannon to left of them,
Cannon behind them
   Volley'd and thunder'd;
Storm'd at with shot and shell,
While horse and hero fell,
They that had fought so well
Came through the jaws of Death
Back from the mouth of Hell,
All that was left of them,
   Left of six hundred.

When can their glory fade?
Oh, the wild charge they made!
   All the world wonder'd.
Honor the charge they made!
Honor the Light Brigade,
   Noble six hundred!

             ALFRED TENNYSON

HERVÉ RIEL

ON THE SEA and at the Hogue, sixteen hundred ninety-two,
   Did the English fight the French,—woe to France!
And, the thirty-first of May, helter-skelter through the blue,
Like a crowd of frightened porpoises a shoal of sharks pursue,
   Came crowding ship on ship to St. Malo on the Rance,
With the English fleet in view.

'T was the squadron that escaped, with the victor in full chase,
   First and foremost of the drove, in his great ship, Damfreville;
      Close on him fled, great and small,
      Twenty-two good ships in all;
And they signalled to the place,
"Help the winners of a race!
   Get us guidance, give us harbor, take us quick,—or, quicker still,
Here's the English can and will!"

Then the pilots of the place put out brisk and leapt on board;
   "Why, what hope or chance have ships like these to pass?" laughed
      they:
"Rocks to starboard, rocks to port, all the passage scarred and scored,
Shall the *Formidable* here with her twelve and eighty guns
   Think to make the river-mouth by the single narrow way,
Trust to enter where 'tis ticklish for a craft of twenty tons,
     And with flow at full beside?

Now, 'tis slackest ebb of tide.
Reach the mooring? Rather say,
While rock stands or water runs,
    Not a ship will leave the bay!"

Then was called a council straight.
Brief and bitter the debate:
"Here's the English at our heels; would you have them take in tow
All that's left us of the fleet, linked together stern and bow,
For a prize to Plymouth Sound?
Better run the ships aground!"
    (Ended Damfreville his speech.)
"Not a minute more to wait!
    Let the Captains all and each
    Shove ashore, then blow up, burn the vessels on the beach!
France must undergo her fate.

"Give the word!" But no such word
Was ever spoke or heard;
    For up stood, for out stepped, for in struck amid all these
—A Captain? A Lieutenant? A Mate—first, second, third?
        No such man of mark, and meet
        With his betters to compete!
    But a simple Breton sailor pressed by Tourville for the fleet,
A poor coasting-pilot he, Hervé Riel the Croisickese.

And, "What mockery or malice have we here?" cries Hervé Riel:
    "Are you mad, you Malouins? Are you cowards, fools, or rogues?
Talk to me of rocks and shoals, me who took the soundings, tell
On my fingers every bank, every shallow, every swell
    'Twixt the offing here and Grève where the river disembogues?
Are you bought by English gold? Is it love the lying's for?
        Morn and eve, night and day,
        Have I piloted your bay,
Entered free and anchored fast at foot of Solidor.
    Burn the fleet and ruin France? That were worse than fifty Hogues!
        Sirs, they know I speak the truth! Sirs, believe me there's a way!
Only let me lead the line,
    Have the biggest ship to steer,
    Get this *Formidable* clear,
Make the others follow mine,
And I lead them, most and least, by a passage I know well,
    Right to Solidor past Grève,
        And there lay them safe and sound;
        And if one ship misbehave,
        —Keel so much as grate the ground,
Why, I've nothing but my life,—here's my head!" cries Hervé Riel.

Not a minute more to wait.
"Steer us in, then, small and great!
    Take the helm, lead the line, save the squadron!" cried its chief.
Captains, give the sailor place!
    He is Admiral, in brief.
Still the north-wind, by God's grace!
See the noble fellow's face
As the big ship, with a bound,
Clears the entry like a hound,
Keeps the passage as its inch of way were the wide seas profound!
    See, safe through shoal and rock,
    How they follow in a flock,
Not a ship that misbehaves, not a keel that grates the ground,
    Not a spar that comes to grief!
The peril, see, is past,
All are harbored to the last,
And just as Hervé Riel hollas "Anchor!"—sure as fate
Up the English come—too late!

So, the storm subsides to calm:
    They see the green trees wave
    On the heights o'erlooking Grève.
Hearts that bled are stanched with balm.
"Just our rapture to enhance,
    Let the English rake the bay,
Gnash their teeth and glare askance
    As they cannonade away!
'Neath rampired Solidor pleasant riding on the Rance!"
How hope succeeds despair on each Captain's countenance!
Out burst all with one accord,
    "This is Paradise for Hell!
        Let France, let France's King
        Thank the man that did the thing!"
What a shout, and all one word,
    "Hervé Riel!"
As he stepped in front once more,
    Not a symptom of surprise
    In the frank blue Breton eyes,
Just the same man as before.

Then said Damfreville, "My friend,
I must speak out at the end,
    Though I find the speaking hard.
Praise is deeper than the lips:
You have saved the King his ships,
    You must name your own reward.
'Faith, our sun was near eclipse!

Demand what'er you will,
France remains your debtor still.
Ask to heart's content and have! or my name's not Damfreville."

Then a beam of fun outbroke
On the bearded mouth that spoke,
As the honest heart laughed through
Those frank eyes of Breton blue:
"Since I needs must say my say,
    Since on board the duty's done,
        And from Malo Roads to Croisic Point, what is it but a run?—
Since 'tis ask and have, I may—
    Since the others go ashore—
Come! A good whole holiday!
    Leave to go and see my wife, whom I call the Belle Aurore!"
    That he asked and that he got,—nothing more.

Name and deed alike are lost:
Not a pillar nor a post
    In his Croisic keeps alive the feat as it befell;
Not a head in white and black
On a single fishing smack,
In memory of the man but for whom had gone to wrack
    All that France saved from the fight whence England bore the bell.
Go to Paris: rank on rank
    Search the heroes flung pell-mell
On the Louvre, face and flank!
    You shall look long enough ere you come to Hervé Riel.
So, for better and for worse,
Hervé Riel, accept my verse!
In my verse, Hervé Riel, do thou once more
Save the squadron, honor France, love thy wife the Belle Aurore!

ROBERT BROWNING

THE INCHCAPE ROCK

No STIR in the air, no stir in the sea,
The ship was still as she could be;
Her sails from heaven received no motion,
Her keel was steady in the ocean.

Without either sign or sound of their shock
The waves flow'd over the Inchcape Rock;
So little they rose, so little they fell,
They did not move the Inchcape Bell.

The Abbot of Aberbrothok
Had placed that bell on the Inchcape Rock;

On a buoy in the storm it floated and swung,
And over the waves its warning rung.

When the rock was hid by the surges' swell,
The mariners heard the warning bell,
And then they knew the perilous rock,
And bless'd the Abbot of Aberbrothok.

The sun in heaven was shining gay,
All things were joyful on that day;
The sea-birds scream'd as they wheel'd round,
And there was joyaunce in their sound.

The buoy of the Inchcape Bell was seen
A darker speck on the ocean green;
Sir Ralph the Rover walk'd his deck,
And he fix'd his eye on the darker speck.

He felt the cheering power of spring,
It made him whistle, it made him sing,
His heart was mirthful to excess,
But the Rover's mirth was wickedness.

His eye was on the Inchcape float;
Quoth he, "My men, put out the boat,
And row me to the Inchcape Rock,
And I'll plague the Abbot of Aberbrothok."

The boat is lower'd, the boatmen row,
And to the Inchcape Rock they go;
Sir Ralph bent over from the boat,
And he cut the bell from the Inchcape float.

Down sank the bell with a gurgling sound,
The bubbles rose and burst around;
Quoth Sir Ralph, "The next who comes to the rock
Won't bless the Abbot of Aberbrothok."

Sir Ralph the Rover sail'd away,
He scour'd the seas for many a day,
And now, grown rich with plunder'd store,
He steers his course for Scotland's shore.

So thick a haze o'erspreads the sky,
They cannot see the sun on high;
The wind hath blown a gale all day,
At evening it hath died away.

On the deck the Rover takes his stand;
So dark it is they see no land.

Quoth Sir Ralph, "It will be lighter soon,
For there is the dawn of the rising moon."

"Canst hear," said one, "the breakers roar?
For methinks we should be near the shore."
"Now, where we are I cannot tell,
But I wish I could hear the Inchcape Bell."

They hear no sound, the swell is strong,
Though the wind hath fallen, they drift along,
Till the vessel strikes with a shivering shock,—
"O Death! it is the Inchcape Rock."

Sir Ralph the Rover tore his hair,
He cursed himself in his despair;
The waves rush in on every side,
The ship is sinking beneath the tide.

But, even in his dying fear,
One dreadful sound could the Rover hear,
A sound as if, with the Inchcape Bell,
The Devil below was ringing his knell.

ROBERT SOUTHEY

AGINCOURT

FAIR stood the wind for France
When we our sails advance,
Nor now to prove our chance
        Longer will tarry;
But putting to the main,
At Kaux, the mouth of Seine,
With all his martial train,
        Landed King Harry.

And taking many a fort,
Furnish'd in warlike sort,
March'd toward Agincourt
        In happy hour—
Skirmishing day by day
With those that stopp'd his way,
Where the French gen'ral lay
        With all his power,

Which in his height of pride,
King Henry to deride,
His ransom to provide
        To the king sending;

Which he neglects the while,
As from a nation vile,
Yet, with an angry smile,
    Their fall portending.

And turning to his men,
Quoth our brave Henry then:
Though they to one be ten,
    Be not amazed;
Yet have we well begun—
Battles so bravely won
Have ever to the sun
    By fame been raised.

And for myself, quoth he,
This my full rest shall be;
England, ne'er mourn for me,
    Nor more esteem me.
Victor I will remain,
Or on this earth lie slain;
Never shall she sustain
    Loss to redeem me.

Poitiers and Cressy tell,
When most their pride did swell,
Under our swords they fell;
    No less our skill is
Than when our grandsire great,
Claiming the regal seat,
By many a warlike feat
    Lopp'd the French lilies.

The duke of York so dread
The eager vaward led;
With the main Henry sped,
    Amongst his henchmen.
Excester had the rear—
A braver man not there:
O Lord! how hot they were
    On the false Frenchmen!

They now to fight are gone;
Armor on armor shone;
Drum now to drum did groan—
    To hear was wonder;
That with the cries they make
The very earth did shake;
Trumpet to trumpet spake,
    Thunder to thunder.

Well it thine age became,
O noble Erpingham!
Which did the signal aim
    To our hid forces;
When, from a meadow by,
Like a storm suddenly,
The English archery
    Struck the French horses,

With Spanish yew so strong,
Arrows a cloth-yard long,
That like to serpents stung,
    Piercing the weather;
None from his fellow starts,
But playing manly parts,
And like true English hearts,
    Stuck close together.

When down their bows they threw,
And forth their bilbows drew,
And on the French they flew,
    Not one was tardy:
Arms were from shoulders sent;
Scalps to the teeth were rent;
Down the French peasants went;
    Our men were hardy.

This while our noble king,
His broadsword brandishing,
Down the French host did ding,
    As to o'erwhelm it;
And many a deep wound lent,
His arms with blood besprent,
And many a cruel dent
    Bruised his helmet.

Glo'ster, that duke so good,
Next of the royal blood,
For famous England stood,
    With his brave brother—
Clarence, in steel so bright,
Though but a maiden knight,
Yet in that furious fight
    Scarce such another.

Warwick in blood did wade;
Oxford the foe invade,
And cruel slaughter made,

Still as they ran up.
Suffolk his axe did ply;
Beaumont and Willoughby
Bare them right doughtily,
　　Ferrers and Fanhope.

Upon Saint Crispin's day
Fought was this noble fray,
Which fame did not delay
　　To England to carry;
Oh, when shall Englishmen
With such acts fill a pen,
Or England breed again
　　Such a King Harry?

MICHAEL DRAYTON

TRAFALGAR

HEARD YE the thunder of battle
　　Low in the South and afar?
Saw ye the flash of the death-cloud
　　Crimson on Trafalgar?

Such another day never
　　England will look on again,
When the battle fought was the hottest,
　　And the hero of heroes was slain!

For the fleet of France and the force of Spain were gather'd for fight—
A greater than Philip their lord, a new Armada in might;
And the sails were aloft once more in the deep Gaditanian bay,
Where *Redoubtable* and *Bucentaure* and great *Trinidada* lay;
Eager-reluctant to close; for across the bloodshed to be
Two navies beheld one prize in its glory—the throne of the sea!
Which were bravest, who should tell? for both were gallant and true;
But the greatest seaman was ours, of all that sail'd o'er the blue.

From Cadiz the enemy sallied: they knew not Nelson was there;
His name a navy to us, but to them a flag of despair.
From Ayamonte to Algeziras he guarded the coast,
Till he bore from Tavira south; and they now must fight, or be lost;
Vainly they steer'd for the Rock and the Midland sheltering sea,
For he headed the Admirals round, constraining them under his lee,
Villeneuve of France, and Gravina of Spain: so they shifted their
　　ground,
They could choose,—they were more than we—and they faced at Trafal-
　　gar round;

Banking their fleet two deep, a fortress-wall thirty-tower'd;
In the midst, four-storied with guns, the dark *Trinidada* lower'd.

So with those.—But meanwhile, as against some dyke that men mas-
sively rear,
From on high the torrent surges, to drive through the dyke as a spear,
Eagle-eyed e'en in his blindness, our chief sets his double array,
Making the fleet two spears, to thrust at the foe, any way . . .

'Anyhow!—without orders, each captain his Frenchman may grapple
perforce:
Collingwood first' (yet the *Victory* ne'er a whit slacken'd her course).
'Signal for action! Farewell! we shall win, but we meet not again!'
—Then a low thunder of readiness ran from the decks o'er the main,
And on—as the message from masthead to masthead flew out like a
flame,
'ENGLAND EXPECTS EVERY MAN WILL DO HIS DUTY'—they came.

—Silent they come—While the thirty black forts of the foeman's array
Clothe them in billowy snow, tier speaking o'er tier as they lay;
Flashes that came and went, as swords when the battle is rife;
But ours stood frowningly smiling, and ready for death as for life.

O in that interval grim, ere the furies of slaughter embrace,
Thrills o'er each man some far echo of England; some glance of some
face!
—Faces gazing seaward through tears from the ocean-girt shore;
Features that ne'er can be gazed on again till the death-pang is
o'er. . . .
Lone in his cabin the Admiral kneeling, and all his great heart
As a child's to the mother, goes forth to the loved one, who bade him
depart
. . . O not for death, but glory! her smile would welcome him home!
Louder and thicker the thunderbolts fall:—and silent they come.

As when beyond Dongola the lion, whom hunters attack,
Stung by their darts from afar, leaps in, dividing them back;
So between Spaniard and Frenchman the *Victory* wedged with a shout,
Gun against gun; a cloud from her decks and lightning went out;
Iron hailing of pitiless death from the sulphury smoke;
Voices hoarse and parch'd, and blood from invisible stroke.
Each man stood to his work, though his mates fell smitten around,
As an oak of the wood, while his fellow, flame-shattered, besplinters
the ground:—
Gluttons of danger for England, but sparing the foe as he lay;
For the spirit of Nelson was on them, and each was Nelson that day.

'She has struck!'—he shouted. 'She burns, the *Redoubtable!* Save whom
we can,

Silence our guns:'—for in him the woman was great in the man,
In that heroic heart each drop girl-gentle and pure,
Dying by those he spared:—and now Death's triumph was sure!
From the deck the smoke-wreath clear'd, and the foe set his rifle in
    rest,
Dastardly aiming, where Nelson stood forth, with the stars on his
    breast—
'In honour I gain'd them, in honour I die with them' . . . Then, in his
    place,
Fell. . . . 'Hardy! 'tis over; but let them not know': and he cover'd his
    face.
Silent, the whole fleet's darling they bore to the twilight below:
And above the war-thunder came shouting, as foe struck his flag after
    foe.

To his heart death rose: and for Hardy, the faithful, he cried in his
    pain—
'How goes the day with us, Hardy?'—' 'Tis ours':—Then he knew, not
    in vain,
Not in vain for his comrades and England he bled: how he left her
    secure,
Queen of her own blue seas, while his name and example endure.
O, like a lover he loved her! for her as water he pours
Life-blood and life and love, given all for her sake, and for ours!
'Kiss me, Hardy!—Thank God!—I have done my duty!'—And then
Fled that heroic soul, and left not his like among men.

> Hear ye the heart of a nation
>   Groan, for her saviour is gone;
> Gallant and true and tender,
>   Child and chieftain in one?
> Such another day never
>   England will weep for again,
> When the triumph darken'd the triumph,
>   And the hero of heroes was slain.

FRANCIS TURNER PALGRAVE

THE EVE OF WATERLOO

There was a sound of revelry by night,
    And Belgium's capital had gathered then
Her beauty and her chivalry, and bright
    The lamps shone o'er fair women and brave men:
A thousand hearts beat happily; and when
    Music arose with its voluptuous swell,
Soft eyes looked love to eyes which spake again,

And all went merry as a marriage-bell;
But hush! hark! a deep sound strikes like a rising knell!

Did ye not hear it?—No; 'twas but the wind,
 Or the car rattling o'er the stony street;
On with the dance! let joy be unconfined;
 No sleep till morn, when youth and pleasure meet
To chase the glowing hours with flying feet. . . .
 But hark!—that heavy sound breaks in once more,
As if the clouds its echo would repeat;
 And nearer, clearer, deadlier than before!
Arm! arm! it is—it is—the cannon's opening roar!

Ah! then and there was hurrying to and fro,
 And gathering tears, and tremblings of distress,
And cheeks all pale, which but an hour ago
 Blushed at the praise of their own loveliness;
And there were sudden partings, such as press
 The life from out young hearts, and choking sighs
Which ne'er might be repeated: who could guess
 If ever more should meet those mutual eyes,
Since upon night so sweet such awful morn could rise?

And there was mounting in hot haste; the steed,
 The mustering squadron, and the clattering car,
Went pouring forward with impetuous speed,
 And swiftly forming in the ranks of war;
And the deep thunder peal on peal afar,
 And near, the beat of the alarming drum
Roused up the soldier ere the morning star;
 While thronged the citizens with terror dumb,
Or whispering with white lips—"The foe! They come! they come!"

And Ardennes waves above them her green leaves,
 Dewy with nature's tear-drops, as they pass,
Grieving, if aught inanimate e'er grieves,
 Over the unreturning brave—alas!
Ere evening to be trodden like the grass,
 Which now beneath them, but above shall grow
In its next verdure, when this fiery mass
 Of living valor, rolling on the foe
And burning with high hope, shall molder cold and low.

Last noon beheld them full of lusty life,
 Last eve in Beauty's circle proudly gay,
The midnight brought the signal-sound of strife,
 The morn, the marshalling in arms—the day,
Battle's magnificently stern array!

The thunder-clouds close o'er it, which when rent,
   The earth is covered thick with other clay,
     Which her own clay shall cover, heaped and pent,
Rider and horse, friend, foe, in one red burial blent.

GEORGE GORDON BYRON

HOMEWARD BOUND

HEAD the ship for England!
   Shake out every sail!
Blithe leap the billows,
   Merry sings the gale.
Captain, work the reckoning;
   How many knots a day?—
Round the world and home again,
   That's the sailor's way!

We've traded with the Yankees,
   Brazilians and Chinese;
We've laughed with dusky beauties
   In shade of tall palm-trees;
Across the line and Gulf-Stream—
   Round by Table Bay—
Everywhere and home again,
   That's the sailor's way!

Nightly stands the North Star
   Higher on our bow;
Straight we run for England;
   Our thoughts are in it now.
Jolly times with friends ashore,
   When we've drawn our pay!—
All about and home again,
   That's the sailor's way!

Tom will to his parents,
   Jack will to his dear,
Joe to wife and children,
   Bob to pipes and beer;
Dicky to the dancing-room,
   To hear the fiddles play;—
Round the world and home again,
   That's the sailor's way!

WILLIAM ALLINGHAM

CHRISTMAS AT SEA

THE sheets were frozen hard, and they cut the naked hand;
The decks were like a slide, where a seaman scarce could stand;
The wind was a nor'-wester, blowing squally off the sea;
And cliffs and spouting breakers were the only things a-lee.

They heard the surf a-roaring before the break of day;
But 'twas only with the peep of light we saw how ill we lay.
We tumbled every hand on deck instanter, with a shout,
And we gave her the maintops'l, and stood by to go about.

All day we tacked and tacked between the South Head and the North;
All day we hauled the frozen sheets, and got no further forth;
All day as cold as charity, in bitter pain and dread,
For very life and nature we tacked from head to head.

We gave the South a wider berth, for there the tide-race roared;
But every tack we made brought the North Head close aboard;
So's we saw the cliffs and houses, and the breakers running high,
And the coastguard in his garden, with his glass against his eye.

The frost was on the village roofs as white as ocean foam;
The good red fires were burning bright in every 'longshore home;
The windows sparkled clear, and the chimneys volleyed out;
And I vow we sniffed the victuals as the vessel went about.

The bells upon the church were rung with a mighty jovial cheer;
For it's just that I should tell you how (of all days in the year)
This day of our adversity was blessèd Christmas morn,
And the house above the coastguard's was the house where I was born.

O well I saw the pleasant room, the pleasant faces there,
My mother's silver spectacles, my father's silver hair;
And well I saw the firelight, like a flight of homely elves,
Go dancing round the china-plates that stand upon the shelves.

And well I knew the talk they had, the talk that was of me,
Of the shadow on the household and the son that went to sea;
And O the wicked fool I seemed, in every kind of way,
To be here and hauling frozen ropes on blessèd Christmas Day.

They lit the high sea-light, and the dark began to fall.
"All hands to loose topgallant sails," I heard the captain call.
"By the Lord, she'll never stand it," our first mate, Jackson, cried.
"It's the one way or the other, Mr. Jackson," he replied.

She staggered to her bearings, but the sails were new and good,
And the ship smelt up to windward, just as though she understood.

As the winter's day was ending, in the entry of the night,
We cleared the weary headland, and passed below the light.

And they heaved a mighty breath, every soul on board but me,
As they saw her nose again pointing handsome out to sea;
But all that I could think of, in the darkness and the cold,
Was just that I was leaving home and my folks were growing old.

ROBERT LOUIS STEVENSON

SONG FOR ALL SEAS, ALL SHIPS

I

To-DAY a rude brief recitative,
Of ships sailing the seas, each with its special flag or ship-signal,
Of unnamed heroes in the ships—of waves spreading and spreading
    far as the eye can reach,
Of dashing spray, and the winds piping and blowing,
And out of these a chant for the sailors of all nations,
Fitful, like a surge.

Of sea-captains young or old, and the mates, and of all intrepid sailors,
Of the few, very choice, taciturn, whom fate can never surprise nor
    death dismay,
Picked sparingly without noise by thee, old ocean, chosen by thee,
Thou sea that pickest and cullest the race in time, and unitest nations,
Suckled by thee, old husky nurse, embodying thee,
Indomitable, untamed as thee.

(Ever the heroes on water or on land, by ones or twos appearing,
Ever the stock preserved and never lost, though rare, enough for seed
    preserved.)

II

Flaunt out, O sea, your separate flags of nations!
Flaunt out visible as ever the various ship-signals!
But do you reserve especially for yourself and for the soul of man one
    flag above all the rest,
A spiritual woven signal for all nations, emblem of man elate above
    death,
Token of all brave captains and all intrepid sailors and mates,
And all that went down doing their duty,
Reminiscent of them, twined from all intrepid captains young or old,
A pennant universal, subtly waving all time, o'er all brave sailors,
All seas, all ships.

WALT WHITMAN

Favorite Poems Of

LEGEND AND FANTASY

THE RIME OF THE ANCIENT MARINER

Part I

An ancient mari-
ner meeteth
three gallants
bidden to a
wedding feast,
and detaineth
one.

It is an ancient mariner,
And he stoppeth one of three,
"By thy long gray beard and glittering eye,
Now wherefore stopp'st thou me?

"The Bridegroom's doors are opened wide,
And I am next of kin;
The guests are met, the feast is set:
May'st hear the merry din."

He holds him with his skinny hand,
"There was a ship," quoth he.
"Hold off! unhand me, gray-beard loon!"
Eftsoons his hand dropt he.

The wedding
guest is spell-
bound by the
eye of the old
seafaring man,
and constrained
to hear his tale.

He holds him with his glittering eye—
The wedding guest stood still,
And listens like a three years child:
The mariner hath his will.

The wedding guest sat on a stone:
He cannot choose but hear;

And thus spake on that ancient man,
The bright-eyed mariner:

"The ship was cheer'd, the harbor clear'd,
Merrily did we drop
Below the kirk, below the hill,
Below the lighthouse top.

*The mariner
tells how the
ship sailed
southward with
a good wind and
fair weather, till
it reached the
Line.*

The sun came up upon the left,
Out of the sea came he!
And he shone bright, and on the right
Went down into the sea.

Higher and higher every day,
Till over the mast at noon—"
The wedding guest here beat his breast,
For he heard the loud bassoon.

*The wedding
guest heareth
the bridal
music; but the
mariner contin-
ueth his tale.*

The bride hath paced into the hall,
Red as a rose is she;
Nodding their heads before her goes
The merry minstrelsy.

The wedding guest he beat his breast,
Yet he cannot choose but hear;
And thus spake on that ancient man,
The bright-eyed mariner:

*The ship drawn
by a storm
toward the
south pole.*

"And now the storm-blast came, and he
Was tyrannous and strong:
He struck with his o'ertaking wings,
And chased us south along.

With sloping masts and dipping prow,
As who pursued with yell and blow
Still treads the shadow of his foe
And forward bends his head,
The ship drove fast, loud roar'd the blast,
And southward aye we fled.

And now there came both mist and snow,
And it grew wondrous cold:
And ice, mast-high, came floating by,
As green as emerald.

*The land of ice,
and of fearful
sounds, where
no living thing
was to be seen.*

And through the drifts the snowy clifts
Did send a dismal sheen:
Nor shapes of men nor beasts we ken—
The ice was all between.

The ice was here, the ice was there,
The ice was all around:
It crack'd and growl'd, and roar'd and howl'd,
Like noises in a swound!

Till a great sea-
bird called the
albatross came
through the
snow-fog, and
was received
with great joy
and hospitality.

At length did cross an albatross,
Thorough the fog it came;
As if it had been a Christian soul,
We hail'd it in God's name.

It ate the food it ne'er had eat,
And round and round it flew.
The ice did split with a thunder-fit;
The helmsman steer'd us through!

And lo! the al-
batross proveth
a bird of good
omen, and fol-
loweth the ship
as it returned
northward
through fog and
floating ice.

And a good south wind sprung up behind;
The albatross did follow,
And every day, for food or play,
Came to the mariners' hollo!

In mist or cloud, on mast or shroud,
It perch'd for vespers nine;
Whiles all the night, through fog-smoke white,
Glimmer'd the white moonshine."

The ancient
mariner inhos-
pitably killeth
the pious bird
of good omen.

"God save thee, ancient mariner!
From the fiends, that plague thee thus!—
Why look'st thou so?" "With my cross-bow
I shot the albatross.

Part II

The Sun now rose upon the right:
Out of the sea came he,
Still hid in mist, and on the left
Went down into the sea.

And the good south wind still blew behind,
But no sweet bird did follow,
Nor any day, for food or play,
Came to the mariners' hollo!

His shipmates
cry out against
the ancient mar-
iner, for killing
the bird of good
luck.

And I had done an hellish thing,
And it would work 'em woe:
For all averr'd I had kill'd the bird
That made the breeze to blow.
Ah wretch! said they, the bird to slay,
That made the breeze to blow!

But when the fog cleared off, they justify the same, and thus make themselves accomplices in the crime.

Nor dim nor red, like God's own head
The glorious Sun uprist:
Then all averr'd I had kill'd the bird
That brought the fog and mist.
'Twas right, said they, such birds to slay,
That bring the fog and mist.

The fair breeze continues; the ship enters the Pacific Ocean, and sails northward, even till it reaches the Line.

The fair breeze blew, the white foam flew,
The furrow follow'd free;
We were the first that ever burst
Into that silent sea.

Down dropt the breeze, the sails dropt down,
'Twas sad as sad could be;
And we did speak only to break
The silence of the sea!

The ship hath been suddenly becalmed;

All in a hot and copper sky,
The bloody Sun, at noon,
Right up above the mast did stand,
No bigger than the Moon.

And the albatross begins to be avenged.

Day after day, day after day,
We stuck, nor breath nor motion;
As idle as a painted ship
Upon a painted ocean.

Water, water, everywhere,
And all the boards did shrink;
Water, water, everywhere,
Nor any drop to drink.

A spirit had followed them; one of the invisible inhabitants of this planet, neither departed souls nor angels; concerning whom the learned Jew Josephus, and the Platonic Constantinopolitan, Michael Psellus, may be consulted. They are very numerous, and there is no climate or element without one or more.

The very deep did rot: O Christ!
That ever this should be!
Yea, slimy things did crawl with legs
Upon the slimy sea.

About, about, in reel and rout,
The death-fires danced at night,
The water, like a witch's oils,
Burnt green, and blue, and white.

And some in dreams assurèd were
Of the spirit that plagued us so;
Nine fathom deep he had follow'd us
From the land of mist and snow.

And every tongue, through utter drought,
Was wither'd at the root;
We could not speak, no more than if
We had been choked with soot.

Ah! well-a-day! what evil looks
Had I from old and young!
Instead of the cross, the albatross
About my neck was hung.

The shipmates, in their sore distress, would fain throw the whole guilt on the ancient mariner; in sign whereof they hang the dead sea-bird round his neck.

Part III

There pass'd a weary time. Each throat
Was parch'd, and glazed each eye.
A weary time! a weary time!
How glazed each weary eye,
When looking westward, I beheld
A something in the sky.

At first it seem'd a little speck,
And then it seem'd a mist;
It moved and moved, and took at last
A certain shape I wist.

The ancient mariner beholdeth a sign in the element afar off.

A speck, a mist, a shape, I wist;
And still it near'd and near'd;
As if it dodged a water-sprite,
It plunged and tack'd and veer'd.

At its nearer approach, it seemeth him to be a ship; and at a dear ransom he freeth his speech from the bonds of thirst.

With throats unslaked, with black lips baked,
We could nor laugh nor wail;
Through utter drought all dumb we stood!
I bit my arm, I suck'd the blood,
And cried, A sail! a sail!

A flash of joy.

With throats unslaked, with black lips baked,
Agape they heard me call;
Gramercy! they for joy did grin,
And all at once their breath drew in,
As they were drinking all.

See! see! (I cried), she tacks no more!
Hither to work us weal;
Without a breeze, without a tide,
She steadies with upright keel!

And horror follows. For can it be a ship that comes onward without wind or tide?

The western wave was all aflame,
The day was well-nigh done!
Almost upon the western wave
Rested the broad bright Sun;
When that strange shape drove suddenly
Betwixt us and the Sun.

It seemeth him but the skeleton of a ship.

And straight the Sun was fleck'd with bars
(Heaven's Mother send us grace!),

As if through a dungeon-grate he peer'd
With broad and burning face.

Alas! (thought I, and my heart beat loud),
How fast she nears and nears!
Are those *her* sails that glance in the Sun,
Like restless gossameres?

And its ribs are seen as bars on the face of the setting sun. The spectre woman and her death-mate, and no other, on board the skeleton-ship. Like vessel, like crew.

Are those *her* ribs through which the Sun
Did peer, as through a grate?
And is that Woman all her crew?
Is that a Death? and are there two?
Is Death that woman's mate?

Her lips were red, *her* looks were free,
Her locks were yellow as gold;
Her skin was as white as leprosy,
The nightmare Life-in-Death was she,
Who thicks man's blood with cold.

Death and Life-in-Death have diced for the ship's crew, and she (the latter) winneth the ancient mariner.

The naked hulk alongside came,
And the twain were casting dice;
"The game is done! I've won, I've won!"
Quoth she, and whistles thrice.

No twilight within the courts of the Sun.

The Sun's rim dips; the stars rush out;
At one stride comes the dark;
With far-heard whisper, o'er the sea,
Off shot the spectre-bark.

At the rising of the moon,

We listen'd and look'd sideways up!
Fear at my heart, as at a cup;
My life-blood seem'd to sip!
The stars were dim, and thick the night,
The steersman's face by his lamp gleam'd white;
From the sails the dew did drip—
Till clomb above the eastern bar
The hornèd Moon, with one bright star
Within the nether tip.

One after another,

One after one, by the star-dogg'd Moon,
Too quick for groan or sigh,
Each turn'd his face with a ghastly pang,
And cursed me with his eye.

His shipmates drop down dead;

Four times fifty living men
(And I heard nor sigh nor groan),
With heavy thump, a lifeless lump,
They dropp'd down one by one.

But Life-in-Death begins her work on the ancient mariner.	The souls did from their bodies fly,— They fled to bliss or woe! And every soul, it pass'd me by, Like the whizz of my cross-bow!"

PART IV

The wedding guest feareth that a spirit is talking to him;	"I fear thee, ancient mariner! I fear thy skinny hand! And thou art long, and lank, and brown, As is the ribb'd sea-sand.
	"I fear thee and thy glittering eye, And thy skinny hand so brown."—
But the ancient mariner assureth him of his bodily life, and proceedeth to relate his horrible penance.	"Fear not, fear not, thou wedding-guest! This body dropt not down. Alone, alone, all, all alone, Alone on a wide, wide sea! And never a saint took pity on My soul in agony.
He despiseth the creatures of the calm.	The many men so beautiful! And they all dead did lie: And a thousand thousand slimy things Lived on; and so did I.
And envieth that they should live, and so may lie dead.	I look'd upon the rotting sea, And drew my eyes away; I look'd upon the rotting deck, And there the dead men lay.
	I look'd to heaven, and tried to pray; But, or ever a prayer had gusht, A wicked whisper came, and made My heart as dry as dust.
	I closed my lids, and kept them close, And the balls like pulses beat; For the sky and the sea, and the sea and the sky, Lay like a load on my weary eye, And the dead were at my feet.
But the curse liveth for him in the eyes of the dead men.	The cold sweat melted from their limbs, Nor rot nor reek did they: The look with which they look'd on me Had never pass'd away.
In his loneliness and fixedness he	An orphan's curse would drag to hell A spirit from on high;

But oh! more horrible than that
Is a curse in a dead man's eye!
Seven days, seven nights, I saw that curse,
And yet I could not die.

The moving Moon went up the sky,
And nowhere did abide:
Softly she was going up,
And a star or two beside—

yearneth towards the journeying moon, and the stars that still sojourn, yet still move onward; and everywhere the blue sky belongs to them, and is their appointed rest, and their native country, and their own natural homes, which they enter unannounced, as lords that are certainly expected, and yet there is a silent joy at their arrival.

Her beams bemock'd the sultry main,
Like April hoar-frost spread;
But where the ship's huge shadow lay,
The charmèd water burnt alway
A still and awful red.

Beyond the shadow of the ship,
I watch'd the water-snakes:
They moved in tracks of shining white,
And when they rear'd, the elfish light
Fell off in hoary flakes.

By the light of the moon he beholdeth God's creatures of the great calm.

Within the shadow of the ship
I watch'd their rich attire:
Blue, glossy green, and velvet black,
They coil'd and swam; and every track
Was a flash of golden fire.

Their beauty and their happiness.

He blesseth them in his heart.

O happy living things! no tongue
Their beauty might declare:
A spring of love gush'd from my heart,
And I bless'd them unaware:
Sure my kind saint took pity on me,
And I bless'd them unaware.

The spell begins to break.

The selfsame moment I could pray;
And from my neck so free
The albatross fell off, and sank
Like lead into the sea.

Part V

Oh sleep! it is a gentle thing,
Beloved from pole to pole!
To Mary Queen the praise be given!
She sent the gentle sleep from Heaven,
That slid into my soul.

By grace of the Holy Mother, the ancient mariner is refreshed with rain.

The silly buckets on the deck,
That had so long remain'd,

I dreamt that they were fill'd with dew;
And when I awoke, it rain'd.

My lips were wet, my throat was cold,
My garments all were dank;
Sure I had drunken in my dreams,
And still my body drank.

I moved, and could not feel my limbs:
I was so light—almost
I thought that I had died in sleep,
And was a blessed ghost.

He heareth sounds, and seeth strange sights and commotions in the sky and the element.

And soon I heard a roaring wind:
It did not come anear;
But with its sound it shook the sails,
That were so thin and sere.

The upper air burst into life!
And a hundred fire-flags sheen,
To and fro they were hurried about!
And to and fro, and in and out,
The wan stars danced between.

And the coming wind did roar more loud,
And the sails did sigh like sedge;
And the rain pour'd down from one black cloud;
The Moon was at its edge.

The thick black cloud was cleft, and still
The Moon was at its side:
Like waters shot from some high crag,
The lightning fell with never a jag,
A river steep and wide.

The bodies of the ship's crew are inspired, and the ship moves on;

The loud wind never reach'd the ship,
Yet now the ship moved on!
Beneath the lightning and the Moon
The dead men gave a groan.

They groan'd, they stirr'd, they all uprose,
Nor spake, nor moved their eyes;
It had been strange, even in a dream,
To have seen those dead men rise.

The helmsman steer'd, the ship moved on;
Yet never a breeze up blew;
The mariners all 'gan work the ropes,
Where they were wont to do;
They raised their limbs like lifeless tools—
We were a ghastly crew.

The body of my brother's son
Stood by me, knee to knee:
The body and I pull'd at one rope,
But he said naught to me."

But not by the
souls of the men,
nor by dæmons
of earth or
middle air, but
by a blessed
troop of angelic
spirits, sent
down by the in-
vocation of the
guardian saint.

"I fear thee, ancient mariner!"
"Be calm, thou wedding guest!
'Twas not those souls that fled in pain,
Which to their corses came again,
But a troop of spirits blest:

For when it dawn'd—they dropp'd their arms,
And cluster'd round the mast;
Sweet sounds rose slowly through their mouths,
And from their bodies pass'd.

Around, around, flew each sweet sound,
Then darted to the Sun;
Slowly the sounds came back again,
Now mix'd, now one by one.

Sometimes a-dropping from the sky,
I heard the skylark sing;
Sometimes all little birds that are,
How they seem'd to fill the sea and air
With their sweet jargoning!

And now 'twas like all instruments,
Now like a lonely flute;
And now it is an angel's song
That makes the heavens be mute.

It ceased; yet still the sails made on
A pleasant noise till noon,
A noise like of a hidden brook
In the leafy month of June,
That to the sleeping woods all night
Singeth a quiet tune.

Till noon we quietly sail'd on,
Yet never a breeze did breathe:
Slowly and smoothly went the ship,
Moved onward from beneath.

The lonesome
spirit from the
south pole car-
ries on the ship
as far as the
Line, in obedi-

Under the keel nine fathom deep,
From the land of mist and snow,
The spirit slid: and it was he
That made the ship to go.
The sails at noon left off their tune,
And the ship stood still also.

ence to the angelic troop, but still requireth vengeance.

The Sun, right up above the mast,
Had fix'd her to the ocean:
But in a minute she 'gan stir,
With a short uneasy motion—
Backwards and forwards half her length
With a short uneasy motion.

Then like a pawing horse let go,
She made a sudden bound:
It flung the blood into my head
And I fell down in a swound.

The Polar Spirit's fellow-dæmons, the invisible inhabitants of the element, take part in his wrong; and two of them relate, one to the other, that penance long and heavy for the ancient mariner hath been accorded to the Polar Spirit, who returneth southward.

How long in that same fit I lay,
I have not to declare;
But ere my living life return'd,
I heard, and in my soul discern'd
Two voices in the air.

'Is it he?' quoth one, 'Is this the man?
By Him who died on cross,
With his cruel bow he laid full low
The harmless albatross.

The spirit who bideth by himself
In the land of mist and snow,
He loved the bird that loved the man
Who shot him with his bow.'

The other was a softer voice,
As soft as honey-dew:
Quoth he, 'The man hath penance done,
And penance more will do.'

PART VI

First Voice:

But tell me, tell me! speak again
Thy soft response renewing—
What makes that ship drive on so fast?
What is the ocean doing?

Second Voice:

Still as a slave before his lord,
The ocean hath no blast;
His great bright eye most silently
Up to the Moon is cast—

If he may know which way to go;
For she guides him smooth or grim.
See, brother, see! how graciously
She looketh down on him.

*The mariner
hath been cast
into a trance:
for the angelic
power causeth
the vessel to
drive northward,
faster than hu-
man life could
endure.*

First Voice:

But why drives on that ship so fast,
Without or wave or wind?

Second Voice:

The air is cut away before,
And closes from behind.

Fly, brother, fly! more high, more high!
Or we shall be belated:
For slow and slow that ship will go,
When the mariner's trance is abated.

*The supernatural
motion is re-
tarded; the mari-
ner awakes, and
his penance be-
gins anew.*

"I woke, and we were sailing on
As in a gentle weather:
'Twas night, calm night, the moon was high;
The dead men stood together.

All stood together on the deck,
For a charnel-dungeon fitter:
All fix'd on me their stony eyes
That in the Moon did glitter.

The pang, the curse, with which they died,
Had never pass'd away:
I could not draw my eyes from theirs,
Nor turn them up to pray.

*The curse is
finally expiated;*

And now this spell was snapt: once more
I view'd the ocean green,
And look'd far forth, yet little saw
Of what had else been seen—

Like one, that on a lonesome road
Doth walk in fear and dread,
And having once turn'd round walks on,
And turns no more his head;
Because he knows a frightful fiend
Doth close behind him tread.

But soon there breathed a wind on me,
Nor sound nor motion made:
Its path was not upon the sea,
In ripple or in shade.

It raised my hair, it fann'd my cheek
Like a meadow-gale of spring—
It mingled strangely with my fears,
Yet it felt like a welcoming.

Swiftly, swiftly flew the ship,
Yet she sail'd softly too:
Sweetly, sweetly blew the breeze—
On me alone it blew.

*And the ancient
mariner behold-
eth his native
country.*

Oh! dream of joy! is this indeed
The lighthouse top I see?
Is this the hill? is this the kirk?
Is this mine own countree?

We drifted o'er the harbor-bar,
And I with sobs did pray—
Oh let me be awake, my God!
Or let me sleep alway.

The harbor-bay was clear as glass,
So smoothly it was strewn!
And on the bay the moonlight lay,
And the shadow of the moon.

The rock shone bright, the kirk no less,
That stands above the rock:
The moonlight steep'd in silentness
The steady weathercock.

*The angelic
spirits leave the
dead bodies,*

And the bay was white with silent light,
Till rising from the same,
Full many shapes, that shadows were,
In crimson colors came.

*And appear in
their own forms
of light.*

A little distance from the prow
Those crimson shadows were:
I turn'd my eyes upon the deck—
O Christ! what saw I there!

Each corse lay flat, lifeless and flat,
And by the holy rood!
A man all light, a seraph man,
On every corse there stood.

This seraph-band, each waved his hand:
It was a heavenly sight!
They stood as signals to the land,
Each one a lovely light;

This seraph-band, each waved his hand,
No voice did they impart—
No voice; but oh! the silence sank
Like music on my heart.

But soon I heard the dash of oars,
I heard the pilot's cheer;
My head was turn'd perforce away,
And I saw a boat appear.

The pilot and the pilot's boy,
I heard them coming fast:
Dear Lord in Heaven! it was a joy
The dead men could not blast.

I saw a third—I heard his voice:
It is the hermit good!
He singeth loud his godly hymns
That he makes in the wood.
He'll shrieve my soul, he'll wash away
The albatross's blood.

PART VII

The hermit of the wood.

This hermit good lives in that wood
Which slopes down to the sea.
How loudly his sweet voice he rears!
He loves to talk with marineres
That come from a far countree.

He kneels at morn, and noon, and eve—
He hath a cushion plump:
It is the moss that wholly hides
The rotted old oak-stump.

The skiff-boat near'd: I heard them talk,
'Why, this is strange, I trow!
Where are those lights so many and fair,
That signal made but now?'

Approacheth the ship with wonder.

'Strange, by my faith!' the hermit said—
'And they answer'd not our cheer!
The planks look'd warp'd! and see those sails
How thin they are and sere!
I never saw aught like to them,
Unless perchance it were

Brown skeletons of leaves that lag
My forest-brook along;
When the ivy-tod is heavy with snow,

And the owlet whoops to the wolf below,
That eats the she-wolf's young.'

'Dear Lord! it hath a fiendish look
(The pilot made reply)—
I am a-fear'd.'—'Push on, push on!'
Said the hermit cheerily.

The boat came closer to the ship,
But I nor spake nor stirr'd;
The boat came close beneath the ship,
And straight a sound was heard.

The ship sud-
denly sinketh.

Under the water it rumbled on,
Still louder and more dread:
It reach'd the ship, it split the bay;
The ship went down like lead.

The ancient
mariner is saved
in the pilot's
boat.

Stunn'd by that loud and dreadful sound,
Which sky and ocean smote,
Like one that hath been seven days drown'd
My body lay afloat;
But swift as dreams, myself I found
Within the pilot's boat.

Upon the whirl, where sank the ship,
The boat spun round and round;
And all was still, save that the hill
Was telling of the sound.

I moved my lips—the pilot shriek'd
And fell down in a fit;
The holy hermit raised his eyes,
And pray'd where he did sit.

I took the oars: the pilot's boy,
Who now doth crazy go,
Laugh'd loud and long, and all the while
His eyes went to and fro.
'Ha! ha!' quoth he, 'full plain I see,
The Devil knows how to row.'

And now, all in my own countree,
I stood on the firm land!

The ancient
mariner ear-
nestly entreateth
the hermit to
shrieve him; and
the penance of
life falls on him.

The hermit stepp'd forth from the boat,
And scarcely he could stand.

'O shrieve me, shrieve me, holy man!'
The hermit cross'd his brow.
'Say quick,' quoth he, 'I bid thee say—
What manner of man art thou?'

Forthwith this frame of mine was wrench'd
With a woeful agony,
Which forced me to begin my tale;
And then it left me free.

And ever and anon throughout his future life an agony constraineth him to travel from land to land.

Since then, at an uncertain hour,
That agony returns:
And till my ghastly tale is told,
This heart within me burns.

I pass, like night, from land to land;
I have strange power of speech;
That moment that his face I see,
I know the man that must hear me;
To him my tale I teach.

What loud uproar bursts from that door!
The wedding-guests are there:
But in the garden-bower the bride
And bride-maids singing are:
And hark the little vesper-bell,
Which biddeth me to prayer!

O wedding-guest! this soul hath been
Alone on a wide wide sea:
So lonely 'twas, that God himself
Scarce seemèd there to be.

Oh sweeter than the marriage-feast,
'Tis sweeter far to me,
To walk together to the kirk
With a goodly company!—

To walk together to the kirk,
And all together pray,
While each to his great Father bends,
Old men, and babes, and loving friends,
And youths and maidens gay!

And to teach, by his own example, love and reverence to all things that God made and loveth.

Farewell, farewell! but this I tell
To thee, thou wedding-guest!
He prayeth well, who loveth well
Both man, and bird, and beast.

He prayeth best, who loveth best
All things both great and small;
For the dear God who loveth us,
He made and loveth all."

The mariner, whose eye is bright,
Whose beard with age is hoar,
Is gone; and now the wedding-guest
Turn'd from the bridegroom's door.

He went like one that hath been stunn'd,
And is of sense forlorn:
A sadder and a wiser man,
He rose the morrow morn.

SAMUEL TAYLOR COLERIDGE

THE RAVEN

ONCE upon a midnight dreary, while I pondered, weak and weary,
Over many a quaint and curious volume of forgotten lore—
While I nodded, nearly napping, suddenly there came a tapping,
As of some one gently rapping, rapping at my chamber door.
" 'Tis some visitor," I muttered, "tapping at my chamber door:
    Only this, and nothing more."

Ah, distinctly I remember, it was in the bleak December,
And each separate dying ember wrought its ghost upon the floor.
Eagerly I wished the morrow; vainly I had sought to borrow
From my books surcease of sorrow—sorrow for the lost Lenore—
For the rare and radiant maiden whom the angels name Lenore—
    Nameless here for evermore.

And the silken, sad, uncertain rustling of each purple curtain,
Thrilled me—filled me with fantastic terrors never felt before;
So that now, to still the beating of my heart, I stood repeating,
" 'Tis some visitor entreating entrance at my chamber door—
Some late visitor entreating entrance at my chamber door:
    This it is, and nothing more."

Presently my soul grew stronger: hesitating then no longer,
"Sir," said I, "or Madam, truly your forgiveness I implore;
But the fact is, I was napping, and so gently you came rapping,
And so faintly you came tapping, tapping at my chamber door,
That I scarce was sure I heard you"—here I opened wide the door;—
    Darkness there, and nothing more!

Deep into that darkness peering, long I stood there, wondering, fearing,
Doubting, dreaming dreams no mortal ever dared to dream before;
But the silence was unbroken, and the darkness gave no token,
And the only word there spoken was the whispered word, "Lenore!"
This I whispered, and an echo murmured back the word "Lenore!"
    Merely this, and nothing more.

Back into the chamber turning, all my soul within me burning,
Soon again I heard a tapping, somewhat louder than before.
"Surely," said I, "surely that is something at my window-lattice;
Let me see then what thereat is, and this mystery explore—
Let my heart be still a moment, and this mystery explore;—
    'Tis the wind, and nothing more!"

Open here I flung the shutter, when, with many a flirt and flutter,
In there stepped a stately Raven of the saintly days of yore.
Not the least obeisance made he; not an instant stopped or stayed he;
But, with mien of lord or lady, perched above my chamber door—
Perched upon a bust of Pallas, just above my chamber door—
    Perched, and sat, and nothing more.

Then this ebony bird beguiling my sad fancy into smiling,
By the grave and stern decorum of the countenance it wore,
"Though thy crest be shorn and shaven, thou," I said, "art sure no craven,
Ghastly, grim, and ancient Raven, wandering from the nightly shore!
Tell me what thy lordly name is on the Night's Plutonian shore!"
    Quoth the Raven, "Nevermore!"

Much I marveled this ungainly fowl to hear discourse so plainly,
Though its answer little meaning—little relevancy bore;
For we cannot help agreeing that no living human being
Ever yet was blessed with seeing bird above his chamber door—
Bird or beast upon the sculptured bust above his chamber door,
    With such name as "Nevermore!"

But the Raven sitting lonely on the placid bust, spoke only
That one word, as if his soul in that one word he did outpour.
Nothing further then he uttered—not a feather then he fluttered—
Till I scarcely more than muttered, "Other friends have flown before—
On the morrow *he* will leave me, as my hopes have flown before."
    Then the bird said, "Nevermore!"

Startled at the stillness broken by reply so aptly spoken,
"Doubtless," said I, "what it utters is its only stock and store,
Caught from some unhappy master, whom unmerciful Disaster
Followed fast and followed faster, till his songs one burden bore—
Till the dirges of his Hope one melancholy burden bore
    Of 'Never—nevermore.' "

But the Raven still beguiling all my sad soul into smiling,
Straight I wheeled a cushioned seat in front of bird, and bust, and door;
Then, upon the velvet sinking, I betook myself to linking
Fancy unto fancy, thinking what this ominous bird of yore—
What this grim, ungainly, ghastly, gaunt, and ominous bird of yore
    Meant in croaking "Nevermore."

This I sat engaged in guessing, but no syllable expressing
To the fowl whose fiery eyes now burned into my bosom's core;
This and more I sat divining, with my head at ease reclining
On the cushion's velvet lining that the lamp-light gloated o'er,
But whose velvet violet lining, with the lamp-light gloating o'er,
  She shall press, ah, nevermore!

Then methought the air grew denser, perfumed from an unseen censer,
Swung by seraphim whose foot-falls tinkled on the tufted floor.
"Wretch," I cried, "thy God hath lent thee—by these angels he hath
  sent thee
Respite—respite and nepenthe from thy memories of Lenore!
Quaff, oh quaff this kind nepenthe, and forget this lost Lenore!"
  Quoth the Raven, "Nevermore!"

"Prophet!" said I, "thing of evil!—prophet still, if bird or devil!
Whether Tempter sent, or whether tempest tossed thee here ashore,
Desolate yet all undaunted, on this desert land enchanted—
On this home by Horror haunted—tell me truly, I implore—
Is there—*is* there balm in Gilead?—tell me—tell me, I implore!"
  Quoth the Raven, "Nevermore."

"Prophet!" said I, "thing of evil!—prophet still, if bird or devil!
By that Heaven that bends above us—by that God we both adore,
Tell this soul with sorrow laden if, within the distant Aidenn,
It shall clasp a sainted maiden, whom the angels name Lenore—
Clasp a rare and radiant maiden, whom the angels name Lenore."
  Quoth the Raven, "Nevermore."

"Be that word our sign of parting, bird or fiend!" I shrieked, upstart-
  ing—
"Get thee back into the tempest and the Night's Plutonian shore!
Leave no black plume as a token of that lie thy soul hath spoken!
Leave my loneliness unbroken!—quit the bust above my door!
Take thy beak from out my heart, and take thy form from off my door!"
  Quoth the Raven, "Nevermore."

And the Raven, never flitting, still is sitting, still is sitting
On the pallid bust of Pallas just above my chamber door;
And his eyes have all the seeming of a demon's that is dreaming,
And the lamp-light o'er him streaming throws his shadow on the floor;
And my soul from out that shadow that lies floating on the floor
  Shall be lifted—nevermore!

        EDGAR ALLAN POE

THE PIED PIPER OF HAMELIN

HAMELIN Town's in Brunswick,
By famous Hanover city;
   The river Weser, deep and wide,
   Washes its wall on the southern side;
   A pleasanter spot you never spied;
But, when begins my ditty,
   Almost five hundred years ago,
   To see the townsfolk suffer so
From vermin was a pity.

   Rats!
They fought the dogs, and kill'd the cats,
   And bit the babies in the cradles,
And ate the cheeses out of the vats,
   And lick'd the soup from the cook's own ladles,
Split open the kegs of salted sprats,
Made nests inside men's Sunday hats,
And even spoil'd the women's chats,
     By drowning their speaking
     With shrieking and squeaking
In fifty different sharps and flats.

At last the people in a body
   To the Town Hall came flocking:
" 'Tis clear," cried they, "our Mayor's a noddy;
   And as for our Corporation—shocking
To think we buy gowns lined with ermine
For dolts that can't or won't determine
What's best to rid us of our vermin!
You hope, because you're old and obese,
To find in the furry civic robe ease?
Rouse up, sirs! Give your brains a racking
To find the remedy we're lacking,
Or, sure as fate, we'll send you packing!"
At this the Mayor and Corporation
Quaked with a mighty consternation.

An hour they sate in counsel,
   At length the Mayor broke silence:
"For a guilder I'd my ermine gown sell;
   I wish I were a mile hence!
It's easy to bid one rack one's brain—
I'm sure my poor head aches again,
I've scratch'd it so, and all in vain.

Oh for a trap, a trap, a trap!"
Just as he said this, what should hap
At the chamber-door but a gentle tap?
"Bless us!" cried the Mayor, "what's that?"
(With the Corporation as he sat,
Looking little though wondrous fat;
Nor brighter was his eye, nor moister
Than a too long-open'd oyster,
Save when at noon his paunch grew mutinous
For a plate of turtle, green and glutinous)
"Only a scraping of shoes on the mat?
Anything like the sound of a rat
Makes my heart go pit-a-pat!"

"Come in!"—the Mayor cried, looking bigger:
And in did come the strangest figure!
His queer long coat from heel to head
Was half of yellow and half of red;
And he himself was tall and thin,
With sharp blue eyes, each like a pin,
And light loose hair, yet swarthy skin,
No tuft on cheek nor beard on chin,
But lips where smiles went out and in—
There was no guessing his kith and kin!
And nobody could enough admire
The tall man and his quaint attire:
Quoth one: "It's as my great-grandsire,
Starting up at the Trump of Doom's tone,
Had walk'd this way from his painted tombstone!"

He advanced to the council-table:
And, "Please your honors," said he, "I'm able,
By means of a secret charm, to draw
All creatures living beneath the sun,
That creep, or swim, or fly, or run,
After me so as you never saw!
And I chiefly use my charm
On creatures that do people harm,
The mole, and toad, and newt, and viper;
And people call me the Pied Piper."
(And here they noticed round his neck
A scarf of red and yellow stripe,
To match with his coat of the selfsame check;
And at the scarf's end hung a pipe;
And his fingers, they noticed, were ever straying
As if impatient to be playing
Upon this pipe, as low it dangled

Over his vesture so old-fangled.)
"Yet," said he, "poor piper as I am,
In Tartary I freed the Cham,
Last June, from his huge swarm of gnats;
I eased in Asia the Nizam
Of a monstrous brood of vampyre bats;
And, as for what your brain bewilders—
If I can rid your town of rats,
Will you give me a thousand guilders?"
"One? fifty thousand!" was the exclamation
Of the astonish'd Mayor and Corporation.

Into the street the piper stept,
   Smiling first a little smile,
As if he knew what magic slept
   In his quiet pipe the while;
Then, like a musical adept,
To blow the pipe his lips he wrinkled,
And green and blue his sharp eyes twinkled,
Like a candle-flame where salt is sprinkled;
And ere three shrill notes the pipe utter'd,
You heard as if an army mutter'd;
And the muttering grew to a grumbling;
And the grumbling grew to a mighty rumbling;
And out of the houses the rats came tumbling.
Great rats, small rats, lean rats, brawny rats,
Brown rats, black rats, gray rats, tawny rats,
Grave old plodders, gay young friskers,
   Fathers, mothers, uncles, cousins,
Cocking tails and pricking whiskers,
   Families by tens and dozens,
Brothers, sisters, husbands, wives—
Follow'd the piper for their lives.
From street to street he piped advancing,
And step for step they follow'd dancing,
Until they came to the river Weser,
Wherein all plunged and perish'd,
Save one who, stout as Julius Cæsar,
Swam across and lived to carry
(As the manuscript he cherish'd)
To Rat-land home his commentary,
Which was, "At the first shrill notes of the pipe,
I heard a sound as of scraping tripe,
And putting apples, wondrous ripe,
Into a cider press's gripe:
And a moving away of pickle-tub boards,
And a leaving ajar of conserve-cupboards,

And a drawing the corks of train-oil flasks,
And a breaking the hoops of butter-casks;
And it seemed as if a voice
(Sweeter far than by harp or by psaltery
Is breathed) call'd out, O rats, rejoice!
The world is grown to one vast drysaltery!
So munch on, crunch on, take your nuncheon,
Breakfast, supper, dinner, luncheon!
And just as a bulky sugar-puncheon,
All ready staved, like a great sun shone
Glorious scarce an inch before me,
Just as methought it said, Come, bore me!
I found the Weser rolling o'er me."

You should have heard the Hamelin people
Ringing the bells till they rock'd the steeple;
"Go," cried the Mayor, "and get long poles!
Poke out the nests and block up the holes!
Consult with carpenters and builders,
And leave in our town not even a trace
Of the rats!"—when suddenly up the face
Of the piper perk'd in the market-place,
With a, "First, if you please, my thousand guilders!"

A thousand guilders! The Mayor look'd blue;
So did the Corporation too.
For council dinners made rare havoc
With Claret, Moselle, Vin-de-Grave, Hock;
And half the money would replenish
Their cellar's biggest butt with Rhenish.
To pay this sum to a wandering fellow
With a gypsy coat of red and yellow!
"Beside," quoth the Mayor, with a knowing wink,
"Our business was done at the river's brink;
We saw with our eyes the vermin sink,
And what's dead can't come to life, I think.
So, friend, we're not the folks to shrink
From the duty of giving you something for drink,
And a matter of money to put in your poke;
But, as for the guilders, what we spoke
Of them, as you very well know, was in joke.
Beside, our losses have made us thrifty;
A thousand guilders! Come, take fifty!"

The piper's face fell and he cried,
"No trifling! I can't wait! beside,
I've promised to visit by dinner-time
Bagdat, and accept the prime

Of the Head Cook's pottage, all he's rich in,
For having left, in the Caliph's kitchen,
Of a nest of scorpions no survivor—
With him I proved no bargain-driver.
With you, don't think I'll bate a stiver!
And folks who put me in a passion
May find me pipe to another fashion."

"How?" cried the Mayor, "d'ye think I'll brook
Being worse treated than a Cook?
Insulted by a lazy ribald
With idle pipe and vesture piebald?
You threaten us, fellow? Do your worst,
Blow your pipe there till you burst!"

Once more he stept into the street;
    And to his lips again
Laid his long pipe of smooth straight cane;
    And ere he blew three notes (such sweet
Soft notes as yet musician's cunning
    Never gave the enraptured air)
There was a rustling, that seem'd like a bustling
Of merry crowds justling at pitching and hustling,
Small feet were pattering, wooden shoes clattering,
Little hands clapping, and little tongues chattering,
And, like fowls in a farm-yard when barley is scattering,
Out came the children running.
All the little boys and girls,
With rosy cheeks and flaxen curls,
And sparkling eyes and teeth like pearls,
Tripping and skipping, ran merrily after
The wonderful music with shouting and laughter.

The Mayor was dumb, and the Council stood
As if they were changed into blocks of wood,
Unable to move a step, or cry
To the children merrily skipping by—
And could only follow with the eye
That joyous crowd at the Piper's back.
But how the Mayor was on the rack,
And the wretched Council's bosoms beat,
As the Piper turn'd from the High Street
To where the Weser roll'd its waters
Right in the way of their sons and daughters!
However, he turned from south to west,
And to Koppelberg Hill his steps address'd,
And after him the children press'd;

Great was the joy in every breast.
"He never can cross that mighty top!
He's forced to let the piping drop,
And we shall see our children stop!"
When, lo, as they reach'd the mountain's side,
A wondrous portal open'd wide,
As if a cavern was suddenly hollow'd;
And the Piper advanced and the children follow'd,
And when all were in to the very last,
The door in the mountain-side shut fast.
Did I say all? No! one was lame,
And could not dance the whole of the way,
And in after years, if you would blame
His sadness, he was used to say,
"It's dull in our town since my playmates left!
I can't forget that I'm bereft
Of all the pleasant sights they see,
Which the Piper also promised me,
For he led us, he said, to a joyous land,
Joining the town and just at hand,
Where waters gush'd and fruit trees grew,
And flowers put forth a fairer hue,
And everything was strange and new;
The sparrows were brighter than peacocks here,
And the dogs outran our fallow deer,
And honey-bees had lost their stings,
And horses were born with eagles' wings;
And just as I became assured
My lame foot would be speedily cured,
The music stopp'd, and I stood still,
And found myself outside the Hill,
Left alone against my will,
To go now limping as before,
And never hear of that country more!"

Alas, alas for Hamelin!
    There came into many a burgher's pate
    A text which says that Heaven's Gate
    Opes to the rich at as easy rate
As the needle's eye takes a camel in!
The Mayor sent east, west, north, and south
To offer the Piper by word of mouth,
    Wherever it was men's lot to find him,
Silver and gold to his heart's content,
If he'd only return the way he went,
    And bring the children behind him.
But when they saw 'twas a lost endeavor,

And Piper and dancers were gone for ever,
They made a decree that lawyers never
    Should think their records dated duly
If, after the day of the month and year,
These words did not as well appear:
"And so long after what happen'd here
    On the twenty-second of July,
    Thirteen hundred and Seventy-six;"
And the better in memory to fix
The place of the children's last retreat,
They call'd it the Pied Piper's Street,
Where any one playing on pipe or tabor
Was sure for the future to lose his labor.
Nor suffer'd they hostelry or tavern
    To shock with mirth a street so solemn,
But opposite the place of the cavern
    They wrote the story on a column,
And on the great church-window painted
The same, to make the world acquainted
How their children were stolen away,
And there it stands to this very day.
And I must not omit to say
That in Transylvania there's a tribe
Of alien people that ascribe
The outlandish ways and dress
On which their neighbors lay such stress,
To their fathers and mothers having risen
Out of some subterranean prison,
Into which they were trepann'd
Long time ago in a mighty band
Out of Hamelin town in Brunswick land,
But how or why, they don't understand.

So, Willy, let you and me be wipers
Of scores out with all men—especially pipers;
And, whether they pipe us free, from rats or from mice,
If we've promised them aught, let us keep our promise.

                    ROBERT BROWNING

WHEN THE SULTAN GOES TO ISPAHAN

When *the Sultan Shah-Zaman*
Goes to the city Ispahan,
Even before he gets so far
As the place where the clustered palm-trees are,

At the last of the thirty palace-gates,
The flower of the harem, Rose-in-Bloom,
Orders a feast in his favorite room—
Glittering squares of colored ice,
Sweetened with syrop, tinctured with spice,
Creams, and cordials, and sugared dates,
Syrian apples, Othmanee quinces,
Limes, and citrons, and apricots,
And wines that are known to Eastern princes;
And Nubian slaves, with smoking pots
Of spicèd meats and costliest fish
And all that the curious palate could wish,
Pass in and out of the cedarn doors;
Scattered over mosaic floors
Are anemones, myrtles, and violets,
And a musical fountain throws its jets
Of a hundred colors into the air.
The dusk Sultana loosens her hair,
And stains with the henna-plant the tips
Of her pointed nails, and bites her lips
Till they bloom again; but, alas, *that* rose
Not for the Sultan buds and blows!
Not for the Sultan Shah-Zaman
When he goes to the city Ispahan.

Then at a wave of her sunny hand
The dancing-girls of Samarcand
Glide in like shapes from fairy-land,
Making a sudden mist in air
Of fleecy veils and floating hair
And white arms lifted. Orient blood
Runs in their veins, shines in their eyes.
And there, in this Eastern Paradise,
Filled with the breath of sandal-wood,
And Khoten musk, and aloes and myrrh,
Sits Rose-in-Bloom on a silk divan,
Sipping the wines of Astrakhan;
And her Arab lover sits with her.
That's when the Sultan Shah-Zaman
Goes to the city Ispahan.

Now, when I see an extra light,
Flaming, flickering on the night
From my neighbors' casement opposite
I know as well as I know to pray,
I know as well as a tongue can say,

That the innocent Sultan Shah-Zaman
Has gone to the city Ispahan.

THOMAS BAILEY ALDRICH

ELDORADO

GAILY bedight,
A gallant knight
In sunshine and in shadow
Had journeyed long,
Singing a song,
In search of Eldorado.

But he grew old—
This knight so bold—
And o'er his heart a shadow
Fell, as he found
No spot of ground
That looked like Eldorado.

And, as his strength
Failed him at length,
He met a pilgrim shadow:
"Shadow," said he,
"Where can it be—
This land of Eldorado?"

"Over the mountains
Of the moon,
Down the valley of the Shadow
Ride, boldly ride,"
The shade replied,
"If you seek for Eldorado!"

EDGAR ALLAN POE

LA BELLE DAME SANS MERCI

OH what can ail thee, knight-at-arms!
Alone and palely loitering?
The sedge has wither'd from the lake,
And no birds sing.

Oh what can ail thee, knight-at-arms!
    So haggard and so woe-begone?
The squirrel's granary is full,
    And the harvest's done.

I see a lily on thy brow,
    With anguish moist and fever dew;
And on thy cheeks a fading rose
    Fast withereth too.

I met a lady in the mead—
    Full beautiful, a fairy's child;
Her hair was long, her foot was light,
    And her eyes were wild.

I made a garland for her head,
    And bracelets too, and fragrant zone;
She look'd at me as she did love,
    And made sweet moan.

I set her on my pacing steed,
    And nothing else saw all day long;
For sidelong would she bend, and sing
    A fairy song.

She found me roots of relish sweet,
    And honey wild, and manna dew;
And sure in language strange she said—
    "I love thee true."

She took me to her elfin grot,
    And there she wept, and sigh'd full sore;
And there I shut her wild, wild eyes
    With kisses four.

And there she lull'd me asleep;
    And there I dream'd—Ah! woe betide!
The latest dream I ever dream'd
    On the cold hill's side.

I saw pale kings and princes too—
    Pale warriors, death-pale were they all;
They cried—"La belle dame sans merci
    Hath thee in thrall!"

I saw their starved lips in the gloam,
    With horrid warning gapèd wide;
And I awoke, and found me here,
    On the cold hill's side.

And this is why I sojourn here,
   Alone and palely loitering,
Though the sedge is wither'd from the lake,
   And no birds sing.

JOHN KEATS

BARBARA ALLEN'S CRUELTY

ALL in the merry month of May,
   When green buds they were swelling,
Young Jemmy Grove on his death-bed lay
   For love of Barbara Allen.

He sent his man unto her then,
   To the town where she was dwelling:
"O haste and come to my master dear,
   If your name be Barbara Allen."

Slowly, slowly she rose up,
   And she came where he was lying;
And when she drew the curtain by,
   Says, "Young man, I think you're dying."

"O it's I am sick, and very, very sick,
   And it's all for Barbara Allen."
"O the better for me you'll never be,
   Tho' your heart's blood were a-spilling!

"O do you not mind, young man," she says,
   "When the red wine you were filling,
That you made the healths go round and round,
   And slighted Barbara Allen?"

He turned his face unto the wall,
   And death with him was dealing:
"Adieu, adieu, my dear friends all;
   Be kind to Barbara Allen."

As she was walking o'er the fields,
   She heard the dead-bell knelling;
And every toll the dead-bell struck,
   Cried, "Woe to Barbara Allen!"

"O mother, mother, make my bed,
   To lay me down in sorrow.
My love has died for me today,
   I'll die for him tomorrow."

ANONYMOUS

MORTE D'ARTHUR

So ALL day long the noise of battle rolled
Among the mountains by the winter sea;
Until King Arthur's table, man by man,
Had fallen in Lyonesse about their Lord,
King Arthur: then, because his wound was deep,
The bold Sir Bedivere uplifted him,
Sir Bedivere, the last of all his knights,
And bore him to a chapel nigh the field,
A broken chancel with a broken cross,
That stood on a dark strait of barren land.
On one side lay the ocean, and on one
Lay a great water, and the moon was full.
    Then spake King Arthur to Sir Bedivere:
"The sequel of to-day unsolders all
The goodliest fellowship of famous knights
Whereof this world holds record. Such a sleep
They sleep—the men I loved. I think that we
Shall never more, at any future time,
Delight our souls with talk of knightly deeds,
Walking about the gardens and the halls
Of Camelot, as in the days that were.
I perish by this people which I made,—
Though Merlin sware that I should come again
To rule once more—but let what will be, be,
I am so deeply smitten through the helm,
That without help I cannot last till morn.
Thou therefore take my brand Excalibur,
Which was my pride: for thou rememberest how
In those old days, one summer noon, an arm
Rose up from out the bosom of the lake,
Clothed in white samite, mystic, wonderful,
Holding the sword—and how I rowed across
And took it, and have worn it, like a king:
And, wheresoever I am sung or told
In after time, this also shall be known:
But now delay not: take Excalibur,
And fling him far into the middle mere:
Watch what thou seest, and lightly bring me word."
    To him replied the bold Sir Bedivere:
"It is not meet, Sir King, to leave thee thus,
Aidless, alone, and smitten through the helm.
A little thing may harm a wounded man.

Yet I thy hest will all perform at full,
Watch what I see, and lightly bring thee word."
    So saying, from the ruined shrine he stepped
And in the moon athwart the place of tombs,
Where lay the mighty bones of ancient men,
Old knights, and over them the sea-wind sang
Shrill, chill, with flakes of foam. He, stepping down
By zigzag paths, and juts of pointed rock,
Came on the shining levels of the lake.
    There drew he forth the brand Excalibur,
And o'er him, drawing it, the winter moon,
Brightening the skirts of a long cloud, ran forth
And sparkled keen with frost against the hilt:
For all the haft twinkled with diamond sparks,
Myriads of topaz-light, and jacinth-work
Of subtlest jewelry. He gazed so long
That both his eyes were dazzled, as he stood,
This way and that dividing the swift mind,
In act to throw: but at last it seemed
Better to leave Excalibur concealed
There in the many-knotted water-flags,
That whistled stiff and dry about the marge.
So strode he back slow to the wounded king.
    Then spake King Arthur to Sir Bedivere:
"Hast thou performed my mission which I gave?
What is it thou hast seen? or what hast heard?"
    And answer made the bold Sir Bedivere:
"I heard the ripple washing in the reeds,
And the wild water lapping on the crag."
    To whom replied King Arthur, faint and pale:
"Thou hast betrayed thy nature and thy name,
Not rendering true answer, as beseemed
Thy fealty, nor like a noble knight:
For surer sign had followed, either hand,
Or voice, or else a motion of the mere.
This is a shameful thing for men to lie.
Yet now, I charge thee, quickly go again
As thou art lief and dear, and do the thing
I bade thee, watch, and lightly bring me word."
    Then went Sir Bedivere the second time
Across the ridge, and paced beside the mere,
Counting the dewy pebbles, fixed in thought;
But when he saw the wonder of the hilt,
How curiously and strangely chased, he smote
His palms together, and he cried aloud,
"And if indeed I cast the brand away,

Surely a precious thing, one worthy note,
Should thus be lost forever from the earth,
Which might have pleased the eyes of many men.
What good should follow this, if this were done?
What harm, undone? deep harm to disobey,
Seeing obedience is the bond of rule.
Were it well to obey then, if a king demand
An act unprofitable, against himself?
The king is sick, and knows not what he does.
What record, or what relic of my lord
Should be to aftertime, but empty breath
And rumors of a doubt? but were this kept,
Stored in some treasure-house of mighty kings,
Some one might show it at a joust of arms,
Saying, 'King Arthur's sword, Excalibur,
Wrought by the lonely maiden of the lake;
Nine years she wrought it, sitting in the deeps
Upon the hidden bases of the hills.'
So might some old man speak in the aftertime
To all the people, winning reverence;
But now much honor and much fame were lost."

     So spake he, clouded with his own conceit,
And hid Excalibur, the second time,
And so strode back slow to the wounded king.
     Then spoke King Arthur, breathing heavily:
"What is it thou hast seen? or what hast heard?"
     And answer made the bold Sir Bedivere:
"I heard the water lapping on the crag
And the long ripple washing in the reeds."
     To whom replied King Arthur, much in wrath:
"Ah, miserable and unkind, untrue,
Unknightly, traitor-hearted! Woe is me!
Authority forgets a dying king,
Laid widowed of the power in his eye
That bowed the will. I see thee what thou art,
For thou, the latest-left of all my knights,
In whom should meet the offices of all,
Thou would'st betray me for the precious hilt;
Either from lust of gold, or like a girl
Valuing the giddy pleasure of the eyes.
Yet, for a man may fail in duty twice,
And the third time may prosper, get thee hence:
But, if thou spare to fling Excalibur,
I will arise and slay thee with my hands."
     Then quickly rose Sir Bedivere, and ran,
And, leaping down the ridges lightly, plunged

Among the bulrush-beds, and clutched the sword,
And strongly wheeled and threw it. The great brand
Made lightnings in the splendor of the moon,
And flashing round and round, and whirled in an arch,
Shot like a streamer of the northern morn,
Seen where the moving isles of winter shock
By night, with noises of the northern sea.
So flashed and fell the brand Excalibur:
But ere he dipped the surface, rose an arm,
Clothed in white samite, mystic, wonderful,
And caught him by the hilt, and brandished him
Three times, and drew him under in the mere.
And lightly went the other to the king.
    Then spoke King Arthur, drawing thicker breath:
"Now see I by thine eyes that this is done.
Speak out: what is it thou hast heard, or seen?"
    And answer made the bold Sir Bedivere:
"Sir King, I closed mine eyelids, lest the gems
Should blind my purpose, for I never saw,
Nor shall see, here or elsewhere, till I die,
Not though I live three lives of mortal men,
So great a miracle as yonder hilt.
Then with both hands I flung him, wheeling him;
But when I looked again, behold an arm,
Clothed in white samite, mystic, wonderful,
That caught him by the hilt, and brandished him
Three times, and drew him under in the mere."
    And answer made King Arthur, breathing hard:
"My end draws nigh; 'tis time that I were gone.
Make broad thy shoulders to receive my weight,
And bear me to the margin; yet I fear
My wound hath taken cold, and I shall die."
    So saying, from the pavement he half rose,
Slowly, with pain, reclining on his arm,
And looking wistfully with wide blue eyes
As in a picture. Him Sir Bedivere
Remorsefully regarded through his tears,
And would have spoken, but he found not words,
Then took with care, and kneeling on one knee,
O'er both his shoulders drew the languid hands,
And rising bore him through the place of tombs.
    But, as he walked, King Arthur panted hard,
Like one that feels a nightmare on his bed
When all the house is mute. So sighed the king,
Muttering and murmuring at his ear, "Quick, quick!
I fear it is too late, and I shall die."

But the other swiftly strode from ridge to ridge,
Clothed with his breath, and looking, as he walked,
Larger than human on the frozen hills.
He heard the deep behind him, and a cry
Before. His own thought drove him like a goad.
Dry clashed his harness in the icy caves
And barren chasms, and all to left and right
The bare black cliff clanged round him, as he based
His feet on juts of slippery crag that rang
Sharp-smitten with the dint of armèd heels—
And on a sudden, lo! the level lake,
And the long glories of the winter moon.
    Then saw they how there hove a dusky barge,
Dark as a funeral scarf from stem to stern,
Beneath them; and descending they were ware
That all the decks were dense with stately forms
Black-stoled, black-hooded, like a dream—by these
Three queens with crowns of gold—and from them rose
A cry that shivered to the tingling stars,
And, as it were one voice, an agony
Of lamentation, like a wind, that shrills
All night in a waste land, where no one comes,
Or hath come, since the making of the world.
    Then murmured Arthur, "Place me in the barge,"
And to the barge they came. There those three queens
Put forth their hands, and took the king, and wept.
But she that rose the tallest of them all
And fairest, laid his head upon her lap,
And loosed the shattered casque, and chafed his hands,
And called him by his name, complaining loud,
And dropping bitter tears against his brow
Striped with dark blood: for all his face was white
And colorless, and like the withered moon
Smote by the fresh beam of the springing east;
And all his greaves and cuisses dashed with drops
Of onset; and the light and lustrous curls—
That made his forehead like a rising sun
High from the dais-throne—were parched with dust;
Or, clotted into points and hanging loose,
Mixed with the knightly growth that fringed his lips.
So like a shattered column lay the king;
Not like that Arthur who, with lance in rest,
From spur to plume a star of tournament,
Shot through the lists at Camelot, and charged
Before the eyes of ladies and of kings.
    Then loudly cried the bold Sir Bedivere:

"Ah! My Lord Arthur, whither shall I go?
Where shall I hide my forehead and my eyes?
For now I see the true old times are dead,
When every morning brought a noble chance,
And every chance brought out a noble knight.
Such times have been not since the light that led
The holy Elders with the gift of myrrh.
But now the whole ROUND TABLE is dissolved
Which was an image of the mighty world;
And I, the last, go forth companionless,
And the days darken round me, and the years,
Among new men, strange faces, other minds."
     And slowly answered Arthur from the barge:
"The old order changeth, yielding place to new,
And God fulfils Himself in many ways,
Lest one good custom should corrupt the world.
Comfort thyself: what comfort is in me?
I have lived my life, and that which I have done
May He within Himself make pure! but thou,
If thou shouldst never see my face again,
Pray for my soul. More things are wrought by prayer
Than this world dreams of. Wherefore, let thy voice
Rise like a fountain for me night and day.
For what are men better than sheep or goats
That nourish a blind life within the brain,
If, knowing God, they lift not hands of prayer
Both for themselves and those who call them friend?
For so the whole round earth is every way
Bound by gold chains about the feet of God.
But now farewell. I am going a long way
With these thou seest—if indeed I go—
For all my mind is clouded with a doubt—
To the island-valley of Avilion;
Where falls not hail, or rain, or any snow,
Nor ever wind blows loudly; but it lies
Deep-meadowed, happy, fair with orchard-lawns
And bowery hollows crowned with summer sea,
Where I will heal me of my grievous wound."
     So said he, and the barge with oar and sail
Moved from the brink, like some full-breasted swan
That, fluting a wild carol ere her death,
Ruffles her pure cold plume, and takes the flood
With swarthy webs. Long stood Sir Bedivere
Revolving many memories, till the hull
Looked one black dot against the verge of dawn,
And on the mere the wailing died away.

ALFRED TENNYSON

THE ENVIABLE ISLES

THROUGH storms you reach them and from storms are free.
    Afar descried, the foremost drear in hue,
But, nearer, green; and, on the marge, the sea
    Makes thunder low and mist of rainbowed dew.

But, inland,—where the sleep that folds the hills
A dreamier sleep, the trance of God, instils,—
    On uplands hazed, in wandering airs aswoon,
Slow-swaying palms salute love's cypress tree
    Adown in vale where pebbly runlets croon
A song to lull all sorrow and all glee.

Sweet-fern and moss in many a glade are here,
    Where, strown in flocks, what cheek-flushed myriads lie
Dimpling in dream, unconscious slumberers mere,
    While billows endless round the beaches die.

HERMAN MELVILLE

KUBLA KHAN

IN XANADU did Kubla Khan
    A stately pleasure-dome decree:
Where Alph, the sacred river, ran
Through caverns measureless to man
    Down to a sunless sea.
So twice five miles of fertile ground
With walls and towers were girdled round:
And there were gardens bright with sinuous rills,
Where blossomed many an incense-bearing tree;
And here were forests ancient as the hills,
Enfolding sunny spots of greenery.

But O! that deep romantic chasm which slanted
Down the green hill athwart a cedarn cover!
A savage place! as holy and enchanted
As e'er beneath a waning moon was haunted
By woman wailing for her demon-lover!
And from this chasm, with ceaseless turmoil seething,
As if this Earth in fast thick pants were breathing,
A mighty fountain momently was forced,
Amid whose swift half-intermitted burst
Huge fragments vaulted like rebounding hail,

Or chaffy grain beneath the thresher's flail:
And 'mid these dancing rocks at once and ever
It flung up momently the sacred river.
Five miles meandering with a mazy motion
Through wood and dale the sacred river ran,
Then reached the caverns measureless to man,
And sank in tumult to a lifeless ocean:
And 'mid this tumult Kubla heard from far
Ancestral voices prophesying war!

 The shadow of the dome of pleasure
 Floated midway on the waves;
 Where was heard the mingled measure
 From the fountain and the caves.
It was a miracle of rare device,
A sunny pleasure-dome with caves of ice!

 A damsel with a dulcimer
 In a vision once I saw:
 It was an Abyssinian maid,
 And on her dulcimer she played,
 Singing of Mount Abora.
 Could I revive within me
 Her symphony and song,
 To such a deep delight 'twould win me
That with music loud and long,
I would build that dome in air,
That sunny dome! those caves of ice!
And all who heard should see them there,
And all should cry, Beware! Beware!
His flashing eyes, his floating hair!
Weave a circle round him thrice,
And close your eyes with holy dread,
For he on honey-dew hath fed,
And drunk the milk of Paradise.

SAMUEL TAYLOR COLERIDGE

Favorite Poems Of

HUMOR AND SATIRE

THE WONDERFUL "ONE-HOSS SHAY"

HAVE you heard of the wonderful one-hoss shay,
That was built in such a logical way
It ran a hundred years to a day,
And then, of a sudden, it—ah, but stay,
I'll tell you what happened without delay,
Scaring the parson into fits,
Frightening people out of their wits,—
Have you ever heard of that, I say?

Seventeen hundred and fifty-five,
Georgius Secundus was then alive,—
Snuffy old drone from the German hive;
That was the year when Lisbon-town
Saw the earth open and gulp her down,
And Braddock's army was done so brown,
Left without a scalp to its crown.
It was on the terrible Earthquake-day
That the Deacon finished the one-hoss shay.

Now in building of chaises, I tell you what,
There is always *somewhere* a weakest spot,—

In hub, tire, felloe, in spring or thill,
In panel, or crossbar, or floor, or sill,
In screw, bolt, thoroughbrace,—lurking still,
Find it somewhere you must and will,—
Above or below, within or without,—
And that's the reason, beyond a doubt,
That a chaise *breaks down*, but doesn't *wear out.*

But the Deacon swore, (as Deacons do,
With an "I dew vum," or an "I tell *yeou*,")
He would build one shay to beat the taown
'N' the keounty 'n' all the kentry raoun';
It should be so built that it couldn't break daown;
"Fur," said the Deacon, "t's mighty plain
That the weakes' place mus' stan' the strain;
'N' the way t' fix it, uz I maintain,
   Is only jist
T' make that place uz strong uz the rest."

So the Deacon inquired of the village folk
Where he could find the strongest oak,
That couldn't be split nor bent nor broke,—
That was for spokes and floor and sills;
He sent for lancewood to make the thills;
The crossbars were ash, from the straightest trees,
The panels of white-wood, that cuts like cheese,
But lasts like iron for things like these;
The hubs of logs from the "Settler's ellum,"—
Last of its timber,—they couldn't sell 'em,
Never an axe had seen their chips,
And the wedges flew from between their lips,
Their blunt ends frizzled like celery-tips;
Step and prop-iron, bolt and screw,
Spring, tire, axle, and linchpin too,
Steel of the finest, bright and blue;
Thoroughbrace bison-skin, thick and wide;
Boot, top, dasher, from tough old hide
Found in the pit when the tanner died.
That was the way he "put her through."—
"There!" said the Deacon, "naow she'll dew!"

Do! I tell you, I rather guess
She was a wonder, and nothing less!
Colts grew horses, beards turned gray,
Deacon and deaconess dropped away,
Children and grandchildren—where were they?
But there stood the stout old one-hoss shay
As fresh as on Lisbon-earthquake-day!

EIGHTEEN HUNDRED;—it came and found
The Deacon's masterpiece strong and sound.
Eighteen hundred increased by ten;—
"Hahnsum kerridge" they called it then.
Eighteen hundred and twenty came;—
Running as usual; much the same.
Thirty and forty at last arrive,
And then came fifty, and FIFTY-FIVE.

Little of all we value here
Wakes on the morn of its hundredth year
Without both feeling and looking queer.
In fact, there's nothing that keeps its youth,
So far as I know, but a tree and truth.
(This is a moral that runs at large;
Take it.—You're welcome.—No extra charge.)

FIRST OF NOVEMBER,—the Earthquake-day
There are traces of age in the one-hoss shay,
A general flavor of mild decay,
But nothing local, as one may say.
There couldn't be,—for the Deacon's art
Had made it so like in every part
That there wasn't a chance for one to start.
For the wheels were just as strong as the thills.
And the floor was just as strong as the sills
And the panels just as strong as the floor,
And the whipple-tree neither less nor more,
And the back-crossbar as strong as the fore,
And spring and axle and hub *encore.*
And yet, *as a whole*, it is past a doubt,
In another hour it will be *worn out!*

First of November, 'Fifty-five!
This morning the parson takes a drive.
Now, small boys, get out of the way!
Here comes the wonderful one-hoss shay,
Drawn by a rat-tailed, ewe-necked bay.
"Huddup!" said the parson.—Off went they.
The parson was working his Sunday's text,—
Had got to *fifthly*, and stopped perplexed
And what the—Moses—was coming next.
All at once the horse stood still,
Close by the meet'n'-house on the hill.
—First a shiver, and then a thrill,
Then something decidedly like a spill,—
And the parson was sitting upon a rock,
At half past nine by the meet'n'-house clock,—

Just the hour of the Earthquake shock!
—What do you think the parson found,
When he got up and stared around?
The poor old chaise in a heap or mound,
As if it had been to the mill and ground!
You see, of course, if you're not a dunce,
How it went to pieces all at once,—
All at once, and nothing first,—
Just as bubbles do when they burst.

End of the wonderful one-hoss shay.
Logic is logic. That's all I say.

                          OLIVER WENDELL HOLMES

THE MOUNTAIN AND THE SQUIRREL

THE MOUNTAIN and the squirrel
Had a quarrel,
And the former called the latter "Little Prig";
Bun replied,
"You are doubtless very big;
But all sorts of things and weather
Must be taken in together,
To make up a year
And a sphere.
And I think it no disgrace
To occupy my place.
If I'm not so large as you,
You are not so small as I,
And not half so spry.
I'll not deny you make
A very pretty squirrel track;
Talents differ; all is well and wisely put;
If I cannot carry forests on my back,
Neither can you crack a nut."

                          RALPH WALDO EMERSON

A WISE OLD OWL

A WISE old owl lived in an oak;
The more he saw the less he spoke;
The less he spoke the more he heard:
Why can't we all be like that bird?

                          EDWARD HERSEY RICHARDS

A BAKER'S DUZZEN UV WIZE SAWZ

THEM ez wants, must choose.
Them ez hez, must lose.
Them ez knows, won't blab.
Them ez guesses, will gab.
Them ez borrows, sorrows.
Them ez lends, spends.
Them ez gives, lives.
Them ez keeps dark, is deep.
Them ez kin earn, kin keep.
Them ez aims, hits.
Them ez hez, gits.
Them ez waits, win.
Them ez *will, kin*.

EDWARD ROWLAND SILL

THE FROG

BE kind and tender to the Frog,
    And do not call him names,
As "Slimy-skin," or "Polly-wog,"
    Or likewise, "Uncle James,"
Or "Gape-a-grin," or "Toad-gone-wrong,"
    Or "Billy Bandy-knees:"
The Frog is justly sensitive
    To epithets like these.

No animal will more repay
    A treatment kind and fair,
At least so lonely people say
Who keep a frog (and, by the way,
    They are extremely rare).

HILAIRE BELLOC

ANIMAL FAIR

I WENT to the animal fair,
The birds and beasts were there.
The big baboon, by the light of the moon,
Was combing his auburn hair.
The monkey, he got drunk,
And sat on the elephant's trunk.

The elephant sneezed and fell on his knees,
And what became of the monk, the monk?
ANONYMOUS

THE YARN OF THE "NANCY BELL"

'Twas on the shores that round our coast
    From Deal to Ramsgate span,
That I found alone, on a piece of stone,
    An elderly naval man.

His hair was weedy, his beard was long,
    And weedy and long was he;
And I heard this wight on the shore recite,
    In a singular minor key:—

"Oh, I am a cook and a captain bold,
    And the mate of the Nancy brig,
And a bo'sun tight, and a midshipmite,
    And the crew of the captain's gig."

And he shook his fists and he tore his hair,
    Till I really felt afraid,
For I couldn't help thinking the man had been drinking,
    And so I simply said:—

"O elderly man, it's little I know
    Of the duties of men of the sea,
And I'll eat my hand if I understand
    How ever you can be

"At once a cook and a captain bold,
    And the mate of the Nancy brig,
And a bo'sun tight, and a midshipmite,
    And the crew of the captain's gig!"

Then he gave a hitch to his trowsers, which
    Is a trick all seamen larn,
And having got rid of a thumping quid,
    He spun this painful yarn:—

" 'Twas in the good ship Nancy Bell
    That we sail'd to the Indian sea,
And there on a reef we come to grief,
    Which has often occurr'd to me.

"And pretty nigh all o' the crew was drown'd
    (There was seventy-seven o' soul);

And only ten of the Nancy's men
   Said 'Here!' to the muster-roll.

"There was me, and the cook, and the captain bold,
   And the mate of the Nancy brig,
And the bo'sun tight and a midshipmite,
   And the crew of the captain's gig.

"For a month we'd neither wittles nor drink,
   Till a-hungry we did feel,
So we draw'd a lot, and, accordin', shot
   The captain for our meal.

"The next lot fell to the Nancy's mate,
   And a delicate dish he made;
Then our appetite with the midshipmite
   We seven survivors stay'd.

"And then we murder'd the bo'sun tight,
   And he much resembled pig;
Then we wittled free, did the cook and me,
   On the crew of the captain's gig.

"Then only the cook and me was left,
   And the delicate question, 'Which
Of us two goes to the kettle?' arose,
   And we argued it out as sich.

"For I loved that cook as a brother, I did,
   And the cook he worshipp'd me;
But we'd both be blow'd if we'd either be stow'd
   In the other chap's hold, you see.

" 'I'll be eat if you dines off me,' says Tom.
   'Yes, that,' says I, 'you'll be.
I'm boil'd if I die, my friend,' quoth I;
   And 'Exactly so,' quoth he.

"Says he: 'Dear James, to murder me
   Were a foolish thing to do,
For don't you see that you can't cook *me*,
   While I can—and will—cook *you*?'

"So he boils the water, and takes the salt
   And the pepper in portions true
(Which he never forgot), and some chopp'd shalot,
   And some sage and parsley too.

" 'Come here,' says he, with a proper pride,
   Which his smiling features tell;

' 'Twill soothing be if I let you see
   How extremely nice you'll smell.'

"And he stirr'd it round and round and round,
   And he sniff'd at the foaming froth;
When I ups with his heels, and smothers his squeals
   In the scum of the boiling broth.

"And I eat that cook in a week or less,
   And as I eating be
The last of his chops, why I almost drops,
   For a wessel in sight I see.—

"And I never larf, and I never smile,
   And I never lark nor play;
But I sit and croak, and a single joke
   I have—which is to say:

"Oh, I am a cook and a captain bold,
   And the mate of the Nancy brig,
And a bo'sun tight, and a midshipmite,
   And the crew of the captain's gig!"

WILLIAM SCHWENCK GILBERT

THE WALRUS AND THE CARPENTER

THE SUN was shining on the sea,
   Shining with all his might:
He did his very best to make
   The billows smooth and bright—
And this was odd, because it was
   The middle of the night.

The moon was shining sulkily,
   Because she thought the sun
Had got no business to be there
   After the day was done—
"It's very rude of him," she said,
   "To come and spoil the fun!"

The sea was wet as wet could be,
   The sands were dry as dry.
You could not see a cloud, because
   No cloud was in the sky:
No birds were flying overhead—
   There were no birds to fly.

The Walrus and the Carpenter
   Were walking close at hand:

They wept like anything to see
    Such quantities of sand.
"If this were only cleared away,"
    They said, "it *would* be grand!"

"If seven maids with seven mops
    Swept it for half a year,
Do you suppose," the Walrus said,
    "That they could get it clear?"
"I doubt it," said the Carpenter,
    And shed a bitter tear.

"O Oysters, come and walk with us!"
    The Walrus did beseech.
"A pleasant talk, a pleasant walk,
    Along the briny beach:
We cannot do with more than four,
    To give a hand to each."

The eldest Oyster looked at him,
    But never a word he said:
The eldest Oyster winked his eye,
    And shook his heavy head—
Meaning to say he did not choose
    To leave the oyster-bed.

But four young Oysters hurried up,
    All eager for the treat:
Their coats were brushed, their faces washed,
    Their shoes were clean and neat—
And this was odd, because, you know,
    They hadn't any feet.

Four other Oysters followed them,
    And yet another four;
And thick and fast they came at last,
    And more, and more, and more—
All hopping through the frothy waves,
    And scrambling to the shore.

The Walrus and the Carpenter
    Walked on a mile or so,
And then they rested on a rock
    Conveniently low:
And all the little Oysters stood
    And waited in a row.

"The time has come," the Walrus said,
    "To talk of many things:
Of shoes and ships and sealing-wax,

Of cabbages and kings;
And why the sea is boiling hot—
  And whether pigs have wings."

"But wait a bit," the Oysters cried,
  "Before we have our chat;
For some of us are out of breath,
  And all of us are fat!"
"No hurry!" said the Carpenter.
  They thanked him much for that.

"A loaf of bread," the Walrus said,
  "Is what we chiefly need:
Pepper and vinegar besides
  Are very good indeed—
Now, if you're ready, Oysters dear,
  We can begin to feed."

"But not on us!" the Oysters cried,
  Turning a little blue.
"After such kindness, that would be
  A dismal thing to do!"
"The night is fine," the Walrus said.
  "Do you admire the view?"

"It was so kind of you to come!
  And you are very nice!"
The Carpenter said nothing but
  "Cut us another slice.
I wish you were not quite so deaf—
  I've had to ask you twice!"

"It seems a shame," the Walrus said,
  "To play them such a trick,
After we've brought them out so far,
  And made them trot so quick!"
The Carpenter said nothing but
  "The butter's spread too thick!"

"I weep for you," the Walrus said:
  "I deeply sympathize."
With sobs and tears he sorted out
  Those of the largest size,
Holding his pocket-handkerchief
  Before his streaming eyes.

"O Oysters," said the Carpenter,
  "You've had a pleasant run!
Shall we be trotting home again?"

But answer came there none—
And this was scarcely odd, because
   They'd eaten every one.

LEWIS CARROLL

ODE ON THE DEATH OF A FAVOURITE CAT, DROWNED IN A TUB OF GOLDFISHES

'TWAS on a lofty vase's side,
Where China's gayest art had dy'd
   The azure flowers, that blow;
Demurest of the tabby kind,
The pensive Selima reclin'd,
   Gazed on the lake below.

Her conscious tail her joy declar'd;
The fair round face, the snowy beard,
   The velvet of her paws,
Her coat, that with the tortoise vies,
Her ears of jet, and emerald eyes,
   She saw; and purr'd applause.

Still had she gaz'd; but 'midst the tide
Two angel forms were seen to glide,
   The Genii of the stream:
Their scaly armour's Tyrian hue
Through richest purple to the view
   Betray'd a golden gleam.

The hapless Nymph with wonder saw:
A whisker first and then a claw,
   With many an ardent wish,
She stretch'd in vain to reach the prize.
What female heart can gold despise?
   What cat's averse to fish?

Presumptuous maid! with looks intent
Again she stretch'd, again she bent,
   Nor knew the gulf between.
(Malignant fate sat by, and smil'd)
The slipp'ry verge her feet beguil'd,
   She tumbled headlong in.

Eight times emerging from the flood
She mew'd to ev'ry watery god,
   Some speedy aid to send.
No dolphin came, no Nereid stirr'd:

Nor cruel Tom, nor Susan heard.
   A fav'rite has no friend!

From hence, ye beauties, undeceiv'd,
Know, one false step is ne'er retriev'd,
   And be with caution bold.
Not all that tempts your wand'ring eyes
And heedless hearts, is lawful prize;
   Nor all, that glisters, gold.

THOMAS GRAY

ELEGY ON THE DEATH OF A MAD DOG

GOOD PEOPLE ALL, of every sort,
   Give ear unto my song;
And if you find it wondrous short,
   It cannot hold you long.

In Islington there was a man
   Of whom the world might say,
That still a godly race he ran—
   Whene'er he went to pray.

A kind and gentle heart he had,
   To comfort friends and foes:
The naked every day he clad—
   When he put on his clothes.

And in that town a dog was found,
   As many dogs there be,
Both mongrel, puppy, whelp, and hound,
   And curs of low degree.

This dog and man at first were friends;
   But when a pique began,
The dog, to gain his private ends,
   Went mad, and bit the man.

Around from all the neighboring streets
   The wondering neighbors ran,
And swore the dog had lost his wits,
   To bite so good a man!

The wound it seemed both sore and sad
   To every Christian eye:
And while they swore the dog was mad,
   They swore the man would die.

But soon a wonder came to light,
    That showed the rogues they lied:—
The man recovered of the bite,
    The dog it was that died!

OLIVER GOLDSMITH

FINNIGIN TO FLANNIGAN

SUPERINTINDINT wuz Flannigan;
Boss av the siction wuz Finnigin;
Whiniver the kyars got offen the thrack
An' muddled up things t' th' divil an' back,
Finnigin writ it to Flannigan,
Afther the wreck wuz all on agin;
That is, this Finnigin
Repoorted to Flannigan.

Whin Finnigin furst writ to Flannigan,
He writed tin pages—did Finnigin,
An' he tould jist how the smash occurred;
Full minny a tajus, blunderin' wurrd
Did Finnigin write to Flannigan
Afther the kyars had gone on agin.
That wuz how Finnigin
Repoorted to Flannigan.

Now Flannigan knowed more than Finnigin—
He'd more idjucation—had Flannigan;
An' it wore'm clane an' complately out
To tell what Finnigin writ about
In his writin' to Musther Flannigan.
So he writed back to Finnigin:
"Don't do sich a sin agin;
Make 'em brief, Finnigin!"

Whin Finnigin got this from Flannigan,
He blushed rosy rid—did Finnigin;
An' he said: "I'll gamble a whole month's pa-ay
That it will be minny an' minny a da-ay
Befoore Sup'rintindint, that's Flannigan,
Gits a whack at this very same sin agin.
From Finnigin to Flannigan
Repoorts won't be long agin."

Wan da-ay on the siction av Finnigin,
On the road sup'rintinded be Flannigan,

A rail gave way on a bit av a curve
An' some kyars wint off as they made the shwerve.
"There's nobody hurted," sez Finnigin,
"But repoorts must be made to Flannigan."
An' he winked at McGorrigan,
As married a Finnigin.

He wuz shantyin' thin, wuz Finnigin,
As minny a railroader's been agin,
An' the shmoky ol' lamp wuz burnin' bright
In Finnigin's shanty all that night—
Bilin' down his repoort, wuz Finnigin!
An' he writed this here: "Musther Flannigan:
Off agin, on agin,
Gone agin.—Finnigin."

STRICKLAND W. GILLILAN

METHUSELAH

METHUSELAH ate what he found on his plate,
And never, as people do now,
Did he note the amount of the calory count:
He ate it because it was chow.
He wasn't disturbed as at dinner he sat,
Devouring a roast or a pie,
To think it was lacking in granular fat
Or a couple of vitamins shy.
He cheerfully chewed each species of food,
Unmindful of troubles or fears
Lest his health might be hurt
By some fancy dessert;
And he lived over nine hundred years.

ANONYMOUS

THE JUMBLIES

THEY went to sea in a sieve, they did;
    In a sieve they went to sea;
In spite of all their friends could say,
On a winter's morn, on a stormy day,
    In a sieve they went to sea.
And when the sieve turned round and round,
And every one cried, "You'll all be drowned!"
They called aloud, "Our sieve ain't big;
But we don't care a button; we don't care a fig:

In a sieve we'll go to sea!"
Far and few, far and few,
Are the lands where the Jumblies live:
Their heads are green, and their hands are blue;
And they went to sea in a sieve.

They sailed away in a sieve, they did,
In a sieve they sailed so fast,
With only a beautiful pea-green veil
Tied with a ribbon, by way of a sail,
To a small tobacco-pipe mast.
And every one said who saw them go,
"Oh! won't they be soon upset, you know?
For the sky is dark, and the voyage is long;
And, happen what may, it's extremely wrong
In a sieve to sail so fast."

The water it soon came in, it did;
The water it soon came in:
So, to keep them dry, they wrapped their feet
In a pinky paper all folded neat:
And they fastened it down with a pin.
And they passed the night in a crockery-jar;
And each of them said, "How wise we are!
Though the sky be dark, and the voyage be long,
Yet we never can think we were rash or wrong,
While round in our sieve we spin."

And all night long they sailed away;
And, when the sun went down,
They whistled and warbled a moony song
To the echoing sound of a coppery gong,
In the shade of the mountains brown,
"O Timballoo! How happy we are
When we live in a sieve and a crockery-jar!
And all night long, in the moonlight pale,
We sail away with a pea-green sail
In the shade of the mountains brown."

They sailed to the Western Sea, they did,—
To a land all covered with trees:
And they bought an owl, and a useful cart,
And a pound of rice, and a cranberry-tart,
And a hive of silvery bees;
And they bought a pig, and some green jackdaws,
And a lovely monkey with lollipop paws,
And forty bottles of ring-bo-ree,
And no end of Stilton cheese:

And in twenty years they all came back,—
　　In twenty years or more;
And everyone said, "How tall they've grown!
For they've been to the Lakes, and the Torrible Zone,
　　And the hills of the Chankly Bore."
And they drank their health, and gave them a feast
Of dumplings made of beautiful yeast;
And every one said, "If we only live,
We, too, will go to sea in a sieve,
　　To the hills of the Chankly Bore."
　　　　Far and few, far and few,
　　　　　Are the lands where the Jumblies live:
　　　　Their heads are green, and their hands are blue;
　　　　　And they went to sea in a sieve.

EDWARD LEAR

EVOLUTION

When you were a tadpole and I was a fish
　　In the Paleozoic time,
And side by side on the ebbing tide
　　We sprawled through the ooze and slime,
Or skittered with many a caudal flip
　　Through the depths of the Carbrian fen,
My heart was rife with the joy of life,
　　For I loved you even then.

Mindless we lived and mindless we loved
　　And mindless at last we died;
And deep in the rift of the Caradoc drift
　　We slumbered side by side.
The world turned on in the lathe of time,
　　The hot lands heaved amain,
Till we caught our breath from the womb of death
　　And crept into light again.

We were amphibians, scaled and tailed,
　　And drab as a dead man's hand;
We coiled at ease 'neath the dripping trees
　　Or trailed through the mud and sand.
Croaking and blind, with our three-clawed feet
　　Writing a language dumb,
With never a spark in the empty dark
　　To hint at a life to come.

Yet happy we lived and happy we loved,
　　And happy we died once more;

Our forms were rolled in the clinging mold
 Of a Neocomian shore.
The eons came and the eons fled
 And the sleep that wrapped us fast
Was riven away in a newer day
 And the night of death was past.

Then light and swift through the jungle trees
 We swung in our airy flights,
Or breathed in the balms of the fronded palms
 In the hush of the moonless nights;
And, oh! what beautiful years were there
 When our hearts clung each to each;
When life was filled and our senses thrilled
 In the first faint dawn of speech.

Thus life by life and love by love
 We passed through the cycles strange,
And breath by breath and death by death
 We followed the chain of change.
Till there came a time in the law of life
 When over the nursing side
The shadows broke and the soul awoke
 In a strange, dim dream of God.

I was thewed like an Auroch bull
 And tusked like the great cave bear;
And you, my sweet, from head to feet
 Were gowned in your glorious hair.
Deep in the gloom of a fireless cave,
 When the night fell o'er the plain
And the moon hung red o'er the river bed
 We mumbled the bones of the slain.

I flaked a flint to a cutting edge
 And shaped it with brutish craft;
I broke a shank from the woodland lank
 And fitted it, head and haft;
Then I hid me close to the reedy tarn,
 Where the mammoth came to drink;
Through the brawn and bone I drove the stone
 And slew him upon the brink.

Loud I howled through the moonlit wastes,
 Loud answered our kith and kin;
From west and east to the crimson feast
 The clan came tramping in.
O'er joint and gristle and padded hoof

We fought and clawed and tore,
And cheek by jowl with many a growl
    We talked the marvel o'er.

I carved that fight on a reindeer bone
    With rude and hairy hand;
I pictured his fall on the cavern wall
    That men might understand.
For we lived by blood and the right of might
    Ere human laws were drawn,
And the age of sin did not begin
    Till our brutal tush were gone.

And that was a million years ago
    In a time that no man knows;
Yet here tonight in the mellow light
    We sit at Delmonico's.
Your eyes are deep as the Devon springs,
    Your hair is dark as jet,
Your years are few, your life is new,
    Your soul untried, and yet—

Our trail is on the Kimmeridge clay
    And the scarp of the Purbeck flags;
We have left our bones in the Bagshot stones
    And deep in the Coralline crags;
Our love is old, our lives are old,
    And death shall come amain;
Should it come today, what man may say
    We shall not live again?

God wrought our souls from the Tremadoc beds
    And furnished them wings to fly;
We sowed our spawn in the world's dim dawn,
    And I know that it shall not die,
Though cities have sprung above the graves
    Where the crook-bone men make war
And the oxwain creaks o'er the buried caves
    Where the mummied mammoths are.

Then as we linger at luncheon here
    O'er many a dainty dish,
Let us drink anew to the time when you
    Were a tadpole and I was a fish.

LANGDON SMITH

UP FROM THE WHEELBARROW

SOME people understand all about machinery,
And to them it is just like beautiful poetry or beautiful
    scenery,
Because they know how to control and handle it,
Because they understandle it,
Yes, when they are confronted with a complicated piece
    of machinery,
Why, they are as cool and collected as a dean sitting in
    his deanery,
And I certainly wish I were among them because if there
    is one thing that makes me terrified and panical,
It is anything mechanical and nowadays everything is
    mechanical.
O thrice unhappy home
Where master doesn't know the difference between a
    watt and an ohm!
O radio glum and silent as a glum and silent burial
When no one knows what to do about the grounding or
    the aerial!
O four-door sedan cantankerous and stubborn and
    Mad Hattery,
With none to give a thought to occasionally changing
    the oil or once in a while checking on the battery!
O telephone and vacuum cleaners and cameras and
    electric toasters and streamlined locomotives and
    artificial refrigeration,
O thermostats and elevators and cigarette-lighters and
    air-conditioning units and all ye other gadgets that
    make ours a mighty nation,
I think you are every one a miracle,
And you do wonderful things and it's probably only
    because I don't see how you do what you do that
    when I think of you I become hystirical,
And of course that is silly of me because what does
    it matter how you function so long as all I have
    to do to get you to function is push a button or
    throw a switch,
Always assuming that I can remember which is which,
So keep on functioning, please,
Because if you don't I shall starve or freeze.

OGDEN NASH

DARIUS GREEN AND HIS FLYING-MACHINE

IF EVER there lived a Yankee lad,
Wise or otherwise, good or bad,
Who, seeing the birds fly, didn't jump
With flapping arms from stake or stump,
    Or, spreading the tail
    Of his coat for a sail
Take a soaring leap from post or rail,
    And wonder why
    He couldn't fly,
And flap and flutter and wish and try—
If ever you knew a country dunce
Who didn't try that as often as once,
All I can say is, that's a sign
He never would do for a hero of mine.

An aspiring genius was D. Green:
The son of a farmer, age fourteen;
His body was long and lank and lean—
Just right for flying, as will be seen;
He had two eyes as bright as a bean,
And a freckled nose that grew between,
A little awry—for I must mention
That he riveted his attention
Upon his wonderful invention,
Twisting his tongue as he twisted the strings,
And working his face as he worked the wings,
And with every turn of gimlet and screw
Turning and screwing his mouth round, too,
    Till his nose seemed bent
    To catch the scent,
Around some corner, of new-baked pies,
And his wrinkled cheeks and his squinting eyes
Grew puckered into a queer grimace,
That made him look very droll in the face,
    And also very wise.

And wise he must have been, to do more
Than ever a genius did before,
Excepting Dædalus of yore
And his son Icarus, who wore
    Upon their backs
    Those wings of wax
He had read of in the old almanacs.

Darius was clearly of the opinion
That the air was also man's dominion,
And that, with paddle or fin or pinion,
   We soon or late shall navigate
The azure as now we sail the sea.
The thing looks simple enough to me;
   And if you doubt it,
Hear how Darius reasoned about it:
   "The birds can fly an' why can't I?
   Must we give in," says he with a grin,
   "That the bluebird an' phoebe
   Are smarter'n we be?
Jest fold our hands an' see the swaller
An' blackbird an' catbird beat us holler?
Does the little chatterin', sassy wren,
No bigger'n my thumb, know more than men?
   Jest show me that!
   Ur prove 't the bat
Hez got more brains than's in my hat,
An' I'll back down, an' not till then!"
He argued further: "Nur I can't see
What's the use o' wings to a bumble-bee,
Fur to get a livin' with, more'n to me;—
   Ain't my business
   Important's his'n is?
   That Icarus
   Made a perty muss—
Him an' his daddy Dædalus
They might 'a' knowed wings made o' wax
Wouldn't stand sun-heat an' hard whacks.
   I'll make mine o' luther,
   Or suthin' or other."
And he said to himself as he tinkered and planned:
"But I ain't goin' to show my hand
To nummies that never can understand
   The fust idee that's big an' grand."

So he kept his secret from all the rest,
Safely buttoned within his vest;
And in the loft above the shed
Himself he locks, with thimble and thread
And wax and hammer and buckles and screws,
And all such things as geniuses use;—
Two bats for a pattern, curious fellows!
A charcoal-pot and a pair of bellows;
An old hoop-skirt or two, as well as
Some wire and several old umbrellas;

A carriage cover, for tail and wings;
A piece of harness; and straps and strings;
   And a big strong box,
   In which he locks
These and a hundred other things.
His grinning brothers, Reuben and Burke
And Nathan and Jotham and Solomon, lurk
Around the corner and see him work—
Sitting cross-legged, like a Turk,
Drawing the wax-end through with a jerk,
And boring the holes with a comical quirk
Of his wise old head, and a knowing smirk.
But vainly they mounted each other's backs,
And poked through knot-holes and pried through cracks;
With wood from the pile and straw from the stacks
He plugged the knot-holes and caulked the cracks;
And a dipper of water, which one would think
He had brought up in the loft to drink
   When he chanced to be dry,
   Stood always nigh,
   For Darius was sly!
And whenever at work he happened to spy
At chink or crevice a blinking eye,
He let the dipper of water fly.
"Take that! an' ef ever ye get a peep,
Guess ye'll ketch a weasel asleep!"
   And he sings as he locks
   His big strong box:
      "The weasel's head is small and trim,
      An' he's little an' long an' slim,
      An' quick of motion an' nimble of limb,
         An' ef you'll be
         Advised by me,
      Keep wide awake when you're ketchin' him!"
   So day after day
He stitched and tinkered and hammered away,
   Till at last 'twas done—
The greatest invention under the sun!
"An' now," says Darius, "hooray fur some fun!"

   'Twas the Fourth of July,
   And the weather was dry,
And not a cloud was on all the sky,
Save a few light fleeces, which here and there,
   Half mist, half air,
Like foam on the ocean went floating by—
Just as lovely a morning as ever was seen

For a nice little trip in a flying-machine.
Thought cunning Darius: "Now I shan't go
Along 'ith the fellers to see the show.
I'll say I've got sich a terrible cough!
And then, when the folks 'ave all gone off
I'll have full swing fur to try the thing,
An' practice a little on the wing."

"Ain't goin' to see the celebration?"
Says brother Nate. "No: botheration!
I've got such a cold—a toothache—I—
My gracious! feel's though I should fly!"
      Said Jotham, "Sho!
      Guess ye better go."
      But Darius said, "No!
Shouldn't wonder 'f you might see me, though,
'Long 'bout noon, if I get red
O' this jumpin', thumpin' pain 'n my head."
For all the while to himself he said:
      "I tell ye what!
I'll fly a few times around the lot,
To see how't seems, then soon's I've got
The hang o' the thing, ez likely's not,
      I'll astonish the nation,
      An' all creation,
By flyin' over the celebration!
      Over their heads I'll sail like an eagle;
I'll balance myself on my wings like a sea-gull.
I'll dance on the chimbleys; I'll stand on the steeple;
I'll flop up to windows and scare the people!
I'll light on the liberty-pole an' crow;
An' I'll say to the gawpin' fools below,
      'What world's this 'ere
      That I've come near?'
Fur I'll make 'em b'lieve I'm a chap f'm the moon;
An' I'll try a race 'ith their ol' balloon!"

      He crept from his bed;
And, seeing the others were gone, he said,
"I'm gittin' over the cold'n my head."
      Away he sped,
To open the wonderful box in the shed.

His brothers had walked but a little way,
When Jotham to Nathan chanced to say,
"What is the feller up to, hey?"
"Don'o'—the's suthin' ur other to pay,

Ur he wouldn't 'a' stayed to hum today."
Says Burke, "His toothache's all 'n his eye!
He never'd miss a F'oth-o-July
Ef he hadn't got some machine to try."
Then Sol, the little one, spoke: "By darn!
Le's hurry back an' hide'n the barn,
An' pay him fur tellin' us that yarn!"
"Agreed!" Through the orchard they creep back,
Along by the fences, behind the stack,
And one by one, through a hole in the wall,
Dressed in their Sunday garments and all;
And a very astonishing sight was that,
When each in his cobwebbed coat and hat
Came up through the floor like an ancient rat.
 And there they hid;
 And Reuben slid
The fastenings back, and the door undid.
"Keep dark!" said he,
"While I squint an' see what the' is to see."

As knights of old put on their mail—
 From head to foot an iron suit,
Iron jacket and iron boot,
Iron breeches, and on the head
No hat, but an iron pot instead,
 And under the chin the bail,
(I believe they call the thing a helm),
Then sallied forth to overwhelm
The dragons and pagans that plague the realm—
 So this *modern* knight
 Prepared for flight,
Put on his wings and strapped them tight;
Jointed and jaunty, strong and light—
Buckled them fast to shoulder and hip;
Ten feet they measured from tip to tip!
And a helmet had he, but that he wore,
Not on his head, like those of yore,
 But more like the helm of a ship.
 "Hush!" Reuben said,
 "He's up in the shed!
He's opened the winder—I see his head!
He stretches it out, an' pokes it about,
Lookin' to see 'f the coast is clear,
 An' nobody near—
Guess he don'o' who's hid in here!
He's riggin' a spring-board over the sill!
Stop laffin', Solomon! Burke, keep still!

He's a-climbin' out now—Of all the things!
What's he got on? I van, it's wings!
An' that 'tother thing? I vum, it's a tail!
An' there he sets like a hawk on a rail!
Steppin' careful, he travels the length
Of his spring-board, and teeters to try its strength,
Now he stretches his wings, like a monstrous bat;
Peeks over his shoulder, this way an' that,
Fur to see 'f the' 's any one passin' by;
But the' 's on'y a ca'f an' a goslin' nigh.
They turn up at him a wonderin' eye,
To see—The Dragon! he's goin' to fly!
Away he goes! Jimminy! what a jump!
    Flop—flop—an' plump
    To the ground with a thump!
Flutt'rin' an' flound'rin', all'n a lump!"

As a demon is hurled by an angel's spear,
Heels over head, to his proper sphere—
Heels over head, and head over heels,
Dizzily down the abyss he wheels—
So fell Darius. Upon his crown,
In the midst of the barn-yard he came down,
In a wonderful whirl of tangled strings,
Broken braces and broken springs,
Broken tail and broken wings,
Shooting stars, and various things;
Barn-yard litter of straw and chaff,
And much that wasn't so sweet by half.
Away with a bellow fled the calf,
And what was that? Did the gosling laugh?
'Tis a merry roar from the old barn-door,
And he hears the voice of Jotham crying,
"Say, Darius! how do you like flyin'?"
Slowly, ruefully where he lay,
Darius just turned and looked that way,
As he staunched his sorrowful nose with his cuff.
"Wal, I like flyin' well enough,"
He said; "but the' ain't sich a thunderin' sight
O' fun in't when ye come to light."

I have just room for the moral here:
And this is the moral—Stick to your sphere.
Or if you insist, as you have a right,
On spreading your wings for a loftier flight,
The moral is—Take care how you light.

JOHN TOWNSEND TROWBRIDGE

THE BLIND MEN AND THE ELEPHANT

IT WAS six men of Indostan
    To learning much inclined,
Who went to see the elephant
    (Though all of them were blind),
That each by observation
    Might satisfy his mind.

The First approached the elephant,
    And, happening to fall
Against his broad and sturdy side,
    At once began to bawl:
"God bless me! but the elephant
    Is nothing but a wall!"

The Second, feeling of the tusk,
    Cried: "Ho! what have we here
So very round and smooth and sharp?
    To me 'tis mighty clear
This wonder of an elephant
    Is very like a spear!"

The Third approached the animal,
    And, happening to take
The squirming trunk within his hands,
    Thus boldly up and spake:
"I see," quoth he, "the elephant
    Is very like a snake!"

The Fourth reached out his eager hand,
    And felt about the knee:
"What most this wondrous beast is like
    Is mighty plain," quoth he;
" 'Tis clear enough the elephant
    Is very like a tree."

The Fifth, who chanced to touch the ear,
    Said: "E'en the blindest man
Can tell what this resembles most;
    Deny the fact who can,
This marvel of an elephant
    Is very like a fan!"

The Sixth no sooner had begun
    About the beast to grope,
Than, seizing on the swinging tail

That fell within his scope,
"I see," quoth he, "the elephant
   Is very like a rope!"

And so these men of Indostan
   Disputed loud and long,
Each in his own opinion
   Exceeding stiff and strong,
Though each was partly in the right,
   And all were in the wrong!

So, oft in theologic wars
   The disputants, I ween,
Rail on in utter ignorance
   Of what each other mean,
And prate about an elephant
   Not one of them has seen!

JOHN GODFREY SAXE

JABBERWOCKY

'Twas brillig, and the slithy toves
   Did gyre and gimble in the wabe;
All mimsy were the borogoves,
   And the mome raths outgrabe.

"Beware the Jabberwock, my son!
   The jaws that bite, the claws that catch!
Beware the Jubjub bird, and shun
   The frumious Bandersnatch!"

He took his vorpal sword in hand:
   Long time the manxome foe he sought,—
So rested he by the Tumtum tree,
   And stood awhile in thought.

And as in uffish thought he stood,
   The Jabberwock, with eyes of flame,
Came whiffling through the tulgey wood,
   And burbled as it came!

One, two! One, two! And through and through
   The vorpal blade went snicker-snack!
He left it dead, and with his head
   He went galumphing back.

"And hast thou slain the Jabberwock?
   Come to my arms, my beamish boy!

O frabjous day! Callooh! Callay!"
    He chortled in his joy.

'Twas brillig, and the slithy toves
    Did gyre and gimble in the wabe;
All mimsy were the borogoves,
    And the mome raths outgrabe.

LEWIS CARROLL

WHEN LOVELY WOMAN

AFTER GOLDSMITH

WHEN lovely woman wants a favor,
    And finds, too late, that man won't bend,
What earthly circumstance can save her
    From disappointment in the end?

The only way to bring him over,
    The last experiment to try,
Whether a husband or a lover,
    If he have feeling is—to cry.

PHOEBE CARY

THE DIVERTING HISTORY OF JOHN GILPIN

JOHN GILPIN was a citizen
    Of credit and renown,
A trainband captain eke was he
    Of famous London town.

John Gilpin's spouse said to her dear,
    "Though wedded we have been
These twice ten tedious years, yet we
    No holiday have seen.

"Tomorrow is our wedding-day,
    And we will then repair
Unto the Bell at Edmonton,
    All in a chaise and pair.

"My sister, and my sister's child,
    Myself, and children three,
Will fill the chaise; so you must ride
    On horseback after we."

He soon replied—"I do admire
    Of womankind but one,
And you are she, my dearest dear,
    Therefore it shall be done.

"I am a linendraper bold,
   As all the world doth know,
And my good friend the calender
   Will lend his horse to go."

Quoth Mrs. Gilpin,—"That's well said;
   And for that wine is dear,
We will be furnished with our own,
   Which is both bright and clear."

John Gilpin kissed his loving wife;
   O'erjoyed was he to find,
That, though on pleasure she was bent,
   She had a frugal mind.

The morning came, the chaise was brought,
   But yet was not allowed
To drive up to the door, lest all
   Should say that she was proud.

So three doors off the chaise was stayed,
   Where they did all get in;
Six precious souls, and all agog
   To dash through thick and thin.

Smack went the whip, round went the wheels,
   Were never folk so glad,
The stones did rattle underneath,
   As if Cheapside were mad.

John Gilpin at his horse's side
   Seized fast the flowing mane,
And up he got, in haste to ride,
   But soon came down again;

For saddletree scarce reached had he,
   His journey to begin,
When, turning round his head, he saw
   Three customers come in.

So down he came; for loss of time,
   Although it grieved him sore,
Yet loss of pence, full well he knew,
   Would trouble him much more.

'T was long before the customers
   Were suited to their mind,
When Betty screaming came down stairs,
   "The wine is left behind!"

"Good lack!" quoth he, "yet bring it me
   My leathern belt likewise,
In which I bear my trusty sword
   When I do exercise."

Now Mistress Gilpin (careful soul!)
   Had two stone bottles found,
To hold the liquor that she loved,
   And keep it safe and sound.

Each bottle had a curling ear,
   Through which the belt he drew,
And hung a bottle on each side
   To make his balance true.

Then over all, that he might be
   Equipped from top to toe,
His long red cloak, well brushed and neat,
   He manfully did throw.

Now see him mounted once again
   Upon his nimble steed,
Full slowly pacing o'er the stones,
   With caution and good heed.

But finding soon a smoother road
   Beneath his well-shod feet,
The snorting beast began to trot,
   Which galled him in his seat.

So "Fair and softly," John he cried,
   But John he cried in vain;
That trot became a gallop soon,
   In spite of curb and rein.

So stooping down, as needs he must
   Who cannot sit upright,
He grasped the mane with both his hands
   And eke with all his might.

His horse, who never in that sort
   Had handled been before,
What thing upon his back had got
   Did wonder more and more.

Away went Gilpin, neck or nought;
   Away went hat and wig;
He little dreamt, when he set out,
   Of running such a rig.

The wind did blow, the cloak did fly,
    Like streamer long and gay,
Till, loop and button failing both,
    At last it flew away.

Then might all people well discern
    The bottles he had slung;
A bottle swinging at each side,
    As hath been said or sung.

The dogs did bark, the children screamed,
    Up flew the windows all;
And every soul cried out, "Well done!"
    As loud as he could bawl.

Away went Gilpin—who but he?
    His fame soon spread around;
"He carries weight!" "He rides a race!"
    " 'T is for a thousand pound!"

And still as fast as he drew near,
    'T was wonderful to view,
How in a trice the turnpike men
    Their gates wide open threw.

And now, as he went bowing down
    His reeking head full low,
The bottles twain behind his back
    Were shattered at a blow.

Down ran the wine into the road,
    Most piteous to be seen,
Which made his horse's flanks to smoke
    As they had basted been.

But still he seemed to carry weight,
    With leathern girdle braced;
For all might see the bottle necks
    Still dangling at his waist.

Thus all through merry Islington,
    These gambols he did play,
Until he came into the Wash
    Of Edmonton so gay;

And there he threw the Wash about,
    On both sides of the way,
Just like unto a trundling mop,
    Or a wild goose at play.

At Edmonton, his loving wife
    From the balcony spied
Her tender husband, wondering much
    To see how he did ride.

"Stop, stop, John Gilpin!—Here's the house!"
    They all at once did cry;
"The dinner waits, and we are tired."—
    Said Gilpin—"So am I!"

But yet his horse was not a whit
    Inclined to tarry there;
For why?—his owner had a house
    Full ten miles off, at Ware.

So like an arrow swift he flew
    Shot by an archer strong;
So did he fly—which brings me to
    The middle of my song.

Away went Gilpin, out of breath,
    And sore against his will,
Till, at his friend the calender's,
    His horse at last stood still.

The calender, amazed to see
    His neighbor in such trim,
Laid down his pipe, flew to the gate,
    And thus accosted him:—

"What news? what news? your tidings tell;
    Tell me you must and shall—
Say why bareheaded you are come,
    Or why you come at all?"

Now Gilpin had a pleasant wit,
    And loved a timely joke;
And thus unto the calender,
    In merry guise, he spoke:—

"I came because your horse would come;
    And, if I well forbode,
My hat and wig will soon be here,—
    They are upon the road."

The calender, right glad to find
    His friend in merry pin,
Returned him not a single word,
    But to the house went in;

When straight he came with hat and wig;
    A wig that flowed behind,

A hat not much the worse for wear,
    Each comely in its kind.

He held them up, and in his turn,
    Thus showed his ready wit:
"My head is twice as big as yours,
    They therefore needs must fit.

"But let me scrape the dirt away
    That hangs upon your face;
And stop and eat, for well you may
    Be in a hungry case."

Said John,—"It is my wedding day,
    And all the world would stare,
If wife should dine at Edmonton,
    And I should dine at Ware."

So turning to his horse, he said,
    "I am in haste to dine;
'T was for your pleasure you came here,
    You shall go back for mine."

Ah! luckless speech, and bootless boast,
    For which he paid full dear;
For while he spake, a braying ass
    Did sing most loud and clear;

Whereat his horse did snort, as he
    Had heard a lion roar,
And galloped off with all his might,
    As he had done before.

Away went Gilpin, and away
    Went Gilpin's hat and wig;
He lost them sooner than at first,
    For why?—they were too big.

Now Mistress Gilpin, when she saw
    Her husband posting down
Into the country far away,
    She pulled out half-a-crown;

And thus unto the youth she said,
    That drove them to the Bell,
"This shall be yours, when you bring back
    My husband safe and well."

The youth did ride, and soon did meet
    John coming back amain;

Whom in a trice he tried to stop
　　By catching at his rein;

But not performing what he meant,
　　And gladly would have done,
The frighted steed he frighted more
　　And made him faster run.

Away went Gilpin, and away
　　Went postboy at his heels,
The postboy's horse right glad to miss
　　The lumbering of the wheels.

Six gentlemen upon the road,
　　Thus seeing Gilpin fly,
With postboy scampering in the rear,
　　They raised the hue and cry:—

"Stop thief! stop thief!—a highwayman!"
　　Not one of them was mute;
And all and each that passed that way
　　Did join in the pursuit.

And now the turnpike-gates again
　　Flew open in short space;
The toll-men thinking as before,
　　That Gilpin rode a race.

And so he did, and won it too,
　　For he got first to town,
Nor stopped till where he had got up
　　He did again get down.

Now let us sing, Long live the King,
　　And Gilpin, long live he;
And when he next doth ride abroad,
　　May I be there to see!

WILLIAM COWPER

THE WELL OF ST. KEYNE

A WELL there is in the west country,
　　And a clearer one never was seen;
There is not a wife in the west country
　　But has heard of the well of St. Keyne.

An oak and an elm tree stand beside,
　　And behind doth an ash tree grow,

And a willow from the bank above
    Droops to the water below.

A traveller came to the well of St. Keyne;
    Joyfully he drew nigh,
For from cock-crow he had been travelling,
    And there was not a cloud in the sky.

He drank of the water so cool and clear,
    For thirsty and hot was he;
And he sat down upon the bank
    Under the willow tree.

There came a man from the house hard by
    At the well to fill his pail;
On the well-side he rested it,
    And he bade the stranger hail.

"Now, art thou a bachelor, stranger?" quoth he;
    "For an if thou hast a wife,
The happiest draught thou hast drank this day
    That ever thou didst in thy life.

"Or has thy good woman, if one thou hast,
    Ever here in Cornwall been?
For an if she have, I'll venture my life,
    She has drank of the well of St. Keyne."

"I have left a good woman who never was here,"
    The stranger he made reply;
"But that my draught should be the better for that,
    I pray you answer me why."

"St. Keyne," quoth the Cornish-man, "many a time
    Drank of this crystal well;
And before the angel summon'd her,
    She laid on the water a spell.

"If the husband of this gifted well
    Shall drink before his wife,
A happy man thenceforth is he,
    For he shall be master for life.

"But if the wife should drink of it first,—
    God help the husband then!"
The stranger stoopt to the well of St. Keyne,
    And drank of the water again.

"You drank of the well, I warrant, betimes?"
    He to the Cornish-man said;
But the Cornish-man smiled as the stranger spake,
    And sheepishly shook his head.

"I hasten'd as soon as the wedding was done,
    And left my wife in the porch;
But i' faith she had been wiser than me,
    For she took a bottle to church."

ROBERT SOUTHEY

PLAIN LANGUAGE FROM TRUTHFUL JAMES

(POPULARLY KNOWN AS *The Heathen Chinee*)

WHICH I wish to remark—
    And my language is plain—
That for ways that are dark
    And for tricks that are vain,
The heathen Chinee is peculiar:
    Which the same I would rise to explain.

Ah Sin was his name;
    And I shall not deny
In regard to the same
    What that name might imply;
But his smile it was pensive and childlike,
    As I frequent remarked to Bill Nye.

It was August the third,
    And quite soft was the skies,
Which it might be inferred
    That Ah Sin was likewise;
Yet he played it that day upon William
    And me in a way I despise.

Which we had a small game,
    And Ah Sin took a hand:
It was euchre. The same
    He did not understand,
But he smiled, as he sat by the table,
    With the smile that was childlike and bland.

Yet the cards they were stocked
    In a way that I grieve,
And my feelings were shocked
    At the state of Nye's sleeve,
Which was stuffed full of aces and bowers,
    And the same with intent to deceive.

But the hands that were played
    By that heathen Chinee,
And the points that he made,
    Were quite frightful to see,—

Till at last he put down a right bower,
    Which the same Nye had dealt unto me.

Then I looked up at Nye,
    And he gazed upon me;
And he rose with a sigh,
    And said, "Can this be?
We are ruined by Chinese cheap labor,"—
    And he went for that heathen Chinee.

In the scene that ensued
    I did not take a hand,
But the floor it was strewed,
    Like the leaves on the strand,
With the cards that Ah Sin had been hiding
    In the game "he did not understand."

In his sleeves, which were long,
    He had twenty-four packs,—
Which was coming it strong,
    Yet I state but the facts;
And we found on his nails, which were taper,
    What is frequent in tapers,—that's wax.

Which is why I remark,—
    And my language is plain,—
That for ways that are dark,
    And for tricks that are vain,
The heathen Chinee is peculiar,—
Which the same I am free to maintain.

FRANCIS BRET HARTE

CASEY AT THE BAT

It looked extremely rocky for the Mudville nine that day;
The score stood two to four, with but one inning left to play.
So, when Cooney died at second, and Burrows did the same,
A pallor wreathed the features of the patrons of the game.

A straggling few got up to go, leaving there the rest,
With that hope which springs eternal within the human breast.
For they thought: "If only Casey could get a whack at that,"
They'd put even money now, with Casey at the bat.

But Flynn preceded Casey, and likewise so did Blake,
And the former was a pudd'n, and the latter was a fake.
So on that stricken multitude a deathlike silence sat;
For there seemed but little chance of Casey's getting to the bat.

But Flynn let drive a "single," to the wonderment of all.
And the much-despisèd Blakey "tore the cover off the ball."
And when the dust had lifted, and they saw what had occurred,
There was Blakey safe at second, and Flynn a-huggin' third.

Then from the gladdened multitude went up a joyous yell—
It rumbled in the mountaintops, it rattled in the dell;
It struck upon the hillside and rebounded on the flat;
For Casey, mighty Casey, was advancing to the bat.

There was ease in Casey's manner as he stepped into his place,
There was pride in Casey's bearing and a smile on Casey's face;
And when responding to the cheers he lightly doffed his hat,
No stranger in the crowd could doubt 'twas Casey at the bat.

Ten thousand eyes were on him as he rubbed his hands with dirt,
Five thousand tongues applauded when he wiped them on his shirt;
Then when the writhing pitcher ground the ball into his hip,
Defiance glanced in Casey's eye, a sneer curled Casey's lip.

And now the leather-covered sphere came hurtling through the air,
And Casey stood a-watching it in haughty grandeur there.
Close by the sturdy batsman the ball unheeded sped;
"That ain't my style," said Casey. "Strike one," the umpire said.

From the benches, black with people, there went up a muffled roar,
Like the beating of the storm waves on the stern and distant shore.
"Kill him! kill the umpire!" shouted someone on the stand;
And it's likely they'd have killed him had not Casey raised his hand.

With a smile of Christian charity great Casey's visage shone;
He stilled the rising tumult, he made the game go on;
He signaled to the pitcher, and once more the spheroid flew;
But Casey still ignored it, and the umpire said, "Strike two."

"Fraud!" cried the maddened thousands, and the echo answered
    "Fraud!"
But one scornful look from Casey and the audience was awed;
They saw his face grow stern and cold, they saw his muscles strain,
And they knew that Casey wouldn't let the ball go by again.

The sneer is gone from Casey's lips, his teeth are clenched in hate,
He pounds with cruel vengeance his bat upon the plate;
And now the pitcher holds the ball, and now he lets it go,
And now the air is shattered by the force of Casey's blow.

Oh, somewhere in this favored land the sun is shining bright,
The band is playing somewhere, and somewhere hearts are light;
And somewhere men are laughing, and somewhere children shout,
But there is no joy in Mudville—Mighty Casey has struck out.

ERNEST LAWRENCE THAYER

Favorite Poems About

FRONTIER DAYS

THE SPELL OF THE YUKON

I WANTED the gold, and I sought it;
   I scrabbled and mucked like a slave.
Was it famine or scurvy—I fought it;
   I hurled my youth into a grave.
I wanted the gold, and I got it—
   Came out with a fortune last fall—
Yet somehow life's not what I thought it,
   And somehow the gold isn't all.

No! There's the land. (Have you seen it?)
   It's the cussedest land that I know,
From the big, dizzy mountains that screen it
   To the deep, deathlike valleys below.
Some say God was tired when He made it;
   Some say it's a fine land to shun;
Maybe; but there's some as would trade it
   For no land on earth—and I'm one.

You come to get rich (damned good reason);
   You feel like an exile at first;
You hate it like hell for a season,
   And then you are worse than the worst.

It grips you like some kinds of sinning;
　　It twists you from foe to a friend;
It seems it's been since the beginning;
　　It seems it will be to the end.

I've stood in some mighty-mouthed hollow
　　That's plumb-full of hush to the brim;
I've watched the big, husky sun wallow
　　In crimson and gold, and grow dim,
Till the moon set the pearly peaks gleaming,
　　And the stars tumbled out, neck and crop;
And I've thought that I surely was dreaming,
　　With the peace o' the world piled on top.

The summer—no sweeter was ever;
　　The sunshiny woods all athrill;
The grayling aleap in the river,
　　The bighorn asleep on the hill.
The strong life that never knows harness;
　　The wilds where the caribou call;
The freshness, the freedom, the farness—
　　O God! how I'm stuck on it all.

The winter! the brightness that blinds you,
　　The white land locked tight as a drum,
The cold fear that follows and finds you,
　　The silence that bludgeons you dumb.
The snows that are older than history,
　　The woods where the weird shadows slant;
The stillness, the moonlight, the mystery,
　　I've bade 'em good-bye—but I can't.

There's a land where the mountains are nameless,
　　And the rivers all run God knows where;
There are lives that are erring and aimless,
　　And deaths that just hang by a hair;
There are hardships that nobody reckons;
　　There are valleys unpeopled and still;
There's a land—oh, it beckons and beckons,
　　And I want to go back—and I will.

They're making my money diminish;
　　I'm sick of the taste of champagne.
Thank God! when I'm skinned to a finish
　　I'll pike to the Yukon again.
I'll fight—and you bet it's no sham-fight;
　　It's hell!—but I've been there before;
And it's better than this by a damsite—
　　So me for the Yukon once more.

There's gold, and it's haunting and haunting;
   It's luring me on as of old;
Yet it isn't the gold that I'm wanting
   So much as just finding the gold.
It's the great, big, broad land 'way up yonder,
   It's the forests where silence has lease;
It's the beauty that thrills me with wonder,
   It's the stillness that fills me with peace.

ROBERT W. SERVICE

THE COWBOY

"WHAT care I, what cares he,
What cares the world of the life we know?
Little they reck of the shadowless plains,
The shelterless mesa, the sun and the rains,
The wild, free life, as the winds that blow."
     With his broad sombrero,
     His worn chapparejos,
       And clinking spurs,
     Like a Centaur he speeds,
     Where the wild bull feeds;
And he laughs, ha, ha!—who cares, who cares!

Ruddy and brown—careless and free—
A king in the saddle—he rides at will
O'er the measureless range where rarely change
The swart gray plains so weird and strange,
Treeless, and streamless, and wondrous still!
     With his slouch sombrero,
     His torn chapparejos,
       And clinking spurs,
     Like a Centaur he speeds
     Where the wild bull feeds;
And he laughs, ha, ha!—who cares, who cares!

He of the towns, he of the East,
Has only a vague, dull thought of him;
In his far-off dreams the cowboy seems
A mythical thing, a thing he deems
A Hun or a Goth as swart and grim!
     With his stained sombrero,
     His rough chapparejos,
       And clinking spurs,
     Like a Centaur he speeds,
     Where the wild bull feeds;
And he laughs, ha, ha!—who cares, who cares!

Often alone, his saddle a throne,
He scans like a sheik the numberless herd;
Where the buffalo-grass and the sage-grass dry
In the hot white glare of a cloudless sky,
And the music of streams is never heard.
  With his gay sombrero,
  His brown chapparejos,
   And clinking spurs,
  Like a Centaur he speeds,
  Where the wild bull feeds;
And he laughs, ha, ha!—who cares, who cares!

Swift and strong, and ever alert,
Yet sometimes he rests on the dreary vasts;
And his thoughts, like the thoughts of other men,
Go back to his childhood days again,
And to many a loved one in the past.
  With his gay sombrero,
  His rude chapparejos,
   And clinking spurs,
  He rests awhile,
  With a tear and a smile,
Then he laughs, ha, ha!—who cares, who cares!

Sometimes his mood from solitude
Harries him, heedless, off to the town!
Where mirth and wine through the goblet shine,
And treacherous sirens twist and twine
The lasso that often brings him down;
  With his soaked sombrero,
  His rent chapparejos,
   And clinking spurs,
  He staggers back
  On the homeward track,
And shouts to the plains—who cares, who cares!

On his broncho's back he sways and swings,
Yet mad and wild with the city's fume;
His pace is the pace of the song he sings,
And the ribald oath that maudlin clings
Like the wicked stench of the harlot's room.
  With his ragged sombrero,
  His torn chapparejos,
   His rowel-less spurs,
  He dashes amain
  Through the trackless rain;
Reeling and reckless—who cares, who cares!

'Tis over late at the ranchman's gate—
He and his fellows, perhaps a score,
Halt in a quarrel o'er night begun,
With a ready blow and a random gun—
There's a dead, dead comrade! nothing more.
  With his slouched sombrero,
  His dark chapparejos,
   And clinking spurs,
  He dashes past
  With face o'ercast,
And growls in his throat—who cares, who cares!

Away on the range there is little change;
He blinks in the sun, he herds the steers;
But a trail on the wind keeps close behind,
And whispers that stagger and blanch the mind
Through the hum of the solemn noon he hears.
  With his dark sombrero,
  His stained chapparejos,
   His clinking spurs,
  He sidles down
  Where the grasses brown
May hide his face, while he sobs—who cares!

But what care I, and what cares he—
This is the strain, common at least;
He is free and vain of his bridle-rein,
Of his spurs, of his gun, of the dull, gray plain;
He is ever vain of his broncho beast!
  With his gray sombrero,
  His brown chapparejos,
   And clinking spurs,
  Like a Centaur he speeds,
  Where the wild bull feeds;
And he laughs, ha, ha!—who cares! who cares!

        JOHN ANTROBUS

THE SHOOTING OF DAN McGREW

A BUNCH of the boys were whooping it up in the Malamute saloon;
The kid that handles the music-box was hitting a jag-time tune;
Back of the bar, in a solo game, sat Dangerous Dan McGrew,
And watching his luck was his light-o'-love, the lady that's known as
 Lou.

When out of the night, which was fifty below, and into the din and the
 glare,

There stumbled a miner fresh from the creeks, dog-dirty, and loaded
    for bear.
He looked like a man with a foot in the grave and scarcely the strength
    of a louse,
Yet he tilted a poke of dust on the bar, and he called for drinks for the
    house.
There was none could place the stranger's face, though we searched our-
    selves for a clue;
But we drank his health, and the last to drink was Dangerous Dan
    McGrew.

There's men that somehow just grip your eyes, and hold them hard like
    a spell;
And such was he, and he looked to me like a man who had lived in hell;
With a face most hair, and the dreary stare of a dog whose day is done,
As he watered the green stuff in his glass, and the drops fell one by one.
Then I got to figgering who he was, and wondering what he'd do,
And I turned my head—and there watching him was the lady that's
    known as Lou.

His eyes went rubbering round the room, and he seemed in a kind of
    daze,
Till at last that old piano fell in the way of his wandering gaze.
The rag-time kid was having a drink; there was no one else on the stool,
So the stranger stumbles across the room, and flops down there like a
    fool.
In a buckskin shirt that was glazed with dirt he sat, and I saw him sway;
Then he clutched the keys with his talon hands—my God! but that
    man could play.

Were you ever out in the Great Alone, when the moon was awful clear,
And the icy mountains hemmed you in with a silence you most could
    hear;
With only the howl of a timber wolf, and you camped there in the cold,
A half-dead thing in a stark, dead world, clean mad for the muck called
    gold;
While high overhead, green, yellow and red, the North Lights swept
    in bars?—
Then you've a hunch what the music meant . . . hunger and night
    and the stars.

And hunger not of the belly kind, that's banished with bacon and
    beans,
But the gnawing hunger of lonely men for a home and all that it means;
For a fireside far from the cares that are, four walls and a roof above;
But oh! so cramful of cosy joy, and crowned with a woman's love—
A woman dearer than all the world, and true as Heaven is true—
(God! how ghastly she looks through her rouge,—the lady that's known
    as Lou.)

Then on a sudden the music changed, so soft that you scarce could hear;
But you felt that your life had been looted clean of all that it once
    held dear;
That someone had stolen the woman you loved; that her love was a
    devil's lie;
That your guts were gone, and the best for you was to crawl away and
    die.
'Twas the crowning cry of a heart's despair, and it thrilled you through
    and through—
"I guess I'll make it a spread misere," said Dangerous Dan McGrew.

The music almost died away . . . then it burst like a pent-up flood;
And it seemed to say, "repay, repay," and my eyes were blind with
    blood.
The thought came back of an ancient wrong, and it stung like a frozen
    lash,
And the lust awoke to kill, to kill . . . then the music stopped with a
    crash,
And the stranger turned, and his eyes they burned in a most peculiar
    way;
In a buckskin shirt that was glazed with dirt he sat, and I saw him sway;
Then his lips went in in a kind of grin, and he spoke, and his voice was
    calm,
And "Boys," says he, "you don't know me, and none of you care a
    damn;
But I want to state, and my words are straight, and I'll bet my poke
    they're true,
That one of you is a hound of hell . . . and that one is Dan McGrew."

Then I ducked my head, and the lights went out, and two guns blazed
    in the dark,
And a woman screamed, and the lights went up, and two men lay stiff
    and stark.
Pitched on his head, and pumped full of lead, was Dangerous Dan
    McGrew,
While the man from the creeks lay clutched to the breast of the lady
    that's known as Lou.

These are the simple facts of the case, and I guess I ought to know.
They say that the stranger was crazed with "hooch," and I'm not deny-
    ing it's so.
I'm not so wise as the lawyer guys, but strictly between us two—
The woman that kissed him and—pinched his poke—was the lady that's
    known as Lou.

ROBERT W. SERVICE

THE FACE UPON THE FLOOR

'Twas a balmy summer evening, and a goodly crowd was there.
Which well-nigh filled Joe's barroom on the corner of the square,
And as songs and witty stories came through the open door
A vagabond crept slowly in and posed upon the floor.

"Where did it come from?" someone said. "The wind has blown it in."
"What does it want?" another cried. "Some whisky, rum or gin?"
"Here, Toby, seek him, if your stomach's equal to the work—
I wouldn't touch him with a fork, he's as filthy as a Turk."

This badinage the poor wretch took with stoical good grace;
In fact, he smiled as though he thought he'd struck the proper place.
"Come, boys, I know there's kindly hearts among so good a crowd—
To be in such good company would make a deacon proud.

"Give me a drink—that's what I want—I'm out of funds, you know;
When I had cash to treat the gang, this hand was never slow.
What? You laugh as though you thought this pocket never held a sou;
I once was fixed as well, my boys, as anyone of you.

"There, thanks; that's braced me nicely; God bless you one and all;
Next time I pass this good saloon, I'll make another call.
Give you a song? No, I can't do that, my singing days are past;
My voice is cracked, my throat's worn out, and my lungs are going fast.

"Say! Give me another whisky, and I'll tell you what I'll do—
I'll tell you a funny story, and a fact, I promise, too.
That I was ever a decent man not one of you would think;
But I was, some four or five years back. Say, give me another drink.

"Fill her up, Joe, I want to put some life into my frame—
Such little drinks, to a bum like me, are miserably tame;
Five fingers—there, that's the scheme—and corking whisky, too.
Well, here's luck, boys; and, landlord, my best regards to you.

"You've treated me pretty kindly, and I'd like to tell you how
I came to be the dirty sot you see before you now.
As I told you, once I was a man, with muscle, frame and health,
And, but for a blunder, ought to have made considerable wealth.

"I was a painter—not one that daubed on bricks and wood
But an artist, and, for my age, was rated pretty good.
I worked hard at my canvas and was bidding fair to rise,
For gradually I saw the star of fame before my eyes.

"I made a picture, perhaps you've seen, 'tis called the 'Chase of Fame,'
It brought me fifteen hundred pounds and added to my name.
And then I met a woman—now comes the funny part—
With eyes that petrified my brain, and sunk into my heart.

"Why don't you laugh? 'Tis funny that the vagabond you see
Could ever love a woman and expect her love for me;
But 'twas so, and for a month or two her smiles were freely given,
And when her loving lips touched mine it carried me to heaven.

"Did you ever see a woman for whom your soul you'd give,
With a form like the Milo Venus, too beautiful to live;
With eyes that would beat the Koh-i-noor, and a wealth of chestnut
    hair?
If so, 'twas she, for there never was another half so fair.

"I was working on a portrait, one afternoon in May,
Of a fair-haired boy, a friend of mine, who lived across the way,
And Madeline admired it, and, much to my surprise,
Said that she'd like to know the man that had such dreamy eyes.

"It didn't take long to know him, and before the month had flown
My friend had stolen my darling, and I was left alone;
And, ere a year of misery had passed above my head,
The jewel I had treasured so had tarnished, and was dead.

"That's why I took to drink, boys. Why, I never saw you smile,
I thought you'd be amused, and laughing all the while.
Why, what's the matter, friend? There's a teardrop in your eye,
Come, laugh, like me; 'tis only babes and women that should cry.

"Say, boys, if you give me just another whisky, I'll be glad,
And I'll draw right here a picture of the face that drove me mad.
Give me that piece of chalk with which you mark the baseball score—
You shall see the lovely Madeline upon the barroom floor."

Another drink, and with chalk in hand the vagabond began
To sketch a face that well might buy the soul of any man.
Then, as he placed another lock upon the shapely head,
With a fearful shriek, he leaped and fell across the picture—dead.

H. ANTOINE D'ARCY

JIM BLUDSO

WALL, NO! I can't tell whar he lives,
    Bekase he don't live, you see;
Leastways, he's got out of the habit
    Of livin' like you an' me.

Whar have you been for the last three year
    That you haven't heard folks tell
How Jimmy Bludso passed in his checks
    The night of the Prairie Belle?

He weren't no saint—them engineers
    Is pretty much all alike—
One wife in Natchez-under-the-Hill
    And another one here in Pike;
A keerless man in his talk was Jim,
    And an awkward hand in a row,
But he never flunked, an' he never lied—
    I reckon he never knowed how.

And this was all the religion he had—
    To treat his engine well;
Never be passed on the river;
    To mind the pilot's bell;
And if ever the Prairie Belle took fire,
    A thousand times he swore
He'd hold her nozzle agin the bank
    Till the last soul got ashore.

All the boats has their day on the Mississip',
    And her day come at last,—
The Movastar was a better boat,
    But the Belle she *wouldn't* be passed.
And so she come tearin' along that night—
    The oldest craft on the line—
With a nigger squat on her safety-valve,
    And her furnace crammed, rosin' an' pine.

The fire bust out as she cl'ared the bar
    And burnt a hole in the night,
And quick as a flash she turned, an' made
    For that willer-bank on the right.
There was runnin' an' cursin', but Jim yelled out
    Over all the infernal roar,
"I'll hold her nozzle agin the bank
    Till the last galoot's ashore!"

Through the hot black breath of the burnin' boat
    Jim Bludso's voice was heard,
An' they all had trust in his cussedness,
    And knowed he would keep his word.
And, sure's you're born, they all got off
    Afore the smokestack fell,—
And Bludso's ghost went up alone
    In the smoke of the Prairie Belle.

He weren't no saint—but at Jedgment
    I'd run my chance with Jim,
'Longside of some pious gentlemen
    That wouldn't shook hands with him.
He seen his duty, a dead-sure thing,—
    And went for it, thar an' then:
And Christ ain't a-goin' to be too hard
    On a man that died for me.

                JOHN HAY

LITTLE BREECHES

I DON'T go much on religion,
    I never ain't had no show;
But I've got a middlin' tight grip, sir,
    On the handful o' things I know.
I don't pan out on the prophets
    An' free-will, an' that sort of thing—
But I b'lieve in God an' the angels,
    Ever sence one night last spring.

I come to town with some turnips,
    An' my little Gabe come along—
No four-year-old in the county
    Could beat him for pretty an' strong,
Peart an' chipper an' sassy.
    Always ready to swear and fight,—
And I'd l'arnt him to chaw terbacker,
    Jest to keep his milk-teeth white.

The snow come down like a blanket
    As I passed by Taggart's store;
I went in for a jug of molasses
    An' left the team at the door.
They scared at something an' started—
    I heard one little squall,
An' hell-to-split over the prairie
    Went team, Little Breeches an' all.

Hell-to-split over the prairie!
    I was almost froze with skeer;
But we rousted up some torches,
    An s'arched for 'em far an' near.
At last we struck horse an' wagon,
    Snowed under a soft white mound,
Upsot, dead beat—but of little Gabe
    No hide nor hair was found.

And here all hope soured on me,
    Of my feller-critter's aid—
I jest flopped down on my marrow-bones
    Crotch-deep in the snow, an' prayed. . . .
By this, the torches wuz played out,
    An' me an' Isrul Parr
Went off for some wood to a sheepfold
    That he said wuz somewhar thar.

We found it at last, an' a little shed
    Where they shut up the lamb at night.
We looked in an' seen them huddled thar,
    So warm an' sleepy an' white;
An' THAR sot Little Breeches an' chirped,
    As peart as ever you see,
"I wants a chaw of terbacky,
    An' that's what's the matter of me."

How did he git thar? Angels.
    He could never have walked in that storm.
They jest scooped down an' toted him
    To whar it was safe an' warm.
An' I think that savin' a little child,
    An' bringin' him to his own,
Is a derned sight better business
    Than loafin' around The Throne.

                                    JOHN HAY

LASCA

I WANT free life and I want fresh air;
And I sigh for the canter after the cattle,
The crack of the whips like shots in a battle,
The medley of horns and hoofs and heads
That wars and wrangles and scatters and spreads;
The green beneath and the blue above,
And dash and danger, and life and love.

And Lasca!

        Lasca used to ride
On a mouse-gray mustang close to my side,
With blue serape and bright-belled spur;
I laughed with joy as I looked at her!
Little knew she of books or of creeds;
An Ave Maria sufficed her needs;
Little she cared, save to be by my side,

To ride with me, and ever to ride,
From San Saba's shore to Lavaca's tide.
She was as bold as the billows that beat,
She was as wild as the breezes that blow;
From her little head to her little feet
She was swayed in her suppleness to and fro
By each gust of passion; a sapling pine,
That grows on the edge of a Kansas bluff,
And wars with the wind when the weather is rough,
Is like this Lasca, this love of mine.
She would hunger that I might eat,
Would take the bitter and leave me the sweet;
But once, when I made her jealous for fun,
At something I'd whispered, or looked, or done,
One Sunday, in San Antonio,
To a glorious girl on the Alamo,
She drew from her garter a dear little dagger,
And—sting of a wasp!—it made me stagger!
An inch to the left, or an inch to the right,
And I shouldn't be maundering here tonight;
But she sobbed, and, sobbing, so swiftly bound
Her torn reboso about the wound,
That I quite forgave her. Scratches don't count
      In Texas, down by the Rio Grande.

Her eye was brown—a deep, deep brown;
Her hair was darker than her eye;
And something in her smile and frown,
Curled crimson lip and instep high,
Showed that there ran in each blue vein,
Mixed with the milder Aztec strain,
The vigorous vintage of Old Spain.
She was alive in every limb
With feeling, to the finger tips;
And when the sun is like a fire,
And sky one shining, soft sapphire,
One does not drink in little sips.

The air was heavy, the night was hot,
I sat by her side, and forgot—forgot;
Forgot the herd that were taking their rest,
Forgot that the air was close opprest,
That the Texas norther comes sudden and soon,
In the dead of night or the blaze of noon;
That once let the herd at its breath take fright,
Nothing on earth can stop the flight;

And woe to the rider, and woe to the steed,
Who falls in front of their mad stampede!

Was that thunder? I grasped the cord
Of my swift mustang without a word.
I sprang to the saddle, and she clung behind.
Away! on a hot chase down the wind!
But never was fox hunt half so hard,
And never was steed so little spared.
For we rode for our lives. You shall hear how we fared
       In Texas, down by the Rio Grande.

The mustang flew, and we urged him on;
There was one chance left, and you have but one;
Halt, jump to ground, and shoot your horse;
Crouch under his carcass, and take your chance;
And, if the steers in their frantic course
Don't batter you both to pieces at once,
You may thank your star; if not, good-by
To the quickening kiss and the long-drawn sigh,
And the open air and the open sky,
        In Texas, down by the Rio Grande!

The cattle gained on us, and, just as I felt
For my old six-shooter behind in my belt,
Down came the mustang, and down came we,
Clinging together, and—what was the rest—
A body that spread itself on my breast.
Two arms that shielded my dizzy head,
Two lips that hard on my lips were prest;
Then came thunder in my ears,
As over us surged the sea of steers,
Blows that beat blood into my eyes,
And when I could rise—
Lasca was dead!

I gouged out a grave a few feet deep,
And there in Earth's arms I laid her to sleep;
And there she is lying, and no one knows,
And the summer shines and the winter snows;
For many a day the flowers have spread
A pall of petals over her head;
And the little gray hawk hangs aloft in the air,
And the sly coyote trots here and there,
And the black snake glides and glitters and slides
Into a rift in a cottonwood tree;
And the buzzard sails on,
And comes and is gone,

Stately and still like a ship at sea;
And I wonder why I do not care
For the things that are like the things that were.
Does half my heart lie buried there
      In Texas, down by the Rio Grande?

FRANK DESPREZ

JESSE JAMES

It was on a Wednesday night, the moon was shining bright,
    They robbed the Glendale train.
And the people they did say, for many miles away,
    'Twas the outlaws Frank and Jesse James.

      Jesse had a wife to mourn all her life,
        The children they were brave.
      'Twas a dirty little coward shot Mister Howard,
        And laid Jesse James in his grave.

It was Robert Ford, the dirty little coward,
    I wonder how he does feel,
For he ate of Jesse's bread and he slept in Jesse's bed,
    Then he laid Jesse James in his grave.

It was his brother Frank that robbed the Gallatin bank,
    And carried the money from the town.
It was in this very place that they had a little race,
    For they shot Captain Sheets to the ground.

They went to the crossing not very far from there,
    And there they did the same;
And the agent on his knees he delivered up the keys
    To the outlaws Frank and Jesse James.

It was on a Saturday night, Jesse was at home
    Talking to his family brave,
When the thief and the coward, little Robert Ford,
    Laid Jesse James in his grave.

How people held their breath when they heard of Jesse's death,
    And wondered how he ever came to die.
'Twas one of the gang, dirty Robert Ford,
    That shot Jesse James on the sly.

Jesse went to his rest with his hand on his breast.
    The devil will be upon his knee.
He was born one day in the county of Clay,
    And came from a solitary race.

ANONYMOUS

BILLY THE KID

I'LL SING you a true song of Billy the Kid,
I'll sing of the desperate deeds that he did
Way out in New Mexico long, long ago,
When a man's only chance was his own forty four.

When Billy the Kid was a very young lad,
In old Silver City he went to the bad;
Way out in the West with a gun in his hand
At the age of twelve years he killed his first man.

Fair Mexican maidens play guitars and sing
A song about Billy, their boy bandit king,
How ere his young manhood had reached its sad end
He'd a notch on his pistol for twenty-one men.

'Twas on the same night when poor billy died
He said to his friends: "I am not satisfied;
There are twenty-one men I have put bullets through
And Sheriff Pat Garrett must make twenty-two."

Now, this is how Billy the Kid met his fate:
The bright moon was shining, the hour was late.
Shot down by Pat Garrett, who once was his friend,
The young outlaw's life had now come to its end.

There's many a man with a face fine and fair
Who starts out in life with a chance to be square,
But just like poor Billy he wanders astray
And loses his life in the very same way.

ANONYMOUS

A HEALTH AT THE FORD

BRONCHO Dan halts midway of the stream,
Sucking up the water that goes tugging at his knees;
High noon and dry noon,—to-day it doesn't seem
As if the country ever knew the blessing of a breeze.
    A torn felt hat with the brim cockled up,
    A dip from the saddle—there you are—
It's the brew of old Snake River in a cowboy's drinking-cup—
    At the ford of Deadman's Bar.

"Now for a toast, a health before we go,—
A health to the life that makes living worth a try;

A long drink, a deep drink, it's bumpers, Dan, you know;
No heel-taps now, old pony, you must drink the river dry!
   Here's to her then,—every sunrise knows her name,
   I've given it away to every star;
Cold water in a hat! Pretty tough, but what of that?—
   It's the best—at Deadman's Bar.

"Where Summer camps all the year by the sea,
By the broad Pacific where your widened waters pour,
Old Snake River, take a message down for me,
Tell the waves that sing to her along the Southern Shore;
   Say that I'm a-rustling, though the trail that leads to wealth
   Is mighty hard to find and dim and far,
But tell her that I love her, and say I drank her health
   To-day at Deadman's Bar."

ROBERT CAMERON ROGERS

THE GOLD-SEEKERS

I saw these dreamers of dreams go by,
I trod in their footsteps a space;
Each marched with his eyes on the sky,
Each passed with a light on his face.

They came from the hopeless and sad,
They faced the future and gold;
Some the tooth of want's wolf had made mad,
And some at the forge had grown old.

Behind them these serfs of the tool
The rags of their service had flung;
No longer of fortune the fool,
This word from each bearded lip rung:

"Once more I'm a man, I am free!
No man is my master, I say;
To-morrow I fail, it may be,—
No matter, I'm freeman to-day."

They go to a toil that is sure,
To despair and hunger and cold;
Their sickness no warning can cure,
They are mad with a longing for gold.

The light will fade from each eye,
The smile from each face;
They will curse the impassable sky,
And the earth when the snow torrents race.

Some will sink by the way and be laid
In the frost of the desolate earth;
And some will return to a maid,
Empty of hand as at birth.

But this out of all will remain,
They have lived and have tossed;
So much in the game will be gain,
Though the gold of the dice has been lost.

HAMLIN GARLAND

DOW'S FLAT

1856

Dow's Flat. That's it's name;
    And I reckon that you
Are a stranger? The same?
    Well, I thought it was true,—
For thar isn't a man on the river as can't spot the place
    at first view.

It was called after Dow,—
    Which the same was an ass;
And as to the how
    That the thing kem to pass,—
Jest tie up your hoss to that buckeye, and sit ye down here
    in the grass.

You see this 'yer Dow
    Had the worst kind of luck;
He slipped up somehow
    On each thing thet he struck.
Why, ef he'd a-straddled thet fence-rail, the derned thing
    'ed get up and buck.

He mined on the bar
    Till he couldn't pay rates;
He was smashed by a car
    When he tunnelled with Bates;
And right on the top of his trouble kem his wife and five
    kids from the States.

It was rough,—mighty rough;
    But the boys they stood by,
And they brought him the stuff
    For a house, on the sly;

And the old woman,—well, she did washing, and took on
    when no one was nigh.

But this 'yer luck of Dow's
    Was so powerful mean
That the spring near his house
    Dried right up on the green;
And he sunk forty feet down for water, but nary a drop to
    be seen.

Then the bar petered out,
    And the boys wouldn't stay;
And the chills got about,
    And his wife fell away;
But Dow in his well kept a peggin' in his usual ridikilous
    way.

One day,—it was June,—
    And a year ago, jest,—
This Dow kem at noon
    To his work like the rest,
With a shovel and pick on his shoulder, and a derringer hid
    in his breast.

He goes to the well,
    And he stands on the brink,
And stops for a spell
    Jest to listen and think:
For the sun in his eyes (jest like this, sir!), you see, kinder
    made the cuss blink.

His two ragged gals
    In the gulch were at play,
And a gownd that was Sal's
    Kinder flapped on a bay:
Not much for a man to be leavin', but his all,—as I've heer'd
    the folks say.

And—That's a peart hoss
    Thet you've got—ain't it now?
What might be her cost?
    Eh? Oh!—Well, then, Dow—
Let's see,—well, that forty-foot grave wasn't his, sir, that
    day, anyhow.

For a blow of his pick
    Sorter caved in the side,
And he looked and turned sick,
    Then he trembled and cried.

For you see the dern cuss had struck—"Water?"—beg your
    parding, young man,—there you lied!

It was *gold,*—in the quartz,
    And it ran all alike;
And I reckon five oughts
    Was the worth of that strike;
And that house with the coopilow's his'n,—which the same
    isn't bad for a Pike.

Thet's why it's Dow's Flat;
    And the thing of it is
That he kinder got that
    Through sheer contrairiness:
For 'twas *water* the derned cuss was seekin', and his luck
    made him certain to miss.

Thet's so! Thar's your way,
    To the left of yon tree;
But—a—look h'yur, say?
    Won't you come up to tea?
No? Well, then the next time you're passin'; and ask after
    Dow,—and thet's *me.*

FRANCIS BRET HARTE

THE OLD CHISHOLM TRAIL

COME ALONG boys, and listen to my tale,
I'll tell you of my troubles on the old Chisholm trail,

I started up the trail October twenty-third,
I started up the trail with the 2-U herd.

O, a ten dollar hoss an' a forty dollar saddle—
And I'm goin' to punchin' Texas cattle.

I woke up one mornin' on the old Chisholm trail,
Rope in my hand and a cow by the tail.

I'm up in the mornin' afore daylight
And afore I sleep the moon shines bright.

Old Ben Bolt was a blamed good boss,
But he'd go see the girls on a sore-backed hoss.

Old Ben Bolt was a fine old man
And you'd know there was whiskey wherever he'd land.

My hoss throwed me off at the creek called Mud,
My hoss throwed me off round the 2-U herd.

Last time I saw him he was goin' 'cross the level
A-kickin' up his heels and a-runnin' like the devil.

It's cloudy in the West, a-lookin' like rain,
And my damned old slicker's in the wagon again.

Crippled my hoss, I don't know how,
Ropin' at the horns of a 2-U cow.

We hit Caldwell and we hit her on the fly,
We bedded down the cattle on the hill close by.

No chaps, no slicker, and it's pouring down rain,
And I swear by God I'll never night-herd again.

Feet in the stirrups and seat in the saddle,
I hung and rastled with them long-horn cattle.

Last night I was on guard and the leader broke the ranks,
I hit my horse down the shoulders and I spurred him in the flanks.

The wind commenced to blow, and the rain began to fall,
Hit looked, by grab, like we wuz goin' to lose 'em all.

I jumped in the saddle and grabbed holt the horn,
Best blamed cow-puncher ever was born.

I popped my foot in the stirrup an' gave a little yell,
The tail cattle broke loose and the leaders went to hell.

I don't give a damn if they never do stop;
I'll ride as long as an eight-day clock.

Foot in the stirrup an' hand on the horn,
Best damned cowboy ever was born.

I herded and I hollered and I done very well,
Till the boss said, "Boys, just let 'em go to hell."

Stray in the herd and the boss said kill it,
So I shot him in the rump with the handle of the skillet.

We rounded 'em up and put 'em on the cars,
And that was the last of the old Two Bars.

Oh, it's bacon an' beans 'most every day,—
I'd as soon be a-eatin' prairie hay.

I'm on my best hoss and I'm goin' at a run,
I'm the quickest shootin' cowboy that ever pulled a gun.

I went to the wagon to get my roll
To come back to Texas, dadburn my soul.

I went to the boss to draw my roll,
He had figured it out I was nine dollars in the hole.

I'll sell my outfit just as soon as I can,
I won't punch cattle for no damned man.

Goin' back to town to draw my money.
Goin' back home to see my honey.

With my knees in the saddle and my seat in the sky,
I'll quit punchin' cows in the sweet by an' by.

ANONYMOUS

OH, MY DARLING CLEMENTINE

IN A CAVERN in a canyon,
    Excavating for a mine,
Dwelt a miner, forty-niner,
    And his daughter, Clementine.

Refrain:
Oh, my darling; oh, my darling;
    Oh, my darling Clementine;
You are lost and gone forever,
    Dreadful sorry Clementine.

Light she was and like a fairy,
    And her shoes were number nine,
Herring boxes, without topses,
    Sandals were for Clementine.

PERCY MONTROSS

THE DYING COWBOY

"OH BURY me not on the lone prairie,"
These words came low and mournfully
From the pallid lips of a youth who lay
On his dying bed at the close of day.

He had waited in pain till o'er his brow
Death's shadows fast were gathering now,
He thought of home and his loved ones nigh,
As the cowboys gathered to see him die.

"Oh bury me not on the lone prairie,
Where the wild cayotes will howl o'er me,
In a narrow grave just six by three,
Oh bury me not on the lone prairie.

"It matters not, I've oft been told,
Where the body lies when the heart grows cold;
Yet grant, oh grant, this wish to me,
Oh bury me not on the lone prairie.

"Oh bury me not on the lone prairie,
Where the owl all night hoots mournfully,
Where the rattlesnakes hiss and the crow flies free,
Where the buffalo paws o'er a lone prairie.
Oh bury me not on the lone prairie."

ANONYMOUS

RED RIVER VALLEY

FROM this valley they say you are going,
 We will miss your bright eyes and sweet smile,
For they say you are taking the sunshine
 That brightens our pathway awhile.

Refrain:
Come and sit by my side if you love me,
 Do not hasten to bid me adieu,
But remember the Red River Valley,
 And the girl that has loved you so true.

Do you think of the valley you're leaving?
 Oh, how lonely, how sad it will be.
Oh, think of the fond heart you're breaking,
 And the grief you are causing me to see.

From this valley they say you are going;
 When you go, may your darling go too?
Would you leave her behind unprotected
 When she loves no other but you?

As you go to your home by the ocean,
 May you never forget those sweet hours
That we spent in the Red River Valley,
 And the love we exchanged 'mid the flowers.

ANONYMOUS

JOHN HENRY

WHEN John Henry was nothin' but a baby
   Sittin' on his mammy's knee,
He said, "De Big Bend tunnel on de C. & O. road
   Is gonna cause de death of me."

De cap'n said to John Henry,
   "Gonna bring me a steam drill aroun';
Gonna take dat steam drill out to de tunnel
   An' gonna mow de mountain down."

John Henry tol' his cap'n
   A man ain't nothin' but a man;
But befo' he'd let dat steam drill beat him
   He'd die wid a hammer in his han'.

John Henry said to his cap'n,
   Lightnin' was in his eye:
"Wid my twelve-poun' hammer an' a four-foot handle
   I'll beat dat steam drill or die."

John Henry went to de tunnel;
   Dey put him in de lead to drive.
De rock so tall an' John Henry so small,
   He put down his hammer an' he cried.

John Henry started on de right side,
   Steam drill started on de lef';
"Befo' I'll let dat steam drill beat me down
   I'll hammer my fool self to death."

Steam drill started workin',
   Was workin' mighty fine;
John Henry drove his fifteen feet,
   An' de steam drill only made nine.

Cap'n said to John Henry,
   "I b'lieve de mountain's sinkin' in."
John Henry said to his cap'n,
   "It's just my hammer suckin' win'."

De hammer dat John Henry swung
   Weighed over thirteen poun'.
He broke a rib in his lef' han' side
   An' his intrails fell on de groun'.

John Henry had a l'l woman,
    Her name was Polly Ann;
On de day dat John Henry drop down dead,
    Polly Ann hammered steel like a man.

Dey took his body to Washin'ton;
    Dey carried it over the lan'.
People f'om de Eas' and people f'om de Wes'
    Dey mourned for dat steel-drivin' man.

ANONYMOUS

KENTUCKY BELLE

SUMMER OF 'SIXTY-THREE, sir, and Conrad was gone away—
Gone to the county town, sir, to sell our first load of hay.
We lived in the log house yonder, poor as ever you've seen;
Roschen there was a baby, and I was only nineteen.

Conrad, he took the oxen, but he left Kentucky Belle;
How much we thought of Kentuck, I couldn't begin to tell—
Came from the Bluegrass country; my father gave her to me
When I rode north with Conrad, away from the Tennessee.

Conrad lived in Ohio—a German he is, you know—
The house stood in broad cornfields, stretching on, row after row;
The old folks made me welcome; they were kind as kind could be;
But I kept longing, longing, for the hills of the Tennessee.

O, for a sight of water, the shadowed slope of a hill!
Clouds that hang on the summit, a wind that never is still!
But the level land went stretching away to meet the sky—
Never a rise, from north to south, to rest the weary eye!

From east to west, no river to shine out under the moon,
Nothing to make a shadow in the yellow afternoon;
Only the breathless sunshine, as I looked out, all forlorn,
Only the "rustle, rustle," as I walked among the corn.

When I fell sick with pining we didn't wait any more,
But moved away from the cornlands out to this river shore—
The Tuscarawas it's called, sir—off there's a hill, you see—
And now I've grown to like it next best to the Tennessee.

I was at work that morning. Someone came riding like mad
Over the bridge and up the road—Farmer Rouf's little lad.
Bareback he rode; he had no hat; he hardly stopped to say,
"Morgan's men are coming, Fraü, they're galloping on this way."

"I'm sent to warn the neighbors. He isn't a mile behind;
He sweeps up all the horses—every horse that he can find;
Morgan, Morgan the raider, and Morgan's terrible men,
With bowie knives and pistols, are galloping up the glen."

The lad rode down the valley, and I stood still at the door—
The baby laughed and prattled, playing with spools on the floor;
Kentuck was out in the pasture; Conrad, my man, was gone;
Near, near Morgan's men were galloping, galloping on!

Sudden I picked up baby and ran to the pasture bar:
"Kentuck!" I called; "Kentucky!" She knew me ever so far!
I led her down the gully that turns off there to the right,
And tied her to the bushes; her head was just out of sight.

As I ran back to the log house at once there came a sound—
The ring of hoofs, galloping hoofs, trembling over the ground,
Coming into the turnpike out from the White-Woman Glen—
Morgan, Morgan the raider, and Morgan's terrible men.

As near they drew and nearer my heart beat fast in alarm;
But still I stood in the doorway, with baby on my arm.
They came; they passed; with spur and whip in haste they sped along;
Morgan, Morgan the raider, and his band six hundred strong.

Weary they looked and jaded, riding through night and through day;
Pushing on east to the river, many long miles away,
To the border strip where Virginia runs up into the west,
And for the Upper Ohio before they could stop to rest.

On like the wind they hurried, and Morgan rode in advance;
Bright were his eyes like live coals, as he gave me a sideways glance;
And I was just breathing freely, after my choking pain,
When the last one of the troopers suddenly drew his rein.

Frightened I was to death, sir; I scarce dared look in his face,
As he asked for a drink of water and glanced around the place;
I gave him a cup, and he smiled—'twas only a boy, you see,
Faint and worn, with dim blue eyes; and he'd sailed on the Tennessee.

Only sixteen he was, sir—a fond mother's only son—
Off and away with Morgan before his life had begun!
The damp drops stood on his temples; drawn was the boyish mouth;
And I thought me of the mother waiting down in the South!

O, pluck was he to the backbone and clear grit through and through;
Boasted and bragged like a trooper; but the big words wouldn't do;
The boy was dying, sir, dying, as plain as plain could be,
Worn out by his ride with Morgan up from the Tennessee.

But, when I told the laddie that I too was from the South,
Water came in his dim eyes and quivers around his mouth.
"Do you know the Bluegrass country?" he wistful began to say,
Then swayed like a willow sapling and fainted dead away.

I had him into the log house, and worked and brought him to;
I fed him and coaxed him, as I thought his mother'd do;
And, when the lad got better, and the noise in his head was gone,
Morgan's men were miles away, galloping, galloping on.

"O, I must go," he muttered; "I must be up and away!
Morgan, Morgan is waiting for me! O, what will Morgan say?"
But I heard a sound of tramping and kept him back from the door—
The ringing sound of horses' hoofs that I had heard before.

And on, on came the soldiers—the Michigan cavalry—
And fast they rode, and black they looked galloping rapidly;
They had followed hard on Morgan's track; they had followed day and
    night;
But of Morgan and Morgan's raiders they had never caught a sight.

And rich Ohio sat startled through all those summer days,
For strange, wild men were galloping over her broad highways;
Now here, now there, now seen, now gone, now north, now east, now
    west,
Through river valleys and corn-land farms, sweeping away her best.

A bold ride and a long ride! But they were taken at last.
They almost reached the river by galloping hard and fast;
But the boys in blue were upon them ere ever they gained the ford,
And Morgan, Morgan the raider, laid down his terrible sword.

Well, I kept the boy till evening—kept him against his will—
But he was too weak to follow, and sat there pale and still;
When it was cool and dusky—you'll wonder to hear me tell—
But I stole down to that gully and brought up Kentucky Belle.

I kissed the star on her forehead—my pretty, gentle lass—
But I knew that she'd be happy back in the old Bluegrass;
A suit of clothes of Conrad's, with all the money I had,
And Kentuck, pretty Kentuck, I gave to the worn-out lad.

I guided him to the southward as well as I knew how;
The boy rode off with many thanks, and many a backward bow;
And then the glow it faded, and my heart began to swell,
As down the glen away she went, my lost Kentucky Belle!

When Conrad came in the evening the moon was shining high;
Baby and I were both crying—I couldn't tell him why—
But a battered suit of rebel gray was hanging on the wall,
And a thin old horse with drooping head stood in Kentucky's stall.

Well, he was kind, and never once said a hard word to me;
He knew I couldn't help it—'twas all for the Tennessee;
But, after the war was over, just think what came to pass—
A letter, sir; and the two were safe back in the old Bluegrass.

The lad had got across the border, riding Kentucky Belle;
And Kentuck she was thriving, and fat, and hearty, and well;
He cared for her, and kept her, nor touched her with whip or spur:
Ah! we've had many horses, but never a horse like her!

CONSTANCE FENIMORE WOOLSON

Favorite

OLD STORY POEMS

MAUD MULLER

MAUD MULLER, on a summer's day,
Raked the meadow sweet with hay.

Beneath her torn hat glow'd the wealth
Of simple beauty and rustic health.

Singing, she wrought, and her merry glee
The mockbird echo'd from his tree.

But, when she glanced to the far-off town,
White from its hillslope looking down,

The sweet song died, and a vague unrest
And a nameless longing fill'd her breast,—

A wish, that she hardly dared to own,
For something better than she had known.

The judge rode slowly down the lane,
Smoothing his horse's chestnut mane.

He drew his bridle in the shade
Of the apple trees to greet the maid,

And ask a draught from a spring that flow'd
Through the meadow across the road.

She stoop'd where the cool spring bubbled up,
And fill'd for him her small tin cup,

And blush'd as she gave it, looking down
On her feet so bare, and her tatter'd gown.

"Thanks!" said the judge; "a sweeter draught
From a fairer hand was never quaff'd."

He spoke of the grass and flowers and trees,
Of the singing birds and the humming bees;

Then talk'd of the haying, and wonder'd whether
The cloud in the west would bring foul weather.

And Maud forgot her brier-torn gown,
And her graceful ankles bare and brown;

And listen'd, while a pleased surprise
Look'd from her long-lash'd hazel eyes.

At last, like one who for delay
Seeks a vain excuse, he rode away.

Maud Muller look'd and sigh'd: "Ah me!
That I the judge's bride might be!

"He would dress me up in silks so fine,
And praise and toast me at his wine.

"My father should wear a broadcloth coat,
My brother should sail a painted boat.

"I'd dress my mother so grand and gay,
And the baby should have a new toy each day.

"And I'd feed the hungry and clothe the poor,
And all should bless me who left our door."

The judge look'd back as he climb'd the hill,
And saw Maud Muller standing still.

"A form more fair, a face more sweet
Ne'er hath it been my lot to meet.

"And her modest answer and graceful air
Show her wise and good as she is fair.

"Would she were mine, and I to-day,
Like her a harvester of hay:

"No doubtful balance of rights and wrongs,
Nor weary lawyers with endless tongues,

"But low of cattle and song of birds,
And health and quiet and loving words."

But he thought of his sisters proud and cold,
And his mother vain of her rank and gold.

So, closing his heart, the judge rode on,
And Maud was left in the field alone.

But the lawyers smiled that afternoon,
When he humm'd in court an old love-tune;

And the young girl mused beside the well,
Till the rain on the unraked clover fell.

He wedded a wife of richest dower,
Who lived for fashion, as he for power.

Yet oft, in his marble hearth's bright glow,
He watch'd a picture come and go;

And sweet Maud Muller's hazel eyes
Look'd out in their innocent surprise.

Oft, when the wine in his glass was red,
He long'd for the wayside well instead;

And closed his eyes on his garnish'd rooms,
To dream of meadows and clover-blooms.

And the proud man sigh'd, with a secret pain,
"Ah, that I were free again!—

"Free as when I rode that day,
Where the barefoot maiden raked her hay."

She wedded a man unlearn'd and poor,
And many children play'd round her door.

But care and sorrow, and childbirth pain,
Left their traces on heart and brain.

And oft, when the summer sun shone hot
On the new-mown hay in the meadow lot,

And she heard the little spring brook fall
Over the roadside, through the wall,

In the shade of the apple tree again
She saw a rider draw his rein.

And, gazing down with timid grace,
She felt his pleased eyes read her face.

Sometimes her narrow kitchen walls
Stretch'd away into stately halls;

The weary wheel to a spinnet turn'd,
The tallow candle an astral burn'd,

And for him who sat by the chimney lug,
Dozing and grumbling o'er pipe and mug,

A manly form at her side she saw,
And joy was duty and love was law.

Then she took up her burden of life again,
Saying only, "It might have been."

Alas for maiden, alas for judge,
For rich repiner and household drudge!

God pity them both! and pity us all,
Who vainly the dreams of youth recall.

For of all sad words of tongue or pen,
The saddest are these: "It might have been!"

Ah, well! for us all some sweet hope lies
Deeply buried from human eyes;

And, in the hereafter, angels may
Roll the stone from its grave away!

JOHN GREENLEAF WHITTIER

THE SKELETON IN ARMOR

"Speak! speak! thou fearful guest!
Who, with thy hollow breast
Still in rude armor drest,
    Comest to daunt me!
Wrapt not in Eastern balms,
But with thy fleshless palms
Stretched, as if asking alms,
    Why dost thou haunt me?"

Then from those cavernous eyes
Pale flashes seemed to rise,
As when the Northern skies
    Gleam in December;
And, like the water's flow
Under December's snow,
Came a dull voice of woe
    From the heart's chamber.

"I was a Viking old!
My deeds, though manifold,
No Skald in song has told,
    No Saga taught thee!
Take heed that in thy verse
Thou dost the tale rehearse,
Else dread a dead man's curse;
    For this I sought thee.

"Far in the Northern Land,
By the wild Baltic's strand,
I, with my childish hand,
    Tamed the gerfalcon;
And, with my skates fast-bound,
Skimmed the half-frozen Sound,
That the poor whimpering hound
    Trembled to walk on.

"Oft to his frozen lair
Tracked I the grisly bear,
While from my path the hare
    Fled like a shadow;
Oft through the forest dark
Followed the were-wolf's bark,
Until the soaring lark
    Sang from the meadow.

"But when I older grew,
Joining a corsair's crew,
O'er the dark sea I flew
    With the marauders.
Wild was the life we led;
Many the souls that sped,
Many the hearts that bled,
    By our stern orders.

"Many a wassail-bout
Wore the long Winter out;
Often our midnight shout
    Set the cocks crowing,
As we the Berserk's tale
Measured in cups of ale,
Draining the oaken pail
    Filled to o'erflowing.

"Once as I told in glee
Tales of the stormy sea,
Soft eyes did gaze on me,

Burning yet tender;
And as the white stars shine
On the dark Norway pine,
On that dark heart of mine
   Fell their soft splendor.

"I wooed the blue-eyed maid,
Yielding, yet half afraid,
And in the forest's shade
   Our vows were plighted.
Under its loosened vest
Fluttered her little breast,
Like birds within their nest
   By the hawk frighted.

"Bright in her father's hall
Shields gleamed upon the wall,
Loud sang the minstrels all,
   Chanting his glory;
When of old Hildebrand
I asked his daughter's hand,
Mute did the minstrels stand
   To hear my story.

"While the brown ale he quaffed,
Loud then the champion laughed,
And as the wind-gusts waft
   The sea-foam brightly,
So the loud laugh of scorn,
Out of those lips unshorn,
From the deep drinking-horn
   Blew the foam lightly.

"She was a Prince's child,
I but a Viking wild,
And though she blushed and smiled,
   I was discarded!
Should not the dove so white
Follow the sea-mew's flight?
Why did they leave that night
   Her nest unguarded?

"Scarce had I put to sea,
Bearing the maid with me,—
Fairest of all was she
   Among the Norsemen!—
When on the white sea-strand,
Waving his armèd hand,

Saw we old Hildebrand,
  With twenty horsemen.

"Then launched they to the blast,
Bent like a reed each mast,
Yet we were gaining fast,
  When the wind failed us;
And with a sudden flaw
Came round the gusty Skaw,
So that our foe we saw
  Laugh as he hailed us.

"And as to catch the gale
Round veered the flapping sail,
'Death!' was the helmsman's hail,
  'Death without quarter!'
Midships with iron keel
Struck we her ribs of steel;
Down her black hull did reel
  Through the black water!

"As with his wings aslant,
Sails the fierce cormorant,
Seeking some rocky haunt,
  With his prey laden,
So toward the open main,
Beating to sea again,
Through the wild hurricane,
  Bore I the maiden.

"Three weeks we westward bore,
And when the storm was o'er,
Cloud-like we saw the shore
  Stretching to leeward;
There for my lady's bower
Built I the lofty tower,
Which, to this very hour,
  Stands looking seaward.

"There lived we many years;
Time dried the maiden's tears;
She had forgot her fears,
  She was a mother;
Death closed her mild blue eyes;
Under that tower she lies;
Ne'er shall the sun arise
  On such another.

"Still grew my bosom then
Still as a stagnant fen!

Hateful to me were men,
   The sunlight hateful!
In the vast forest here,
Clad in my warlike gear,
Fell I upon my spear,
   Oh, death was grateful!

"Thus, seamed with many scars,
Bursting these prison bars,
Up to its native stars
   My soul ascended!
There from the flowing bowl
Deep drinks the warrior's soul,
Skoal! to the Northland! *skoal!*"
   Thus the tale ended.

HENRY WADSWORTH LONGFELLOW

AUX ITALIENS

AT PARIS it was, at the opera there;—
   And she look'd like a queen in a book that night,
With the wreath of pearl in her raven hair,
   And the brooch on her breast so bright.

Of all the operas that Verdi wrote,
   The best, to my taste, is the Trovatore;
And Mario can soothe, with a tenor note,
   The souls in purgatory.

The moon on the tower slept soft as snow;
   And who was not thrill'd in the strangest way,
As we heard him sing, while the gas burn'd low,
   "Non ti scordar di me"?*

The emperor there, in his box of state,
   Look'd grave, as if he had just then seen
The red flag wave from the city gate,
   Where his eagles in bronze had been.

The empress, too, had a tear in her eye:
   You'd have said that her fancy had gone back again,
For one moment, under the old blue sky,
   To the old glad life in Spain.

Well, there in our front-row box we sat
   Together, my bride betroth'd and I;

* Do not forget me.

My gaze was fixed on my opera hat,
   And hers on the stage hard by.

And both were silent, and both were sad;
   Like a queen she lean'd on her full white arm,
With that regal, indolent air she had,
   So confident of her charm!

I have not a doubt she was thinking then
   Of her former lord, good soul that he was,
Who died the richest and roundest of men,
   The Marquis of Carabas.

I hope that, to get to the kingdom of heaven,
   Through a needle's eye he had not to pass.
I wish him well, for the jointure given
   To my lady of Carabas.

Meanwhile, I was thinking of my first love,
   As I had not been thinking of aught for years,
Till over my eyes there began to move
   Something that felt like tears.

I thought of the dress that she wore last time,
   When we stood 'neath the cypress trees together,
In that lost land, in that soft clime,
   In the crimson evening weather;

Of that muslin dress (for the eve was hot),
   And her warm white neck in its golden chain,
And her full, soft hair, just tied in a knot,
   And falling loose again;

And the jasmine flower in her fair young breast,
   (Oh, the faint, sweet smell of that jasmine flower!)
And the one bird singing alone to his nest,
   And the one star over the tower.

I thought of our little quarrels and strife,
   And the letter that brought me back my ring;
And it all seem'd then, in the waste of life,
   Such a very little thing!

For I thought of her grave below the hill,
   Which the sentinel cypress tree stands over,
And I thought, "Were she only living still,
   How I could forgive her, and love her!"

And I swear, as I thought of her thus, in that hour,
   And of how, after all, old things were best,

That I smelt the smell of that jasmine flower
   Which she used to wear in her breast.

It smelt so faint, and it smelt so sweet,
   It made me creep, and it made me cold;
Like the scent that steals from the crumbling sheet
   Where a mummy is half unroll'd.

And I turned, and looked. She was sitting there
   In a dim box, over the stage; and dressed
In that muslin dress with that full soft hair,
   And that jasmine in her breast!

I was here; and she was there;
   And the glittering horseshoe curved between:—
From my bride-betrothed, with her raven hair,
   And her sumptuous scornful mien,

To my early love, with her eyes downcast,
   And over her primrose face the shade
(In short from the Future back to the Past),
   There was but a step to be made.

To my early love from my future bride
   One moment I looked. Then I stole to the door,
I traversed the passage; and down at her side
   I was sitting, a moment more.

My thinking of her, or the music's strain,
   Or something which never will be expressed,
Had brought her back from the grave again,
   With the jasmine in her breast.

She is not dead, and she is not wed!
   But she loves me now, and she loved me then!
And the very first word that her sweet lips said,
   My heart grew youthful again.

The Marchioness, there, of Carabas,
   She is wealthy, and young, and handsome still,
And but for her . . . well, we'll let that pass,
   She may marry whomever she will.

But I will marry my own first love,
   With her primrose face: for old things are best,
And the flower in her bosom, I prize it above
   The brooch in my lady's breast.

The world is filled with folly and sin,
   And Love must cling where it can, I say:

For Beauty is easy enough to win;
   But one isn't loved every day.

And I think, in the lives of most women and men,
   There's a moment when all would go smooth and even,
If only the dead could find out when
   To come back, and be forgiven.

But O the smell of that jasmine-flower!
   And O that music! and O the way
That voice rang out from the donjon tower,
   Non ti scordar di me,
     Non ti scordar di me!

            EDWARD ROBERT BULWER LYTTON

THE LEGEND OF THE ORGAN-BUILDER

DAY BY DAY the Organ-Builder in his lonely chamber wrought;
Day by day the soft air trembled to the music of his thought,

Till at last the work was ended; and no organ-voice so grand
Ever yet had soared responsive to the master's magic hand.

Ay, so rarely was it builded that whenever groom and bride,
Who in God's sight were well pleasing, in the church stood side by side

Without touch or breath the organ of itself began to play,
And the very airs of heaven through the soft gloom seemed to stray.

He was young, the Organ-Builder, and o'er all the land his fame
Ran with fleet and eager footsteps, like a swiftly rushing flame.

All the maidens heard the story; all the maidens blushed and smiled,
By his youth and wondrous beauty and his great renown beguiled.

So he sought and won the fairest, and the wedding day was set:
Happy day—the brightest jewel in the glad year's coronet!

But when they the portal entered he forgot his lovely bride—
Forgot his love, forgot his God, and his heart swelled high with pride.

"Ah!" thought he; "how great a master am I! When the organ plays,
How the vast cathedral arches will re-echo with my praise!"

Up the aisle the gay procession moved. The altar shone afar,
With every candle gleaming through soft shadows like a star.

But he listened, listened, listened, with no thought of love or prayer,
For the swelling notes of triumph from his organ standing there.

All was silent. Nothing heard he save the priest's low monotone,
And the bride's robe trailing softly o'er the floor of fretted stone.

Then his lips grew white with anger. Surely God was pleased with him
Who had built the wondrous organ for His temple vast and dim!

Whose the fault, then? Hers—the maiden standing meekly at his side!
Flamed his jealous rage, maintaining she was false to him—his bride.

Vain were all her protestations, vain her innocence and truth;
On that very night he left her to her anguish and her ruth.

Far he wandered to a country wherein no man knew his name;
For ten weary years he dwelt there, nursing still his wrath and shame.

Then his haughty heart grew softer, and he thought by night and day
Of the bride he had deserted, till he hardly dared to pray;

Thought of her, a spotless maiden, fair and beautiful and good;
Thought of his relentless anger, that had cursed her womanhood;

Till his yearning grief and penitence at last were all complete,
And he longed, with bitter longing, just to fall down at her feet.

Ah! how throbbed his heart when, after many a weary day and night,
Rose his native towers before him, with the sunset glow alight!

Through the gates into the city, on he pressed with eager tread;
There he met a long procession—mourners following the dead.

"Now, why weep ye so, good people? and whom bury ye today?
Why do yonder sorrowing maidens scatter flowers along the way?

"Has some saint gone up to heaven?" "Yes," they answered, weeping
    sore;
"For the Organ-Builder's saintly wife our eyes shall see no more;

"And because her days were given to the service of God's poor,
From his church we mean to bury her. See! yonder is the door."

No one knew him; no one wondered when he cried out, white with
    pain;
No one questioned when, with pallid lips, he poured his tears like rain.

" 'Tis some one whom she has comforted, who mourns with us," they
    said,
As he made his way unchallenged, and bore the coffin's head;

Bore it through the open portal, bore it up the echoing aisle,
Let it down before the altar, where the lights burned clear the while:

When, oh, hark! the wondrous organ of itself began to play
Strains of rare, unearthly sweetness never heard until that day!

All the vaulted arches rang with the music sweet and clear;
All the air was filled with glory, as of angels hovering near;

And ere yet the strain was ended, he who bore the coffin's head,
With the smile of one forgiven, gently sank beside it—dead.

They who raised the body knew him, and they laid him by his bride;
Down the aisle and o'er the threshold they were carried, side by side,

While the organ played a dirge that no man ever heard before,
And then softly sank to silence—silence kept for evermore.

JULIA C. R. DORR

THE DESTRUCTION OF SENNACHERIB

THE ASSYRIAN came down like the wolf on the fold,
And his cohorts were gleaming in purple and gold;
And the sheen of their spears was like stars on the sea,
When the blue wave rolls nightly on deep Galilee.

Like the leaves of the forest when summer is green,
That host with their banners at sunset were seen:
Like the leaves of the forest when autumn hath blown,
That host on the morrow lay withered and strown.

For the Angel of Death spread his wings on the blast,
And breathed in the face of the foe as he passed;
And the eyes of the sleepers waxed deadly and chill,
And their hearts but once heaved, and forever grew still!

And there lay the steed with his nostril all wide,
But through it there rolled not the breath of his pride:
And the foam of his gasping lay white on the turf,
And cold as the spray of the rock-beating surf.

And there lay the rider distorted and pale,
With the dew on his brow, and the rust on his mail;
And the tents were all silent, the banners alone,
The lances unlifted, the trumpet unblown.

And the widows of Ashur are loud in their wail,
And the idols are broke in the temple of Baal;
And the might of the Gentile, unsmote by the sword,
Hath melted like snow in the glance of the Lord!

GEORGE GORDON BYRON

CLEOPATRA DYING

Sɪɴᴋs the sun below the desert,
    Golden glows the sluggish Nile;
Purple flame crowns Spring and Temple,
    Lights up every ancient pile
Where the old gods now are sleeping;
    Isis and Osiris great,
Guard me, help me, give me courage
    Like a Queen to meet my fate.

"I am dying, Egypt, dying,"
    Let the Caesar's army come—
I will cheat him of his glory,
    Though beyond the Styx I roam;
Shall he drag this beauty with him—
    While the crowd his triumph sings?
No, no, never! I will show him
    What lies in the blood of Kings.

Though he hold the golden scepter,
    Rule the Pharaoh's sunny land,
Where old Nilus rolls resistless
    Through the sweeps of silvery sand—
He shall never say I met him
    Fawning, abject, like a slave—
I will foil him, though to do it
    I must cross the Stygian wave.

Oh, my hero, sleeping, sleeping—
    Shall I meet you on the shore
Of Plutonian shadows? Shall we
    In death meet and love once more?
See, I follow in your footsteps—
    Scorn the Caesar in his might;
For your love I will leap boldly
    Into realms of death and night.

Down below the desert sinking,
    Fades Apollo's brilliant car;
And from out the distant azure
    Breaks the bright gleam of a star.
Venus, Queen of Love and Beauty,
    Welcomes me to death's embrace,
Dying, free, proud, and triumphant,
    The last sovereign of my race.

Dying, dying! I am coming,
  Oh, my hero, to your arms;
You will welcome me, I know it—
  Guard me from all rude alarms.
Hark! I hear the legions coming,
  Hear the cries of triumph swell,
But, proud Caesar, dead I scorn you—
  Egypt, Antony, farewell.

THOMAS STEPHENS COLLIER

MARY, QUEEN OF SCOTS

I LOOKED far back into other years, and lo, in bright array
I saw, as in a dream, the form of ages passed away.
It was a stately convent with its old and lofty walls,
And gardens with their broad green walks, where soft the footstep falls;
And o'er the antique dial stones the creeping shadows passed,
And all around the noonday sun a drowsy radiance cast.
No sound of busy life was heard, save from the cloisters dim
The tinkling of the silver bell, or the sisters' holy hymn.
And there five noble maidens sat beneath the orchard trees,
In that first budding spring of youth, when all its prospects please;
And little recked they, when they sang, or knelt at vesper prayers,
That Scotland knew no prouder names—held none more dear than theirs;
And little even the loveliest thought, before the Virgin's shrine,
Of royal blood and high descent from the ancient Stuart line;
Calmly her happy days flew on, uncounted in their flight,
And as they flew they left behind a long-continuing light.

The scene was changed: it was the court, the gay court of Bourbon,
And 'neath a thousand silver lamps a thousand courtiers throng;
And proudly kindles Henry's eye—well pleased I ween, to see
The land assemble all its wealth of grace and chivalry;
But fairer far than all the rest who bask in fortune's tide,
Effulgent in the light of youth is she, the new-made bride!
The homage of a thousand hearts—the fond, deep love of one—
The hopes that dance around a life whose charms are but begun—
They lighten up her chestnut eye, they mantle o'er her cheek,
They sparkle on her open brow, and high-souled joy bespeak.
Ah, who shall blame, if scarce that day, through all its brilliant hours,
She thought of the quiet convent's calm, its sunshine and its flowers?

The scene was changed: it was a barque that slowly held its way,
And o'er its lee the coast of France in light of evening lay;
And on its deck a lady sat, who gazed with tearful eyes

Upon the fast-receding hills that, dim and distant, rise.
No marvel that the lady wept—there was no land on earth
She loved like that dear land, although she owed it not her birth.
It was her mother's land, the land of childhood and of friends,
It was the land where she had found for all her griefs amends;
The land where her dead husband slept, the land where she had known
The tranquil convent's hushed repose, and the splendors of a throne.
No marvel that the lady wept—it was the land of France,
The chosen home of chivalry, the garden of romance.
The past was bright, like those dear hills so far behind her barque;
The future, like the gathering night, was ominous and dark.
One gaze again—one long, last gaze, "Adieu, fair France, to thee!"
The breeze comes forth—she is alone on the unconscious sea!

The scene was changed: it was an eve of raw and surly mood,
And in a turret chamber high of ancient Holyrood
Sat Mary, listening to the rain and sighing with the winds
That seemed to suit the stormy state of men's uncertain minds.
The touch of care had blanched her cheek, her smile was sadder now,
The weight of royalty had pressed too heavy on her brow;
And traitors to her councils came, and rebels to the field;
The Stuart sceptre well she swayed, but the sword she could not wield.
She thought of all her blighted hopes, the dreams of youth's brief day,
And summoned Rizzio with his lute, and bade the minstrel play
The songs she loved in early years—the songs of gay Navarre,
The songs perchance that erst were sung by gallant Chattilor.
They half beguiled her of her cares, they soothed her into smiles,
They won her thoughts from bigot zeal and fierce domestic broils;
But hark, the tramp of armed men, the Douglas' battle cry!
They come! they come! and lo, the scowl of Ruthven's hollow eye!
The swords are drawn, the daggers gleam, the tears and words are vain—
The ruffian steel is in his heart, the faithful Rizzio's slain!
Then Mary Stuart dashed aside the tears that trickling fell:
"Now for my father's arm!" she cried; "my woman's heart farewell!"

The scene was changed: a royal host a royal banner bore,
And the faithful of the land stood round their smiling Queen once
  more;
She stayed her steed upon a hill—she saw them marching by—
She heard their shouts—she read success in every flashing eye.
The tumult of the strife begins—it roars—it dies away;
And Mary's troops and banners now—and courtiers—where are they?
Scattered and strewn, and flying far, defenceless and undone!
Alas! to think what she had lost, and all that guilt had won!
Away! Away! thy noble steed must act no laggard's part;
Yet vain his speed, for thou dost bear the arrow in thy heart!

The scene was changed: it was a lake, with one small lonely isle,

And there, within the prison walls of its baronial pile,
Stern men stood menacing their queen, till she should stoop to sign
The traitorous scroll that snatched the crown from her ancestral line;
"My lords, my lords," the captive said, "were I but once more free,
With ten good knights on yonder shore to aid my cause and me,
This parchment would I scatter wide to every breeze that blows,
And once more reign a Stuart queen o'er my remorseless foes!"
A red spot burned upon her cheek, streamed her rich tresses down,
She wrote the words, she stood erect, a queen without a crown!

The scene was changed: beside the block a sullen headsman stood,
And gleamed the broad axe in his hand, that soon must drip with
    blood.
With slow and steady step there came a Lady through the hall,
And breathless silence chained the lips and touched the hearts of all.
I knew that queenly form again, though blighted was its bloom;
I saw that grief and decked it out—an offering for the tomb!
I knew that eye, though faint its light, that once so brightly shone;
I knew the voice, though feeble now, that thrilled with every tone;
I knew the ringlets almost grey, once threads of living gold;
I knew that bounding grace of step, that symmetry of mould!

Even now I see her far away in that calm convent aisle,
I hear her chant her vesper hymn, I mark her holy smile;
Even now I see her bursting forth upon the bridal morn,
A new star in the firmament, to light and glory born!
Alas, the change! she placed her foot upon a triple throne,
And on the scaffold now she stands—beside the block—alone!
The little dog that licks her hand the last of all the crowd
Who sunned themselves beneath her glance, and round her footsteps
    bowed.
Her neck is bared—the blow is struck—the soul is passed away!
The bright—the beautiful—is now a bleeding piece of clay.
The dog is moaning piteously; and, as it gurgles o'er,
Laps the warm blood that trickling runs unheeded to the floor.
The blood of beauty, wealth and power, the heart-blood of a queen,
The noblest of the Stuart race, the fairest earth has seen,
Lapped by a dog! Go think of it, in silence and alone;
Then weigh against a grain of sand the glories of a throne.

HENRY GLASSFORD BELL

YUSSOUF

A STRANGER came one night to Yussouf's tent,
  Saying, "Behold one outcast and in dread,
  Against whose life the bow of power is bent,

Who flies, and hath not where to lay his head;
I come to thee for shelter and for food,
To Yussouf, called through all our tribes 'The Good.' "

"This tent is mine," said Yussouf, "but no more
Than it is God's; come in, and be at peace;
Freely shalt thou partake of all my store
As I of His who buildeth over these
Our tents his glorious roof of night and day,
And at whose door none ever yet heard Nay."

So Yussouf entertained his guest that night,
And, waking him ere day, said: "Here is gold;
My swiftest horse is saddled for thy flight;
Depart before the prying day grow bold."
As one lamp lights another, nor grows less,
So nobleness enkindleth nobleness.

That inward light the stranger's face made grand,
Which shines from all self-conquest; kneeling low,
He bowed his fore head upon Yussouf's hand,
Sobbing: "O Sheik, I cannot leave thee so;
I will repay thee; all this thou hast done
Unto that Ibrahim who slew thy son!"

"Take thrice the gold," said Yussouf, "for with thee
Into the desert, never to return,
My one black thought shall ride away from me;
First-born, for whom by day and night I yearn,
Balanced and just are all of God's decrees;
Thou art avenged, my first-born, sleep in peace!"

JAMES RUSSELL LOWELL

TWO PICTURES

Two PICTURES hung on the dingy wall
Of a grand old Florentine hall—

One of a child of beauty rare,
With a cherub face and golden hair;
The lovely look of whose radiant eyes
Filled the soul with thoughts of Paradise.

The other was a visage vile
Marked with the lines of lust and guile,
A loathsome being, whose features fell
Brought to the soul weird thoughts of hell.

Side by side in their frames of gold,
Dingy and dusty and cracked and old,
This is the solemn tale they told:

A youthful painter found one day,
In the streets of Rome, a child at play,
And, moved by the beauty it bore,
The heavenly look that its features wore,
On a canvas, radiant and grand,
He painted its face with a master hand.

Year after year on his wall it hung;
'Twas ever joyful and always young—
Driving away all thoughts of gloom
While the painter toiled in his dingy room.

Like an angel of light it met his gaze,
Bringing him dreams of his boyhood days,
Filling his soul with a sense of praise.

His raven ringlets grew thin and gray,
His young ambition all passed away;
Yet he looked for years in many a place,
To find a contrast to that sweet face.

Through haunts of vice in the night he stayed
To find some ruin that crime had made.
At last in a prison cell he caught
A glimpse of the hideous fiend he sought.

On a canvas weird and wild but grand,
He painted the face with a master hand.
His task was done; 'twas a work sublime—
An angel of joy and a fiend of crime—
A lesson of life from the wrecks of time.

O Crime: with ruin thy road is strewn;
The brightest beauty the world has known
Thy power has wasted, till in the mind
No trace of its presence is left behind.

The loathsome wretch in the dungeon low,
With a face of a fiend and a look of woe,
Ruined by revels of crime and sin,
A pitiful wreck of what might have been,
Hated and shunned, and without a home,
Was the *child* that played in the streets of Rome.

ANONYMOUS

THE MAN ON THE FLYING TRAPEZE

ONCE I was happy, but now I'm forlorn,
Like an old coat, all tattered and torn,
Left in this wide world to fret and to mourn,
Betrayed by a wife in her teens.
Oh, the girl that I loved she was handsome,
I tried all I knew her to please,
But I could not please one quarter as well
As the man on the flying trapeze.

Chorus:

He would fly through the air
With the greatest of ease,
This daring young man
On the flying trapeze;
His movements were graceful,
All girls he could please,
And my love he purloined away.

Her father and mother were both on my side,
And very hard tried to make her my bride.
Her father he sighed, and her mother she cried
To see her throw herself away.
'Twas all no avail, she'd go there every night
And throw him bouquets on the stage,
Which caused him to meet her; how he ran me down
To tell you would take a whole page.

One night I as usual called at her dear home,
Found there her father and mother alone.
I asked for my love, and soon they made known
To my horror that she'd run away.
She packed up her goods and eloped in the night
With him with the greatest of ease;
From three stories high he had lowered her down
To the ground on his flying trapeze.

Some months after this, I chanced in a hall,
Was greatly surprised to see on the wall
A bill in red letters that did my heart gall,
That she was appearing with him.
He taught her gymnastics and dressed her in tights
To help him to live at his ease,
And made her assume a masculine name,
And now she goes on the trapeze.

Chorus:

She floats through the air
With the greatest of ease,
You'd think her a man
On the flying trapeze.
She does all the work
While he takes his ease,
And that's what became of my love.

GEORGE LEYBOURNE

CASABIANCA

THE BOY stood on the burning deck,
Whence all but him had fled;
The flame that lit the battle's wreck
Shone round him o'er the dead.

Yet beautiful and bright he stood,
As born to rule the storm;
A creature of heroic blood,
A proud though childlike form.

The flames rolled on; he would not go
Without his father's word;
That father, faint in death below,
His voice no longer heard.

He called aloud, "Say, Father, say,
If yet my task be done!"
He knew not that the chieftain lay
Unconscious of his son.

"Speak, Father!" once again he cried,
"If I may yet be gone!"
And but the booming shots replied,
And fast the flames rolled on.

Upon his brow he felt their breath,
And in his waving hair,
And looked from that lone post of death
In still yet brave despair;

And shouted but once more aloud,
"My father! must I stay?"
While o'er him fast, through sail and shroud,
The wreathing fires made way.

They wrapt the ship in splendor wild,
　　They caught the flag on high,
And streamed above the gallant child,
　　Like banners in the sky.

There came a burst of thunder sound;
　　The boy,—Oh! where was *he?*
Ask the winds, that far around
　　With fragments strewed the sea,—

With mast and helm and pennon fair,
　　That well had borne their part,—
But the noblest thing that perished there
　　Was that young, faithful heart.

FELICIA D. HEMANS

CURFEW MUST NOT RING TONIGHT

SLOWLY ENGLAND'S SUN was setting o'er the hilltops far away,
Filling all the land with beauty at the close of one sad day;
And the last rays kissed the forehead of a man and maiden fair,
He with footsteps slow and weary, she with sunny floating hair;
He with bowed head, sad and thoughtful, she with lips all cold and
　　white,
Struggling to keep back the murmur, "Curfew must not ring tonight!"

"Sexton," Bessie's white lips faltered, pointing to the prison old,
With its turrets tall and gloomy, with its walls, dark, damp and cold—
"I've a lover in the prison, doomed this very night to die
At the ringing of the curfew, and no earthly help is nigh.
Cromwell will not come til' sunset": and her face grew strangely white
As she breathed the husky whisper, "Curfew must not ring tonight!"

"Bessie," calmly spoke the sexton—and his accents pierced her heart
Like the piercing of an arrow, like a deadly poisoned dart—
"Long, long years I've rung the curfew from that gloomy, shadowed
　　tower;
Every evening, just at sunset, it has told the twilight hour;
I have done my duty ever, tried to do it just and right—
Now I'm old I still must do it: Curfew, girl, must ring tonight!"

Wild her eyes and pale her features, stern and white her thoughtful
　　brow,
And within her secret bosom Bessie made a solemn vow.
She had listened while the judges read, without a tear or sigh,
"At the ringing of the curfew, Basil Underwood must die."

And her breath came fast and faster, and her eyes grew large and bright,
As in undertone she murmured, "Curfew must not ring tonight!"

With quick step she bounded forward, sprang within the old church door,
Left the old man threading slowly paths he'd often trod before;
Not one moment paused the maiden, but with eye and cheek aglow
Mounted up the gloomy tower, where the bell swung to and fro
As she climbed the dusty ladder, on which fell no ray of light,
Up and up, her white lips saying, "Curfew shall not ring tonight!"

She has reached the topmost ladder, o'er her hangs the great dark bell;
Awful is the gloom beneath her like the pathway down to hell;
Lo, the ponderous tongue is swinging. 'Tis the hour of curfew now,
And the sight has chilled her bosom, stopped her breath and paled her brow;
Shall she let it ring? No, never! Flash her eyes with sudden light,
And she springs and grasps it firmly: "Curfew shall not ring tonight!"

Out she swung, far out; the city seemed a speck of light below;
She 'twixt heaven and earth suspended as the bell swung to and fro;
And the sexton at the bell rope, old and deaf, heard not the bell,
But he thought it still was ringing fair young Basil's funeral knell.
Still the maiden clung more firmly, and, with trembling lips and white,
Said, to hush her heart's wild beating, "Curfew shall not ring tonight!"

It was o'er; the bell ceased swaying, and the maiden stepped once more
Firmly on the dark old ladder, where for hundred years before
Human foot had not been planted; but the brave deed she had done
Should be told long ages after—often as the setting sun
Should illume the sky with beauty, aged sires, with heads of white,
Long should tell the little children, "Curfew did not ring that night."

O'er the distant hills came Cromwell; Bessie sees him, and her brow,
Full of hope and full of gladness, has no anxious traces now.
At his feet she tells her story, shows her hands all bruised and torn;
And her face so sweet and pleading, yet with sorrow pale and worn,
Touched his heart with sudden pity—lit his eye with misty light;
"Go, your lover lives!" said Cromwell; "Curfew shall not ring tonight!"

ROSE HARTWICK THORPE

CARCASSONNE

"I'M GROWING OLD, I've sixty years;
    I've labored all my life in vain.
In all that time of hopes and fears

I've failed my dearest wish to gain.
I see full well that here below
    Bliss unalloyed there is for none;
My prayer would else fulfillment know—
    Never have I seen Carcassonne!

"You see the city from the hill,
    It lies beyond the mountains blue;
And yet to reach it one must still
    Five long and weary leagues pursue,
And, to return, as many more.
    Had but the vintage plenteous grown——
But, ah! the grape withheld its store.
    I shall not look on Carcassonne!

"They tell me every day is there
    Not more or less than Sunday gay;
In shining robes and garments fair
    The people walk upon their way.
One gazes there on castle walls
    As grand as those of Babylon;
A bishop and two generals!
    What joy to dwell in Carcassonne!

"The vicar's right: he says that we
    Are ever wayward, weak, and blind;
He tells us in his homily
    Ambition ruins all mankind.
Yet could I there two days have spent,
    While still the autumn sweetly shone,
Ah, me! I might have died content
    When I had looked on Carcassonne.

"Thy pardon, Father, I beseech,
    In this my prayer if I offend;
One something sees beyond his reach
    From childhood to his journey's end.
My wife, our little boy, Aignan,
    Have traveled even to Narbonne;
My grandchild has seen Perpignan;
    And I—have not seen Carcassonne!"

So crooned, one day, close by Limoux,
    A peasant, double-bent with age.
"Rise up, my friend," said I; "with you
    I'll go upon this pilgrimage."
We left, next morning, his abode,
    But (Heaven forgive him!) halfway on

The old man died upon the road—
He never gazed on Carcassonne.

GUSTAVE NADAUD
Translated by John R. Thompson

THE FOOL'S PRAYER

THE ROYAL FEAST was done; the King
  Sought some new sport to banish care,
And to his jester cried: "Sir Fool,
  Kneel now, and make for us a prayer!"

The jester doffed his cap and bells,
  And stood the mocking court before;
They could not see the bitter smile
  Behind the painted grin he wore.

He bowed his head, and bent his knee
  Upon the monarch's silken stool;
His pleading voice arose: "O Lord,
  Be merciful to me, a fool!

"No pity, Lord, could change the heart
  From red with wrong to white as wool:
The rod must heal the sin; but, Lord,
  Be merciful to me, a fool!

" 'T is not by guilt the onward sweep
  Of truth and right, O Lord, we stay;
'T is by our follies that so long
  We hold the earth from heaven away.

"These clumsy feet, still in the mire,
  Go crushing blossoms without end;
These hard, well-meaning hands we thrust
  Among the heart-strings of a friend.

"The ill-timed truth we might have kept—
  Who knows how sharp it pierced and stung!
The word we had not sense to say—
  Who knows how grandly it had rung!

"Our faults no tenderness should ask,
  The chastening stripes must cleanse them all;
But for our blunders—oh, in shame
  Before the eyes of heaven we fall.

"Earth bears no balsam for mistakes;
  Men crown the knave, and scourge the tool

That did his will; but Thou, O Lord,
    Be merciful to me, a fool!"

The room was hushed; in silence rose
    The King, and sought his gardens cool,
And walked apart, and murmured low,
    "Be merciful to me, a fool!"

EDWARD ROWLAND SILL

THE SIDEWALKS OF NEW YORK

DOWN IN FRONT of Casey's old brown wooden stoop
On a Summer's evening we formed a merry group;
Boys and girls together, we would sing and waltz
While the "Ginnie" played the organ
On the sidewalks of New York.

That's where Johnny Casey and little Jimmie Crowe,
With Jakey Krause, the baker, who always had the dough,
Pretty Nellie Shannon, with a dude as light as cork,
First picked up the waltz-step
On the sidewalks of New York.

Things have changed since those times,
Some are up in "G,"
Others they are wand'rers, but they all feel just like me.
They'd part with all they've got could they but once more walk
With their best girl and have a twirl
On the sidewalks of New York.

East side, west side, all round the town,
The tots sang "Ring-a-rosie," "London Bridge is falling down";
Boys and girls together, me and Mamie Rorke
Tripped the light fantastic
On the sidewalks of New York.

CHARLES B. LAWLOR AND JAMES W. BLAKE

Indexes

Index of Authors

(The page numbers in this index refer to the page on which poems begin. The authors' names will be found at the end of each poem.)

Index of Titles

Index of First Lines

A broken wagon wheel that rots away beside the river, 136

A bunch of the boys were whooping it up in the Malamute saloon, 417

A cheer and salute for the Admiral, and here's to the Captain bold, 138

A cloud possessed the hollow field, 120

A hundred years from now, dear heart, 15

A life on the ocean wave, 288

A little work, a little play, 71

A song to the oak, the brave old oak, 237

A stranger came one night to Yussouf's tent, 457

A well there is in the west country, 408

A wet sheet and a flowing sea, 293

A wise old owl lived in an oak, 378

Abide with me: fast falls the eventide, 80

Abou Ben Adhem (may his tribe increase), 58

Across the narrow beach we flit, 226

Ah, happy youths, ah, happy maid, 44

Alas, how easily things go wrong!, 11

All day I did the little things, 154

All in the merry month of May, 366

All paths lead to you, 20

"All quiet along the Potomac," they say, 115

Alter? When the hills do, 40

And what is so rare as a day in June?, 213

Anger in its time and place, 188

Announced by all the trumpets of the sky, 239

As a fond mother, when the day is o'er, 285

As I rummaged thro' the attic, 162

As I wandered round the homestead, 166

At evening when the lamp is lit, 192

At Paris it was, at the opera there, 448

At the muezzin's call for prayer, 80

Ay, tear her tattered ensign down!, 104

Backward, turn backward, O time, in your flight, 153

Be kind and tender to the Frog, 379

Be strong!, 52

Behind him lay the gray Azores, 90

Believe me, if all those endearing young charms, 19

Beneath the shadow of dawn's aerial cape, 72

Better trust all and be deceived, 55

Between the dark and the daylight, 148

Blessings on thee, little man, 149

Break, break, break, 286

Bring me men to match my mountains, 140

Broncho Dan halts midway of the stream, 428

By the flow of the inland river, 126

By the rude bridge that arched the flood, 106

Carry me back to old Virginny, 170

Come along boys, and listen to my tale, 432

Come listen to me, you gallants so free, 316